BERLIN

CONTENTS

Barrierefrei durch Berlin
Step-free access

🛗 Aufzug
lift

🛗 nur zur S-Bahn
only to urban rail

🛗 nur zur U-Bahn
only to underground

🛗 nur zum Bahn-Regionalverkehr
only to regional rail

🔲 Rampe
ramp

🔲 nur zur S-Bahn
only to urban rail

🔲 nur zum Bahn-Regionalverkehr
only to regional rail

Stand: 9. Februar 2017
Redaktionsschluss: 2. Februar 2017

BERLIN

To Sachsenhausen
Memorial & Museum

Berlin Wall
Sights

Prenzlauer
Berg

Scheunenviertel

Reichstag

Museum
Island

Alexander-
platz

Charlottenburg
Palace

Brandenburg
Gate

Unter
den Linden

Spree River

City West

Potsdamer Platz
& Kulturforum

Fascism &
Cold War Sights

Jewish
Museum

Kreuzberg

To
Potsdam

Welcome to Rick Steves' Europe

Travel is intensified living—maximum thrills per minute and one of the last great sources of legal adventure. Travel is freedom. It's recess, and we need it.

I discovered a passion for European travel as a teen and have been sharing it ever since—through my tours, public television and radio shows, and travel guidebooks. Over the years, I've taught thousands of travelers how to best enjoy Europe's blockbuster sights—and experience "Back Door" discoveries that most tourists miss.

This book offers a balanced mix of Berlin's serious, historical sights and lively people zones. And it's selective—rather than listing dozens of neighborhoods to explore, I recommend only the best ones—Prenzlauer Berg and Scheunenviertel. My self-guided museum tours and city walks give insight into Berlin's vibrant history and today's living, breathing culture.

I advocate traveling simply and smartly. Take advantage of my money- and time-saving tips on sightseeing, transportation, and more. Try local, characteristic alternatives to expensive hotels and restaurants. In many ways, spending more money only builds a thicker wall between you and what you traveled so far to see.

We visit Berlin to experience it—to become temporary locals. Thoughtful travel engages us with the world, as we learn to appreciate other cultures and new ways to measure quality of life.

Judging from the positive feedback I receive from readers, this book will help you enjoy a fun, affordable, and rewarding vacation—whether it's your first trip or your tenth.

Gute Reise! Happy travels!

Rick Steves

INTRODUCTION

Berlin is a city of leafy boulevards, grand Neoclassical buildings, world-class art, glitzy shopping arcades, and funky graffitied neighborhoods with gourmet street food. It's big and bombastic—the showcase city of kings and kaisers, of the Führer and 21st-century commerce.

Huge names have left their mark here, from the 18th-century King Frederick the Great, who turned Prussia from a purely militaristic state to a cultural hotspot, to Otto von Bismarck, whose over-the-top egotism unified modern Germany, then drove it—and all of Europe—into a devastating Great War.

Of course, Berlin is still largely defined by its tumultuous 20th century. The city was Europe's counterculture capital during the cabaret years, but drastically changed course when Hitler came to power in 1933—ultimately leaving Berlin (and much of Europe) in ruins. In the post-WWII years, Berlin became the front line of a new global conflict, the Cold War between Soviet-style communism and American-style capitalism. The East-West division was set in stone in 1961, when the East German government surrounded West Berlin with the Berlin Wall.

Since the fall of the Wall in 1989, Berlin has been a constant construction zone. Standing on ripped-up streets and under a canopy of cranes, visitors have witnessed the city's reunification and rebirth. Today Berlin is a world capital once again—the nuclear fuel rod of a great nation. Berliners joke that they don't need to travel anywhere because their city's always changing. A 10-year-old guidebook on Berlin covers a different place.

As one of Europe's top destinations, Berlin welcomes more visitors annually than Rome. There's no shortage of diversions. In the city's top-notch museums, you can walk through an enormous Babylonian gate amid rough-and-tumble ancient statuary, fondle a chunk of the concrete-and-rebar Berlin Wall, and peruse canvases by Dürer and Rembrandt. A series of thought-provoking memorials directly confront some of Germany's most difficult past of the last century. And some of the best history exhibits anywhere—covering everything from Prussian princes to Nazi atrocities to life under communism—have a knack for turning even those who claim to hate history into armchair experts.

Beyond its tangible sights and its enthralling history, Berlin is simply a pleasurable place to hang out. It's captivating, lively, fun-loving—and easy on the budget. The city vibrates with an anything's-possible buzz. It's a magnet for young expats from around the world who want to live in a dynamic and trendy city, but can't afford London rents. Entire neighborhoods have been overtaken by Americans, Brits, and Aussies—many of whom get by just fine without ever bothering to learn German.

Spend a day here...or a week. Go for a pedal in a park, or a lazy cruise along the delightful Spree riverfront. Step across what was the Berlin Wall and through the iconic Brandenburg Gate. Nurse a stein of brew in a rollicking beer hall, slurp a bowl of ramen at a foodie hotspot, or do like the Berliners do, and dive into a cheap *Currywurst*. Ponder present-day "street art" (a.k.a. graffiti) on your way to see the famous bust of Nefertiti or a serene Vermeer. Grab a drink from a sidewalk vendor, find a bench along the river, watch the sun set over a skyline of domes and cranes...and simply bask in Berlin.

ABOUT THIS BOOK

Rick Steves Berlin is a personal tour guide in your pocket. The book divides Berlin into convenient neighborhoods (shown on the "Berlin Sightseeing Modules" map on page 9). Inside, you'll find the following chapters:

Orientation to Berlin has specifics on public transportation, helpful hints, local tour options, easy-to-read maps, and tourist information. The "Planning Your Time" section suggests a schedule for how to best use your limited time.

Sights in Berlin describes the top attractions and includes their cost and hours.

The **Self-Guided Walks** cover Berlin's main historic and touristy zones—the Reichstag

and Brandenburg Gate, Unter den Linden, the communist sights of the former East Berlin, and Fascism and Berlin Wall sights south of downtown—as well as two of its most enjoyable-to-explore residential neighborhoods, Prenzlauer Berg and the Scheunenviertel.

The **Self-Guided Tours** lead you through Berlin's most fascinating museums and sights: the museums of Museum Island, including the Pergamon Museum; the German History Museum; the Berlin Wall Memorial; and the Gemäldegalerie and Kulturforum.

Sleeping in Berlin describes my favorite hotels in appealing neighborhoods, from good-value deals to cushy splurges.

Eating in Berlin serves up a buffet of options, from street food to inexpensive cafés to upscale splurges, arranged by neighborhood.

Shopping in Berlin gives you tips for shopping painlessly and enjoyably, without letting it overwhelm your vacation or ruin your budget.

Entertainment in Berlin is your guide to fun, including live music, cabaret, and more—from tango dancing in the park to swing dancing in a century-old ballroom.

Berlin Connections lays the groundwork for your arrival and departure, covering transportation by train and plane, with detailed information on Berlin's airports and main train station (Berlin Hauptbahnhof).

Day Trips from Berlin include the opulent palaces and lush parks at Potsdam, the sobering concentration camp memorial at Sachsenhausen, and Martin Luther's hometown, Wittenberg—each within an hour's train ride of downtown Berlin.

Germany: Past & Present gives you a quick overview of the country's tumultuous history and contemporary challenges.

The **Practicalities** chapter near the end of this book is a traveler's tool kit, with my best advice about money, sightseeing, sleeping, eating, staying connected, and transportation.

The **appendix** has the nuts and bolts: useful phone numbers and websites, a holiday and festival list, recommended books and films, a climate chart, a handy packing checklist, and German survival phrases.

Throughout this book, you'll find money- and time-saving tips for sightseeing, transportation, and more. Some businesses—especially hotels and walking tour companies—offer special discounts to my readers, indicated in their listings.

Browse through this book and select your favorite sights. Then have a *wunderbar* trip! Traveling like a temporary local, you'll get the absolute most out of every mile, minute, and dollar. As you visit places I know and love, I'm happy that you'll be meeting my favorite Berliners.

INTRODUCTION

Planning

This section will help you get started planning your trip—with advice on trip costs, when to go, and what you should know before you take off.

TRIP COSTS

Five components make up your trip costs: airfare to Europe, transportation in Europe, room and board, sightseeing and entertainment, and shopping and miscellany.

Airfare to Europe: A basic round-trip flight from the US to Berlin can cost, on average, about $1,000-2,000 total, depending on where you fly from and when (cheaper in winter). If Berlin is part of a longer European trip, consider saving time and money by flying into one city and out of another; for instance, into Berlin and out of Munich. Overall, Kayak.com is the best place to start searching for flights on a combination of mainstream and budget carriers.

Transportation in Europe: For a typical one-week visit, allow about $30 for transit tickets and a couple of day trips by train. To get between Berlin and the airport, figure around $4 per trip by bus, or closer to $30-40 for a taxi.

Room and Board: You can thrive in Berlin on $100 a day per person for room and board. This allows $10 for lunch, $20 for dinner, $5 for beer and *Eis* (ice cream), and $65 for lodging (based on two people splitting the cost of a $130 double room). Students and tightwads can enjoy Germany for as little as $65 a day ($35 for a bed in a hostel, $30 for cheap meals and picnics).

Sightseeing and Entertainment: Consider the Museum Pass Berlin, which covers many sights in the city (for more information, see page 14). You'll pay about $30 for a three-day pass. Without a Museum Pass, figure about $10-15 per major sight, and $5-10 for minor ones. Add $20-60 for bus tours and splurge experiences (such as walking tours and concerts). An overall average of $40 a day works for most people. Don't skimp here. After all, this category is the driving force behind your trip—you came to sightsee, enjoy, and experience Berlin.

Shopping and Miscellany: Figure $3 per ice cream cone, coffee, or soft drink. Shopping can vary in cost from nearly nothing to a small fortune. Good budget travelers find that this category has little to do with assembling a trip full of lifelong memories.

WHEN TO GO

May, June, September, and October are my favorite months for Berlin—most likely to be not too hot, not too cold. However, these are also the most crowded months; there can be lines at sights and higher prices at hotels.

Summers (July and August) are lively—Berliners love to hang out in parks and along riverbanks, as if enjoying a continuous open-air party. Be aware that the city can get unpleasantly hot and humid. If you wilt in the heat, look for a room with air-conditioning (which can be scarce).

Berlin is a decent winter getaway—its museums are ample and offer an escape from bad weather. However, many of the important historical sights are outdoors. And in general, Berlin is an exuberantly outdoor-oriented city—a scene that wintertime visitors miss out on. Night draws the shades on your sightseeing early, and you'll want to dress warmly, with layers. Expect cold (even freezing lows) and rain (hats, gloves, scarves, umbrellas, and thick-soled shoes are essential). For specific temperatures, see the climate chart in the appendix.

Before You Go

You'll have a smoother trip if you tackle a few things ahead of time. For more information on these topics, see the Practicalities chapter (and www.ricksteves.com, which has helpful travel tips and talks).

Make sure your passport is valid. If it's due to expire within six months of your ticketed date of return, you need to renew it. Allow up to six weeks to renew or get a passport (www.travel.state. gov).

Arrange your transportation. Book your international flights. You won't want a car in congested Berlin, but if you'll be touring the countryside beyond, figure out your main form of transportation: You can buy train tickets as you go, get a rail pass, rent a car, or book a cheap flight. (You can wing it in Europe, but it may cost more.)

Book rooms well in advance, especially if your trip falls during peak season or any major holidays or festivals.

Reserve or buy tickets ahead for major sights, saving you from long ticket-buying lines. To visit the **Reichstag dome,** reserve a free entry slot online a week or so in advance (see page 29); if you don't reserve ahead, you'll have to line up for tickets, then go back later to enter. The **Pergamon Museum** also accepts reservations, which can be a good idea to avoid lines (see page 142).

Consider travel insurance. Compare the cost of the insurance to the cost of your potential loss. Check whether your existing insurance (health, homeowners, or renters) covers you and your possessions overseas.

Call your bank. Alert your bank that you'll be using your debit and credit cards in Europe. Ask about transaction fees, and get the

INTRODUCTION

∩ **Stick This Guidebook in Your Ear!** ∩

My free Rick Steves Audio Europe app makes it easy for you to download my audio tours of many of Europe's top attractions and listen to them offline during your travels. My Berlin City Walk audio tour links several key sights through the city center, from the Brandenburg Gate to Alexanderplatz. Sights covered by my audio tour are marked in this book with this symbol: ∩. The app also offers insightful travel interviews from my public radio show with experts from Germany and around the globe. It's all free! You can download the app via Apple's App Store, Google Play, or Amazon's Appstore. For more info, see www.ricksteves.com/audioeurope.

PIN number for your credit card. You don't need to bring euros for your trip; you can withdraw euros from cash machines in Europe.

Use your smartphone smartly. Sign up for an international service plan to reduce your costs, or rely on Wi-Fi in Europe instead. Download any apps you'll want on the road, such as maps, translation, transit schedules, and Rick Steves Audio Europe (see sidebar).

Pack light. You'll walk with your luggage more than you think. I travel for weeks with a single carry-on bag and a daypack. Use the packing checklist in the appendix as a guide.

Travel Smart

If you have a positive attitude, equip yourself with good information (this book), and expect to travel smart, you will.

Read—and reread—this book. To have an "A" trip, be an "A" student. As you study up on sights, note opening hours, closed days, crowd-beating tips, and whether reservations are required or advisable. Check the latest at www.ricksteves.com/update.

Be your own tour guide. As you travel, get up-to-date info on sights, reserve tickets and tours, reconfirm hotels and travel arrangements, and check transit connections. Visit local tourist information offices (TIs). Upon arrival, lay the groundwork for a smooth departure; confirm the train, bus, or road you'll take when you leave.

Outsmart thieves. Pickpockets abound in crowded places where tourists congregate. Treat commotions as smokescreens for theft. Keep your cash, credit cards, and passport secure in a money belt tucked under your clothes; carry only a day's spending money in your front pocket. Don't set valuable items down on counters or café tabletops, where they can be quickly stolen or easily forgotten.

Minimize potential loss. Keep expensive gear to a minimum. Bring photocopies of important documents (passport and cards) to aid in replacement if they're lost or stolen.

Guard your time and energy. Taking a taxi can be a good value if it saves you a long wait for a cheap bus or an exhausting walk across town. To avoid long lines, follow my crowd-beating tips, such as making advance reservations, or sightseeing early or late. Before taking day-trips, check the hours and closed days for the sights you plan to visit.

Be flexible. Even if you have a well-planned itinerary, expect changes, strikes, closures, sore feet, bad weather, and so on. Your Plan B could turn out to be even better.

Attempt the language. Many Germans—especially in the tourist trade and in cities—speak English, but if you learn some German, even just a few phrases, you'll get more smiles and make more friends. Practice the survival phrases near the end of this book, and even better, bring a phrase book.

Connect with the culture. Interacting with locals carbonates your experience. Enjoy the friendliness of the German people. Ask questions; most locals are happy to point you in their idea of the right direction. Set up your own quest for the best *Currywurst*, microbrew, or jazz club. When an opportunity pops up, make it a habit to say "yes."

Berlin…here you come!

ORIENTATION TO BERLIN

Berlin is a sprawling city (pop. 3.4 million), built on a huge scale. Take a deep breath, then use this orientation to prepare for your trip. The day plans—for visits of one to seven days—will help you prioritize the many sights. You'll tap into Berlin's information sources for current events. Most important, you'll learn to navigate Berlin by subway, bus, taxi, bicycle, or on foot. With the proper approach and a measure of patience, you'll have Berlin by the tail.

BERLIN: A VERBAL MAP

Berlin is huge. Though it's a major metropolis, it's not a city of skyscrapers packed into a single, dense urban core. Rather, Berlin is spread out—a series of pleasant neighborhoods, with broad boulevards, long blocks, and low five-story buildings.

Berlin's "downtown" alone stretches five miles, following the west-to-east flow of the Spree River. In the center sits the vast park called Tiergarten. Most tourist sights lie east of the park, in the central zone known as "Mitte." To make sprawling Berlin easier to digest, this book's coverage is organized by compass direction, radiating out from the historic core. (This organization has nothing to do with the old, Cold War-era "East Berlin" and "West Berlin" designations; in fact, virtually everything mentioned here other than "Western Berlin" was in the former East.)

Historic Core: Berlin's one-mile sightseeing axis runs west-to-east along **Unter den Linden** boulevard—the city's "Champs-Élysées"—with a mix of 19th-century Neoclassical grandeur and

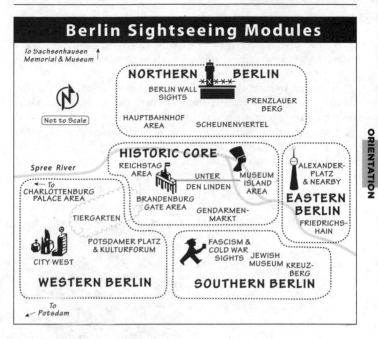

Berlin Sightseeing Modules

To Sachsenhausen
Memorial & Museum

NORTHERN BERLIN

BERLIN WALL
SIGHTS

PRENZLAUER
BERG

Not to Scale

HAUPTBAHNHOF
AREA

SCHEUNENVIERTEL

HISTORIC CORE

REICHSTAG
AREA

Spree River

UNTER
DEN LINDEN

MUSEUM
ISLAND
AREA

ALEXANDER-
PLATZ
& NEARBY

← To
CHARLOTTENBURG
PALACE AREA

BRANDENBURG
GATE AREA

GENDARMEN-
MARKT

EASTERN
BERLIN

TIERGARTEN

FRIEDRICHS-
HAIN

POTSDAMER PLATZ
& KULTURFORUM

FASCISM &
COLD WAR
SIGHTS

JEWISH
MUSEUM

KREUZ-
BERG

CITY WEST

WESTERN BERLIN

SOUTHERN BERLIN

To
Potsdam

ORIENTATION

21st-century glitz. At the western edge, you'll find the historic **Brandenburg Gate,** the **Reichstag** (Germany's domed parliament), and a scattering of poignant memorials. Unter den Linden passes the grand squares called Gendarmenmarkt and Bebelplatz before it terminates at **Museum Island**—the birthplace of Berlin and today home to a cluster of the city's top museums: the ancient wonders of the Pergamon and Neues museums, and German paintings in the Old National Gallery.

Besides art, within this core are Berlin's towering Cathedral, the German History and DDR museums, and the re-creation of Berlin's former royal palace. While this area is where most tourists spend their time, there's little local life here; for that, venture to the areas described next.

Northern Berlin: The trendy **Scheunenviertel** ("Barn Quarter") neighborhood, near the Hackescher Markt transit hub, is a short walk north of Unter den Linden; here you'll find eateries, shopping, and Jewish history. Farther out is the even hipper **Prenzlauer Berg** residential area, with recommended hotels, restaurants, and shopping. Also in this zone are the **Berlin Wall Memorial**—the best place in town to learn more about the Wall—and the **Hauptbahnhof** (main train station).

Southern Berlin: South of Unter den Linden, **fascism and Cold War sights** dominate, anchored by Checkpoint Charlie (the former border crossing through the Wall) and the Topography of

Terror (documenting Nazi atrocities). Further south and east is the sprawling, diverse, and fun-to-explore **Kreuzberg** neighborhood with characteristic mini-neighborhoods known as *Kieze;* the main sight here is the Jewish Museum Berlin.

Eastern Berlin: East of Museum Island, Unter den Linden changes its name to Karl-Liebknecht-Strasse and leads to **Alexanderplatz**—formerly the hub of communist East Berlin, still marinated in brutal architecture, and marked by its impossible-to-miss TV Tower. Farther east sits the gentrifying **Friedrichshain** neighborhood, with the East Side Gallery (a mile-long stretch of surviving Berlin Wall, now slathered in graffiti).

Western Berlin: Just west of the Brandenburg gate is the entrance to Berlin's huge central park, **Tiergarten.** South of the park, **Potsdamer Platz** is home to Berlin's 21st-century glitz, with skyscrapers and shopping plazas. Down the street, the **Kulturforum** is a cluster of museums dedicated to painting (starring Rembrandt, Dürer, and more), decorative-arts treasures, and classic musical instruments.

West of the park is **City West**—the former heart of communist-era West Berlin, lined up along the boulevard named Kurfürstendamm ("Ku'damm" for short). Today this modern area feels more like a classy suburb, with a few sights (including the Berlin Zoological Garden) and several recommended hotels. Finally, to the north is **Charlottenburg Palace,** with a mediocre royal interior but excellent 20th-century art museums nearby.

PLANNING YOUR TIME

While most European capitals have a handful of clear-cut "must-see" sights, Berlin is more of a "choose your own adventure" destination. There's plenty to see and do here. Art lovers could spend days museum-hopping, never once thinking about Hitler or the Berlin Wall. History buffs could be on cloud nine without ever looking at a single canvas. And plenty of visitors have a blast just hanging out in Berlin's funky neighborhoods and leafy parks, never stepping through a turnstile. My suggested plans incorporate a bit of everything. Though jam-packed, they work if you're energetic and well-organized. If you have more time, spread out these priorities to give yourself some breathing room.

Berlin in One Insane Day

9:00	Ascend the Reichstag dome (reserve in advance).
10:00	Follow my Reichstag & Brandenburg Gate Walk.
11:30	Follow my Unter den Linden Walk.
13:00	Grab a quick *Currywurst* lunch near Museum Island.
13:30	Do an "express tour" of the Pergamon, Neues Museum, and Old National Gallery; or, if you prefer history, tour the German History Museum and/or DDR Museum.
16:00	Follow my Communist East Berlin Walk.
17:00	Ride the S-Bahn from Alexanderplatz to Nordbahnhof and take my Berlin Wall Memorial Tour.
18:30	Ride tram #M10 to Prenzlauer Berg for dinner.
20:00	Explore Prenzlauer Berg before collapsing at your hotel.

Berlin in Two Days

Day 1

9:00	Ascend the Reichstag dome (reserve in advance).
10:00	Follow my Reichstag & Brandenburg Gate Walk.
11:30	Follow my Unter den Linden Walk.
13:00	Grab a takeaway lunch to enjoy on a Spree River cruise.
14:30	Choose from these Museum Island area sights: Pergamon, Neues Museum, Old National Gallery, German History Museum, or DDR Museum.
17:00	Follow my Communist East Berlin Walk (or stretch your museum time).
18:00	Head to Hackescher Markt (take the S-Bahn from Alexanderplatz, or walk from Museum Island) for my Scheunenviertel Walk.
19:00	Have dinner in the Scheunenviertel.

Day 2

9:00	Follow my Fascism & Cold War Walk from Checkpoint Charlie to Potsdamer Platz.
11:00	Take my Gemäldegalerie & Kulturforum Tour; have lunch at a museum café or on Potsdamer Platz.
15:00	Ride the U-Bahn (U2 from Potsdamer Platz to Senefelderplatz) and take my Prenzlauer Berg Walk.
16:30	Take tram #M10 to Nordbahnhof for my Berlin Wall Memorial Tour.
18:00	Return to Prenzlauer Berg (tram #M10 or walk along the rest of the Memorial) for dinner.

ORIENTATION

Berlin in Three (or More) Days

Day 1

9:00	Ascend the Reichstag dome (reserve in advance).
10:00	Follow my Reichstag & Brandenburg Gate Walk.
11:30	Take my Unter den Linden Walk.
13:00	Take a Spree River cruise with a picnic lunch.
14:30	Follow my Communist East Berlin Walk.
15:30	Take the U-Bahn to Senefelderplatz for my Prenzlauer Berg Walk.
17:00	Take tram #M10 to Nordbahnhof for my Berlin Wall Memorial Tour.
18:30	Head back to Prenzlauer Berg (tram #M10 or walk along the rest of the Memorial) for dinner.

Day 2

The timing of this day depends on how much museum-going you want.

Morning: Binge on your choice of Museum Island-area museums: Pergamon, Neues, Old National Gallery, German History Museum, or DDR Museum.

Midday: If you're still going strong with museums, take a lunch break at the Bode Museum café or under the S-Bahn tracks on Georgenstrasse; if you're done early, walk to the Scheunenviertel for lunch.

Afternoon: Take my Scheunenviertel Walk, then visit the Palace of Tears; with additional time, choose from the "Days 4-7" options, later.

Evening: Have dinner in the Scheunenviertel or Prenzlauer Berg.

Day 3

9:00	Follow my Fascism & Cold War Walk, from Checkpoint Charlie to Potsdamer Platz.
11:00	Follow my Gemäldegalerie & Kulturforum Tour; have lunch at the museum café or Potsdamer Platz.
15:00	Your choice: Take bus #200 to City West for sightseeing and dinner; or head to the Jewish Museum and/or Berlinische Galerie, then to Kreuzberg for exploring and dinner.

Days 4-7

Choose from:

City West sights: Kaiser Wilhelm Memorial Church, Käthe Kollwitz Museum, strolling Ku'damm, and browsing KaDeWe and Bikini Berlin stores; with more time, extend your explorations into the adjacent **Schöneberg** district

Jewish Museum and/or **Berlinische Galerie**

    Kreuzberg (you could add on **Treptower Park** or **Tempelhof Field**)

    Charlottenburg Palace and nearby **modern art museums**

    Friedrichshain and **20th-century sights:** East Side Gallery, Stasi Museum, and/or Karl-Marx-Allee; Treptower Park is also nearby

    Day-trip to **Sachsenhausen Memorial and Museum**

    Day-trip to the palaces at **Potsdam**

    Day-trip to the Martin Luther sights at **Wittenberg**

Overview

TOURIST INFORMATION

Berlin's tourist offices (abbreviated as "TI" in this book) are for-profit agencies that are only marginally helpful (tel. 030/250-025, www.visitberlin.de). You'll find them at the **Hauptbahnhof** (daily 8:00-22:00, by main entrance on Europaplatz), in City West at **Europa Center** (Mon-Sat 10:00-20:00, closed Sun, hidden inside the shopping mall ground floor at Tauentzienstrasse 9); nearby "info box" kiosk on Rankestrasse across from **Kaiser Wilhelm Memorial Church** (daily 10:00-18:00, until 16:00 Nov-March), at the **Brandenburg Gate** (daily 9:30-19:00, until 18:00 Nov-March), in the Park Inn hotel lobby at **Alexanderplatz** (Mon-Sat 7:00-21:00, Sun 8:00-18:00, Alexanderplatz 7), and at **Tegel Airport** (daily 8:00-21:00). A separately run TI—focusing on Prenzlauer Berg, and generally more useful—is at the **Kulturbrauerei** (daily 11:00-19:00). See the map on page VII for most locations.

Skip the TI's €1 map, and instead browse the walking tour company brochures—many include nearly-as-good maps for free. Most hotels provide free city maps. If you're staying (or spending lots of time) in Prenzlauer Berg, ask for the free *Pankow Entdecken* booklet, with lots of local insights.

While the TI sells the three-day Museum Pass Berlin (see "Helpful Hints" below), it's also available at major museums. If you take a walking tour, your guide is likely a better source of nightlife or shopping tips than the TI.

ARRIVAL IN BERLIN

For a comprehensive rundown of the city's train stations and airports, and for information on parking a car, see the Berlin Connections chapter.

HELPFUL HINTS

Medical Help: The US Embassy has a list of local English-speaking doctors (tel. 030/83050, https://de.usembassy.gov, search for "English-speaking services").

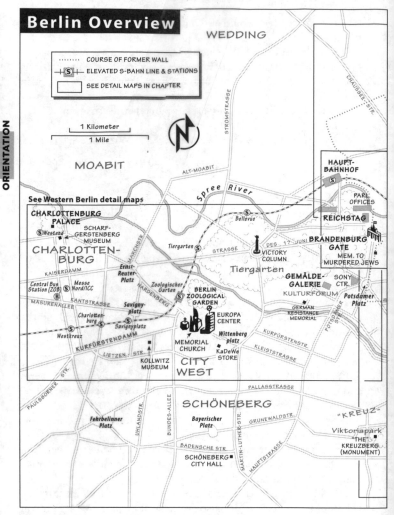

Berlin Overview

WEDDING

········· COURSE OF FORMER WALL

⊢⑤⊣ ELEVATED S-BAHN LINE & STATIONS

☐ SEE DETAIL MAPS IN CHAPTER

1 Kilometer

1 Mile

N

MOABIT

ALT-MOABIT

STROMSTRASSE

CHAUSSEE-STR.

HAUPT-BAHNHOF

PARL. OFFICES

Spree River

See Western Berlin detail maps

Bellevue

REICHSTAG

CHARLOTTENBURG PALACE

SCHARF-GERSTENBERG MUSEUM

⑤ Westend

Tiergarten ⑤

STRASSE DES 17. JUNI

VICTORY COLUMN

BRANDENBURG GATE

MEM. TO MURDERED JEWS

CHARLOTTEN-BURG

KAISERDAMM

Tiergarten

GEMÄLDE-GALERIE

SONY CTR.

MARKCHSTR.

Ernst-Reuter-Platz

KULTURFORUM

Central Bus Station (ZOB) ⑤ Messe Nord/ICC

HARDENBERG

Zoologischer Garten

BERLIN ZOOLOGICAL GARDEN

GERMAN RESISTANCE MEMORIAL

Potsdamer Platz

POTSDAMER STRASSE

KANTSTRASSE

MASURENALLEE

Savigny-platz

EUROPA CENTER

Charlotten-burg ⑤

Savignyplatz

Wittenberg platz

KURFÜRSTENSTR.

Westkreuz ⑤

MEMORIAL CHURCH

KaDeWe STORE

KLEISTSTRASSE

KURFÜRSTENDAMM

LIETZEN-STR.

KOLLWITZ MUSEUM

CITY WEST

PAULSBORNER STR.

PALLASSTRASSE

SCHÖNEBERG

"KREUZ-

Fehrbelliner Platz

UHLANDSTR.

BUNDES-ALLEE

Bayerischer Platz

MARTIN-LUTHER-STR.

GRUNEWALDSTR.

Viktoriapark

"THE KREUZBERG (MONUMENT)

BADENSCHE STR.

HAUPTSTRASSE

SCHÖNEBERG CITY HALL

Museum Closures: The Berlin Wall Memorial Visitors Center and Documentation Center, the Old National Gallery, and the Gemäldegalerie are closed on Monday.

Museum Passes: Of Berlin's three different passes, the €29 **Museum Pass Berlin** is best for serious museumgoers—it covers nearly all the city sights for three days (including everything covered by the one-day Museum Island Pass). The Museum Pass Berlin is a great value and pays for itself in a hurry. It gets you into more than 45 museums, including the national museums and most of the recommended biggies (though not the German History Museum), on three consecutive days. Covered sights include the five Museum Island museums

(Old National Gallery, Neues, Altes, Bode, and Pergamon), Gemäldegalerie, and the Jewish Museum, along with more minor sights. Buy it at any participating museum or a TI. The pass generally lets you skip the line and go directly into the museum (except at the Pergamon, where you can prebook a time slot).

The €18 **Museum Island Pass** (not sold at TIs) covers all the sights on Museum Island and is a fine value—but for just €11 more, the three-day Museum Pass Berlin gives you triple the days and many more entries.

There's also the **WelcomeCard,** a transportation pass that includes discounts for the Berlin Cathedral, DDR Museum,

German History Museum, Museum of the Wall at Checkpoint Charlie, Jewish Museum, and others (pass described later, under "Getting Around Berlin").

Addresses: Be warned that many Berlin streets are numbered with odd and even numbers on the same side of the street, often with no connection to the other side (for example, Ku'damm #212 can be across the street from #14).

Festivals: Berlin hosts a near-constant string of events; see the appendix for key holiday and festival dates.

Cold War Terminology: What Americans called "East Germany" was technically the German Democratic Republic—the Deutsche Demokratische Republik, or DDR. You'll still see those initials around what was once East Germany. The name for what was "West Germany"—the Federal Republic of Germany (Bundesrepublik Deutschland, or BRD)—is now the name shared by all of Germany.

Laundry: You'll find several self-service launderettes near my recommended hotels (generally daily 6:00-22:00). In Prenzlauer Berg, try **Eco-Express Waschsalon** (Danziger Strasse 7) or **Schnell & Sauber Waschcenter** (Oderberger Strasse 1); for locations see the map on page 262. In the Scheunenviertel, there are two launderettes around the corner from Rosenthaler Platz: **Waschsalon 115** (Wi-Fi, Torstrasse 115) and **Eco-Express Waschsalon** (Torstrasse 109); for locations see the map on page 266.

GETTING AROUND BERLIN

The city is vast. Berlin's sights spread far and wide. Right from the start, commit yourself to the city's fine public-transit system.

By Public Transit

Berlin's transit system uses the same ticket for its many modes of transportation: buses, trams *(Strassenbahn)*, and trains. There are two types of trains: The U-Bahn—like a subway, making lots of short hops around town—is run by the local transit authority (BVG); the S-Bahn, a light rail that goes faster and stops only at major stations, is operated by German Railways (Deutsche Bahn).

For all types of transit, there are three lettered zones: A, B, and C. Most of your sightseeing will be in zones A and B (the city proper); you may enter zone

C if you're going to Potsdam, Sachenhausen, Schönefeld airport, or other outlying areas.

Information: Timetables and prices are available on the helpful BVG website or app (www.bvg.de), VBB, the public transportation authority for Berlin and Brandenburg, offers a handy website and free app especially good for on-the-go trip routing, as it includes U-Bahn, S-Bahn, and tram connections (www.vbb.de).

Sections of the U-Bahn or S-Bahn sometimes close temporarily for repairs, with a bus route replacing the train (*Ersatzverkehr,* or "replacement transportation"; *zwischen* means "between").

Within Berlin, Eurail passes are good only on S-Bahn connections from the train station when you arrive and to the station when you depart.

ORIENTATION

Ticket Options

The €2.80 **basic single** ticket *(Einzelfahrschein)* covers two hours of travel in one direction. It's easy to make this ticket stretch to cover several rides...as long as they're in the same direction.

The €1.70 **short-ride** ticket *(Kurzstrecke Fahrschein)* covers a single ride of up to six bus/tram stops or three subway stations (one transfer allowed on subway). You can save on

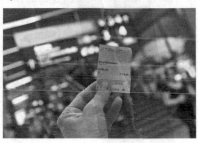

short-ride tickets by buying them in groups of four (€5.60).

The €9 **four-trip** ticket *(4-Fahrten-Karte)* is the same as four basic single tickets at a small discount.

The **day pass** *(Tageskarte)* is good until 3:00 the morning after you buy it (€7 for zones AB, €7.40 for zones ABC). For longer stays, consider a seven-day pass *(Sieben-Tage-Karte;* €30 for zones AB, €37.50 for zones ABC), or the WelcomeCard (options from 2 to 6 days; described below). The *Kleingruppenkarte* lets groups of up to five travel all day (€19.90 for zones AB, €20.80 for zones ABC).

If you've already bought a ticket for zones A and B, and later decide to go to zone C (such as to Potsdam), you can buy an **"extension ticket"** *(Anschlussfahrschein)* for €1.60, which covers 1.5 hours of travel in that zone.

If you plan to cover a lot of ground using public transportation during a two- or three-day visit, the **WelcomeCard** is usually the best deal (available at TIs; www.visitberlin.de/welcomecard). It covers all public transportation and gives you up to 50 percent discounts on lots of minor and a few major museums, sightseeing tours (including 25 percent off the recommended Original Berlin

ORIENTATION

Berlin Public Transportation

SACHSEN-HAUSEN ■
#804
Oranienburg **S1**

TEGEL AIRPORT ✈
Alt-Tegel **U6**

Beussel-strasse Ⓢ

Jungfern-heide Ⓢ
Wedding **U**

Reinickendorfer Strasse **U**

Schwarzkopf-strasse

Naturkunde-museum **U**   #M10 & 12

Oranien-burger Tor

Hauptbahnhof Ⓢ   S5 & S7

Spree   River

CHARLOTTENBURG PALACE ■   #M45   Bellevue Ⓢ   REICHSTAG ■
#100
BRANDENBURG GATE 🏛
Brand. Tor

Westend Ⓢ   Ernst Reuter Platz   Tiergarten Ⓢ   **MEMORIAL TO MURDERED JEWS**

Ruhleben **U2**   Messe Nord / ICC   U2   VICTORY COLUMN ■

To Spandau   Deutsche Oper   S5   Potsdamer Platz

Westkreuz Ⓢ   Savigny-platz   Zoolo-gischer Garten Ⓢ Ⓤ   **BERLIN ZOO** ■   *Tiergarten*   KULTURFORUM ■

Charlottenburg   Mend. Ⓤ Ⓢ

To Potsdam   Uhland-strasse **U1**   #100 & 200   Gleisdreieck

KURFÜRSTENDAMM   **CITY WEST**   U1 & U2   U1 Anhalter Bahnhof

WESTERN BERLIN   #200   S1 & S2

Wittenberg-platz Ⓤ   Nollendorf-platz Ⓤ   Bülow-strasse Ⓤ

SCHÖNEBERG   Yorckstrasse Ⓢ

Not all lines, stops, or stations are shown

Schöneberg Ⓢ   Südkreuz Ⓢ

S1 Wannsee
To Potsdam, change to S7

S2 Blankenfelde

Legend

- ━Ⓢ━ S-Bahn Spine (S5 & S7)
- ─Ⓢ─ S-Bahn 1 & 2
- ─Ⓢ─ S-Bahn Outer Circle
- ━Ⓤ━ U-Bahn 1, 2, 6 & 8
- ┼─●─┼ Tram Lines
- ‑ ‑ ‑ Bus #100
- - - - - Other Buses

Walks and Insider Tour), and music and theater events. It's especially smart for families, as each adult card also covers up to three kids under age 15. The Berlin-only card covers transit zones AB (€19.90/48 hours, €27.90/72 hours, also 4-, 5-, and 6-day options). For multiple trips beyond the city center, there's a Berlin-with-Potsdam card (zones ABC, €21.90/48 hours, €29.90/72 hours, also 4-, 5-, and 6-day options). If you're a museum junkie, consider the **WelcomeCard+Museumsinsel** (€44/72 hours), which combines

ORIENTATION

travel in zones A and B with unlimited access to the five museums on Museum Island (€46/72 hours for the ABC version).

Buying Tickets

You can buy U-Bahn/S-Bahn tickets from machines at stations. Tickets are also sold at BVG pavilions at train stations and at the TI, from machines onboard trams, and on buses from drivers, who'll give change. You'll need coins or paper bills (only German

"EC" credit cards are accepted as payment at transit ticket machines or retailers).

To use a ticket machine, start by pressing the flag icon, and then tap the British flag for English instructions. Next, select the zone (AB, ABC, or "short-distance journey" for a zoneless short-ride ticket) and the type of ticket you want (single, day, or four-trip; for seven-day tickets, select the "season tickets" option), then feed in coins or bills. Most travelers want the AB ticket—either single or all-day ticket. Note that "adult" *(Erwachsener)* means anyone 14 or older.

Boarding Transit

As you board the bus or tram or enter the subway, validate your ticket in a clock machine (or risk a €60 fine; with a pass, stamp it only the first time you ride). Tickets are checked periodically, often by plainclothes inspectors. You may be asked to show your ticket when boarding the bus.

Useful Transit Lines

If you learn a few key transit lines, it will help shrink this vast city.

Several **S-Bahn lines** converge along a single east-west axis—flowing like a high-speed river through the heart of the city. Get used to this, and you'll zip quickly between key stops: Savignyplatz (hotels in western Berlin), Zoologischer Garten—also known as "Zoo Station" (zoo, City West, Ku'damm), Hauptbahnhof, Friedrichstrasse (near the heart of Unter den Linden), Hackescher Markt (Museum Island, Scheunenviertel, connection to Prenzlauer Berg), and Alexanderplatz (eastern end of the historic core).

Buses #100, #200, and **#TXL** travel east-west along Unter den Linden between the Reichstag/Brandenburg on one end and Alexanderplatz on the other. There are stops every few blocks, with buses every 10 minutes or so.

On the S-Bahn, lines **S1** and **S2** travel north-south between Nordbahnhof (Berlin Wall Memorial), Friedrichstrasse, Brandenburger Tor, and Potsdamer Platz (Kulturforum).

On the U-Bahn, line **U2** cuts diagonally across the city from Prenzlauer Berg (hotels) to Potsdamer Platz, stopping near Checkpoint Charlie at Stadtmitte. Other handy U-Bahn lines include **U6** (running north-south through downtown, offering a quick connection to Kreuzberg) and **U1** (cutting east-west through southern Berlin, connecting City West, Kreuzberg, and Friedrichshain). The still-under-construction **U5** will eventually connect the Hauptbahnhof, Reichstag, and strategic stops along the city's main sightseeing spine: Brandenburger Tor, Unter den Linden (near Babelplatz), Museum Island, Rotes Rathaus (City Hall, near the Nikolai Quarter), and Alexanderplatz.

Tram **#M1** is helpful for getting to and around Prenzlauer

Berg—connecting the Hackescher Markt S-Bahn station with key stops along the main drag Kastanienallee up to the Eberswalder Strasse U-Bahn station. Useful tram **#12** overlaps with the middle part of this route.

Tram **#M10** connects stops along the Berlin Wall Memorial, from Nordbahnhof all the way to the Mauerpark and the Eberswalder Strasse U-Bahn station.

By Taxi

Cabs are easy to flag down, and taxi stands are common. A typical ride within town costs around €10, and a crosstown trip (for example, Savignyplatz to Alexanderplatz) will run about €20. Tariff 1 is for a *Kurzstrecke* ticket (see below). All other rides are tariff 2 (€3.90 drop plus €2/km for the first seven kilometers, then €1.50/km after that). If possible, use cash: Credit card payment comes with a surcharge.

For any ride of less than two kilometers (about a mile), you can save several euros if you take advantage of the *Kurzstrecke* (short-stretch) rate. To get this rate, it's important that you flag down the cab on the street—not at or even near a taxi stand. You must ask for the *Kurzstrecke* rate as soon as you hop in: Confidently say "*Kurzstrecke, bitte*" (KOORTS-shtreh-keh, BIT-teh), and your driver will grumble and flip the meter to a fixed €5 rate (for a ride that would otherwise cost €8).

Local laws require Berlin's Uber drivers to charge the same rates as taxis; there's no financial advantage to using Uber over just hailing a cab.

By Bike

Flat Berlin is a very bike-friendly city, but be careful—motorists don't brake for bicyclists (and bicyclists don't brake for pedestrians). Fortunately, many roads and sidewalks have special red-painted bike lanes. Don't ride on the regular sidewalk—it's *verboten* (though locals do it all the time). Better yet, to get out of the city on two wheels, rent a bike, take it on the subway (requires extra €1.90 ticket) to the pleasant Potsdam/Wannsee parkland area west of town, then ride through forests and along skinny lakes to the vast Grünewald park, then back into the city. (During the Cold War, Grünewald was the West Berliners' playground, while East Berliners communed with nature at the Müggelsee, to the east.) Bike shops can suggest a specific route.

ORIENTATION

The majority of Berlin hotels rent bikes to guests, which could be your easiest choice (ask when you book). But for a more serious bike, consider the following options.

Fat Tire Bikes rents good bikes at two handy locations—in the east (at the base of the TV Tower near Alexanderplatz; see map on page 276), and in the west (at Zoologischer Garten—leaving the station onto Hardenbergplatz, turn left and walk 100 yards to the big bike sign; see map on page 270). Rates are the same at both locations (€14/day, cheaper for 2 or more days, trekking and e-bikes available, free luggage storage; Zoologischer Garten location open daily May-Sept 9:30-20:00, April and Oct until 18:00, shorter hours or by appointment only Nov-March; Alexanderplatz location open daily March-Nov and sporadically off-season; tel. 030/2404-7991, www.berlinbikerental.com).

In central Berlin, **Take a Bike**—near the Friedrichstrasse S-Bahn station—is owned by a knowledgeable Dutch-German with a huge inventory (3-gear bikes: €8/4 hours, €12.50/day, €19/2 days, slightly cheaper for longer rentals, more for better bikes, includes helmets, daily 9:30-19:00, Nov-March closed Tue-Thu, Neustädtische Kirchstrasse 8—see map on page 276, tel. 030/2065-4730, www.takeabike.de). To find it, leave the S-Bahn station via the Friedrichstrasse exit, turn right, go through a triangle-shaped square, and hang a left on Neustädtische Kirchstrasse.

Bike Rental Berlin is a good option if you're sleeping in the Prenzlauer Berg neighborhood (€10/day, €16/2 days, helmets-€1, kids' bikes and child seats available, daily 10:00-17:00, often closed off-season—call ahead, Kastanienallee 55—see map on page 262, tel. 030/7153-3020, http://bike-rental-berlin.de).

Simple **Rent a Bike** stands are outside countless Berlin shops, restaurants, and hotels. Most charge €10-12 a day and are super-convenient, given their ubiquitous availability—but these bikes don't come with the reliable quality, advice, helmets, or maps offered by the full-service rental shops listed above.

Tours in Berlin

▲▲▲BUS TOURS

Berlin lends itself to a bus-tour orientation. Several companies offer essentially the same routine: a circuit of the city with unlimited, all-day hop-on, hop-off privileges for about €20 (two days for a few euros more, check for WelcomeCard discounts). Buses make about 15 stops at

ORIENTATION

Do-It-Yourself Bus #100 Tour

Running from the Berlin Zoological Garden to Alexanderplatz, Berlin's city bus #100 laces together the major sights in a kind of poor man's self-guided bus tour. Since a basic, single bus ticket is good for two hours of travel in one direction and buses leave every few minutes, hopping on and off works great. Bus #100 stops at Zoologischer Garten station, the Berlin Zoo, the Victory Column, the Reichstag, Unter den Linden, the Brandenburg Gate, the Pergamon Museum, and Alexanderplatz.

Here's a quick review of what you'll see: Leaving from Zoologischer Garten, you'll spot the bombed-out hulk of the **Kaiser Wilhelm Memorial Church,** with its jagged spire and postwar sister church. Next, on the left, the elephant gates mark the entrance to the venerable and much-loved **Berlin Zoo** and aquarium. After a left turn, you cross the canal and pass Berlin's **embassy row.**

The bus then enters the **Tiergarten** city park and loops around the **Victory Column** (Siegessäule; with the gilded angel). A block beyond the Victory Column (on the left) is the 18th-century late-Rococo **Bellevue Palace,** the residence of the federal president (if the flag's out, he's in).

Driving along the Spree River (on the left), you'll see several striking **national government** buildings. A metal Henry Moore sculpture entitled *Butterfly* (a.k.a. "The Drinker's Liver") floats in front of the slope-roofed House of World Cultures. Through the trees on the left is the **Chancellery**—Germany's "White House." The big open space is the **Platz der Republik,** where the Victory Column (which you passed earlier) stood until Hitler moved it. The Hauptbahnhof (Berlin's vast main train station, marked by its tall tower with the *DB* sign) is across the field between the Chancellery and the **Reichstag** (Germany's parliament—the old building with the new dome).

Hop off at the next stop (Reichstag/Bundestag) if you'd like to follow my ⬛ Reichstag & Brandenburg Gate Walk (see page 86). If you stay on the bus, you'll zip by the next string of sights, in this order:

Unter den Linden, the main east-west thoroughfare, stretches from the **Brandenburg Gate** through Berlin's historic core to the TV Tower in the distance. You'll pass the **Russian Embassy** (right). Crossing **Friedrichstrasse,** look right for a Fifth Avenue-style conga line of big, glitzy department stores. Later, on the left, are the **German History Museum, Museum Island,** and the **Berlin Cathedral;** on the right is the construction site of the **Humboldt Forum** (a resurrected Prussian palace/cultural complex). You'll rumble to a final stop at the transit hub of **Alexanderplatz.**

the city's major tourist spots (Potsdamer Platz, Museum Island, Brandenburg Gate, Kaiser Wilhelm Memorial Church, and so on). For specifics, look for brochures in your hotel lobby or at the TI, or check the websites for the dominant outfits: **CitySightseeing Berlin,** a.k.a. Berlin City Tour, runs red buses and yellow-and-green buses (www.berlin-city-tour.de). **City Circle Sightseeing,** a.k.a. BEX, runs yellow-and-black buses marked with a "Grayline" logo (www.berlinerstadtrundfahrten.de).

Buses come with cursory narration in English and German by a live, sometimes tired guide, or a dry recorded commentary. Try to catch a bus with a live guide rather than a recorded spiel. In season, buses run at least four times per hour (generally April-Oct daily 10:00-18:00, last bus leaves all stops around 16:00, 2-hour loop; Nov-March 2/hour, last departure around 15:00).

Before handing over your money, consider following my self-guided "Bus #100 tour" instead (see previous page), which costs only the price of a transit ticket.

▲▲▲WALKING TOURS

Berlin's fascinating and complex history can be challenging to appreciate on your own, but a good Berlin tour guide makes the city's dynamic story come to life.

Unlike many European countries, Germany has no regulations controlling who can give city tours. This can make guide quality hit-or-miss, ranging from brilliant history buffs who've lived in Berlin for years while pursuing their PhDs, to new arrivals who memorize a script and start leading tours after being in town for just a couple of weeks. To improve your odds of landing a great guide, try one of my recommendations.

Most outfits offer walks that are variations on the same themes: general **introductory** walk, **Third Reich** walk (Hitler and Nazi sites), and day trips to **Potsdam** and the **Sachsenhausen Memorial and Museum.** Most tours cost about €12-15 and last about three to four hours (longer for side-trips to Potsdam and Sachsenhausen); public-transit tickets and entrances to sights are extra. For more details than I've given here—including prices, specific schedules, and other themed tours—see each company's website or pick up brochures at TIs, hotel reception desks, cafés, and shops.

Original Berlin Walks

With a strong commitment to quality guiding, Original Berlin's Discover Berlin walk offers a good overview in four hours (daily at 10:30 except no walks on Tue Nov-March, April-Oct also daily at 14:00). They also offer a Third Reich walking tour (Hitler's Germany), themed walks, and tours to Potsdam, Sachsenhausen, and Wittenberg. Get a €1 discount per tour with this book. Tours depart from opposite the Hackescher Markt S-Bahn station, outside the Weihenstephaner restaurant (tour info: tel. 030/301-9194, www.berlinwalks.de).

Brewer's Berlin Tours

Specializing in in-depth walks, this company was started by the late, great Terry Brewer, who once worked for the British diplomatic service in East Berlin. Terry left the company to his guides. Led by enthusiastic historians, their city tours are intimate, relaxed, and can flex with your interests. Their Best of Berlin introductory tour, billed at six hours, can last for eight (daily at 10:30). They also do a shorter 3.5-hour tour (free, tip expected, daily at 13:00), an all-day Potsdam tour (Wed and Sat May-Oct), and others. All tours depart from Bandy Brooks ice cream shop at the Friedrichstrasse S-Bahn station (tel. 0177-388-1537, www.brewersberlintours.com).

Insider Tour

This well-regarded company runs the full gamut of itineraries: introductory walk (daily), themed and museum tours, as well as Sachsenhausen, Potsdam, and a day trip to Dresden. Their tours have two meeting points: in Western Berlin, in front of the McDonald's outside the Zoologischer Garten station; and in the Scheunenviertel neighborhood, outside the AM to PM Bar at the Hackescher Markt S-Bahn station (tel. 030/692-3149, www.insidertour.com).

Berlin Underworlds Association
(Berliner Unterwelten Verein)

Much of Berlin's history lies beneath the surface, and this group is devoted to what's hidden underground. Their Dark Worlds tour takes you into a WWII air-raid bunker (year-round). The "From Flak Towers to Mountains of Debris" tour enters the Humboldthain air defense tower (April-Oct only). The "Subways and Bunkers in the Cold War" tour visits a fully functional nuclear emergency bunker in former West Berlin (year-round). Meet in the hall of the Gesundbrunnen U-Bahn/S-Bahn station—follow signs to the *Humboldthain/Brunnenstrasse* exit, and find Brunnenstrasse 105 (tour times and prices at www.berliner-unterwelten.de).

Alternative Berlin Tours

Specializing in cutting-edge street culture and art, this company emphasizes the bohemian chic that flavors the city's ever-changing urban scene. Their basic three-hour tour (daily at 11:00 and 13:00) is tip-based; other tours cost €12-20 (all tours meet at Starbucks on Alexanderplatz under the TV Tower, mobile 0162-819-8264, www.alternativeberlin.com).

ORIENTATION

"Free" Tours

You'll see ads for "free" introductory tours all over town. Popular with students (free is good), it's a business model that has spread across Europe: English-speaking students (often Aussies and Americans) deliver a memorized script before a huge crowd lured in by the promise of a free tour. The catch: Guides expect to be "tipped in paper" (€5/person minimum is encouraged). While the guides can be entertaining, better ones typically move on to more serious tour companies. These tours are fine, but as with many things, you get what you pay for.

"Free" tour companies also offer **pub crawls** that are wildly popular with visiting college students (see page 307).

Local Guides

Berlin guides are generally independent contractors who work with tour companies (such as those listed here) but can also be hired privately (generally charging around €50-60/hour or €200-300/day, confirm when booking). I've personally worked with and can strongly recommend each of the following guides: Archaeologist **Nick Jackson** (mobile 0171-537-8768, www. jacksonsberlintours.com, info@ jacksonsberlintours.com, nick.

jackson@berlin.de); **Lee Evans** (makes 20th-century Germany a thriller, mobile 0177-423-5307, lee.evans@berlin.de); **Torben Brown** (a walking Berlin encyclopedia, mobile 0176-5004-2572, tfbrown@web.de, www.berlinperspectives.com); journalist **Holger Zimmer** (a cultural connoisseur who also guides my groups, mobile 0163-345-4427, explore@berlin.de); **Carlos Meissner** (a historian with a professorial earnestness, mobile 0175-266-0575, carlos_meissner@hotmail.com, www.berlinperspectives.com); young British expat **Maisie Hitchcock** (mobile 01763-847-2717, maisiehitchcock@hotmail.com); **Caroline Marburger** (a sharp historian who has lived and studied abroad, mobile 0176-7677-9920, caroline@berlinlocals.com, www.berlinlocals.com); and **Bernhard Schlegelmilch** (the only guide listed here who grew up behind the Wall, mobile 0176-6422-9119, www.steubentoursberlin.com, info@steubentoursberlin.com).

Guides can get booked up—especially in the summer—so reserve ahead. Many of these guides belong to a guiding federation called Bündnis Berliner Stadtführer, which is a great source for connecting with even more guides (www.guides-berlin.org).

BIKE TOURS
Fat Tire Bike Tours
Fat Tire offers several different guided bike tours from April through October (most €28, 4-6 hours, 6-10 miles, check schedules at www.fattiretours.com/berlin): City Tour (daily; also available as a more expensive e-bike version), Berlin Wall Tour, Third Reich, evening food tour (€49), Modern Berlin Tour (countercultural, creative aspects of contemporary Berlin), an all-day Potsdam Gardens and Palaces Tour, and private tours for families and small groups. Meet at the TV Tower at Alexanderplatz (reservations smart, tel. 030/2404-7991).

▲▲SPREE RIVER CRUISES
Several boat companies offer €14 trips up and down the river. In one relaxing hour, you'll listen to excellent English audio-

guides, see lots of wonderful new government-commissioned architecture, and enjoy the lively park action fronting the river. Boats leave from docks clustered near the bridge behind the Berlin Cathedral (just off Unter den Linden, near the DDR Museum). For better views, go for a two-story boat with open-deck seating. While you have many essentially interchangeable options, I enjoyed the Historical Sightseeing Cruise from **Stern und Kreisschiffahrt** (mid-March-Nov daily 10:00-19:00, leaves from Nikolaiviertel Dock—cross bridge from Berlin Cathedral toward Alexanderplatz and look right; not all boats have English commentary—ask; tel. 030/536-3600, www.sternundkreis.de).

TOUR PACKAGES FOR STUDENTS
Andy Steves (Rick's son) runs Weekend Student Adventures (WSA Europe), offering 3-day and 10-day budget travel packages across Europe including accommodations, skip-the-line sightseeing, and unique local experiences. Locally guided and DIY options are available for student and budget travelers in 13 of Europe's most popular cities, including Berlin (guided trips from €199, see www.wsaeurope.com for details). Check out Andy's tips, resources, and podcast at www.andysteves.com.

SIGHTS IN BERLIN

Many visitors view Berlin through a Hitler or Berlin Wall lens—fixating on only the 20th century. But there's a lot more to the city: Its sightseeing ranks right up there alongside London, Paris, and Rome in both variety and quality—offering everything from German history, to great works of art by European masters, to world-famous treasures from the ancient world (the Pergamon altar and bust of Nefertiti). To help you prioritize, I've chosen what I think are the best of Berlin's many sights, organized geographically for more efficient sightseeing. To get you beyond the museums and into the "real Berlin," I've also described some fun-to-explore neighborhoods—from posh City West to funky Kreuzberg.

When you see a 📖 in a listing, it means the sight is described in greater detail in one of my self-guided walks or tours. This is why some of Berlin's greatest sights get the least coverage in this chapter—we'll explore them later in the book, where you'll also find crucial info on avoiding lines, saving money, and finding a decent bite to eat nearby.

A 🎧 means that the sight is covered by my free Berlin City Walk audio tour (via my Rick Steves Audio Europe app—see page 6). For these, you can choose whether to read or to listen (though the chapters in this book offer a bit more depth).

For general tips on sightseeing, see page 390. Check www.ricksteves.com/update for any significant changes that may have occurred since this book was printed.

Central Berlin (The Historic Core)

Much of Berlin's sightseeing is concentrated in this central strip, stretching along a mile-long corridor from the Tiergarten Park to Museum Island.

REICHSTAG AND BRANDENBURG GATE AREA

This area is covered in detail in the 📖 Reichstag & Brandenburg Gate Walk chapter and my free 🎧 Berlin City Walk audio tour.

▲▲▲Reichstag

Germany's historic parliament building—completed in 1894, burned in 1933, sad and lonely in a no-man's land throughout the

Cold War, and finally rebuilt and topped with a glittering glass cupola in 1999—is a symbol of a proudly reunited nation. Visit here to spiral up the remarkable dome and gaze across Berlin's rooftops, and to watch today's parliament in action. Because of security concerns, you'll need a reservation.

SIGHTS

Cost and Hours: Free, reservations required—see below, daily 8:00-24:00, last entry at 22:00, metal detectors, no big luggage allowed, Platz der Republik 1; S- or U-Bahn: Friedrichstrasse, Brandenburger Tor, or Bundestag; tel. 030/2273-2152, www.bundestag.de.

Reservations: You must make a free reservation. It's easy to do online, but book early—spots often book up several days in advance. Go to www.bundestag.de, and from the "Visit the Bundestag" menu, select "Online registration." You have two choices: "Visit to the dome" includes a good audioguide and is plenty for most; the 90-minute guided tour provides more in-depth information. After choosing your preferred date and time, you'll be sent an email link to a website where you'll enter details for each person in your party. A final email will contain your reservation (with a letter you must print out and bring with you).

Without a Reservation: Tickets may be available even when online sales are "sold out"—inquire at the tiny visitors center on the Tiergarten side of Scheidemannstrasse, across from Platz der Republik (open daily 8:00-20:00, until 18:00 Nov-March; bookings from 3 hours to 2 days in advance, go early to avoid lines). When booking, the whole party must be present and ID is required.

Another option for visiting the dome, though a bit pricey, is to have lunch or dinner at the extremely expensive rooftop restaurant, **$$$$** Käfer Dachgarten (daily 9:00-16:30 & 18:30-24:00, last access at 22:00, reserve well in advance at tel. 030/2262-9933 or www.feinkost-kaefer.de/berlin).

Getting In: Report 15 minutes before your appointed time to the temporary-looking entrance facility in front of the Reichs'

Berlin at a Glance

▲▲▲**Reichstag** Germany's historic parliament building, topped with a striking modern dome you can climb (reservations required). **Hours:** Daily 8:00-24:00. See page 29.

▲▲▲**Brandenburg Gate** One of Berlin's most famous landmarks, a massive columned gateway, at the former border of East and West. See page 35.

▲▲▲**Pergamon Museum** World-class museum of classical antiquities on Museum Island, partially closed through 2025 (including its famous Pergamon Altar). **Hours:** Daily 10:00-18:00, Thu until 20:00. See page 39.

▲▲▲**German History Museum** The ultimate swing through Germany's tumultuous story. **Hours:** Daily 10:00-18:00. See page 41.

▲▲▲**Berlin Wall Memorial** A "docu-center" with videos and displays, several outdoor exhibits, and lone surviving stretch of an intact Wall section. **Hours:** Tue-Sun 10:00-18:00, closed Mon; outdoor areas accessible daily 24 hours. See page 48.

▲▲**Memorials near the Reichstag** Tributes to Nazi victims, including Jews, disabled people, and politicians. See page 34.

▲▲**Memorial to the Murdered Jews of Europe** Holocaust memorial with almost 3,000 symbolic pillars, plus an exhibition about Hitler's Jewish victims. **Hours:** Memorial always open; information center Tue-Sun 10:00-20:00, Oct-March until 19:00, closed Mon year-round. See page 35.

▲▲**Unter den Linden** Leafy boulevard in the heart of former East Berlin, lined with some of the city's top sights. See page 35.

▲▲**Neues Museum** Egyptian antiquities collection and proud home of the exquisite 3,000-year-old bust of Queen Nefertiti. **Hours:** Daily 10:00-18:00, Thu until 20:00. See page 39.

▲▲**Old National Gallery** German paintings, mostly from the Romantic Age. **Hours:** Tue-Sun 10:00-18:00, Thu until 20:00, closed Mon. See page 40.

▲▲**DDR Museum** Quirky collection of communist-era artifacts. **Hours:** Daily 10:00-20:00, Sat until 22:00. See page 41.

▲▲**Courtyards** *(Höfe)* Interconnected courtyards with shops, eateries, and museums, best explored in the Scheunenviertel neighborhood. See page 45.

▲▲**Prenzlauer Berg** Lively, colorful neighborhood with hip cafés, restaurants, boutiques, and street life. See page 49.

▲▲**Topography of Terror** Chilling exhibit documenting the Nazi perpetrators, built on the site of the former Gestapo/SS headquarters. **Hours:** Daily 10:00-20:00. See page 54.

▲▲**Kreuzberg** *Kieze* Eclectic, trendy micro neighborhoods in the colorful Kreuzberg district, with diverse roots, popular eateries, and the Turkish street market. See page 58.

▲▲**Gemäldegalerie** Germany's top collection of 13th- through 18th-century European paintings, featuring Holbein, Dürer, Cranach, Van der Weyden, Rubens, Hals, Rembrandt, Vermeer, Velázquez, Raphael, and more. **Hours:** Tue-Fri 10:00-18:00, Thu until 20:00, Sat-Sun 11:00-18:00, closed Mon. See page 74.

▲**Gendarmenmarkt** Inviting square bounded by twin churches (one with a fine German history exhibit), a chocolate shop, and a concert hall. See page 38.

▲**Palace of Tears** Once a border crossing and place of sad good-byes, now a museum about life in divided Germany. **Hours:** Tue-Fri 9:00-19:00, Sat-Sun 10:00-18:00, closed Mon. See page 47.

▲**Museum of the Wall at Checkpoint Charlie** Stories of brave Cold War escapes, near the site of the famous former East-West border checkpoint; the surrounding street scene is almost as interesting. **Hours:** Daily 9:00-22:00. See page 52.

▲**East Side Gallery** Largest surviving stretch of the Berlin Wall, now covered with murals. See page 67.

▲**Museum of Decorative Arts** Applied arts bric-a-brac from porcelain to fashion, including elaborate reliquaries. **Hours:** Tue-Fri 10:00-18:00, Sat-Sun 11:00-18:00, closed Mon. See page 75.

▲**Kaiser Wilhelm Memorial Church** Bombed-out church ruins from World War II kept as a memorial alongside a meditative modern church. **Hours:** Church—daily 9:00-19:00—or until 18:00 if there's a concert; Memorial Hall—Mon-Fri 10:00-18:00, Sat 10:00-17:30, Sun 12:00-17:30. See page 76.

▲**Charlottenburg Palace** Baroque former home of the royal family, with large collection of 17th-century French frescoes. **Hours:** Tue-Sun 10:00-18:00, Nov-March until 17:00, closed Mon year-round. See page 82.

SIGHTS

Historic Core

······ Former Course of the Wall

500 Meters

500 Yards

HAUPTBAHNHOF & EURAIDE

Spree River

FÜRST-BISMARCK-STR.

KAPELLE UFER

OTTO-VON-BISMARCK-ALLEE

Bundestag

CHANCELLERY

To Berlin Zoo via Bus #100

Platz der Republik #100

SCHEIDEMANNSTR.

PARLIAMENT OFFICES

REICHSTAG

REICHSTAG VISITORS CENTER

BRANDENBURG GATE

Pariser Platz

To Victory Column

SOVIET WAR MEM.

STRASSE DES 17 JUNI

MEMORIAL TO THE MURDERED JEWS OF EUROPE

Tiergarten

TUNNEL TIERGARTEN

HOMOSEXUAL MEMORIAL

To Kultur-forum

LENNÉSTR.

EBERTSTRASSE

LUISENSTR.

SCHUMANNSTR.

REINHARD-STR.

MARIENSTR.

ELEVATED RAILWAY

SCHIFFBAUERDAMM

ALBRECHTSTR.

Oranienburger Tor BOROS COLLECTION

PALACE OF TEARS

Friedrich-strasse

FRIEDRICHSTRASSE

Oranienburger Strasse

JOHANNISSTR.

ZIEGELSTR.

AM WEIDEN-DAMM

PLANK

GEORGENSTR.

DOROTHEEN- STRASSE

Branden-burger Tor

HOTEL ADLON

US EMB.

DZ BANK

BRITISH EMBASSY

ACAD. OF ART

HANNAH-ARENDT-STR.

UNTER DEN LINDEN

RUSSIAN EMBASSY

BEHRENSTRASSE

WILHELMSTR.

MAUERSTR.

SCHADOW

MITTELSTR.

NEUSTÄDT.

FRIEDRICH-STR.

KOMISCHE OPER

Französische Strasse

GLINKASTR.

JÄGERSTR.

TAUBENSTR.

MOHRENSTR.

To Potsdamer Platz

To Checkpoint Charlie

Mohren-strasse

GESCHWISTER-SCHOLL-STR.

#M1 & 12 Universitäts-strasse

UNIVERSITÄTS STR.

CHARLOTTENSTR.

RITTER SPORT

FRANZÖSISCHE STR.

GALERIES LAFAYETTE

CONCERT HALL

F & R

Stadt-mitte

and be ready to show ID and your reservation print-out. After passing through a security check, you'll wait with other visitors for a guard to take you to the Reichstag entrance.

📖 For more on the building's exterior and history, see the Reichstag & Brandenburg Gate Walk chapter.

Visiting the Reichstag: The open, airy **lobby** towers 100 feet high, with 65-foot-tall colors of the German flag. See-through glass doors show the central legislative chamber. The message: There will be no secrets in this government. Look inside. Spreading his wings behind the podium is a stylized German eagle, the *Bundestagsadler* (affectionately nicknamed the "Fat Hen"), representing the Bundestag (each branch of government has its own symbolic eagle). Notice the doors

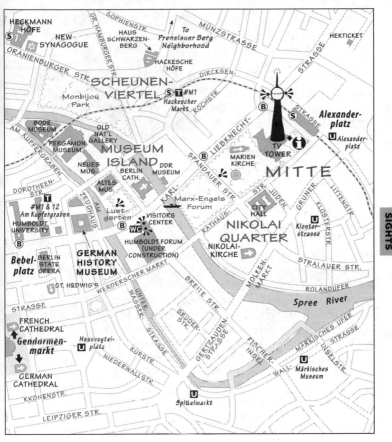

marked *Ja* (Yes), *Nein* (No), and *Enthalten* (Abstain)...an homage to the Bundestag's traditional "sheep jump" way of counting votes by exiting the chamber through the corresponding door. (For critical votes, however, they vote with electronic cards.)

Germany's Bundestag (comparable to the US House of Representatives) meets here. Its 631 members are elected to four-year terms. They in turn elect the chancellor. Unlike America's two-party system, Germany has a handful of significant parties, so they must form coalitions to govern effectively. Bundestag members have offices in the building to the left of the Reichstag.

Ride the elevator to the base of the **glass dome.** The dome is 80 feet high, 130 feet across, and weighs a quarter of a million pounds. It uses about 33,000 square feet of glass, or nearly enough to cover a football field.

Study the photos and read the circle of captions (around the base of the central funnel) telling the Reichstag story. Then study the surrounding architecture: a broken collage of new on old, torn between antiquity and modernity, like Germany's history. Notice the dome's giant and unobtrusive sunscreen that moves as necessary with the sun. Peer down through the skylight to look over the shoulders of the elected representatives at work. For Germans, the best view from here is down—keeping a close eye on their government.

Start at the **ramp** nearest the elevator and wind up to the top of the double ramp. Take a 360-degree survey of the city as you hike: The big park is the Tiergarten, the "green lungs of Berlin." Beyond that is the Teufelsberg ("Devil's Hill"). Built of rubble from the destroyed city in the late 1940s, it was famous during the Cold War as a powerful ear of the West—notice the telecommunications tower on top. Knowing the bombed-out and bulldozed story of their city, locals say, "You have to be suspicious when you see the nice, green park."

Find the Victory Column (Siegessäule), glimmering in the middle of the park. Hitler moved it there in the 1930s from in front of the Reichstag as part of his grandiose vision for postwar Berlin. Next, scenes of the new Berlin spiral into view—Potsdamer Platz, marked by the conical glass tower that houses Sony's European headquarters. Continue circling left, and find the green chariot atop the Brandenburg Gate. Just to its left is the curving fish-like roof of the DZ Bank building, designed by the unconventional American architect Frank Gehry. The Memorial to the Murdered Jews of Europe stretches south of the Brandenburg Gate. Next, you'll see former East Berlin and the city's next huge construction zone, with a forest of 300-foot-tall skyscrapers in the works. Notice the TV Tower, the Berlin Cathedral's massive dome, and the golden dome of the New Synagogue.

Follow the train tracks in the distance to the left toward Berlin's huge main train station, the Hauptbahnhof. Complete your spin-tour with the blocky, postmodern Chancellery, the federal government's headquarters. Continue spiraling up. You'll come across all the same sights again, twice, from higher vantage points.

▲▲Memorials near the Reichstag

The area immediately surrounding the Reichstag is rich with memorials. Within a few steps, you'll find monuments to politicians who opposed Hitler; to the various groups targeted by the Nazis (Jews, Roma, homosexuals, and people with disabilities); to victims of the Berlin Wall; and even to the Soviet soldiers who liberated Berlin from Hitler—plunging it into the deep end of the Cold War. For more on these monuments, see the sidebar on page 92.

Most of these memorials are within (or facing) the sprawling park called the Tiergarten, which extends west from the Brandenburg Gate. For more on the Tiergarten, see the listing later in this chapter.

▲▲▲Brandenburg Gate

The icon of Berlin, this majestic gateway has seen more than its share of history. Armies from Napoleon to Hitler have marched

under its gilded statues, and for more than 25 years, it sat forlorn in the Berlin Wall's death strip. Today it's a symbol of Berlin's rejuvenated capital.

Just inside (east of) the Brandenburg gate is the tidy "Parisian Square"—Pariser Platz. This prime real estate is ringed by governmental buildings, banks, historic plush hotels, the Academy of Arts, and the heavily fortified US Embassy.

▲▲Memorial to the Murdered Jews of Europe (Denkmal für die Ermordeten Juden Europas)

This labyrinth of 2,711 irregularly shaped pillars memorializes the six million Jewish people who were executed by the Nazis. Loaded

with symbolism, it's designed to encourage a pensive moment in the heart of a big city. At its information center, you can learn more about the Nazis' crimes and see items belonging to the victims.

Cost and Hours: Memorial—free and always open; information center—open Tue-Sun 10:00-20:00, Oct-March until 19:00, closed Mon year-round, last entry 45 minutes before closing, brief security screening at entry, audioguide-€4; S-Bahn: Brandenburger Tor or Potsdamer Platz, tel. 030/2639-4336, www.stiftung-denkmal.de.

UNTER DEN LINDEN

Berlin's main boulevard—"Under the Linden Trees"—has been the city's artery since the 15th century. Today, it's a well-tended place to stroll. This main drag is covered in detail in the ☐ Unter den Linden Walk chapter and my free ⌖ Berlin City Walk audio tour.

SIGHTS

Nazi and World War II Sites

Many people come to Berlin hoping to see sites from World War II. These fall into two broad categories: Nazi and Hitler sites, and memorials to their greatest crime, the Holocaust.

Nazi and Military Sights

Hitler left Berlin in ruins, so there's not much left to see of his capital city. If you're determined, track down these sights (described in the ◫ Reichstag & Brandenburg Gate Walk and ◫ Fascism & Cold War Walk chapters).

Hitler's Bunker: The site where Hitler committed suicide at the end of the war is marked by a simple plaque.

Topography of Terror: On the site of the Gestapo and SS headquarters, this has Berlin's best exhibit documenting Nazi crimes.

German History Museum: Visit for excellent exhibits about Hitler and the Nazis.

Former Air Ministry: Once the base for Hermann Göring's Luftwaffe, this is one of only a few still-standing Nazi-built governmental buildings.

Tempelhof Airport: Another massive, blocky, Nazi-built structure.

German Resistance Memorial: This memorial near Kulturforum chronicles Germans who attempted to fight Hitler from within.

Neue Wache: This former guardhouse now holds Käthe Kollwitz's *pietà*, memorializing Germany's victims of tyranny—from soldiers to concentration camp victims.

Kaiser Wilhelm Memorial Church: In City West, this church has

▲▲Strolling Unter den Linden

On this showcase street, you'll sense echoes of the Prussian kings and kaisers who shaped Berlin (and modern Germany). Along the way, you'll discover DDR-era S-Bahn stations, the Russian Embassy, nostalgic *Ampelmännchen* traffic lights, a futuristic VW showroom, and a statue of Frederick the Great—

been left in ruins as a reminder of WWII destruction.

Holocaust Sights

Memorials: Groups targeted by the Nazis are honored with memorials, most near Brandenburg Gate.

Stolpersteine (stumbling stones): Small brass plaques embedded

in the pavement throughout Berlin identify buildings where Holocaust victims lived. (For details, see page 185.)

Scheunenviertel Landmarks: New Synagogue (partially rebuilt after the war) and a **Jewish cemetery** along Grosse Hamburger Strasse are reminders of the Jewish community that once thrived here. (□ See the Scheunenviertel Walk chapter.) Prenzlauer Berg also has a Jewish cemetery and a synagogue (on Rykestrasse) that managed to survive Kristallnacht.

Haus Schwarzenberg Courtyard Museums: Also in the Scheunenviertel are two powerful museums honoring Nazi victims: The **Museum of Otto Weidt's Workshop for the Blind,** celebrating a Berliner who employed blind and deaf Jews to save them from the Nazis, and the **Silent Heroes Memorial Center,** with more stories of resistance.

The Jewish Museum: While dedicated to the full breadth of Germany's Jewish experience, this museum thoughtfully recalls the Holocaust, both in its modern building's design and in its exhibits.

Sachsenhausen Concentration Camp Memorial: At this powerful site outside of Berlin, you can learn more about the Nazis' methods and honor their victims.

the 18th-century king who put his hometown on the world map. And you're sure to see lots of construction along this street—which, like Berlin itself, is continually reinventing itself.

Farther east—as you approach Museum Island—are two poignant landmarks. The square called Bebelplatz was designed by Frederick the Great to showcase his idealistic and enlightened vision for Berlin as a cultural capital, with a university library, an opera house, and the first Catholic church built in Prussia after the Reformation. Later, Hitler chose this as the place to torch 20,000 forbidden books in 1933 (look for the glass window in the middle of the square, and peer into a subterranean room of empty bookshelves). Across Unter den Linden and a few steps toward Museum Island, the Neue Wache royal barracks houses a powerful *pietà* by Berlin sculptor Käthe Kollwitz, honoring the toll Germany's 20th century took on its people.

▲Gendarmenmarkt

Berlin's finest square sits two blocks south of Unter den Linden (and one block south of Bebelplatz). The square, like its name ("Square of the Gens d'Armes," Freder-

ick the Great's French guard), is a hybrid of Prussia and France. The square is bookended by two matching churches: the German Cathedral (with a free exhibit on the German parliamentary system) and the French Cathedral (with a dome climb and an exhibit on the French Hugue-nots who found refuge in Prussia). Gendarmenmarkt's centerpiece is the Concert Hall (Konzerthaus), commissioned by Frederick the Great and built by his favorite architect, Karl Friedrich Schinkel. While the square is more about simply enjoying a genteel space than it is about sightseeing, you can dip into its church/museums or visit a pair of fun chocolate shops nearby.

MUSEUM ISLAND AREA

Filling a spit of land in the middle of the Spree River, Museum Island has perhaps Berlin's highest concentration of serious sightseeing. The island's centerpiece is the grassy square called Lustgarten, ringed by five museums and the hulking Berlin Cathedral.

This neighborhood is covered in more detail in the 📖 Unter den Linden Walk chapter and my free 🎧 Berlin City Walk audio tour. For cruises on the Spree River from near Museum Island, see page 27.

Museum Island (Museumsinsel)

Five of Berlin's top museums—featuring art and artifacts from around the world—are just a

few steps apart on Museum Island. These museums are described in great depth in the 📖 Museum Island Tour and 📖 Pergamon Museum Tour chapters.

Cost and Hours: Each museum has its own admission

(€10-12, includes audioguide). If you're visiting at least two museums here, invest in the €18 Museum Island Pass (which covers all 5; also covered by the €24 Museum Pass Berlin—see page 14). The museums are open 10:00-18:00 (until 20:00 on Thu). The Pergamon and Neues museums are open daily; the Old National Gallery, Bode Museum, and Altes Museum are open Tue-Sun, closed Mon.

Avoiding Crowds: The always-busy Pergamon is most crowded in the morning, on weekends, and when it rains; Thursday evenings are the least crowded. You can also book a timed-entry ticket (or, if you have a pass, a reservation), tel. 030/266-424-242, www. smb.museum.

Getting There: The island is a 10-minute walk from the Hackescher Markt or Friedrichstrasse S-Bahn stations. Trams #M1 and #12 connect to Prenzlauer Berg. Buses #100 and #200 run along Unter den Linden, stopping near the museums at the Lustgarten stop.

Expect Construction: A new visitors center (the James-Simon-Galerie) will connect the complex with tunnels, possibly by 2024.

▲▲▲Pergamon Museum (Pergamonmuseum)

This world-class museum contains Berlin's Collection of Classical Antiquities (Antikensammlung)—in other words, full-sized buildings from the most illustrious civilizations of the ancient world. Its namesake and highlight—the gigantic Pergamon Altar—is under renovation and off-limits to visitors until 2025. In the meantime, there's still plenty to see: the massive Babylonian Processional Way and Ishtar Gate (slathered with glazed blue tiles, from the sixth century B.C.); artifacts from the Assyrians (7th-10th century B.C.); the full-sized market gate from the ancient Roman settlement of Miletus (first century B.C.); and, upstairs, an extensive collection of treasures from the Islamic world. Take advantage of the excellent, included audioguide.

▲▲Neues (New) Museum

This beautifully renovated museum, featuring objects from the prehistoric (i.e., pre-Pergamon) world, contains three collections. Most visitors focus on the Egyptian Collection, with the famous and even-more-stunning-in-person bust of Queen Nefertiti. But it's also worth a walk through the Museum of Prehistory and Early History (see an actual Neanderthal skull and an exquisitely decorated, nearly three-foot-tall hat made of gold), and some items from the Collection of Classical Antiquities (artifacts from ancient Troy—famously excavated by German adventurer Heinrich Schliemann—and Cyprus). Everything is well-described in English (fine audioguide included with admission; for more on the museum, see www.neues-museum.de).

▲▲Old National Gallery (Alte Nationalgalerie)

Of Berlin's many top-notch art collections, this is the best for *German* art—mostly paintings from the 19th century, the era in which "German culture" first came to

mean something. For a concise visit, focus on the Romantic German paintings (top floor), where Caspar David Friedrich's hauntingly beautiful canvases offer an insightful glimpse into German landscapes...and the German psyche. With more time, peruse the French and German Impressionists and German Realists on the first and second floors.

Bode Museum

This fine building—at the northern tip of the island—contains a hodgepodge of collections: Byzantine art, historic coins, ecclesiastical art, sculptures, and medals commemorating the fall of the Berlin Wall and German reunification. While this museum is too deep a dive for casual sightseers, avid museumgoers find plenty to excite here—including the stunning Ravenna Mosaic, transplanted here from the Byzantine world of sixth-century Italy. For a free, quick look at its lavish interior, climb the grand staircase under a sweeping dome to the charming café on the first floor.

Altes (Old) Museum

Of the five Museum Island collections, this is the least exciting—unless you're an enthusiast of obscure Etruscan, Roman, and Greek art and artifacts.

Berlin Cathedral (Berliner Dom)

This bulky stone structure, with its rusted-copper dome, looms over Museum Island like the home church of a Prussian kaiser...because it was. Kaiser Wilhelm II built this to epitomize his bigger-is-better aesthetic.

While pricey to enter, the lavish interior has some fine details and the opportunity to climb 270 steps for sweeping views. Skip the crypt.

Cost and Hours: €7 includes dome gallery access, not covered by Museum Island Pass, Mon-Sat 9:00-20:00, Sun from 12:00, until 19:00 Oct-March, closes around 17:30 on concert days, interior closed but dome open during services, last entry one hour before closing, audioguide-€3, tel. 030/2026-9136, www.berliner-dom.de.

Humboldt Forum Visitors Center

Communists replaced the Prussian palace on this site with a giant "brutalist" conference center. Now, that DDR-era building is being replaced with a cultural complex that essentially resurrects the original palace. The visitors center (in the big, boxy structure along the street) hosts models and illustrations of the construction plans, and offers views of Museum Island.

Cost and Hours: Free, daily 10:00-18:00, www.humboldt forum.com.

Near Museum Island

The German History Museum is on Unter den Linden, immediately west of Museum Island; and the DDR Museum is (fittingly) just east of Museum Island, on the riverbank facing the back of the Berlin Cathedral. The Nikolai Quarter is a five-minute walk to the south, down the river (facing Museum Island). For locations, see the map on page 121.

▲▲▲German History Museum
(Deutsches Historisches Museum)

This impressive museum offers the best look at German history under one roof, anywhere. The permanent collection packs 9,000 artifacts into two huge rectangular floors of the old arsenal building. You'll stroll through insightfully described historical objects, paintings, photographs, and models—all intermingled with multimedia stations. The 20th-century section—on the ground floor—is far better than any of the many price-gouging historical Nazi or Cold War "museums" all over town. A thoughtful visit here provides valuable context for your explorations of Berlin (and Germany).

Cost and Hours: €8, daily 10:00-18:00, good €3 audioguide, Unter den Linden 2, tel. 030/2030-4751, www.dhm.de.

📖 See the German History Museum Tour chapter.

▲▲DDR Museum

While overpriced, crammed with school groups, and frustrating to local historians, the DDR Museum has a knack for helping

SIGHTS

Cold War, Berlin Wall, and DDR Sights

When visiting Berlin, it's hard not to get caught up in Cold War intrigue. The city has several sights relating to East Berlin from the 1940s to the 1990s; each is covered in depth elsewhere in this book.

To learn more about the Cold War, see the ∩ Fascism & Cold War Walk and ∩ Communist East Berlin Walk chapters.

Berlin Wall Sights

Berlin Wall Memorial: The best all-around place to learn about the Wall is at the memorial along Bernauer Strasse, with two visitors centers and information boards.

Checkpoint Charlie: While tacky and touristy, the spot where people crossed between West and East is still evocative. The **Museum of the Wall at Checkpoint Charlie** is dated but offers engaging stories of escapes.

Stretch of Wall Along Niederkirchnerstrasse: A short stretch of the Wall is next to the Topography of Terror and a nearby surviving watchtower.

East Side Gallery: This nearly mile-long stretch of surviving Wall is still painted with vivid graffiti (east of the center, in Friedrichshain).

"Life in the DDR" Sights

Several good, somewhat overlapping museums illuminate various aspects of life in East Germany (a.k.a., the DDR).

DDR Museum: Near Museum Island, its hands-on approach makes East German lifestyles accessible to outsiders.

Everyday Life in the DDR: An exhibit in Prenzlauer Berg, this is equally good, though more intellectually rigorous and geared to a German audience.

Palace of Tears: The building where people crossed between East and West (next to Friedrichstrasse Station) has a good exhibit about DDR life.

Stasi Museum: Farther out in Friedrichshain, this museum fills the former headquarters of the DDR secret police with a dense exhibit about their crimes.

Other Cold War Sights

German History Museum: Excellent exhibits include the Cold War period.

Architecture: The socialist aesthetic is on display around **Alexanderplatz,** the **TV Tower,** and **Karl-Marx-Allee.**

Platz der Luftbrücke: "Air Bridge Square," in front of Tempelhof Field, has a towering monument celebrating the 1948-49 Berlin Airlift.

USSR-Built Memorials: The Russian soldiers who died to free Berlin from Hitler are honored with the **Soviet War Memorial** (in Tiergarten park) and the much bigger and more dramatic **Treptower Park** (farther out, just east of Kreuzberg).

JFK Sights: The **Kennedys Museum** and the front steps of **Schöneberg City Hall**—where the president famously proclaimed, *"Ich bin ein Berliner"*—are good stops for JFK fans.

Potsdam: This posh town outside of Berlin holds the **Cecilienhof Palace,** where Truman, Churchill, and Stalin met in the famous 1945 Potsdam Conference; and a **KGB Prison Memorial,** on the site of a Russian "counterintelligence" facility.

Potsdamer Platz, the **Reichstag,** and the **Brandenburg Gate:** These sights were once stranded within or near the Berlin Wall's death strip, and today are some of the city's most vital spaces.

More Cold War

This book also covers the Berlin Wall (page 212) and its fall (page 177); the Berlin Airlift (page 63); the Stasi (page 69); communist-era apartment blocks (page 175); and DDR-era Trabant cars (known as Trabi; page 230).

U6 Cold War Spine: The U6 subway line conveniently links up several powerful Cold War-era sights, in roughly chronological order. For a busy day of Cold War sightseeing, begin at the **Platz der Luftbrücke** to see the monument and Tempelhof Airport where the Berlin Airlift took place. Then ride to the **Checkpoint Charlie** stop to see the most famous border crossing at the Berlin Wall. Next is the **Friedrichstrasse** station, near the Palace of Tears. And finally, the **Nordbahnhof** is at the start of the Berlin Wall Memorial.

outsiders (rather than "Ost-algic" Germans) understand life in communist East Germany (the *Deutsche Demokratische Republik,* or DDR). Visitors walk through a reconstructed home—peeking into bathroom cabinets and wardrobes—and are encouraged to pick up and handle anything that isn't behind glass. The museum is well-stocked with kitschy everyday items from the DDR period, plus photos, video clips, and concise English explanations.

Cost and Hours: €9.50, daily 10:00-20:00, Sat until 22:00, just across the Spree from Museum Island at Karl-Liebknecht-Strasse 1, tel. 030/847-123-731, www.ddr-museum.de.

Visiting the Museum: Inside, you can crawl through a Trabant car (known as a "Trabi"; take it for a virtual test drive) and pick up some DDR-era black humor ("East Germany had 39 newspapers, four radio stations, two TV channels...and one opinion"). You'll learn how many East Germans—with limited opportunities to travel abroad—vacationed on Hungary's Lake Balaton or on the Baltic Coast, where nudism was all the rage (as a very revealing display explains). Lounge in DDR cinema chairs as you view a subtitled propaganda film or clips from beloved-in-the-East TV shows, including the popular kids' show *Sandmännchen*—"Little Sandman." The highlight is a tourable reconstructed communist-era home, where you can open drawers and cupboards to find both information panels and the trappings of a typical DDR home. You can even climb into a rickety old "elevator" and get jostled around.

Nikolai Quarter (Nikolaiviertel)

The Nikolai Quarter marks the original medieval settlement of Cölln, which would eventually become Berlin. Huddled around the twin spires of the Nikolaikirche (along the river, but tucked behind blocky buildings—as if hidden from the main road), the area was destroyed during the war, then rebuilt for Berlin's 750th birthday in 1987. It has a cute and cobbled old-town feel...Middle Ages meets Socialist Realism. Today most of the buildings are occupied by touristy shops and restaurants—giving it a soulless, cut-rate Epcot vibe. Still, if you aren't exploring any small towns (such as Wittenberg) on your visit to Germany, this zone is worth a stroll. You can duck into the Nikolaikirche to see its pristinely renovated interior, which now houses a museum. There's also a small, pricey-but-interesting museum dedicated to Heinrich Zille, a local photographer and illustrator who captured engaging slices of Berlin life in the early 20th century (€7, daily 11:00-19:00, Nov-March until 18:00, http://zillemuseum-berlin. de). Perhaps the best reason to come here is to visit its old-fashioned beer hall—the recommended Brauhaus Georgbräu, with seating along the river.

Northern Berlin

THE SCHEUNENVIERTEL ("BARN QUARTER")
Immediately northeast of the Spree River is the Scheunenviertel ("Barn Quarter") neighborhood, packed with intriguing shops and fun eateries. This is also one of the most important areas for Berlin's historic Jewish community—offering insights into a culture that thrived here until the 1940s. On a sunny day, a stroll through this bursting-with-life area, and onward to Prenzlauer Berg, can be as engaging as any museum in town.

📖 For a self-guided walk through this fine area—including the first two sights listed below—see the Scheunenviertel Walk chapter.

▲▲Courtyards (Höfe)
The Scheunenviertel is a particularly handy place to explore Berlin's unique *Höfe*—interconnected courtyards that burrow through city blocks, today often filled

with trendy shops and cateries. Two starkly different examples are nearly next door, and just steps from the Hackescher Markt transit hub: the upscale, *Jugendstil* Hackesche Höfe (Rosenthaler Strasse 40), with eye-pleasing architectural flourishes and upscale shops; and the funky Haus Schwarzenberg (Rosenthaler Strasse 39), with museums honoring Berliners who defied the Nazis to save Jews—including Otto Weidt, who employed blind and deaf Jews in his workshop.

New Synagogue (Neue Synagogue)
Marked by its golden dome, this large, mid-19th-century synagogue is now a modest museum, memorializing the Berlin Jewish community that was decimated by the Nazis. While the exhibits

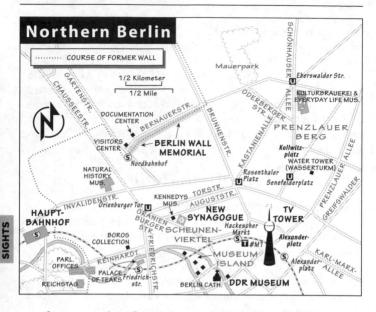

are of interest only to Jewish history buffs, the beautiful shimmering dome makes a bold statement.

Cost and Hours: Main exhibit–€5, dome–€3, combo-ticket for both–€6, April-Sept Mon-Fri 10:00-18:00, Sun until 19:00; Oct-March dome closed, exhibit open Sun-Thu 10:00-18:00, Fri until 15:00; closed Sat year-round; audioguide–€3, Oranienburger Strasse 28, S-Bahn: Oranienburger Strasse, tel. 030/8802-8300 and press 1, www.cjudaicum.de.

Visiting the Synagogue: Enter through the low-profile door in the modern building to the right of the domed synagogue facade. Inside, past tight security, a small but moving permanent exhibit with good English descriptions recounts the Berlin Jewish community through the centuries. Under the soaring dome, a cutaway model shows the entire synagogue. Skip the stair climb to the dome (past temporary exhibits, separate entry fee); it's unimpressive from the inside and has ho-hum views.

The Kennedys Museum

This crisp collection (in a former Jewish girls' school building) recalls John F. Kennedy's 1963 Germany trip with photos and video clips, as well as a photographic shrine to the Kennedy clan in America. Among the interesting mementos are old campaign buttons and posters, and JFK's notes with the phonetic pronunciation "Ish bin ein Bearleener." Jacqueline Kennedy commented on how strange it was that this—not even in his native language—was her husband's most quotable quote. The highlight: a newsreel of Kennedy's historic speech (20 minutes, plays continuously).

Cost and Hours: €5, Tue-Fri 10:00-18:00, Sat-Sun from 11:00, closed Mon, tel. 030/2065-3570, www.thekennedys.de.

Getting There: Look for a huge red-brick building with red-and-white-striped doors (Auguststrasse 13, on the opposite end of the block from the New Synagogue, museum is on the second floor). For a shortcut from the synagogue, cut through the Heckmann Höfe courtyard (at Oranienburger Strasse 32) and turn right on Auguststrasse.

▲Palace of Tears (Tränenpalast) at Friedrichstrasse Station

Just south of the Scheunenviertel (cross the river on Weidendammer Brücke and bear right) stands this impactful Cold War site.

The Friedrichstrasse train station—situated within East Berlin, but accessible by train from West Berlin—was one of the few places where Westerners were allowed to cross into the East. And when crossing back into the free world, this was where they'd take leave of their East German loved ones. The scene of so many sad farewells, it earned the nickname "Tränenpalast" (palace of tears). The 1962 building—an unassuming, boxy, bureaucratic structure that was once attached by a corridor to the station—has now been converted into a museum about everyday life in a divided Germany, with a fascinating peek into the paranoid border-control world of the DDR. Ample artifacts—such as suitcases and their contents—illustrate the story. You'll learn about contraband that was smuggled over the border (and the guards who played a constant cat-and-mouse game with the smugglers), and watch archival footage from the era. Of the many "life in the Cold War" sights in Berlin, this is the one most closely linked to a specific location.

Cost and Hours: Free, includes excellent audioguide, Tue-Fri 9:00-19:00, Sat-Sun 10:00-18:00, closed Mon, on the river side of the Friedrichstrasse station—look for the building with large glass windows and blue trim, Reichstagufer 17, tel. 030/4677-7790, www.hdg.de/traenenpalast.

Boros Collection (Sammlung Boros)

An aboveground air-raid bunker, dating from 1942, sits just west of the Oranienburger Tor U-Bahn stop. Since 2007, it's been a venue for a private collection of contemporary art (1990s to present), visitable only on a guided tour.

Cost and Hours: €12, reservations required—book on website, English tours Thu-Sun hourly at :30 past each hour 10:00-17:00, closed Mon-Wed, Reinhardstrasse 20, www.sammlung-boros.de.

BERLIN WALL SIGHTS

At the far-northern edge of Mitte, brushing up against Prenzlauer Berg, is Berlin's most famous sight, the Berlin Wall Memorial.

▲▲▲Berlin Wall Memorial (Gedenkstätte Berliner Mauer)

This is Berlin's most substantial and educational sight relating to its gone-but-not-forgotten Wall. Exhibits line up along several blocks of Bernauer Strasse, stretching more than a mile northeast from the Nordbahnhof S-Bahn station (one of the DDR's "ghost stations") to Schwedter Strasse and the Mauerpark. For a targeted visit, focus on the engaging sights clustered near the Nordbahnhof: two museums (with films, photos, and harrowing personal stories); various open-air exhibits and memorials; original Wall fragments; and observation tower views into the only preserved, complete stretch of the Wall system (with a Cold War-era "death strip"). Begin at the Nordbahnhof, pick up an informational pamphlet from the Visitors Center, head up Bernauer Strasse, visit the exhibits and memorials that interest you, then ride home from the Bernauer Strasse U-Bahn station. For a longer visit, walk several more blocks all the way to the Mauerpark. The entire stretch is lined with informational posts (some with video or audio clips) and larger-than-life images from the Wall, painted on the sides of buildings.

Cost and Hours: Free; outdoor areas accessible daily 24 hours; Visitors Center and Documentation Center both open Tue-Sun 10:00-18:00, closed Mon, memorial chapel closes at 17:00; on Bernauer Strasse at #119 (Visitors Center) and #111 (Documentation Center), tel. 030/4679-86666, www.berliner-mauer-gedenkstaette.de.

📖 See the Berlin Wall Memorial Tour chapter.

Mauerpark

Where the eastern reaches of the Berlin Wall Memorial run into the western edge of Prenzlauer Berg, you'll hit the Mauerpark (Wall Park). Once part of the Wall's death strip, today it's a Prenzlauer Berg green space. The park is particularly entertaining on Sundays, when it hosts a rummage market and a giant karaoke party. Along the bluff, below the old DDR soccer stadium, runs a bit of the Wall covered in graffiti art.

📖 For more on the Mauerpark, see the Prenzlauer Berg Walk.

PRENZLAUER BERG

This thriving district, worth ▲▲, offers an ideal opportunity to see a corner of today's "real Berlin," just beyond the core tourist zone but still easily accessible. Prenzlauer Berg (PRENTS-low-er behrk) was largely untouched by World War II bombs, fell into disrepair during DDR days, and has since been completely rejuvenated. The neighborhood fans out to the north and east from Rosenthaler Platz; the most appealing bit is along Kastanienallee, which connects Rosenthaler Platz to the Eberswalder Strasse U-Bahn tracks (and is served by tram #M1, which begins its run at Hackescher Markt S-Bahn station). The area just to the east, around Kollwitzplatz, is also enjoyable. Key landmarks include the Wasserturm (Industrial Age water tower); trendy Kollwitzplatz (with its upscale playgrounds); the Kulturbrauerei and Everyday Life in the DDR museum (both described next); lively Kastanienallee and livable Oderberger Strasse; and Berlin Wall sights in and near the Mauerpark. For locations, see the map on page 194. Prenzlauer Berg is also a great place to sleep, eat, shop, and enjoy nightlife—all of which are covered in those chapters.

📖 See the Prenzlauer Berg Walk chapter.

Kulturbrauerei

The "Culture Brewery" is a onetime brewery-turned-cultural center that fills an evocative old industrial space with a handful of interesting shops, breezy restaurants, a movie theater, grocery store, and TI, plus a Sunday food market (12:00-18:00),

winter Christmas market, and other outdoor events (Schönhauser Allee 36, tel. 030/4435-2170). Of most interest is the museum described next.

▲Everyday Life in the DDR (Alltag in der DDR)

This museum, tucked in a passage at the northern end of the Kulturbrauerei, recounts the quotidian reality of communist East Germany. The thoughtful, well-curated collection—organized by theme—displays original artifacts, videos, photos, art, and mock storefronts that rise above the kitsch factor to give a real sense of the disparity between the socialist ideal and the grinding reality. It's designed not for casual tourists, but for aging Germans eager to teach their kids and grandkids about how they once lived. (The

DDR Museum near Museum Island—described earlier—is less substantial, but also more tourist-friendly.) Although tricky to appreciate, this museum is free and well worth a visit, particularly if you're well-versed in DDR history.

Cost and Hours: Free, Tue-Sun 10:00-18:00, Thu until 20:00, closed Mon; enter at Knaackstrasse 97, tel. 030/4677 7790, www.hdg.de.

Visiting the Museum: As you explore, tune into details that offer insight into the DDR daily reality. The rack of magazines—all published to coincide with the big "Workers' Day" May 1 holiday—make it clear that freedom of the press was an illusion. A humble pub's short, handwritten menu demonstrates how limited even basic foodstuffs were—often relying on ersatz, miserable knock-offs (look for the "Kaffee-Mix," containing

51 percent actual coffee...and 49 percent fillers). Better-quality goods were mostly exported to bring in hard Western currency. People with loved ones in the West looked forward to receiving an occasional Westpaket—a care package of Western goods (minus whatever was seized by Stasi mail inspectors). Even the clothing was government-controlled. Peek inside the typical, circa-1979 Datsche—a simple countryside "allotment garden" cottage (owned by one in six East Germans) used for weekend retreats from the grimy city. You'll also learn about vacations (even just visiting Hungary's Lake Balaton—see the big postcards near the Trabi—came with bureaucratic hurdles); the Stasi secret police, who kept a close eye on all citizens; party propaganda, often through organizations like the Free German Youth (FDJ—scouts who were co-opted by communist messaging); and the organization of various workplaces into "collectives" where everyone was supposedly equal, yet somebody was in charge.

HAUPTBAHNHOF AREA
Hauptbahnhof

Berlin's main train station is a sight in itself—a postmodern temple of slick transportation. Even if you're not arriving or departing here, it's worth a quick visit to ogle the soaring main hall, peer down into a canyon of crisscrossing platforms connecting Berlin to the rest of Germany and beyond, and do a little shopping. (On Sundays, this is where you'll find the highest concentration of open shops.) It's also home to the handy, American-run EurAide office—the most user-friendly place in town to book train tickets and reservations. For more on the Hauptbahnhof, see the Berlin Connections chapter.

Natural History Museum (Museum für Naturkunde)

Between the Hauptbahnhof and the Berlin Wall Memorial, this museum contains one of the best-preserved, most complete T-Rex skeletons ever assembled. While you're there, meet "Bobby" the stuffed ape, and tour shelf after shelf of animals preserved in ethanol (about a million all together). Kid-friendly interactive displays include the "History of the Universe in 120 Seconds" exhibit and virtual-reality "Jurascope" glasses that put meat and skin on the dinosaur skeletons.

Cost and Hours: €8, €5 for kids, Tue-Fri 9:30-18:00, Sat-Sun 10:00-18:00, closed Mon, Invalidenstrasse 43, U6: Naturkundemuseum, tel. 030/2093-8591, www.naturkundemuseum-berlin.de.

SIGHTS

Southern Berlin

The following sights are listed roughly north to south (as you'd reach them from Unter den Linden).

FASCISM AND COLD WAR SITES NEAR CHECKPOINT CHARLIE

A variety of fascinating sites relating to Germany's tumultuous 20th century cluster south of Unter den Linden.

📖 For a guided walk connecting these, see the Fascism and Cold War Walk chapter (includes a visit inside the Topography of Terror).

▲Checkpoint Charlie

Famous as the place where many visiting Westerners crossed into East Berlin during the Cold War, the original Checkpoint Charlie is long gone. But today

a reconstructed guard station—with big posters of American and Soviet guards, and a chilling "You are leaving the American sector" sign—attracts curious tourists for a photo op. Nothing here is original (except for the nearby museum—described next), and the whole area feels like a Cold War theme park, with kitschy communist-themed attractions, Trabi rides, hucksters, buskers, and sleazy vendors who charge through the nose for a DDR stamp in your passport. Those nostalgic for the Cold War enjoy seeing this historic site and visit-

Southern Berlin

To Unter den Linden
Stadtmitte
Potsdamer Platz
CHECKPOINT CHARLIE
Kochstrasse
KOCH
BERLINISCHE GALERIE
TOPOGRAPHY OF TERROR
JEWISH MUSEUM
ORANIENSTRASSE
KREUZBERG
Mariannenplatz
Spree River
OST-BAHNHOF
MERCEDES-BENZ ARENA
EAST SIDE GALLERY
MÜHLENSTR.
Warschauer Strasse
MARKTHALLE NEUN
WRANGELSTR.
Schlesisches Tor
OBERBAUM-BRÜCKE
WRANGELKIEZ
Görlitzer Park
Halleschesches Tor
GITSCHINER STR.
Kottbusser Tor
"KREUZBERG 36"
Görlitzer Bahnhof
Landwehr Canal
Mehringdamm
GRAEFEKIEZ
PAUL-LINCKE-UFER
Gneisenaustr.
URBANSTR.
DIEFFEN
MAYBACHUFER
To Treptower Park
GNEISENAUSTR.
MITTEN
GRIMM
GRAEFESTR.
Viktoriapark
MARHEINEKE MARKTHALLE
"THE KREUZBERG" (MONUMENT)
"KREUZBERG 61"
BERGMANNKIEZ
TURKISH STREET MARKET (TUE & FRI)
Platz der Luftbrücke
TEMPELHOF FIELD & "AIR BRIDGE" MEMORIAL
Tempelhof Park
COLUMBIADAMM
NEUKÖLLN

1 Kilometer
1 Mile
········ COURSE OF FORMER WALL

ing the museum, but for a more serious look at the Berlin Wall, visit the official Berlin Wall Memorial (described earlier).

▲Museum of the Wall at Checkpoint Charlie (Mauermuseum Haus am Checkpoint Charlie)

This ragtag but riveting celebration of the many ways desperate East Germans managed to slip through the Wall to freedom has stood here since 1963...taunting DDR authorities. Today East Germany and its Wall are long gone, but the museum is still going strong. Some of the displays have yellowed, the place is cramped and confusing, and the ticket prices are way too high, but the museum retains a special sense of history. Visiting here, you'll learn about the creation of the Wall and the many escape attempts (including several of the actual items used by clever escapees). If you're pressed for time, visit after dinner, when most other museums are closed. Compared to the soberly academic official Berlin Wall Memorial near the Nordbahnhof, this museum has more personality, buoyed by a still-defiant spirit.

Cost and Hours: €12.50, daily 9:00-22:00, last entry one hour before closing, audioguide-€5, U6 to Kochstrasse or U2 to Stadtmitte, Friedrichstrasse 43, tel. 030/253-7250, www.mauermuseum.de.

Visiting the Museum: The first (cramped) room gets you

right into it. A VW bug shows how people were smuggled through Checkpoint Charlie—note the mannequin behind the spare tire.

The timeline on the wall behind the car takes you through the events that made Checkpoint Charlie necessary. It's 1946 and the war's over, but the USSR possesses half of Berlin. Churchill warns the world that an Iron Curtain is descending (see the video). In 1949, West Berlin is blockaded (another video), but the city is saved by the US airlift. Still, people are becoming trapped under repressive Soviet rule. The section called "Raoul Wallenberg lives" honors the Swedish diplomat who saved tens of thousands of Jews during World War II, then disappeared under Soviet arrest. Countless others (names in binders) were similarly lost to Soviet work camps.

Upstairs, photos of June 17, 1953 show the brutal suppression of an East German revolt. (The big boulevard through Tiergarten park is named for this date.)

In the next room, the divide between East and West widens. In 1955, West Germany joined NATO, while the East joined the Warsaw Pact. In 1956, a Hungarian uprising was crushed by Soviet tanks; 1957 saw the arms race and a "Missile Gap." The split between East and West finally hardened into concrete and rebar when the Wall went up in 1961. You'll see a model of the Wall and its fortified and booby-trapped death strip. When the Wall went up, so did the famous Checkpoint Charlie guard station—the first (or last) stop in American territory.

The rest of the museum focuses largely on many ingenious escape attempts: A beat-up armor-plated car, side-by-side suitcases that a woman squeezed into, a makeshift zip line for crossing over (rather than through) the border, a gas tank just big enough for one escapee, a wooden cart designed to go through the famous "Tunnel 57" (see page 221), a hot-air balloon that floated two families to safety, a primitive homemade ultralight aircraft, a mini-submarine, a child smuggled in a shopping bag, and many more. Photos show brave escapees and their helpers, such as American John P. Ireland, who posed as an eccentric antiques collector so he could transport refugees in his modified Cadillac.

Other exhibits chronicle the terror of life for those trapped in the East. A list names the 43,000 people who died in "Internal Affairs" internment camps from 1945-1950. Artwork inspired by the Wall includes a large painting of USSR premier Leonid Brezhnev and DDR premier Erich Honecker sharing the traditional "fraternal kiss" between comrades. And you'll see a memorial to Rainer Hildebrandt, who founded this museum shortly after the Wall went up in 1961.

On the **top floor** (skippable if time is short), you'll find a grab bag of exhibits on freedom movements across the globe: the 1956 Uprising in Hungary, 1968's Prague Spring, the 1980s Solidarity movement in Poland, even Gandhi's protests in India. An extensive exhibit celebrates Pablo Picasso's antiwar painting, *Guernica.* A room honors US President Ronald ("Tear Down This Wall") Reagan, displaying his cowboy hat and boots. A room in the corner of the museum—with the huge "You are leaving" sign—offers a nice view over Checkpoint Charlie.

Finally, on your way out—near the sculpture of a Russian cellist who played at the newly opened Wall—a video captures those heady days when people-power tore down the Wall, and Checkpoint Charlie was history. It's hard not to get a little emotional watching teary-eyed Germans finally embracing their long-lost loved ones.

▲▲Topography of Terror (Topographie des Terrors)

SIGHTS

A rare undeveloped patch of land in central Berlin, right next to a surviving stretch of Wall, was once the nerve center for the Gestapo and the SS—the most despicable elements of the Nazi government. Today this site hosts a modern documentation center, along with an outdoor exhibit in the Gestapo headquarters' excavated foundations. While there isn't much in the way of original artifacts, the exhibit does a good job of telling this

powerful story, in the place where it happened. The information is a bit dense, but WWII historians (even armchair ones) find it fascinating. For a self-guided tour of the exhibit, see the 🕮 Fascism & Cold War Walk chapter.

Cost and Hours: Free, includes audioguide (ID required), daily 10:00-20:00, outdoor exhibit closes at dusk and closed entirely mid-Oct-mid-April, Niederkirchnerstrasse 8, U-Bahn: Potsdamer Platz or Kochstrasse, S-Bahn: Anhalter Bahnhof or Potsdamer Platz, tel. 030/254-5090, www.topographie.de.

Nearby: Immediately next door is an unusually long surviving stretch of the Berlin Wall. A block beyond that is the looming, very fascist-style Former Air Ministry—built by Hitler to house his Luftwaffe (Nazi air force), later the DDR's "Hall of Ministries," today the German Finance Ministry, still adorned with cheery 1950s communist propaganda. And a short walk away is a surviving DDR Watchtower, which kept careful vigil over the Wall.

MUSEUMS SOUTH OF UNTER DEN LINDEN
▲Jewish Museum Berlin (Jüdisches Museum Berlin)

Combining a remarkable building with a thoughtful permanent exhibit, this is the most educational Jewish-themed sight in Ber-

lin—easily worth ▲▲ (and the effort to reach it) for those with an interest in Jewish history. The exhibit provides a detailed overview of the rich culture and history of Europe's Jewish community. And the building itself—which enhances the overall experience—is packed with symbolism and offers several spaces designed for pondering what you've learned. To really dig into the place, give yourself at least two hours here. English explanations interpret both the exhibits and the building, but the excellent €3 audioguide—with four hours of commentary—is essential to fully appreciate the collection.

Cost and Hours: €8, ask for discount if also going to Berlinische Galerie, daily 10:00-20:00, Mon until 22:00, closed on Jewish holidays. Tight security includes bag check and metal detectors. Tel. 030/2599-3300, www.jmberlin.de.

Getting There: It's in a nondescript residential neighborhood (halfway between Checkpoint Charlie and the happening Kreuzberg scene). Take the U-Bahn to Hallesches Tor, find the exit marked *Jüdisches Museum*, exit straight ahead, then turn right on Franz-Klühs-Strasse. The museum is a five-minute walk ahead on your left, at Lindenstrasse 9.

Eating: The museum's **$$** restaurant offers good Jewish-style meals, albeit not kosher.

Visiting the Museum: Designed by American architect Daniel Libeskind (the master planner for the redeveloped World Trade Center in New York), the zinc-walled **building** has a zigzag shape pierced by voids symbolic of the irreplaceable cultural loss caused by the Holocaust. Enter the 18th-century Baroque building next door, then go through an underground tunnel to reach the museum interior.

Before you reach the exhibit, your visit starts with three **memorial spaces.** Follow the Axis of Exile—lined with the names of cities where the Jewish diaspora settled— to a disorienting slanted garden with 49 pillars. Next, the Axis of Holocaust—lined with names of concentration camps and artifacts from Jews imprisoned and murdered by the Nazis—leads to an eerily empty tower shut off from the outside world. Finally, the Axis of Continuity takes you to stairs and the main exhibit. A detour partway up the long stairway leads (through temporary exhibits) to the Memory Void, a compelling space of "fallen leaves": heavy metal faces that you walk on, making inhuman noises with each step.

Finish climbing the stairs to the top of the museum and stroll chronologically through the 2,000-year story of Judaism in Germany. The engaging exhibit, with lots of artifacts, spans two large floors. Interactive bits make it lively for kids: Spell your name in Hebrew, or write a prayer and hang it from a tree.

The **top floor** focuses on everyday life in Ashkenaz (medieval German-Jewish lands). The nine-minute movie *A Thousand Years Ago* sets the stage. The Middle Ages were a positive time for Jewish culture, which flourished then in many areas of Europe. But around 1500, many Jews were expelled from the countryside and moved into cities. Viewing stations feature short, lively videos that pose provocative questions about faith. And you'll learn about Berlin philosopher Moses Mendelssohn's role in the late-18th-century Jewish Enlightenment (Haskalah), which gave rise to Reform Judaism. The Tradition and Change exhibit analyzes how subgroups of the Jewish faith adapted to a changing world.

Downstairs, on the **middle floor,** exhibits detail the rising tide of anti-Semitism in Germany through the 19th century—at a time when many Jews were so secularized that they celebrated Christmas right along with Hanukkah. Berlin's glory days (1890-1933) were also a boom time for many Jews, despite the challenge of reconciling the reformed ways of assimilated western (German) Jews with those of more traditional Eastern European Jews. The exhibit segues into the dark days of Hitler, including the horrific night of November 9, 1938, when, throughout Germany, hateful mobs destroyed Jewish-owned businesses, homes, synagogues, and even entire villages—called "Crystal Night" (Kristallnacht) for the broken glass that glittered in the streets.

Finally, the displays bring us to the present day, with the question: How do you keep going after six million of your people have been murdered? In the last segment, devoted to Jewish life today, German Jews describe their experiences growing up in the postwar years.

▲Berlinische Galerie

Berlin was avant-garde long before there were Kreuzberg hipsters. The Berlinische Galerie, a gorgeous, well-presented museum (with an oversized word-search puzzle out front), showcases modern and contemporary art created in this eclectic city. The main draw is the permanent exhibit upstairs, offering an intriguing, chronological, and easily digestible look at art generated in Berlin from 1880 to

1980. The collection begins with Conservative (i.e., realistic) art, then gives way to the shimmering Berlin Secession (starting in 1892), and evolves from there. You'll meet Margarette Kubicka (1891-1984), with her colorful, curvy, Cubist-inspired style; and Klimt-like, avant-garde Expressionism, including works by Otto Dix (the biggest name here). You'll get a lesson in the Weimar-era "New Objectivity" (where artists focused on everyday scenes, intentionally objectifying their subjects in response to the abstraction trend). And you'll see how historical events shaped the art: works created under the Nazis (capturing confusion and alienation); scenes of postwar destruction; Cold War-era abstraction; and perspectives on the Wall from West Berlin artists.

Cost and Hours: €8, ask for discount if also going to the Jewish Museum, Wed-Mon 10:00-18:00, closed Tue, Alte Jakobstrasse 124, tel. 030/7890-2600, www.berlinischegalerie.de.

KREUZBERG

The sprawling Kreuzberg (KROYTS-behrk) neighborhood, just south of the center, is most often described as Berlin's "Turkish neighborhood," or its "edgy multicultural district." And it is those things—but much more. It's a delight to explore Kreuzberg's fascinating little *Kieze* (small neighborhoods)—each with its own personality. (Note that the Jewish Museum and Berlinische Galerie—described previously—are technically in Kreuzberg, but in a nondescript zone between Unter den Linden and the more colorful Kreuzberg *Kieze* described below.)

Background: Kreuzberg expanded like crazy to house workers in the late 19th century (much like Prenzlauer Berg, to the north). During the Cold War, it was in the West but surrounded on three sides by the Wall. Its buildings, already damaged by bombs, became further dilapidated as property owners—fishing for government support—refused to invest in repairs. All of this made Kreuzberg the least desirable neighborhood in West Berlin. Its bad reputation and low rents attracted two groups: immigrants, largely Turkish guest workers trying to scrape together a living in their adopted country; and draft-dodging West German punks, who squatted in Kreuzberg's ramshackle tenements. In more recent years, Kreuzberg has been in transition, as Berliners have been

Berlin's *Kiez* Culture

Berliners have a strong sense of community. They manage this in a big city by enjoying a strong neighborhood identity. Your neighborhood is called your *Kiez* ("keets"). This doesn't refer to a large swath of the city (like Prenzlauer Berg or Kreuzberg), but a microscopic sub-sub-sub-neighborhood. A Kiez can be just a few blocks, barely big enough to contain a smattering of key services (grocery store, school, park), and typically named for a major street or square. People tend to live lives very focused on their *Kiez*, and rarely stray. Some Berliners venture to other *Kieze* only when entertaining out-of-town visitors.

Each *Kiez* has its own personality—but things are definitely in flux. As a traditionally low-rent district, once surrounded on three sides by the Berlin Wall, Kreuzberg used to be thought of as being home to two types of people: draft-dodging, alternative-lifestyle German squatters and hard-working, lower-middle-class Turkish immigrants. And to an extent, you'll still see both groups in Kreuzberg. However, over the last decade or so, several Kreuzberg *Kieze* have gone through a predictable life cycle of gentrification: Artists and hipsters, lured by the *Kiez*'s low rents and ramshackle funkiness, move in. They open up gourmet ramen shops and fair-trade coffee houses, stoking a buzz. As these areas become hip and desirable, rents increase—often forcing out long-time residents and ultimately changing the face of the *Kiez*.

As you talk to Berliners, you'll learn that these issues of class, gentrification, and socioeconomic stratification are a huge preoccupation. Some make a hobby of chasing the latest trendy neighborhoods around town before they "go mainstream." Others grow disgruntled at having to move farther and farther from the center, priced out by über-rich yuppies. Throughout its history, Berlin has been a city in transition. I imagine that for just as long, the local pastime has been complaining about those changes...and today is no exception.

priced out of more expensive, central neighborhoods and moved south. While it still retains some of its Turkish and squatter roots, Kreuzberg has blossomed into one of the most diverse and trendy parts of town—and rapidly gentrified. And yet, the district remains true to its alternative roots: Kreuzberg is Germany's only electoral district with a directly elected Green delegate in parliament.

▲▲Kreuzberg *Kieze*

Kreuzberg is huge (four square miles, with about 150,000 residents), and broken into two general areas—each named for its postal code: "Kreuzberg 61" (or SW61), roughly north and west, is thought of as sleepy and more bourgeois. "Kreuzberg 36" (or SO36), loosely between Kottbusser Tor and the river, was traditionally the grittier area—with more immigrants and anarchists—but in recent years, several parts, including Graefekiez, have gentrified dramatically. Kreuzberg is well served by the north-south U6 line and the east-west U1 line; these cross at the epicenter of Kreuzberg, Kottbusser Tor.

Below are some *Kieze* of Kreuzberg that you might enjoy exploring (mostly in Kreuzberg 36); I've listed the handiest U-Bahn stop for each. You can easily walk (or ride the U-Bahn or bus) between several *Kieze*. Kreuzberg is also emerging as a foodie hotspot: You could combine your visit here with a meal (for suggestions, see the Eating in Berlin chapter).

While these parts of Kreuzberg are relatively safe, dazed and homeless people do hang out near U-Bahn stations (generally if you ignore them, they ignore you). After dark, I'd avoid getting too far off the main thoroughfares (or, for example, wandering in Görlitzer Park).

Kottbusser Tor (U1/U6: Kottbusser Tor): Nicknamed "Kotti" by locals, this area is a lesson in contrasts. The area immediately around the station is seedy. You'll see police vans (and homeless relief causes handing out donations) at the northwest edge of the square, in front of Casino 36. But after a few minutes' walk in each direction, things become more pleasant: Some of Berlin's highest-rent areas are a short stroll away. The giant, semicircular apartment block—wrapping around the northern part of the square—was built as a sound barrier for a planned major highway, which (thanks to local protests) was never built.

From Kottbusser Tor, the next several areas fan out. I've explained where each one is located (in case you'd like a long walk), but also noted the nearest U-Bahn stop for each one.

Landwehr Canal and the Graefekiez (U8: Schönleinstrasse): A few short blocks south of Kottbusser Tor is one of Kreuzberg's most enjoyable areas to explore, with two big draws: the Turkish street market and the trendy Graefekiez neighborhood. Berlin is the largest Turkish city outside of Turkey itself...and you'll know it when you come here. Twice each week, the Turkish street market sprawls along canalside Maybachufer street (Tue and Fri, described in the Shopping in Berlin chapter).

Nearby is the delightful-to-explore Graefekiez area. The

Graefekiez has more than its share of gourmet ice cream shops—thanks partly to Berlin's baby boom (notice all the strollers). For an enjoyable loop from Kottbusser Brücke, at the start of the Turkish street market, head down engaging Graefestrasse, passing lots of tempting shops, cafés, and eateries. Turn right on Dieffenbach-strasse—with distinctive little basement shops—then right again when you hit the big, park-like Grimmstrasse. Work your way up Grimmstrasse to the Landwehr Canal, at a broad bridge (Admiralsbrücke) that's absolutely packed with locals on a sunny summer day. (This bridge was the site of "The Battle of the Fraenkelufer," a 1980 rumble between squatters—who had taken over some 160 area buildings—and the police, with riots, barricades, and beatings.) Turn right and follow the Planufer embankment back to Kottbusser Brücke (noticing the historic synagogue across the river).

Paul-Lincke-Ufer (between U8: Schönleinstrasse and U1: Görlitzer Bahnhof): The sunny northern embankment of the Landwehr Canal—across from the Turk-ish street market, stretching east all the way to about Liegnitzer Strasse—is a pleasant, largely residential area to stroll and enjoy some of Berlin's trendiest restaurants (de-scribed in the Eating in Berlin chapter). Just up Lausitzer Strasse is the funky, artsy squatters' courtyard called Regenbogenfab-rik ("Rainbow Factory"), still run as a collec-tive with its own cinema, kindergarten, and bike-repair shop. Between Forster Strasse and Liegnitzer Strasse are popular public *boules* (lawn bowling) courts. At any point along the Paul-Lincke-Ufer, you can peel off and head north to Görlitzer Park (safe by day), and beyond it, to Markthalle Neun or the Wrangelkiez (both described later).

Oranienstrasse (U1/U8: Kottbusser Tor): From Kottbusser Tor, head a couple of blocks north to reach this main east-west drag. It feels less upscale and more authentic, with lots of Turkish and Middle Eastern restaurants, as well as cheap bars catering to hordes of young, drunk tourists. You can take Oranienstrasse east (passing the famous punk club SO36) to the octagonal intersection at Mari-annenstrasse. Here, detour a couple of blocks north and pass the firefighters monument to reach Mariannenplatz. On the left side of this huge park, the turreted building is a former hospital-turned-arts center, called Kunstquartier Bethanien. Its courtyard hosts an atmospheric restaurant/beer garden and a summer outdoor movie series (www.kunstquartier-bethanien.de). At the northeast edge of this long park, just beyond the Sankt-Thomas-Kirche, is a strange little nub of land where the Wall once ran. A Kreuzberg resident realized that this land belonged to the East, but somehow wound up just outside the Wall, so he claimed it for his own—eventually building a treehouse here, which stands to this day.

Markthalle Neun (U1: Görlitzer Bahnhof): This area, just north of the Görlitzer Bahnhof U-Bahn station, is one of the most appealing places to get a taste of Kreuzberg, thanks to the wonderful Markthalle Neun, a restored brick market hall where foodie stalls rub shoulders with traditional vendors (for details on the Markthalle Neun and the least-seedy route to get there, see the Eating in Berlin chapter).

Wrangelkiez (U1: Schlesisches Tor): Wrangelstrasse, running between Markthalle Neun and the river, is a trendy drag that defines another up-and-coming neighborhood, the Wrangelkiez. This tidy grid-planned zone feels equal parts young Turks, German hipsters, and, yes, a few Turkish hipsters. Among Berliners, the Wrangelkiez is a cautionary tale of gentrification: It happened here a few years back, fast. Falckensteinstrasse (the main cross-street to Wrangelstrasse) sprouted a row of obnoxious, tourist-pub-crawl-type bars, earning it the nickname "Party Mile." To get things under control, local authorities banned new bars and restaurants from opening. You may see red paint or rude graffiti splashed on some of the trendier eateries: Locals tapping the brakes on the transformation of their 'hood. Görlitzer Park, at the southern edge of this area, is fine by day—but after dark, it's best avoided.

Note that the Wrangelkiez (and the Schlessisches Tor station) is just across the river (on the picturesque Oberbaumbrücke—the Oberbaum Bridge) from the East Side Gallery—an easy add-on (see page 67).

Bergmannkiez (U7: Gneisenaustrasse): The most upscale of the Kreuzberg *Kieze* (and the only one in the posh "Kreuzberg 61"), the Bergmannkiez gentrified before gentrification was hot. This is where many Kreuzberg revolutionaries from the 1970s and 1980s moved once they grew up and calmed down a bit. From the Gneisenaustrasse U-Bahn stop, exit toward *Mittenwalder Strasse*, do a U-turn out of the staircase, and turn left (south) down Mittenwalder Strasse. After a couple of blocks, you'll pop out in a leafy playground square next to the glass-walled Marheineke Markthalle. While the renovated market hall building is soulless, the vendors inside are top-quality, and the square out front (Marheinekeplatz) is a total delight. A block to the east is a classic, parklike Prussian cemetery with a fine little café.

Back on Marheinekeplatz, head west down the neighborhood's main artery, Bergmannstrasse—a fun place to browse. Don't miss the pleasant side-streets, with inviting little shops. Just uphill and to the south, Chamissoplatz feels almost Parisian.

At the intersection with busy Mehringdamm, you can take your pick. Heading right (north) up Mehringdamm a few blocks takes you to the Mehringdamm U-Bahn station; nearby are two of Berlin's favorite street food restaurants, Curry 36 and Mustafa's Gemüse Kebab. Alternatively, carry on straight across Mehringdamm and continue up Kreuzbergstrasse to Viktoriapark, where a sturdy hike takes you up to "the" Kreuzberg—a frilly pillar with a cross *(Kreuz)* on top of a steep hill *(Berg)*, designed by Karl Friedrich Schinkel to commemorate the Franco-Prussian War—which gave its name to this whole area. After the hike, reward yourself with a tankard at the Golgatha Gaststätten beer garden (near the stadium, behind the hill).

Tempelhof Field

Adolf Hitler built the world's first modern airport terminal here in the late 1930s. After the war, Tempelhof Field was pressed into service 24/7 with airplanes landing, unloading, and taking off again—supplying the blockaded city of West Berlin (see "The Berlin Airlift" sidebar). In 2008—after decades as a commercial airstrip—Tempelhof closed for good. Today, the looming fascist-style terminal stands empty, and the airfield's former runways are a gigantic park—filled with Berliners on a sunny day, enjoying the wide-open spaces and the history.

Visiting the Airfield: Tempelhof is huge and time-consuming to visit—come here only if you're fascinated by the Berlin Airlift or by Nazi-era architecture. First, ride the U6 line to **Platz der Luftbrücke,** a small park where the focal point is a sweeping monument honoring the "air bridge" that supplied the city during the Berlin Airlift. (A similar monument—representing the other end of the air bridge—is at the Frankfurt Airport.) The names of those who died in the effort are carved into the base. Nearby is the gigantic **terminal building**—boxy and severe. The head of the Nazi eagle that once topped the airport sits out front.

It's possible to circle all the way around the terminal building to see the runways and park—but it's a very long (20-minute) walk. Facing the terminal building, head left, then turn right on

The Berlin Airlift

The first big post-WWII showdown between the Western Allies and the Soviet Union took place in Berlin, years before the Berlin Wall went up.

On June 24, 1948, the Soviets cut off all land access to West Berlin—which was completely surrounded by East German territory. The Soviets hoped that, through this modern-day siege, West Berliners would come to them for assistance, which would only be given to those who committed to the Soviet cause. The end game was to gradually absorb West Berliners into the East, wiping out the very idea of "West Berlin."

To beat the blockade, the Western Allies dedicated themselves to supplying the two million people of West Berlin—mostly civilians—the only way they could: by air. American, British, Canadian, and other British Commonwealth forces began a yearlong campaign of flying supply sorties back and forth between West Berlin's Tempelhof Field (among others) and big airports in West Germany. They carried not only food, but medicine, fuel, and other critical resources.

In one famous photograph, American airman Gail Halvorsen flies over West Berlin, dropping candy in little parachutes into the outstretched arms of German kids. (Over the course of the airlift, the "Candy Bomber" dropped more than 20 tons of candy on West Berlin.) The photo—and the Berlin Airlift itself—was highly symbolic: The Western Allies, who just a few years prior used their planes to drop bombs, were now using them to keep Germans alive.

At the airlift's peak, a plane landed in West Berlin every 30 seconds, around the clock. Larger planes could carry as much as 8,000 tons per flight. Taking off and landing an overloaded aircraft was dangerous. Over the course of the blockade, 101 people died (in 25 plane crashes and other incidents). And yet, they persevered. Imagine: In a year, there were more than 270,000 flights, delivering a total of 2 million tons of supplies (at a cost, in today's dollars, of between 2.5 and 5 billion).

On May 12, 1949, the USSR lifted the blockade. The Berlin Airlift had succeeded. And it was a turning point in relations between the Western Allies and West Germany: After the Berlin Airlift, it was clear that the Americans and Brits were not here as occupiers, like the Soviets. They were here to help.

Columbiadamm street. You'll walk alongside the massive building, passing (across the street on your left), a small rust-colored **kiosk** at corner with Golssener Strasse. This is a monument to Columbia Concentration Camp—one of the earliest in the Nazi system. Finally, you reach the entrance to the vast **park,** where people stroll, bike, and picnic on former runways. You'll likely see a few historic airplanes, along with biergartens, softball fields, and (just over the fence) the minaret of one of Berlin's biggest mosques. On a sunny day, the park is packed.

Why has the city preserved this sprawling property—a square mile-and-a-half of prime real estate so close to the city center—as an oversized park? In a 2015 referendum, Berliners (perhaps fatigued by the city's treadmill of construction) jilted would-be developers when they voted decisively to keep this as a park. As for the gigantic building itself, it remains vacant as city leaders debate what to do with it. Syrian refugees are temporarily housed in its hangars.

Alternate Approach: If you're more interested in the park than in the airport building and "Air Bridge" monument, it's more pleasant (and easier) to approach it from nearby neighborhoods. Kreuzberg's upscale Bergmannkiez (U7: Gneisenaustrasse) is just to the north, while the up-and-coming Neukölln neighborhood (U8: Boddinstrasse) faces the park's eastern edge. On a nice day, combine exploring one of those neighborhoods with a walk in the park.

Treptower Park

For a taste of Moscow-style monumentalism in Berlin, head for Treptower Park. This was one of three major monuments erected in the postwar era to honor the Soviet soldiers who liberated Berlin (the others are in Tiergarten park—see page 92—and Schönholzer Heide in Pankow, north of Prenzlauer Berg). In the Battle of Berlin (April and May, 1945), an estimated 80,000 Soviet troops were killed in the fight to topple Hitler. Opened just four years later, the monument at Treptower Park epitomizes the USSR's bombastic knack for celebrating the fallen heroes of the "Great Patriotic War." Specifically, this monument represents the collective grave of 5,000 unknown soldiers. People who are really into grand Soviet architecture find this worth ▲▲▲; for others, it's simply an oversized curiosity.

Cost and Hours: Free, always open.

Getting There: While Treptower Park has its own S-Bahn station, it's a tedious 15-minute walk from there to the core of the monument itself. Instead, take the U-Bahn to Schlesisches Tor (in Kreuzberg's Wrangelkiez neighborhood), then take bus #165 or #265 to the Herkomerstrasse stop, at the side entrance to the park (along Am Treptower Park road). Enter through the gateway and you'll see the "Motherland" statue.

Visiting the Monument: From the statue of an anguished mother(land), a tree-lined boulevard leads through a ceremonial gateway (shaped like Soviet flags) and past 32 symbolic sarcophagi (carved with reliefs of wartime hardship and courage) to a 40-foot-tall statue of a victorious Soviet solider. One arm crushes a swastika with a giant sword; the other gently cradles a toddler. In the small memorial room at the statue's base, visitors lay fresh flowers under a mosaic-red-star ceiling. You'll see the monument's theme carved into its stone (in German and in Russian): "The homeland will not forget its heroes."

Notice how well cared-for this monument is. Despite East Berliners' tumultuous relationship with the USSR, the sacrifice of 80,000 soldiers to free Europe from Hitler is still respected. The "Two Plus Four Agreement" (1990)—which relieved Germany of its post-WWII obligations to permit reunification—provided for the preservation of Soviet war monuments in perpetuity. Berlin's large Russian expat community fills this park each year on May 8—the anniversary of the day that the Red Army took Berlin.

Eastern Berlin

ALEXANDERPLATZ AND NEARBY

This area is of interest mostly to those nostalgic for the DDR era.

📖 For more details on this—and the many other socialist landmarks in this area—see the Communist East Berlin Walk chapter.

▲Alexanderplatz

Marking the eastern end of the Unter den Linden/Karl-Liebknecht-Strasse thoroughfare, this kitschy-futuristic space was the main square of DDR-era East Berlin. Named (fittingly) for a Russian czar, under communist rule the square was turned into a model of Soviet aesthetics—with stern, blocky

SIGHTS

facades; a showpiece department store; a transit hub for trams and trains; and a trippy "World Time Clock." Nearby is the start of the severely socialist-style Karl-Marx-Allee; originally named Stalinallee, it would have been more at home in Moscow than in Berlin.

TV Tower (Fernsehturm)

One of Berlin's main landmarks, this 1,200-foot-tall massive spike is topped by a giant glittering disco ball. You'll see it from just about anywhere in the city, and riding the elevator to the observation deck comes with sweeping (but almost too-high) views. The tower also has a TI, and various walking and bike tours leave from here.

Cost and Hours: €13, more expensive skip-the-line "fast track" tickets available online, daily 9:00-24:00, Nov-Feb from 10:00, Panoramastrasse 1A, www.tv-turm.de.

Karl-Liebknecht-Strasse

This wide boulevard—connecting Alexanderplatz to Museum Island, and named for an early German communist pioneer—is lined with DDR-era landmarks, including the TV Tower, Marien Kirche (historic church kept open—barely—during communism), Rotes Rathaus ("Red City Hall" of former East Berlin), and stat- of communism founders Karl Marx and Friedrich Engels, who in Berlin.

FRIEDRICHSHAIN

This neighborhood—just east of the core "Mitte" area—is quickly transforming, with a sea of construction cranes erecting super-modern buildings (such as the 17,000-seat Mercedes-Benz Arena, and the glitzy East Side Mall). The Warschauer Strasse S- and U-Bahn station area, while gritty, offers a glimpse into this neighborhood. Just uphill is a grungy but gentrifying neighborhood, fanning out from Boxhagener Platz, a scruffy square ringed by creative cheap eats; the street between here and Wühlischstrasse teem with creative eateries and shops. Just downhill from the Warschauer Strasse station is a striking bridge and the start of the East Side Gallery.

▲East Side Gallery

The biggest remaining stretch of the Wall is now the "world's longest outdoor art gallery." This segment of the Wall makes a meaningful walk—for those interested in street art and/or Berlin Wall history, it's worth ▲▲. The gallery stretches for nearly a mile and is covered with murals painted by artists from around the world. The murals (classified as protected monuments) got a facelift in 2009, when the city invited the original artists back to re-create their work for the 20th anniversary of the fall of the Wall. For the history of the East Side Gallery, see www.eastsidegallery-berlin.de.

Visiting the East Side Gallery: The most interesting stretch is its easternmost end, near the Oberbaumbrücke (Oberbaum

Bridge), which crosses the Spree between Friedrichshain's Warschauer Strasse station (U1 or S5/S7/S75) and Kreuzberg's Wrangelkiez neighborhood (U1: Schlesisches Tor). From either station, head for the Friedrichshain side of the bridge and find the start of the East Side Gallery (facing Mühlenstrasse).

The fanciful bridge, a sight in itself, is a marvelous example of Brandenburg Neo-Gothic brickwork. Its fun neon "rock, paper, scissors" installment pokes fun at the futility of the Cold War (visible only after dark).

From the bridge, head along the East Side Gallery. Close to the start of the Wall, a gap leads to an overpriced "Wall museum" (multimedia displays in 13 stuffy rooms—skip it in favor of better museums elsewhere in Berlin). About 50 yards farther is a funky souvenir shop; supposedly, the owner was the first person to sell a piece of the original Wall. A mural on the side of the shop features iconic DDR-era scenes: a border guard leaping over barbed wire to freedom, and a bold escape that sheared off the top of a car—but safely delivered its driver to the West.

From here, follow the Wall and its creative graffiti as far as you'd like—perhaps its entire length, just under a mile to the Ostbanhof (where the S5/S7/S75 line can take you back to the center). Or get a brief taste, then double back to either Warschauer Strasse or Schlesisches Tor.

Several sections are protected by chain-link fence—a drag for photographers, but necessary to deter "artists" who want to add their own flair to these historic works of art. Along the way, watch for some iconic scenes. Just past the souvenir shop, you'll see Dmitri Vrubel's "fraternal kiss" between DDR and USSR leaders (Honecker and Brezhnev), with the message in Russian and German: "Dear God, help me to survive this deadly love." While the painting is based on an actual photograph, this ritual—designed to show the comradeship between leaders of communist countries—is frequently parodied to show other world leaders in cahoots with each other (for example, Donald Trump French-kissing Vladimir Putin).

Farther along, tune into a few more highlights. The black-and-white portrait *Danke, Andrej Sacharow* honors the Soviet dissident and human rights activist. The work titled *Es Gilt Viele Mauern Abzubauen* comes with a message: "Tearing down applies to many walls." One of the longest works—a row of colorful heads with *Simpsons* overbites—is by French artist Thierry Noir, one of the first street artists who gained fame using the Wall as his canvas. *Test the Rest* shows a Trabi car bursting through the Wall. And Kani Alavi's *It Happened in November* shows the sea of humanity flowing through the wall the night it opened.

▲Stasi Museum

This extensive, thoughtfully presented exhibit tells the story of how the communist-era Ministry for State Security (a.k.a. Stasi)—headquartered in these very buildings—infiltrated all aspects of East German life. While the museum is quite dry and out of the way, it's the best place in Berlin to learn about the Stasi—worth the effort for those interested in this chapter of history.

Cost and Hours: €6, Mon-Fri 10:00-18:00, Sat-Sun 11:00-18:00, tel. 030/553-6854, www.stasimuseum.de. It's a long haul from the center, at Ruschestrasse 103. Take the U5 to Magdalenenstrasse and exit toward *Rusches-*

The Stasi

Initially formed to investigate and prosecute Nazi crimes, the DDR government's Ministerium für Staatssicherheit (MfS, "Ministry for State Security")—nicknamed the "Stasi" (SHTAH-zee)—quickly became a means of suppressing dissent as civil liberties dwindled in communist Germany. The Stasi considered themselves "the sword and shield of the party."

Modeled after the Soviet Union's secret police, the Stasi actively recruited informants from every walk of life, often intimidating them into cooperating by threatening their jobs, their children's education, or worse. They eventually gathered an army of some 600,000 "unofficial employees" *(inoffizielle Mitarbeiter)*, nearly 200,000 of whom were still active when communism fell in 1989. At its peak, an estimated one in seven East Germans was cooperating with the Stasi. These "employees" were coerced into reporting on the activities of their co-workers, friends, neighbors, and even their immediate family members.

Preoccupied with keeping track of "nonconformist" behavior, the Stasi collected whatever bits of evidence they could—including saliva, handwriting, odors, and voice recordings—and wound up with vast amounts of files.

What was the Stasi's goal? Quite simply, to be in control...of everything. Sometimes they'd pursue criminal prosecution and imprisonment. And the worst offenders might be deported. But most often, the Stasi simply harassed. They wanted suspects to *know* that they were being watched—to destabilize and marginalize them. Often no formal accusation ever came of these investigations, but lives were ruined nonetheless.

Soon after the Wall fell, DDR authorities scrambled to destroy the copious illicit information their agents and informants had collected about the people of East Germany. But the new government mandated that these records be preserved as evidence of DDR crimes, and the documents are now managed by the Federal Commissioner for Stasi Records.

These days, German citizens can read the files that were once kept on them. People struggle with the decision: Request a full view of their record—and likely find out that friends and loved ones had been reporting on them—or never know the truth. For a film that brilliantly captures the paranoid Stasi culture, see the 2006 Oscar winner *The Lives of Others*.

SIGHTS

trasse. Up on the street, turn right up Ruschestrasse and watch on the right for the yellow sign—the museum is tucked far back in a courtyard.

Visiting the Museum: Exhibits fill three floors of the building where Stasi Minister Erich Mielke had his office. Everything is described in English, with lots of reading and several artifacts.

At the entrance, check out the sprawling **model** of this neighborhood. The Stasi operation filled entire city blocks—essentially creating a city-within-the-city (54 acres, 50 buildings, 7,000 employees) for the sole purpose of surveilling its citizens. On official maps of East Berlin, this area showed up as blank space.

Upstairs, **floor 1** explains the mission and methods of the Stasi—including the "unofficial employees" who were recruited to report on their coworkers, neighbors, and loved ones. On **floor 2,** you can tour the offices of the Stasi leadership (including Mielke's private study) as it was furnished during its heyday. Seeing these anonymous, bureaucratic spaces, you realize that "the banality of evil" did not end with Hitler. And on **floor 3,** you'll learn more about some of the tools and methods used by the Stasi: Tiny microphones and cameras that could be hidden inside walls, handbags, neckties, watering cans, belts, and buttons. An infrared camera built into the door of a car. X-ray machines for seeing inside care packages sent from the West. In a glass jar, a yellow cloth suffused with the body scent of a suspect—which could be used with trained dogs to track the suspect. And endless stacks of index cards filled with mundane details about the lives of others.

Out in the parking lot is a **photo exhibit** about the events of 1989 that brought this painful chapter to a close: the Peaceful Revolution and the fall of the Berlin Wall.

Other Stasi Sights: If you're particularly keen, you can trek a bit north to the Stasi Prison, where "enemies of the state" served time (€6, visits possible only with tour, often guided by former inmates; English tours daily March-Oct at 10:30, 12:30, and 14:30, Nov-Feb at 11:30 and 14:30—call to confirm before making the trip; Genslerstrasse 66, reachable via tram from downtown—see website for specifics, tel. 030/9860-8230, www.stiftung-hsh.de).

Western Berlin

TIERGARTEN PARK

Berlin's "Central Park" stretches two miles from the Reichstag and Brandenburg Gate to Berlin Zoological Garden. This vast, 400-acre park, once a royal hunting ground, is now packed with cycling paths, joggers, and—on hot days—nude sunbathers.

The main boulevard through its middle—Strasse des 17 Juni—commemorates a bold 1953 uprising in the communist DDR. This series of strikes and protests culminated on June 17, when 40,000 protesters in East Berlin were dispersed by Soviet and East German tanks. Dozens, or possibly hundreds, were killed. While the East brushed the revolt under the rug, June 17 became a national holiday in West Germany—the Day of German Unity.

The Tiergarten's centerpiece—faintly visible in the distance from the Brandenburg Gate—is the **Victory Column** (Siegessäule). This was built to commemorate the Prussian defeat of Denmark in 1864...then reinterpreted after the defeat of France in 1870. The pointy-helmeted Germans rubbed it in, decorating the tower with French cannons and paying for it all with francs received as war reparations. The three lower rings commemorate Otto von Bismarck's victories (see page 162). I imagine the statues of German military greats—which lurk among the trees nearby—goose-stepping around the floodlit angel at night.

Originally standing at the Reichstag, in 1938 the tower was moved to this position and given a 25-foot lengthening by Hitler's architect, Albert Speer, in anticipation of the planned re-envisioning of Berlin as "Welthauptstadt Germania"—the capital of a worldwide Nazi empire. Streets leading to the circle are flanked by surviving Nazi guardhouses, built in the stern style that fascists loved. At the memorial's first level, notice how WWII bullets chipped the fine marble columns. From 1989 to 2003, the column was the epicenter of the Love Parade (Berlin's citywide techno-hedonist street party), and it was the backdrop for Barack Obama's summer 2008 visit to Germany as a presidential candidate.

Climbing the column's 270 steps earns you a breathtaking Berlin-wide view and a close-up of the gilded bronze statue of the goddess Victoria (€3, daily April-Oct 9:30-18:30, until 19:00 Sat-Sun, Nov-March 10:00-17:00, closes for rain, no elevator, tel. 030/391-2961). You might recognize Victoria from Wim Wenders' 1987 art-house classic

Wings of Desire, or the *Stay (Faraway, So Close!)* video he directed for the rock band U2.

SOUTH OF TIERGARTEN PARK

This area, a 15-minute walk from the Brandenburg Gate, is divided into the skyscraper zone of Potsdamer Platz and the arts-and-culture complex called the Kulturforum. For history buffs, the German Resistance Museum sits just beyond the Kulturforum.

Potsdamer Platz Area

This immense, 150-acre square is home to sleek skyscrapers, shopping malls, a transportation hub, several major corporate headquarters, upscale restaurants, and a few museums.

SIGHTS

▲Potsdamer Platz

The architectural face of Potsdamer Platz has changed drastically over time: Berlin's busiest intersection before World War II, it was bombed flat and remained a devastated wasteland until the 1990s, then quickly sprouted a forest of glassy skyscrapers, as if to trumpet the victory of capitalism. Visiting today, you'll see a skyscraper panorama, a replica of Europe's first traffic light, a boldly modern train station, a few chunks of the Berlin Wall, and the Sony Center shopping/entertainment complex. A good place to view it all is from the intersection of Potsdamer Strasse and Ebertstrasse. (From the S-Bahn or U-Bahn, exit following *Leipziger Platz* signs.) The next two sights are also nearby. A quick look at Potsdamer Platz also works well in conjunction with the nearby Kulturforum.

📖 For more details on Potsdamer Platz and Sony Center, plus a detailed map of the area, see the Fascism & Cold War Walk chapter.

▲Deutsche Kinemathek Film and TV Museum

This exhibit is the most interesting place to visit within the Sony Center. Many early pioneers in filmmaking were German (including Fritz Lang, F. W. Murnau, Ernst Lubitsch, and the Austrian-born Billy Wilder)—and many became influential in Hollywood—making this a fun visit for cinephiles from anywhere. Your admission ticket gets you into several floors of exhibits made meaningful by the essential English audioguide.

Cost and Hours: €7, free Thu 16:00-20:00; open Tue-Sun 10:00-18:00, Thu until 20:00, closed Mon; audioguide-€2, Potsdamer Strasse 2, tel. 030/300-9030, www.deutsche-kinemathek.de.

Visiting the Museum: From the ticket desk, ride the elevator up to the third floor, where you can turn left (into the film section, floors 3 and 2) or right (into the TV section, floors 3 and 4).

In the **film section,** you'll walk back in time to the German film industry's beginnings, with an emphasis on the Weimar Republic period in the 1920s, when Berlin rivaled Hollywood. Influential films included the early German Expressionist masterpiece *The Cabinet of Dr. Caligari* (1920) and Fritz Lang's seminal *Metropolis* (1927). Three rooms are dedicated to Marlene Dietrich, who was a huge star both in Germany and, later, in Hollywood.

Another section examines Nazi use of film as propaganda, including Leni Riefenstahl's masterful documentary of the 1936 Berlin Olympics and her earlier, chillingly propagandistic *Triumph des Willens* (*Triumph of the Will*, 1935).

The exhibit's finale highlights today's influential German filmmakers—including Wolfgang Petersen *(Das Boot, Air Force One, The Perfect Storm)* and Werner Herzog (documentaries such as *Grizzly Man* and the drama *Rescue Dawn*). If a visit here gets you curious about German cinema, see the recommendations in the appendix.

The **TV section** tells the story of *das Idioten Box* from its infancy (when it was primarily used as a Nazi propaganda tool) to today. The 30-minute kaleidoscopic review—kind of a frantic fast-forward montage of greatest hits in German TV history, both East and West—is great fun even if you don't understand a word of it (it plays all day long, with 10-minute breaks). Otherwise, the TV section is a little more challenging for non-German speakers to appreciate. Upstairs (on the fourth floor) is a TV archive where you can dial through a wide range of new and classic German TV standards.

Nearby: The Kino Arsenal theater downstairs shows offbeat art-house films in their original language.

Panoramapunkt

Across Potsdamer Strasse from the Deutsche Kinemathek museum, you can ride what's billed as the "fastest elevator in Europe" to skyscraping rooftop views. You'll travel at nearly 30 feet per second to the top of the 300-foot-tall Kollhoff Tower. Its sheltered-but-open-air view deck provides a fun survey of Berlin's changing skyline.

Cost and Hours: €7.50, €11.50 VIP ticket lets you skip the line, cash only, daily 10:00-20:00, until 18:00 in winter, last elevator 30 minutes before closing, in red-brick building at Potsdamer Platz 1, tel. 030/2593-7080, www.panoramapunkt.de.

Kulturforum

Berlin's *other* ensemble of museums (after Museum Island) fills a purpose-built facility just beyond Potsdamer Platz. Here you'll find a variety of impressive museums and other cultural institutions, including exquisite European Masters at the Gemäldegalerie, musical instruments, and decorative arts. Its New National Gallery (which houses modern art) is closed, likely through 2021.

Combo-Tickets: All Kulturforum sights are covered by a €12 combo-ticket (can cost more if a special exhibit is on, www.kulturforum-berlin.de).

Getting There: Ride the S-Bahn or U-Bahn to Potsdamer Platz, then walk along Potsdamer Platz; from Alexanderplatz or Zoologischer Garten, you can take bus #200 to Philharmonie (though this can be slow during rush hour).

　The Gemäldegalerie and other museums mentioned here are covered by the Gemäldegalerie & Kulturforum Tour chapter.

▲▲Gemäldegalerie

This "Painting Gallery" is one of Germany's top collections of great works by European masters. The Gemäldegalerie shows off fine works from the 13th through 18th century. While there's no one famous piece of art, you'll get an enticing taste of just about all the big names. In the North Wing are painters from Germany (Albrecht Dürer, Hans Holbein, Lucas Cranach), the Low Countries (Jan van Eyck, Pieter Brueghel, Peter Paul Rubens, Anthony van Dyck, Frans Hals, Johannes Vermeer), Britain (Thomas Gainsborough), France (Antoine Watteau), and an impressive hall of Rembrandts. The South Wing is the terrain of Italian greats, including Giotto, Botticelli, Titian, Raphael, and Caravaggio.

Cost and Hours: €10, includes audioguide, covered by Kulturforum combo-ticket, Tue-Fri 10:00-18:00, Thu until 20:00, Sat-Sun 11:00-18:00, closed Mon, clever little loaner stools, great salad bar in cafeteria upstairs, Matthäikirchplatz 4, tel. 030/266-424-242, www.smb.museum.

▲Musical Instruments Museum (Musikinstrumenten Museum)

Music lovers appreciate this beautifully displayed collection of 600 different items, going back to the 1500s. The included audioguide brings the collection to life and lets you actually hear a few of the instruments in action.

Cost and Hours: €6, covered by Kulturforum combo-ticket, Tue-Fri 9:00-17:00, Thu until 20:00, Sat-Sun 10:00-17:00, closed Mon, Tiergartenstrasse 1, www.sim.spk-berlin.de.

Nearby: Berlin's yellow Philharmonic Concert Hall sits just beyond the Musical Instruments Museum. Appreciate its bold architecture (inspired by a ship at sea, and different from each angle) and step into the lobby to consider a performance during your stay (ticket office open Mon-Fri 15:00-18:00, Sat-Sun 11:00-14:00 except closed July-Aug, tel. 030/2548-8999—answered daily 9:00-18:00, www.berliner-philharmoniker.de).

▲Museum of Decorative Arts (Kunstgewerbemuseum)

Berlin's answer to London's Victoria and Albert Museum collects applied arts over a millennium—from shimmering reliquaries (the Guelph Treasure) and delicate porcelain to Art Deco and *Jugendstil* furnishings, and much more. The highlights are the Dome Reliquary (an elaborately decorated, church-shaped container for saints' bones) and an appealing collection of women's fashions over the centuries.

Cost and Hours: €8, covered by Kulturforum combo-ticket, Tue-Fri 10:00-18:00, Sat-Sun 11:00-18:00, closed Mon, Matthäikirchplatz, www.smb.museum.

Near the Kulturforum
German Resistance Memorial
(Gedenkstätte Deutscher Widerstand)

This memorial and museum, located in the former Bendlerblock military headquarters, tells the story of several organized German resistance movements and the more than 42 separate assassination attempts against Hitler. While the exhibit has no real artifacts, the building itself is important: One of the most thoroughly planned schemes to kill Hitler was plotted here (the actual attempt occurred in Rastenburg, eastern Prussia). That attempt failed, and several leaders of the conspiracy, including Claus Schenk Graf von Stauffenberg, were shot here in the courtyard.

Cost and Hours: Free, Mon-Fri 9:00-18:00, Thu until 20:00, Sat-Sun 10:00-18:00, free and good English audioguide, no crowds; near Kulturforum at Stauffenbergstrasse 13, enter through courtyard, door on left, main exhibit on second floor up; bus #M29, tel. 030/2699-5000, www.gdw-berlin.de.

CITY WEST

These sights—in the heart of the former "West Berlin"—cluster near Kurfürstendamm boulevard. To get here, ride the S-Bahn to Zoologischer Garten. For a map, see page 71.

▲Kurfürstendamm

Kurfürstendamm boulevard (nicknamed "Ku'damm") starts at Kaiser Wilhelm Memorial Church and does a commercial cancan for two miles. In the 1850s, when Berlin became a wealthy and important capital, her "new rich" chose Kurfürstendamm as their street. In the 1870s, Bismarck made it Berlin's Champs-Élysées. In the 1920s, it was a stylish and fashionable drag of cafés and boutiques. During the Third Reich it was home to an international community of diplomats and journalists, and throughout the Cold War, economic subsidies from the West ensured that capitalism thrived here. Today, Berlin's focus has shifted east and Ku'damm feels more "international-touristy" than "authentic Berlin"—with a Hard Rock Café and a Käthe Wohlfahrt Christmas ornament superstore. But it remains a fine place to enjoy elegant shops (around Fasanenstrasse), department stores, and people-watching.

▲Kaiser Wilhelm Memorial Church (Gedächtniskirche)

This church was originally dedicated to the first emperor of Germany, Wilhelm I. Reliefs and mosaics show great events in the

life of Germany's favorite kaiser, from his coronation in 1871 to his death in 1888. The church's bombed-out ruins have been left standing as a memorial to Berlin's destruction in World War II, with a new church constructed next door. Start your visit by picking up the English flier for information on both churches.

Cost and Hours: Church—free, daily 9:00-19:00—or until 18:00 if there's a concert; Memorial Hall—free, Mon-Fri 10:00-18:00, Sat 10:00-17:30, Sun 12:00-17:30. Located on Breitscheidplatz, U2/U9 and S-Bahn: Zoologischer Garten or U1/U9: Kurfürstendamm, www. gedaechtniskirche-berlin.de.

Visiting the Church: The church is an ensemble of buildings: a new church, the matching bell tower, a meeting hall, and the ruins of the old church, with its Memorial Hall.

Bullet holes dot the exterior of the **ruined church.** After the war, some Berliners wanted to tear down the ruins, but instead the ruins were kept as a Memorial Hall. Inside, under a Neo-Romanesque mosaic ceiling, you'll find a small photo exhibit and before-and-after models of the church.

To replace the ruined church, the authorities held a competition to design a contemporary annex. The winning entry—the short, **modern church** (1961) across from the Memorial Hall—offers a meditative world of 11,000 little blue windows. The blue glass was

In the West

The area now called City West has seen a lot of history. When Berlin's zoo was built here in the 1840s, this area was farm fields. But as Berlin boomed in the late 19th century, the area developed at a fast clip: In 1882, the Zoologischer Garten (Zoo Station) train station opened, and in 1886, Otto von Bismarck inaugurated the newly broadened and spiffed-up Kurfürstendamm boulevard (known as Ku'damm).

By the 1890s, this area was known as the *Neue Westen*—the "New West." Back then, "West" was associated with modernity. And the *Neue Westen* was where Berlin's famous artistic, alternative cabaret scene was at its most colorful. It was here that Bertolt Brecht and Marlene Dietrich gained fame; it was here that Christopher Isherwood set many of his *Berlin Stories* (later adapted into the musical and film *Cabaret*); and it was here that influential early filmmakers established the "German Hollywood" in the nascent days of motion pictures. The adjacent Schöneberg district became a popular residential zone for young people eager to be a part of the thriving arts scene. And it was during this era that several "West" landmarks popped up, including the Kaufhaus des Westens (KaDeWe department store) and the Theater des Westens (Theater of the West).

With the advent of the Cold War and the Berlin Wall, this area embraced the "West" in a different sense: capitalism and democracy. Ku'damm became West Berlin's main drag. The West German government poured funds into building Europa Center—glittering skyscrapers to house the headquarters of international businesses, a bold outpost of capitalism. The Schöneberg City Hall became the seat of West Berlin government, and the site of JFK's famous visit. Thirty years ago, Zoo Station was the first stop for any traveler arriving in Berlin; from here, you'd venture cautiously into the East, before retreating to the safety of Ku'damm.

With the fall of the Berlin Wall, things changed again. West Berlin was passé. Investors poured funds into developing previously inaccessible swaths of the East. High-rises on Potsdamer Platz and along Friedrichstrasse eclipsed the ones at Europa Center. Zoo Station—previously the city's de facto main train station—was supplanted by the futuristic new Hauptbahnhof.

Rebranded as City West, this area has bounced back and seems comfortable with its revised identity. No longer the center of the action, City West is content to be an upscale suburb with an illustrious history.

given to the church by the French as a reconciliation gift. As you enter, turn immediately right to find a simple charcoal sketch of the Virgin Mary wrapped in a shawl. During the Battle of Stalingrad, German combat surgeon Kurt Reuber rendered the Virgin on the back of a stolen Soviet map to comfort the men in his care. On the right are the words "Light, Life, Love" from the gospel of John; on the left, "Christmas in the cauldron 1942"; and at the bottom, "Fortress Stalingrad." Though Reuber died in captivity a year later, his sketch was flown out of Stalingrad on the last medical evacuation flight, and postwar Germany embraced it as a symbol of the wish for peace. Copies of the drawing, now known as the *Stalingrad Madonna,* hang in the Berlin Cathedral, in St. Michael's Cathedral in Coventry, England, and in the Kozan Cathedral in Russia's Volgograd (formerly Stalingrad) as a sign of reconciliation among nations. Every Friday at 13:00 a "Prayers for Peace" service is held simultaneously here and at the cathedral in Coventry.

Nearby: The lively square between the churches and the Europa Center attracts street musicians and performers—especially in the summer. Berliners call the funky fountain the "Wet Meatball." Overlooking the scene is the newly renovated Bikini Berlin shopping mall, with a mix of local and international shops, pop-up stores, and an upstairs terrace peering down into the zoo.

▲Käthe Kollwitz Museum

This local artist (1867-1945), who experienced much of Berlin's stormiest century, conveyed powerful, deeply felt emotions about motherhood, war, and suffering through the stark faces of her art. This small yet fine collection consists of three floors of charcoal drawings and woodcuts, topped by an attic with a handful of sculptures.

Cost and Hours: €7, daily 11:00-18:00, a block off Ku'damm at Fasanenstrasse 24, U-Bahn: Uhlandstrasse, tel. 030/882-5210, www.kaethe-kollwitz.de.

Visiting the Museum: Head up the stairwell, with a timeline of events in Kollwitz's life. **Floor 1** focuses on the relatively happy first half of her life, when she drew from interactions with the poor to create some of her most moving works. You'll see how she gained confidence and found her artistic voice in her depictions of the Peasants' Revolt (1520s) and the Weavers' Revolt (1844). **Floor 2** continues the story, with the turning point in her life: 1914, when her first-born son died in battle on Flanders Fields. You'll see her transition to a woodcut technique, focusing on depictions of war colored by her personal loss. Posters from this era show her social conscience—shaming Germans into helping feed their starving compatriots. Her self-portraits from the 1930s are imbued with a world-weariness that will only intensify with the death of her grandson, fighting in Russia, in World War II. (These losses inspired her to create her most famous work, the powerful *pietà* inside Germany's war memorial at the Neue Wache—see page 113.) **Floor 3** displays her sculptures. While best known during her lifetime for her prints, Kollwitz favored sculpting. But lack of access to materials meant that she produced relatively few works. Some that you see here were cast (from her designs) only after her death. Taken together, Kollwitz's evocative oeuvre testifies to her struggle to define the duties of wife, mother, and artist.

Note that Kollwitz didn't live in this building; she and her husband made their home across the city in Prenzlauer Berg (near Kollwitzplatz, the square named in her honor—see page 199).

Berlin Zoological Garden (Zoologischer Garten) and Aquarium

More than 1,500 kinds of animals call Berlin's famous zoo home... or so the zookeepers like to think. The zoo and the world-class

adjacent aquarium draw gaggles of school kids and their frazzled chaperones. For a free look into the monkey enclosure, head inside the nearby Bikinihaus shopping center, where the ground-floor windows offer an eye-level glimpse at the playful primates (or for a delightful bird's-eye view, head to the mall's rooftop terrace).

Cost and Hours: Zoo-€14.50, aquarium-€14.50, €20 for both, kids half-price, daily 9:00-18:30, until 16:30 in winter, aquarium closes at 18:00 year-round; feeding times—*Fütterungszeiten*—posted just inside entrance, the best feeding show is the sea lions—generally at 15:15; enter zoo near Europa Center in front of Hotel Palace or opposite Zoologischer Garten station on Hardenbergplatz, Budapester Strasse 34, tel. 030/254-010, www.zoo-berlin.de, www.aquarium-berlin.de.

Kaufhaus des Westens (KaDeWe)

The "Department Store of the West" has been a Berlin tradition for more than a century. With a staff of 2,100 to help you sort through its vast selection of 450,000 items (up 70,000 items from my visit last year), KaDeWe claims to be the biggest department store on the Continent. You can get everything from a haircut (third floor) to souvenirs (fourth floor). The cash-only theater and concert box office on the sixth floor charges an 18 percent booking fee, but they know all your options. The sixth floor is a world of gourmet taste treats. The biggest selection of deli and exotic food in Germany offers plenty of classy opportunities to sit down and eat. Ride the glass elevator to the seventh floor's glass-domed Winter Garden, a self-service cafeteria—fun but pricey.

Hours: Mon-Thu 10:00-20:00, Fri until 21:00, Sat 9:30-20:00, closed Sun, S-Bahn: Zoologischer Garten or U-Bahn: Wittenbergplatz, tel. 030/21210, www.kadewe.de.

Nearby: The Wittenbergplatz U-Bahn station (in front of KaDeWe) is a unique opportunity to see an old-time station. The first subway station in Berlin (1902), its interior still has classic advertisements decorating its venerable walls. On the KaDeWe side of the station, a sign lists sites of Nazi concentration camps—one of many examples of present-day Germans ensuring that the crimes of their ancestors are never forgotten.

The Wittenbergplatz station also marks the boundary of the adjacent Schöneberg district, described next.

Schöneberg

Those with an interest in Jewish and Cold War history might enjoy a walk through the Schöneberg district, immediately southeast of the Ku'damm corridor. While largely rebuilt after the war, and therefore less architecturally striking than Ku'damm and Savignyplatz, Schöneberg packs in some powerful history.

Background: Around the turn of the 20th century—when Berlin was booming and the cabaret scene was taking off along the Ku'damm—Schöneberg was *the* place for youthful, alternative flappers to hang their hats. (It was sort of the original "hipster neighborhood," a century before its time.) Many young Jews also moved from the Scheunenviertel to this happening spot; plaques mark the homes of Albert Einstein, filmmaker Billy Wilder, and philosopher/psychologist Erich Fromm, all of whom later fled to the United States to continue their seminal work. Fancy Schöneberg even had its own little neighborhood U-Bahn line (U4). After Hitler's government swept Jews out of this area, several Nazi officials decided to move in—which is why Schöneberg was hammered by World War II bombs. After the war, the Schöneberg City Hall became the de facto seat of the West Berlin city government. It was on the city hall's front steps, on June 26, 1963, that John F. Kennedy stood in solidarity with the people of West Berlin: *"Ich bin ein Berliner."* In the 1990s, creative locals erected a series of particularly moving memorials to local residents lost in the Holocaust. And from the 1990s through to today, Schöneberg (especially around Fuggerstasse and Motzstrasse) has been the epicenter of Berlin's thriving gay community—as it was back in cabaret days.

Visiting Schöneberg: While the history is substantial, the sights are subtle. For a quick taste of Schöneberg, ride the U4 or

U7 to **Bayerischer Platz,** and explore. This square and the streets around it (with names like Münchener Strasse, Salzburger Strasse, and Innsbrucker Strasse) were inspired by places in Bavaria and the alpine region. The Café Haberland—just above the U-Bahn stop, and named for the urban planner behind this neighborhood—has a fine and free little local history museum. Photos and descriptions inside the U-Bahn station itself add to the story.

On and near Bayerischer Platz, keep an eye out for this neighborhood's unique style of **Holocaust memorials.** Eighty signs feature an image of local life on the front, and on the back, a story (in German only) of how that object was involved in the Holocaust. (For example, near a local bakery, the flipside of a picture of bread recounts how Jews were only allowed to buy groceries between 4 and 5 o'clock in the afternoon—after all the best goods had already been sold.) These signs appeared overnight (thanks to a local artists' collective) in 1993, during a wave of Neo-Nazism and the 60th anniversary of Hitler's rise to power. At first, many residents were offended by these in-your-face reminders of everyday anti-Semitism. But the signs were quickly embraced as people realized... that's exactly the point.

A few blocks southeast of Bayerischer Platz is the **Schöneberg City Hall** (Rathaus)—with a modern, rebuilt tower, holding a "Freedom Bell" that was donated by US forces after World War II. At the front steps where JFK delivered one of his most famous speeches, you'll find a plaque commemorating that day. Just five months later, Berliners flocked here again, this time to mourn the assassinated president. Deep inside City Hall is the "We Were Neighbors" exhibit about the Jewish and Holocaust heritage of Schöneberg (all in German).

Several blocks north, Schöneberg meets the Ku'damm at the historic Wittenbergplatz U-Bahn stop.

CHARLOTTENBURG PALACE AREA

Halfway to the airport, tucked in an upscale residential neighborhood at the northwestern edge of the city, sits Charlottenburg Palace—once a suburban residence of Prussian royalty (including Frederick the Great—see page 106). While there are far better palaces in Germany—including just out of town in Potsdam (see the Day Trips from Berlin chapter)—Charlottenburg offers an easy and accessible look at a royal interior. For art lovers, this area is even more appealing for its cluster of three museums just across the street from the palace, which combine to present a remarkable array of early-20th-century art: Surrealism (Scharf-Gerstenberg Collection); Picasso, Matisse, and Klee (Museum Berggruen); and furniture and decorative arts in the *Jugendstil* and Art Deco styles (Bröhan Museum).

Getting There: Ride U7 to Richard-Wagner Platz or U2 to Sophie-Charlotte Platz and walk 10 minutes up the tree-lined boulevard Schlossstrasse (from either stop, follow signs to *Schloss*), or—much faster—catch bus #M45 (direction: Spandau) direct from Zoologischer Garten or bus #109 from along Ku'damm (direction: Flughafen Tempel). You can also take the S-Bahn to Westend, then ride bus #M45 (or walk 10 minutes). From any bus, you want the Schloss Charlottenburg stop.

Eating: For lunch on Luisenplatz just east of the palace, try the traditional German grub at Brauhaus Lemke brewpub or sample Russian specialties at Samowar (both open daily).

▲Charlottenburg Palace (Schloss Charlottenburg)

Charlottenburg Palace is the largest former residence of the royal Hohenzollern family in Berlin, and contains the biggest collection of 17th-century French fresco painting outside France. If you've seen the great palaces of Europe, this Baroque palace comes in at about number 10. I'd rate it behind Potsdam, too, though Charlottenburg is arguably a more pleasant outing: It's easy to reach, involves no timed tickets, has good included audioguides, and is across the street from a pair of great art museums. The palace has several parts: the central "Old Palace" (Altes Schloss), renovated in 2017; the New Wing (Neue Flügel); a variety of other royal pavilions; and sprawling gardens.

Cost and Hours: New Wing-€10, Old Palace-€12, prices include audioguides, smaller buildings-€4 each, combo-ticket for everything-€17; all buildings open Tue-Sun 10:00-18:00, Nov-March until 17:00, closed Mon year-round; tel. 0331/969-4200, www.spsg.de.

Visiting the Palace: The **New Wing** (Neue Flügel, a.k.a. the Knobelsdorff Wing) features Rococo royal apartments and fine paintings. First you'll head upstairs and walk through the sumptuous, gold-crusted State Rooms. The highlight is the 105-foot-long

Charlottenburg Palace Area

Golden Gallery, a real-life Cinderella ballroom with rich green walls, faux marble, gold flourishes, glittering chandeliers, and different details over each doorway and window frame. You'll also see Frederick the Great's apartments (the concert chamber where he played and composed on the flute, and his study and bedroom). Retracing your steps, you'll enter the Winter Rooms, dating from after Frederick's time—warm and rich, and cozy with tapestries. Rooms of royal portraits lead to the old wing, with more Frederick the Great apartments and collections of silver and porcelain. Back downstairs is a painting gallery, with two highlights: In the antechamber, look for the painting of a huge parade in front of Unter den Linden's Neue Wache. Then, at the end of this wing, don't miss the famous *Napoleon Crossing the Alps*—one of five originals done by Jacques-Louis David.

When open, the **Altes Schloss**' highlight is its Porcelain Cabinet—a crazy melding of trompe l'oeil painting and 3-D stucco work.

Out back are sprawling **gardens** that are fun and free to wander in good weather, with a few skippable royal pavilions. The one that may be worth considering—past the end of the New Wing—is the **New Pavilion,** offering a concise and accessible look at the two big names of German Romanticism: the paintings of Caspar David Friedrich and Karl Friedrich Schinkel.

▲Scharf-Gerstenberg Collection

This pleasant museum houses more than 250 works of Surrealist and pre-Surrealist art. The collection is thoughtfully organized by theme, as if these great artists are in conversation. Note that these are "deep cuts" rather than "greatest hits," making this worth ▲▲ for someone with an affinity for this kind of art, but not worth the trip for those with a casual interest.

Cost and Hours: €10 combo-ticket includes audioguide and Museum Berggruen, can be more during special exhibits, Tue-Fri 10:00-18:00, Sat-Sun from 11:00, closed Mon, Schlossstrasse 70, tel. 030/266-424-242, www.smb.museum.

Visiting the Museum: At the start of the collection stands the huge Kalabsha Gate, salvaged from an ancient Egyptian temple before it was moved to make way for the Aswan Dam. Then head into the exhibits, with works by big names including Joan Miró, Salvador Dalí, Paul Klee, Jean Dubuffet, and Francisco de Goya, juxtaposed with lesser-known Germanic artists, such as Otto Dix, Max Ernst, and George Grosz. The *Surreal Worlds* exhibit shows just how freaky the world looked to artists—a jumbled existence of subjects and emotions.

▲Museum Berggruen

This tidy museum—with lesser-known works by some big-name modern artists (especially Picasso)—is a pleasant surprise. It's worth ▲▲ for fans of Picasso or Paul Klee, and would be a big deal in a city with fewer blockbuster sights.

Cost and Hours: €10 combo-ticket includes audioguide and Scharf-Gerstenberg Collection, Tue-Fri 10:00-18:00, Sat-Sun from 11:00, closed Mon, Schlossstrasse 1, tel. 030/266-424-242, www.smb.museum.

Visiting the Museum: The highlight here is the fun, substantial, best-in-Germany collection of Picassos. The first floor features some of his earlier works: Blue Period, newspaper collages, and early Cubism (including a study for the seminal *Les Demoiselles d'Avignon*). The second (top) floor shows off how the prolific artist dabbled in virtually every medium: ceramic, mixed media, doodles, pencil sketches, and, of course, painting. The ground floor has a fine collection of Italian sculptor Alberto Giacometti. In the annex are notable works by Henri Matisse, Paul Cézanne, and a huge collection of pieces by Paul Klee. Everything is thoughtfully described in English.

▲Bröhan Museum

This beautifully understated museum displays decorative arts from the early 20th century on three floors (permanent exhibits on ground floor, temporary exhibits upstairs). This collection makes you wish you were furnishing a 1900s Berlin apartment. Wander through a dozen Jugendstil and Art Deco living rooms, a curvy and eye-pleasing organic world of lamps, glass, silver, and posters. English descriptions are posted in some rooms, and the included audioguide does a fair job describing the rest. Rotating exhibits feature various subjects associated with the design history of the Art Deco and Art Nouveau movements.

Cost and Hours: €8, more with special exhibits, Tue-Sun 10:00-18:00, closed Mon, Schlossstrasse 1A, tel. 030/3269-0600, www.broehan-museum.de.

REICHSTAG & BRANDENBURG GATE WALK

Trace Germany's turbulent 20th-century history on this walk, as we weave together a cluster of must-see sights near Berlin's most famous landmark, the Brandenburg Gate. We'll start at the Reichstag—symbol of Germany's nascent turn-of-the-century democracy—and learn how that democracy was toppled by the rise of Nazism. We'll see sites associated with Hitler, remember the destructive consequences of World War II, and ponder a moving memorial to Jewish victims of the Holocaust. We'll remember how postwar Berlin was split in two by the Berlin Wall. And finally, we'll see gleaming new buildings, announcing how Berlin has risen from those difficult years once again.

Orientation

Length of This Walk: Allow about 1.5 hours.

Tours: ⌒ Download my free Berlin City Walk audio tour, which narrates much of the same information covered on this walk.

When to Go: This walk is designed to be done early in your stay in Berlin—to help get your bearings to some key landmarks. It can be done at any time of day, but note open hours for the information center at the Jewish memorial (below). If you'd like to ascend the Reichstag dome, reserve a time in advance, then plan this walk around it. (Without a reservation, try to book a slot while on this walk, and circle back later.)

Getting There: The Reichstag is easiest to reach on bus #100 (Reichstag/Bundestag stop). You can also take the S-Bahn to Brandenburger Tor and walk 10 minutes (through the Brandenburg Gate, then turn right). Or, from the Hauptbahnhof or Brandenburger Tor, ride the U55 line to Bundestag and exit

Create Your Own Berlin City Walk

If you have a limited time in Berlin—or just want to spend your first few hours getting a solid orientation to the sightseeing spine of this sprawling city—consider linking this **Reichstag and Brandenburg Gate Walk** with the ▭ **Unter den Linden Walk,** followed by the ▭ **Communist East Berlin Walk,** to create one big "Berlin City Walk." Following all three walks takes you from the Reichstag to Alexanderplatz and beyond, and can take up to five hours—or fill a whole day if you visit museums along the way.

🎧 I've recorded a condensed version of this whole handy route as a free **Berlin City Walk audio tour** (just under 1.5 hours; see page 6).

Whether on paper or in your ear, this "Berlin City Walk" route sets you up to enjoy a fun and smartly planned visit to Germany's capital.

toward *Reichstagsgebäude* (this option will become far more convenient once the U5 line is complete, likely in 2020).

Reichstag: Free, reservations required—see page 29, daily 8:00-24:00.

Memorial to the Murdered Jews of Europe: Free and always open. The information center is open Tue-Sun 10:00-20:00, Oct-March until 19:00, closed Mon year-round; last entry 45 minutes before closing, brief security screening at entry; S-Bahn: Brandenburger Tor or Potsdamer Platz, tel. 030/2639-4336, www.stiftung-denkmal.de. A €4 audioguide augments the experience.

Services: There are pay WCs in the Berlin Pavillon across the street from the Reichstag, and free WCs in the basement of the Academy of Arts on Pariser Platz.

Eateries: This is not a great area for a satisfying meal. In a pinch, you'll find mostly overpriced, tourist-oriented eateries, especially on Pariser Platz (Starbucks, Dunkin Donuts, and a basic *Currywurst* stand in the median in front of Hotel Adlon).

Starring: Germany's tumultuous 20th century, including its parliament building, its definitive landmark, and its most poignant memorial.

The Walk Begins

• *Begin directly in front of the Reichstag, the giant domed building dominating the big park called Platz der Republik. Stand in the park about 100 yards from the grand Reichstag and take in your surroundings.*

❶ Reichstag

The Reichstag is the heart of Germany's government. It's where the Bundestag—the lower house of parliament—meets to govern the nation (similar to the US House of Representatives).

Berlin has always been Germany's capital, whatever the form of government: from the first Dukes of Brandenburg in medieval times to the democracy of today. In between, this city was the seat of the kings and emperors of Prussia, the Weimar Republic of the 1920s, Hitler and the Nazis, and communist East Germany.

Think of the history the Reichstag has seen. When the building was inaugurated in 1895, Germany was still a kingdom, ruled by the Hohenzollern family that had reigned here for nearly 500 years. Back then, the Reichstag was far from the real center of power—that was a mile east of here, at the royal palace. Kaiser Wilhelm II disdainfully called this place the *Reichsaffenhaus*—the "Imperial Monkey House." But after the emperor was deposed in World War I, the German Republic was proclaimed right on this spot. Look above the columns to see the promise they carved into the facade: *Dem Deutschen Volke*—"To the German People."

That first democracy, known as the Weimar Republic, proved weak. Meanwhile, the storm of National Socialism was growing—the Nazis. Soon the Reichstag had dozens of duly elected National Socialists, and Adolf Hitler seized power. Then, in 1933, the Reichstag building caught fire and nearly burned down. No one's entirely sure how it happened. The Nazis blamed the communists. But many believe it was a setup, and that Hitler planned the fire as an excuse to frame the communists and grab power for himself.

Whatever happened, it worked. With Hitler as *Führer* and real democracy a thing of the past, the Reichstag was hardly used. But it remained a powerful symbol. That's why, after Hitler led Germany into World War II, the Reichstag was a prime target for Allied bombers. It survived, but you can still see the bomb damage: Look closely at the inscription above the door, and notice the lighter stone patches where they repaired it. As World War II wound down, and Soviet troops advanced on the city, it was here at the Reichstag that 1,500 German troops made their last stand before Berlin fell. An Iwo Jima-like photograph of Soviet troops raising the hammer-and-sickle on the Reichstag's roof is—at least in the Russian world—an iconic image of that war's end.

After the war, Berlin was divided into East and West. The

Reichstag & Brandenburg Gate Walk

To Hauptbahnhof

OTTO-VON-BISMARCK-ALLEE

CHANCELLERY

Bundestag **U**

PARLIAMENT OFFICES

LUISENSTRASSE

SCHIFFBAUERDAMM

PAUL-LÖBE-ALLEE

Spree River

REICHSTAGUFER

100 Meters
100 Yards

Platz der Republik

WALK BEGINS

REICHSTAG ❶

POLITICIANS WHO
OPPOSED HITLER MEM. ❷

❸

DOROTHEENSTRASSE

SCHEIDEMANNSTR.

REICHSTAG
TICKET OFFICE
& **WC**

BERLIN WALL
VICTIMS MEM.

ROOM OF
SILENCE

MURDERED
SINTI AND ROMA
MEM.

*Pariser
Platz*

*Brandenburger
Tor* **S** **U**

SOVIET
WAR MEM.

To
Victory
Column

STRASSE DES 17 JUNI

BRANDENBURG
GATE

❹

❻

UNTER DEN LINDEN

WALK ENDS

HOTEL
ADLON

BRITISH
EMBASSY

DZ BANK
BUILDING

ACADEMY
OF ARTS

U.S.
EMBASSY

BEHRENSTR.

WILHELMSTR.

#200 & N2

B

❾

❺

Tiergarten

EBERTSTRASSE

HANNAH-ARENDT-STR.

GERTRUD-
KOLMAR-
STR.

WC (PAY)

❼ **i**

MURDERED JEWS
OF EUROPE MEM.

SITE
OF
HITLER'S
BUNKER

❽

HOMOSEXUAL
MEMORIAL

To
"Euthanasia"
Memorial

IN DEN MINISTERGÄRTEN

❶ Reichstag

❷ Memorial to Politicians
Who Opposed Hitler

❸ Berlin Wall Victims
Memorial

❹ Brandenburg Gate

❺ Tiergarten

❻ Pariser Platz

❼ Memorial to the Murdered
Jews of Europe

❽ Site of Hitler's Bunker

❾ Wilhelmstrasse

REICHSTAG & BRANDENBURG GATE WALK

Berlin Wall ran right behind the Reichstag. Now in a kind of no-man's land, the Reichstag fell into disuse, and the West German capital was moved from Berlin to the remote city of Bonn.

When the Berlin Wall fell in 1989 and Germany was reunited, the Reichstag became the focus of the new nation. It was renovated by British architect Norman Foster, who added the glass dome, or cupola. In 1999, the new Reichstag reopened, and the parliament reconvened. To many Germans, the proud resurrection of their Reichstag symbolizes the end of a terrible chapter in their country's history.

Look now at the Reichstag's modern **dome.** The cupola rises 155 feet above the ground. Inside the dome, a cone of 360 mirrors

reflects natural light into the legislative chamber below, and an opening at the top allows air to circulate. Lit from inside after dark, it gives Berlin a memorable nightlight. Entering the Reichstag is free but requires a reservation; once inside, you can climb the spiral ramp all the way to the top of the dome for a grand city view (for details on reservations, and what you'll see from up top, see page 29).

Facing the Reichstag, do a 360-degree spin to find some other big landmarks. To the left of the Reichstag, at the Bundestag U-Bahn stop, the long, partly transparent building houses parliamentary offices. Beyond that, in the distance, is the tower of the huge main train station, the Hauptbahnhof (marked *DB* for Deutsche Bahn, the German rail company). Farther left is the mammoth, white, concrete-and-glass Chancellery (nicknamed "the Washing Machine"). This is the office of Germany's most powerful person, the

chancellor. To remind the chancellor who he or she works for, Germany's Reichstag (housing the parliament) is about six feet taller than the Chancellery.

Beyond the Chancellery—and curling behind the Reichstag—is the **Spree River.** When kings ruled Prussia, government buildings crowded

right up to its banks. But today, the riverscape is a people-friendly zone.

• *Walk up closer to the Reichstag, turn right, walk nearly to the street, and find a small memorial next to the shipping-container-like entrance buildings. It's a row of slate stones sticking out of the ground—it looks like a bike rack. This is the...*

❷ Memorial to Politicians Who Opposed Hitler

These 96 slabs remember the 96 members of the Reichstag who spoke out against Adolf Hitler and the rising tide of fascism. When Hitler became chancellor, these critics were persecuted and murdered. Each slate slab memorializes one man. You'll see his name and political party—most are KPD (Communists) and SPD (Social Democrats). There's also the date and location of his death; *KZ* denotes those who died in concentration camps. These courageous politicians are honored here, in front of the building in which they worked.

This memorial is only the first of several we'll see on this walk. (For even more memorials near here, see the sidebar on the next page.) Berlin is a city with a troubled past, which its citizens commemorate with moving monuments. Just up ahead is a memorial to the next dark chapter in Berlin's history: communism.

• *Walk east, along the right side of the Reichstag, on busy Scheidemannstrasse, toward the rear of the building. When you reach the intersection at the back of the Reichstag, turn right and cross the street. Once across, you'll see a row of white crosses along the sidewalk.*

❸ Berlin Wall Victims Memorial

The Berlin Wall once stood right here, running north-south down what is now busy Ebertstrasse, dividing the city in two. This side

(near the crosses) was democratic West Berlin. On the other side was the Soviet-controlled East. The row of white crosses commemorates a few of the many brave East Berliners who died trying to cross the Wall to freedom.

Think about the events that caused Berlin to become so horribly divided: At the end of World War II, Hitler was defeated, and the city was essentially destroyed. In May 1945, Berlin was finally taken by the Soviet army. As had been agreed at the Yalta Conference, the city was divided into four sectors, one for each victorious Allied power: the USSR, the USA, Britain, and France.

In short order, it became clear that Berliners preferred the Western Allies to the Soviet sector—and it didn't take long for the paranoid Soviets to begin closing off free passage. Their first bold move came in 1949, when Soviets blockaded road and rail access into West Berlin; the Western Allies responded by supplying the entire city with food, fuel, and medicine by airplane (the Berlin Airlift—see page 63). Eventually the Soviets relented—and

Memorials to the Victims of Germany's 20th Century

Modern Germans are painfully aware of the many tragic victims of their forebears. And, particularly in the years since the Berlin Wall came down, the German government has thoughtfully erected monuments to various victims in its capital city. Here are six memorials to very different groups, all within walking distance of the Brandenburg Gate—listed in the order you reach them, heading south from the Reichstag. (The first two and the Memorial to the Murdered Jews of Europe are also described on my Reichstag & Brandenburg Gate walk.)

In the paved area immediately in front of the Reichstag, the low-profile **Memorial to Politicians Who Opposed Hitler** recalls those who dared to defy a rising tyrant. Across the street, at the corner of the vast Tiergarten park, simple white crosses constitute the **Berlin Wall Victims Memorial.**

In the park just behind the Berlin Wall Victims Memorial is the **Monument to the Murdered Sinti and Roma of Europe**—commemorating the roughly 500,000 victims of the Holocaust who identify as "Sinti" and "Roma" (the main tribes and politically correct terms for the group often called "Gypsies"). These groups were as persecuted by the Nazis as were the Jews, and they lost the same percentage of their population to Hitler. The opaque glass wall, with a timeline in English and German, traces the Nazi abuse and atrocities. To learn more, enter through the rusty steel portal to reach a circular reflecting pool surrounded by stone slabs, some containing the names of the death camps. In the water along the rim of the pool is the heart-wrenching poem "Auschwitz," by composer and writer Santino Spinelli, an Italian Roma. Dissonant music evokes the tragedy of the Sinti and Roma genocide.

Also in the park—in the opposite direction, toward the Victory Column—is the **Soviet War Memorial,** adorned with hammers-and-sickles and Cyrillic lettering. This monument honors the 80,000 Red Army soldiers who died in their successful attack on Hitler's capital, which brought World War II to a decisive conclusion. Erected just months after the war's end—within the British sector of the city, but before the Wall went up—this monument makes a statement that still fills some Berliners with unease. While today the Soviet Union is often thought of as a hated oppressor, these brave young men fought valiantly to defeat one of the world's greatest threats. Is their sacrifice less worthy of remembrance because of the flag they fought under? Either way, the monument is in impeccable repair, and often adorned with fresh flowers (Berlin has many Russian residents, and even more Russian tourists). If this interests you, a much bigger Soviet war memorial is at Treptower Park (see page 64).

Farther south—immediately south of the Brandenburg Gate—is the **Memorial to the Murdered Jews of Europe** (see the description in the walk).

Across the street from the Jewish memorial is the stark **Memorial to the Homosexuals Persecuted Under the National Socialist Regime** (access it from the Jewish memorial's southwest corner, across Ebertstrasse from Hannah-Arendt-Strasse). Nazis particularly targeted gay men, whom they considered both "too weak to fight" and unable to increase the Aryan birth rate (a Nazi priority). Concentration camps attempted to "cure" homosexuality through hard work, medical experimentation, or castration. An untold number of gay people died during the Holocaust; unlike the other groups, homosexual executions were not as carefully documented. This memorial is simply a dark-gray concrete box, tucked into a corner of the park. Through a small window, you can watch a film loop of same-sex couples kissing—a reminder that life and love are precious.

And finally, quite a bit farther south (in front of the philharmonic, facing the Tiergarten), is the **Memorial to the Victims of Nazi "Euthanasia."** Even before the Holocaust began in earnest, as early as 1940, Hitler sought to rid German society of "useless eaters"—people with physical and mental disabilities. Doctors were required to register newborns with birth defects, and parents were prodded to authorize their murder. Over time—in the "T4" program, which was administered from a building that once stood on this site (Tiergartenstrasse 4)—the Nazis involuntarily "euthanized" 300,000 German citizens. (While the Nazis called it "euthanasia," implying a humane act, many of the victims died painful deaths, sometimes by starvation.) This monument—consisting of a long, transparent, blue wall, information panels, and portraits of 10 victims—is yet another powerful reminder of the many victims of the Third Reich.

the flow of people from East to West increased. Finally, in 1961, the political division became a physical reality when the East built an imposing barrier: the Berlin Wall *(Berliner Mauer)*, which encircled West Berlin in concrete, rebar, and barbed wire. (For more, see "The Berlin Wall: The Basics" on page 212.)

During the 28 years the Wall was up, around 5,000 people managed to escape—but an estimated 136 were killed trying to do so. Those are the people honored by this monument. Read some of the crosses. The last person killed while trying to escape was 20-year-old Chris Gueffroy. He died a mere nine months before the Wall fell in 1989. He was shot through the heart just a few steps away from here.

• *Continue south down Ebertstrasse toward the Brandenburg Gate, tracing the former course of the Berlin Wall. While the Wall is long gone, you can see a thin strip of memorial bricks embedded in the pavement of Ebertstrasse indicating where it once stood.*

Ebertstrasse spills into a busy intersection dominated by the imposing Brandenburg Gate. To take in this scene, cross the Berlin Wall bricks to the piazza in front of the...

❹ Brandenburg Gate

This massive classical-looking monument is the grandest—and last survivor—of the 14 original gates in Berlin's old city wall. (This

one led to the neighboring city of Brandenburg.) The majestic four-horse chariot on top is driven by the Goddess of Peace. When Napoleon conquered Prussia in 1806, he took this statue to the Louvre in Paris. Then, after the Prussians defeated Napoleon, they got it back (in 1813)...and the Goddess of Peace was renamed the "Goddess of Victory."

The gate straddles the major east-west axis of the city. The western segment—behind you—stretches four miles, running through Tiergarten Park to the Olympic Stadium. To the east—on the other side of the gate—the street is called Unter den Linden. That's where we're headed. In the distance (if you jockey for position), you can see the red-and-white spire of the TV Tower that marks the end of Berlin's main axis.

Historically, the Brandenburg Gate was just another of this city's many stately Prussian landmarks. But in our lifetime, it became *the* symbol of Berlin—of its Cold War division and its reunification. That's because, from 1961 to 1989, the gate was stranded in the no-man's land between East and West. For an entire generation, scores of German families were divided—some on this side of the Wall, some on the other. This landmark stood tantalizingly close to both East and West...but was completely off-limits to all.

By the 1980s, it was becoming clear that the once-mighty Soviet empire was slowly crumbling from within. On June 12, 1987,

US President Ronald Reagan stood right here and said, "Mr. Gorbachev, tear down this wall."

And then, two and a half years later—almost out of the blue—the ecstatic moment arrived. On November 9, 1989, the world rejoiced at the sight of happy Berliners standing atop the Wall. They chipped away at it with hammers, passed beers to their long-lost cousins on the other side, and adorned the Brandenburg Gate with flowers like a parade float. (For more on this story, see "The Wall Comes Down" on page 177.) A month and a half later, on December 22, West German Chancellor Helmut Kohl led a triumphant procession through the Brandenburg Gate to shake hands with his (soon-to-be-defunct) East German counterpart—the literal opening of a big gateway that marked the symbolic closing of a heinous era. Eventually, the Wall was physically dismantled, and Berliners—East and West—could now enjoy total freedom.

• *Turn 180 degrees and take in the vast, green expanse of the park called...*

❺ Tiergarten

Look down the long boulevard (Strasse des 17. Juni) that bisects the 500-acre park called Tiergarten ("Animal Garden"). In the distance is the 220-foot **Victory Column,** topped with a golden statue that commemorates the three big military victories that established Prussia as a world power in the late 1800s—over France, Denmark, and Austria—and kicked off Berlin's golden age. The boulevard's name comes from the 17th of June, 1953, when brave East Germans rose up against their communist leaders. The rebellion was crushed, and East Berliners had to wait another 36 years for the kind of freedom you can enjoy next. (For more on Tiergarten and the Victory Column, see page 70).

• *Walk through the Brandenburg Gate, entering what for years was forbidden territory. Just past the gate, there's a small TI on the right, and on the left is the Room of Silence, dedicated to quiet meditation on the cost of freedom. As you emerge on the other side of the gate, you enter a grand square known as...*

❻ Pariser Platz

Pariser Platz marks the start of Unter den Linden, the broad boulevard that stretches before you. "Parisian Square" was so named

after the Prussians defeated France and Napoleon in 1813. The square was once filled with important government buildings, but all were bombed to smithereens in World War II. For decades, it was an unrecognizable, deserted no-man's-land, cut off from both East and West by the Wall. But now it's rebuilt, and the banks and hotels that were here before the bombing have reclaimed their original places, with a few modern additions. And the winners of World War II—the US, France, Great Britain, and Russia—continue to enjoy this prime real estate: Their embassies are all on or near this square.

Check out some of the buildings facing the square (on the right as you come through the gate). The **US Embassy** reopened here in its original location on July 4, 2008. The building has been controversial: For safety's sake, Uncle Sam wanted more of a security zone around the building. But the Germans wanted to keep Pariser Platz a welcoming people zone. The compromise: The extra security the US wanted is built into the structure itself. Easy-on-the-eyes barriers keep potential car bombs at a distance, and the front door is actually on the back side of the building—farthest from the Brandenburg Gate.

To the left of the US Embassy is the **DZ Bank Building,** built as a conference center in 2001 by Canadian-American architect Frank Gehry. Gehry fans who enjoy his attention-grabbing forms and colors might be surprised at the bank building's low-profile exterior. Structures on Pariser Platz are designed so as not to draw attention away from the Brandenburg Gate. To get your fix of wild and colorful Gehry, step into the building's lobby. The undulating interior is like a big, slithery fish.

Two doors past the bank is the ritzy **Hotel Adlon.** The original hotel was demolished after World War II, and rebuilt in 1997.

Over the years, this place has hosted celebrities and VIPs from Charlie Chaplin to Albert Einstein. And, yes, this was where pop star Michael Jackson shocked millions by dangling his infant son over the railing (from the second balcony up). The Hotel Adlon was also the setting for the classic film *Grand Hotel*, in which Greta Garbo uttered the immortal line, "I vant to be alone."

• *And I say, "I vant to move along," because we have a lot more to see. The most direct route to our next stop is by passing through the **Academy of Arts** (Akademie der Künst) building—it's between Hotel Adlon and the DZ Bank, at Pariser Platz 4. (If the Academy of Arts is closed, loop to the left, circling around the Hotel Adlon to Behrenstrasse.)*

Enter the glassy Academy of Arts (WC in basement) and start making your way to the back. Just past the ground-floor café is the former office of Albert Speer, Hitler's chosen architect. Continue on, passing Speer's favorite statue, Prometheus *(from around 1900). This is the kind of art that turned Hitler on: a strong, soldierly, vital man, defending the homeland.*

As you exit out the back of the building, veer right on Behrenstrasse and cross the street. You'll wind up at our next stop, a sprawling field of stubby concrete pillars.

❼ Memorial to the Murdered Jews of Europe

This memorial consists of 2,711 coffin-shaped pillars covering an entire city block. It remembers the six million Jews who were

killed by the Nazis during World War II. Completed in 2005 by the Jewish-American architect Peter Eisenman, this was the first formal, German-government-sponsored Holocaust memorial. Using the word "murdered" in the title was intentional, and a big deal. Germany, as a nation, was admitting to a crime.

Start walking through, aiming for the information center in the far-left corner. As you enter the memorial, notice that people seem to appear and disappear between the columns. No matter where you are, the exit always seems to be up. The memorial is thoughtfully lit at night and guarded. The pillars are made of hollow concrete. They stand in a gently sunken area, which can be entered from any side. The number of pillars isn't symbolic of anything—it's simply how many fit on the provided land. The memorial's location—where the Wall once stood—is also coincidental.

Over 160,000 Jewish people lived in Berlin when Hitler took power. Tens of thousands fled the Nazi regime, and many thousands more were arrested, sent to nearby Sachsenhausen Concentration Camp (see the Berlin Day Trips chapter), and eventually killed. Murdered.

Inside the **information center,** exhibits trace the rise of Nazism and how it led to World War II. Six portraits, representing the six million Jewish victims, put a human face on the staggering numbers. You'll see diaries, letters, and final farewells penned by Holocaust victims. And you'll learn about 15 Jewish families from very different backgrounds, who all met the same fate. A continually running soundtrack recites victims'

names. To read them all aloud would take more than six and a half years.

The meaning of the Memorial to the Murdered Jews of Europe is open to interpretation. Is it a symbolic cemetery full of gravestones? An intentionally disorienting labyrinth? Like death, you enter it alone. It's up to the visitor to derive the meaning, while pondering this horrible chapter in human history.

Please be discreet at this powerful site...obviously. Or maybe not so obviously: Recently, young international visitors have taken to snapping irreverent selfies on this hallowed ground. A local artist started a selfie-shaming initiative called "YOLOcaust," which digitally replaces the blocks in the background with piles of dead bodies. Today's Germans—even several generations removed from the atrocities of their ancestors—still live by the ethic: "Never forget."

• *At the far-left corner, a little beyond the information center, you eventually emerge on the street corner. Our next stop is about a block further. Carefully jaywalk across Hannah-Arendt-Strasse (named for the writer who originated the phrase "banality of evil" to describe the Nazis' gruesome efficiency) and continue straight (south) down Gertrud-Kolmar-Strasse. On the left side of the street, you'll reach a rough parking lot. At the far end of the lot is an information plaque labeled* Führerbunker. *This marks the...*

❽ Site of Hitler's Bunker

You're standing atop the buried remains of the *Führerbunker*. In early 1945, as Allied armies advanced on Berlin and Nazi Germany lay in ruins, Hitler and his staff retreated to this bunker complex behind the former Reich Chancellery. He stayed here for two months. Meanwhile, Berlin was laid to waste by Allied bombing. Tens of thousands of Berliners lost their lives, and hundreds of thousands were forced to evacuate to the countryside.

It was here, on April 30, 1945—as the Soviet army tightened its noose on the Nazi capital—that Hitler and Eva Braun, his wife

of less than 48 hours, committed suicide. A week later, the war in Europe was over. The information board here explains the rest of the story. It shows a detailed floorplan of the bunker complex, which stood right about where the plaque is today. A timeline traces the bunker's history and ultimate fate. After the war, the roof was removed, and the bunker was filled with dirt and covered over.

Though the site of Hitler's Bunker is certainly thought-provoking, there really isn't much to see here. And that's on purpose. No one wants to turn Hitler's final stronghold into a tourist attraction. Present-day Germans still treat the touchy subject of Hitler with extraordinary sensitivity. There's an understandable concern about stoking the fires of neo-Nazism, which never seems to die... in Germany, or around the world. They've been wary of making Hitler's book, *Mein Kampf,* available on a mass level. It took Berlin 65 years for the German History Museum to hold its first exhibit on Hitler's life. Schoolkids are taught the hard lessons of history. But when it comes to Hitler memorabilia and Hitler sites, there's a distinct shortage. It's a balancing act—remembering Hitler, without glorifying the memory.

• *We'll return to Unter den Linden and the Hotel Adlon. Backtrack up Gertrud-Kolmar-Strasse, and turn right on Hannah-Arendt Strasse. Then take your first left (at the traffic light) on...*

❾ Wilhelmstrasse

This street was the traditional center of the German power, beginning back when Germany first became a nation in the 19th century. It was lined with stately palaces housing foreign embassies and government offices. This was the home of the Reich Chancellery, where the nation's chief executive presided. When the Nazis took control, this street was where Hitler waved to his adoring fans, and where Joseph Goebbels had his Ministry of Propaganda.

During World War II, Wilhelmstrasse was the nerve center of the German war command. From here, Hitler directed the war, and ordered the Blitz (the air raids that destroyed London). As the war turned to the Allies' side, the British began returning the favor. Wilhelmstrasse and the neighborhood around it was heavily bombed. Most of the stately palaces were destroyed, and virtually nothing historic survives today.

Case in point is the **British Embassy** (two blocks up Wilhelmstrasse, on the left, with the smooth, stony facade). When World War II broke out, the British closed their embassy. Then it was bombed by the Allies. After the war, the West German capital was moved to the city of Bonn...and the British Embassy went with it. But in the 1990s, when the seat of government returned to Berlin, Wilhelmstrasse was completely

modernized, and the British Embassy was rebuilt. (The building's purplish color is what you get when you mix the red, white, and blue of the Union Jack together.) This is now just one of the nearly 150 embassies in the globalized city that is today's modern capital of Germany.

• *Wilhelmstrasse spills out onto Berlin's main artery, the tree-lined Unter den Linden, next to the Hotel Adlon.*

Our walk is finished, and you're standing right in front of the Brandenburger Tor S- and U-Bahn station. To continue Berlin's story with a walk down Unter den Linden, turn to the next chapter.

UNTER DEN LINDEN WALK

From Pariser Platz to Museum Island

Before reunification, before communism, and before Hitler, Berlin was a grandiose imperial capital, a city built to impress world leaders and intimidate would-be enemies. Prussia, founded in the 13th century by the Teutonic Knights, gradually became both a military and a cultural power, and later grew into the "Second German Reich" and the cornerstone of a modern, unified state of Germany.

Berlin's imperial past is often overshadowed by its compelling 20th-century history. But along and near Unter den Linden is where you'll hear the loudest echoes of the kaisers. This walk, a one-mile stroll from Pariser Platz to Museum Island (with some worthwhile detours), takes you through the heart of Berlin's 18th- and 19th-century glory—past Neoclassical remnants of the enlightened Prussian rulers. It also includes three of Berlin's most monumental squares—Gendarmenmarkt, Bebelplatz, and Lustgarten—and the Berlin Cathedral, which attests to the over-the-top egotism of the Prussian kaisers who sparked World War I. The walk ends on Museum Island in the Spree River—birthplace of Berlin, home of Prussian princes, and showcase of past rulers' artistic treasures.

Orientation

Tours: ∩ Download my free Berlin City Walk audio tour, which narrates much of the route of this walk.

Length of This Walk: Allow about 1.5 hours. This walk is designed to be done immediately after my 📖 **Reichstag & Brandenburg Gate Walk** (previous chapter). And if you're interested in the communist period, it's easy to continue to the 📖 **Communist East Berlin Walk.** (For more about linking these three walks, see "Create Your Own Berlin City Walk" on page 87).

When to Go: This walk can be done at any time. Those who plan on touring any of Museum Island's many sights (covered in the next three chapters) should begin the walk early enough to allow plenty of sightseeing time. You could also use this walk to get your bearings in Berlin, then circle back to the museums on another day.

Getting There: This walk picks up right where my Reichstag & Brandenburg Gate Walk leaves off, near Pariser Platz. To get here directly, take the U-Bahn, S-Bahn, or bus (#100, #200, or #TXL) to Brandenburger Tor. Buses also follow the route of this walk—handy for skipping ahead or backtracking. And once the new U5 line is complete (likely 2020), it will zip (underground) along this same axis.

Pickpocket Warning: As Berlin's most touristy gauntlet, Unter den Linden has more than its share of pickpockets (especially around Museum Island). Use caution.

Drive Volkswagen Group Forum: Daily 10:00-20:00, Friedrichstrasse 84, www.drive-volkswagen-group.com.

German Cathedral: Exhibit—free, Tue-Sun 10:00-19:00, Oct-April until 18:00, closed Mon year-round, tel. 030/2273-0432.

French Cathedral: Huguenot Museum—€3.50, Tue-Sat 12:00-17:00, Sun from 11:00, closed Mon, enter around right side, tel. 030/229-1760; dome climb—€3, daily 10:00-18:00, Nov-March until 17:30, 254 steps, enter through door facing square, tel. 030/2064-9922, www.franzoesischer-dom.de.

Humboldt Forum Visitors Center: Free, daily 10:00-18:00, www.humboldtforum.com.

Berlin Cathedral: €7, includes interior and access to dome gallery, not covered by Museum Island ticket, Mon-Sat 9:00-20:00, Sun from 12:00, daily until 19:00 Oct-March, interior closed but dome open during services (Sat-Sun after 17:00).

Services: You'll find free WCs in the basement of the Academy of Arts (on Pariser Platz, near the beginning of this walk); in the basement of the Galeries Lafayette department store on Friedrichstrasse; and in the Humboldt Forum visitors center, near the end of the walk.

Eateries: We'll pass several recommended eateries on or near Gendarmenmarkt.

Expect Construction: The U5 subway extension and the Humboldt Forum on Museum Island may be under construction during your visit.

Starring: Berlin's kaiser-built main boulevard, and a trio of its most impressive squares.

The Walk Begins

• *We'll begin where Pariser Platz (the big square just inside the Brandenburg Gate) meets Unter den Linden. Stand on the sidewalk in front of Hotel Adlon to get a view down this big boulevard.*

❶ Unter den Linden

This boulevard is the heart of imperial Germany. During Berlin's golden age in the late 1800s, this was one of Europe's grand boule-

vards—the Champs-Élysées of Berlin, a city of nearly 2 million people. It was lined with linden trees, so as you promenaded down, you'd be walking *"unter den Linden."* The street got its start in the 15th century as a way to connect the royal palace (a half-mile down the road, at the end of this walk) with the

king's hunting grounds (today's big Tiergarten Park, out past the Brandenburg Gate). Over the centuries, aristocrats moved into this area so their palaces could be close to their king's.

Many of the grandest landmarks we'll pass on this walk are thanks to Frederick the Great, who ruled from 1740 to 1786, and put his kingdom (Prussia) and his capital (Berlin) on the map. We'll also see a few signs of modern times; after World War II, this part of Berlin fell under Soviet influence, and Unter den Linden was the main street of communist East Berlin. The first two stops on this walk date from that period.

• *Turn your attention to the subway stop in front of the Hotel Adlon (labeled* Brandenburger Tor*).*

❷ Brandenburger Tor S-Bahn Station

For a time-travel experience back to DDR days, head down the stairs into this station (no ticket necessary). As you go down the stairs, keep to the right (toward the S-Bahn, not the U-Bahn), to the subway tracks. You can walk along the platform about 200 yards, before popping back up to the surface.

For decades, the Brandenburger Tor S-Bahn station was unused—one of Berlin's "ghost stations." While

Unter den Linden Walk

1 Unter den Linden
2 Brandenburger Tor S-Bahn Station
3 Russian Embassy
4 Strolling Unter den Linden
5 Friedrichstrasse
6 Gendarmenmarkt
7 Bebelplatz
8 Statue of Frederick the Great
9 Neue Wache
10 Museum Island
11 Museum Island Sights
12 Spree River Sights

UNTER DEN LINDEN WALK

you're down under, notice how mid-20th-century the station still looks. There's the original 1930s green tilework on the walls, and harsh fluorescent lighting. Some old signs (on the central pillars) still have *Unter den Linden* written in old Gothic lettering. During the Cold War, the line dividing East and West Berlin was anything but straight—which meant that some existing train lines crossed the border underground. To make a little hard Western cash, the East German government allowed a few trains to cut under East Berlin on their way between Western destinations. The only catch: No one could get on or off while the train was in East Berlin. For 28 years, stations like this were unused, as Western trains slowly passed through, and passengers saw only East German guards...and lots of cobwebs. Then, in 1989, literally within days of the fall of the Wall, these stations were reopened.

• *At the far end of the platform, ascend the escalator, bear right, and head up the stairs to exit. You'll emerge at the Russian Embassy's front yard, situated on the right side of Unter den Linden (at #63). Belly up to the bars and look in.*

❾ Russian Embassy

Built from the ashes of World War II, this imposing building—it's

Prussian King Frederick the Great
(1712-1786)

Berlin was the capital of Prussia, a large kingdom that became the leading force and cornerstone of German unification in the late 19th century. While Prussia—which no longer exists in any form—can be hard to get your head around, it's easier to understand through the lens of its most influential leader, King Frederick the Great. It was largely Frederick who set forth the ideals that defined Prussia and its successor states.

Frederick the Great's father, the "Soldier King" Frederick William I (1688-1740), believed a strong army was the keystone of a great state. And so—like ancient Sparta—he was preoccupied with the militarization of Prussia. Voltaire famously said, "Whereas some states have an army, the Prussian army has a state."

When Frederick II came to power in 1740, he honored his father's military legacy. He extended Prussian territory (taking chunks out of Austria and Poland) and prevailed in the Seven Years' War (1754-1763). But Frederick also wanted Prussia to be a cultural and intellectual leader. As king, he became both a ruthless military tactician and a cultured lover of the arts.

"Old Fritz," as he was nicknamed, was a prodigy on the flute, spoke six languages, and counted Voltaire among his friends. He built over-the-top pleasure palaces at nearby Potsdam. Frederick invited musicians and composers to Berlin. C.P.E. Bach, the son of the more famous Johann Sebastian Bach, moved here around 1740 to play harpsichord in a band organized by Frederick—helping to make Berlin Europe's music capital at the time. Under Frederick's rule, Berlin grew wealthy and cosmopolitan.

But Frederick was also enlightened in other, more impactful

Europe's largest embassy—made it clear to East Berliners who was now in charge: the Soviet Union. It was the first big postwar building project in East Berlin, built in the powerful, simplified Neoclassical style that Stalin liked. Standing here, imagine Unter den Linden as a depressing Cold War era cul-de-sac, dead-ending at the walled-off Brandenburg Gate. After the fall of the Soviet Union in 1991, this building became the ways. The "Sun King," Louis XIV of France, famously said, *"L'état, c'est moi"*—I am the state, and all of this is for me. But Frederick had a different spin: *"Ich bin der erste Diener meines Staates"*—I am the first *servant* of my state. Frederick felt an obligation to better the lives of his subjects, through the arts and education.

Frederick wanted Enlightenment ideals to be accessible to all. He believed in social mobility, the rule of law via an independent judiciary, and the Protestant work ethic—by which even the poorest of the poor could improve their lives. The museums and other cultural institutions he built weren't just for his personal pleasure, but to enable the betterment of his subjects.

And that didn't apply only to native-born Protestant Germans. In an age when religious and ethnic minorities were being driven out of many other states, Frederick actively invited talented immigrants to come and contribute to Prussian society. When he annexed Catholic Silesia (from Austria), rather than forcibly convert his new subjects to Protestantism, he integrated them as-is into Prussian life—even allowing them to build churches in the capital.

Frederick was also a practical problem-solver. During a famine in the 1760s, it was Frederick who introduced the potato (then virtually unknown in Germany) as a highly nutritious crop. Germans have been potato eaters ever since.

Architecturally, Frederick left his mark all over Berlin (particularly the historic core). His custom-built square, today's Bebelplatz, best embodies his values: a university library, an opera house, and St. Hedwig's Church (built by those French Catholic émigrés).

In short, many of the characteristics we associate with modern Germany—hardworking, intelligent, well-cultured, effective problem-solvers, at times ruthlessly efficient, and, yes, really into potatoes—originated with Frederick the Great.

UNTER DEN LINDEN WALK

Russian Embassy, flying the white, blue, and red flag. Find the hammer-and-sickle motif decorating the window frames—a reminder of the days when Russia was part of the USSR.
• *Keep walking down the boulevard, for two blocks.*

❹ Strolling Unter den Linden

This part of Unter den Linden has traditionally been its business section. And to this day, much of what we'll pass in these early blocks are dull banks, tacky trinket shops, and a few high-end boutiques (Herend and Meissen both sell porcelain here). But as we go along, the scene grows more cultural—the university, the opera, and so on. That's intentional: The Prussian kings wanted to have culture closer to their palace.

As you walk, think of how this boulevard has evolved. In the 19th century, Unter den Linden was a leafy promenade lined with linden trees (also known in English as lime trees). Linden trees can live for centuries. But most of the trees we see today are not that old. Hitler cut down many of the venerable trees—some of them 250 years old—and replaced them with Nazi flags. Popular discontent among Berliners (even Nazi Berliners) drove him to replant the trees.

Look for big, colorful water pipes running above ground. (If you don't happen to see any along here, you're sure to see them elsewhere around town.) Berlin's high water table means that anytime they're digging into foundations, it requires lots of pumping out. And construction is always ongoing in this city, which seems obsessed with reinventing itself. Berliners accept flux as the status quo. As historian Karl Scheffler put it a century ago, "Berlin is a city cursed always to *become*, never to *be*."

• *Pause when you reach the intersection with...*

❺ Friedrichstrasse

You're standing at perhaps the most central crossroads in Berlin—named for, you guessed it, Frederick the Great. Before World War II, Friedrichstrasse was the heart of cultural Berlin. In the Roaring Twenties, it was home to anything-goes nightlife and cabarets where entertainers like Marlene Dietrich, Bertolt Brecht, and Josephine Baker performed. And since the fall of the Wall, it's become home to super-sized department stores and big-time hotels. For that reason, the next few blocks of Unter den Linden are pretty dull. So we're taking a detour, following "Frederick's Street" to Frederick's finest square.

Cross the street, then immediately turn right down Friedrichstrasse and duck into #84: the free **Drive Volkswagen Group Forum.** This futuristic, souped-up showroom trumpets the many VW brands: Audi, Bugatti, Bentley, Porsche, Ducati, Lamborghini, and so on. On display are classic models, currently available hot rods, and futuristic prototypes (electric and self-driving cars). As you check your reflection in the chrome, think about Volkswagen's surprisingly dark history: It was founded in the fateful year of 1937. Meaning "Car of the People," Volkswagen began as a populist initiative of none other than Adolf Hitler, who sought an affordable automobile for the masses.

Back out on the street, continue down Friedrichstrasse. At the next intersection—with **Behrenstrasse**—notice something strange: No traffic lights. No stop signs. No crosswalks. Studies have shown that, when drivers, pedestrians, and cyclists are given no instructions about how to handle an intersection, it forces them all to pay attention and carefully negotiate with each other—and statistically reduces the number of accidents. Berlin is converting some of its intersections to this approach, hoping that a fleeting moment of confusion keeps everyone safer.

Keep heading...carefully...down Friedrichstrasse. A half-block after crossing Französische Strasse, duck into the grand **Galeries Lafayette** department store (on your left). Inside, you can ogle a huge glass-domed atrium—a miniature version of the Reichstag cupola. After the fall of the Wall, investors wanted Friedrichstrasse to compete with the glitz of Kurfürstendamm, which—throughout the Cold War—was the main commercial boulevard of West Berlin (see page 75). But the plan never really took off. Berlin is a neighborhood-oriented city, and sterile Friedrichstrasse isn't appealing to many locals. They'd rather hang out in more colorful neighborhoods farther out, such as Prenzlauer

Berg, Kreuzberg, Friedrichshain, and—yes—Kurfürstendamm. But this area still has some showcase shopping. (Before moving on, note that there's a WC and a handy designer food court in the basement.)

• *Inside Galeries Lafayette, turn left, exit onto Französische Strasse, and turn right. You'll pass a shop for **Ritter Sport**—Germany's favorite mass-market chocolate (see page 298) and then emerge behind a church. Circle around the church to find yourself in a grand square. Go to the middle, stand directly in front of the statue of poet/philosopher Friedrich Schiller, and take in...*

❻ Gendarmenmarkt

Berlin's finest square feels like a wonderfully symmetrical stage set—bounded by twin churches, with the Berlin Symphony's Concert Hall in the middle. In summer, Gendarmenmarkt also hosts a few outdoor cafés, *Biergartens*, and occasional outdoor concerts.

The hybrid name of the square is part French and part German (after the *Gens d'Armes*, Frederick the Great's royal guard, who were headquartered here)—a reminder that, in the 17th century, a fifth of all Berliners were French émigrés. Frederick the Great's tolerant Prussia was a magnet for the persecuted (and their money). Protestant Huguenots fleeing Catholic France revitalized Berlin with new ideas, practical knowledge, and deep pockets.

The **Concert Hall** (Konzerthaus) was designed by Karl Friedrich Schinkel, the man who put the Neoclassical stamp on Berlin. We'll see more of his works on this walk, and you can see his paintings in the Old National Gallery on Museum Island. This is one of Berlin's two main classical music venues (the other is the Berlin Philharmonic, at the Kulturforum). Thanks to its uniquely divided history, it seems Berlin has two of everything: Two symphonies, two operas, two great museum ensembles, and so on.

The church at the north end of the square (to your right, as you face the concert hall) is the **French Cathedral** (Französischer

Dom), which offers a humble museum on the Huguenots and a viewpoint in the dome up top. To peek into the austere interior of the church, you can circle around the left side and head up the stairs (organ concerts advertised at the entrance).

Facing that, at the south end of the square, is the **German Cathedral** (Deutscher Dom). This church was bombed flat in the war and rebuilt only in the 1980s. Inside, you can peer up into the brick-and-concrete dome, and tour the free, thought-provoking "Milestones, Setbacks, Sidetracks" *(Wege, Irrwege, Umwege)* exhibit. This traces the history of the German parliamentary system, from the revolutionary days of 1848 to the 1920s, and then more deeply through the tumultuous 20th century (it's all in German, but you can borrow the excellent and free English audioguide). The German government invests mightily in educating its populace with initiatives like this. Germany is all too aware that a dumbed-down electorate, manipulated by rabble-rousing politicians who think they get to pick and choose which "facts" are real, can be a very dangerous thing.

By the way, neither of these churches is a true "cathedral"— because neither was the seat of a bishop. Remember Frederick the

Great's penchant for mixing German and French? In this case, the German name *Dom* (cathedral) is simply a play on the French word *dôme* (cupola).

Before leaving the square, consider checking out the elite **Fassbender & Rausch** chocolate shop (behind the German Cathedral, with the green awnings—see page 297). This area is also a good place to grab lunch; for recommendations, see page 279.

UNTER DEN LINDEN WALK

• *Go around the right side of the French Cathedral and walk one block straight up Markgrafenstrasse. Turn right on Behrenstrasse, and in a half-block, you'll emerge at another dramatic square, Bebelplatz. Head for the center of the square, until you find a glass window set into the pavement. Stand there in the center and survey the impressive buildings around you (noticing that you're back at Unter den Linden—it's running along the top of the square).*

❼ Bebelplatz—The Square of the Books

Frederick the Great built this square to show off Prussian ideals: education, the arts, improvement of the individual, and a tolerance for different groups—provided they're committed to the betterment of society. This square was the cultural center of Frederick's capital. In many ways, it still is. Spin counterclockwise to take in the cultural sights, some of which date back to Frederick's time.

Start by looking across Unter den Linden. That's **Humboldt University,** one of Europe's greatest. Marx and Engels both studied here before going on to start the communist movement. Other distinguished alums include the Brothers Grimm and more than two dozen Nobel Prize winners. Albert Einstein taught here until he fled Germany to join the faculty at Princeton in 1932. Today, it has more than 100,000 students.

Continue panning left. Fronting Bebelplatz is the **former state library**—which was funded by Frederick the Great. After the library was damaged in World War II, communist authorities decided to rebuild it in the original style...but only because Lenin studied here during much of his exile from Russia. Inside, on the second floor, is a 1968 vintage stained-glass window that depicts Lenin's life's work with almost biblical reverence.

As you continue your spin, the square is closed by one of Berlin's swankiest lodgings—**Hotel de Rome,** housed in a historic bank building.

Next, the green-domed structure is **St. Hedwig's Church** (nicknamed the "Upside-Down Teacup"). It stands as a symbol of Frederick the Great's religious and cultural tolerance. The pragmatic king wanted to encourage the integration of Catholic Silesians into Protestant Prussia after he annexed their region in 1742. And so this—the first Catholic church in Berlin since the Reformation—was built. It's dedicated to St. Hedwig, the patron saint of Silesia (a region now shared by Germany, Poland, and the Czech Republic). But Frederick's progressivism had its limits: St. Hedwig's is set back from the street, suggesting its inferiority to Protestant churches.

Up next is the **Berlin State Opera** (Staatsoper)—originally established in Frederick the Great's time. Frederick believed that the arts were essential to having a well-rounded populace. He moved the opera house from inside the castle to this showcase square. To make it even more accessible, the king set aside a few budget-priced tickets for every performance. Over the centuries, the opera has survived, but the building has been repeatedly damaged and rebuilt. It was bombed in 1941, rebuilt to bolster German morale and to celebrate its centennial two years later in 1943, and bombed again in 1945. Its latest renovation is scheduled to wrap up in 2018.

Now look down through the glass window in the pavement, which gives a glimpse at what appears to be a room of empty

bookshelves. This **book-burning memorial** commemorates a notorious event that took place here during the Nazi years. It was on this square in 1933 that staff and students from the university built a bonfire. Into the flames they threw 20,000 newly forbidden books—books authored by the likes of Einstein, Hemingway, Freud, and T.S. Eliot. Overseeing it all was the Nazi propaganda minister, Joseph Goebbels. Goebbels himself tossed books onto the fire. As the flames rose up, he declared, "The era of extreme Jewish intellectualism has come to an end, and the German revolution has again opened the way for the true essence of being German."

Think of it: Hitler purposely chose this square—built by Frederick the Great to embody culture and enlightenment—to symbolically demonstrate that the era of tolerance and openness was over.

A plaque nearby has a quote by the 19th-century German poet Heinrich Heine. The Nazis despised Heine because—even though he converted to Christianity—he was born a Jew. His books were among those that went up in flames on this spot. Read Heine's prophetic quote, written in 1820: "Where they burn books, in the end they will also burn people." Put in other words (by Voltaire, a friend of Frederick the Great's): "Those who can make you believe absurdities can make you commit atrocities."

• *Leave Bebelplatz toward Unter den Linden, angling left to reach an equestrian statue, in the median of the boulevard.*

❽ Statue of Frederick the Great

This statue honors the one man from Berlin's early history who matters most: Frederick the Great. Frederick ruled as king of Prussia in the mid-1700s. He turned his capital, Berlin, into a world-class city. (For more on Frederick, see the sidebar, earlier in this chapter.)

Notice which way the statue of Frederick is pointing: east. He's facing the epicenter of Prussian imperial power, where his royal palace once stood. We're now entering the stretch of Unter den Linden that best represents Frederick's legacy.

• *Cross to the university side, and continue heading east down Unter den Linden. You'll pass in front of Humboldt University's main gate, where sellers of used books set up their tables. Immediately in front of the gate, embedded in the cobbles, notice the row of square, bronze plaques—each one bearing the name of a university student who was executed by the Nazis. You'll*

see similar **Stolpersteine** *("stumbling stones") all over Berlin (for more, see page 185).*

About 30 yards further, notice the playful **Berliner Wasserbetriebe** *manhole cover, decorated with city icons. These, too, are all over the city.*

Our next destination is just beyond the university on the left— a building that looks like a Greek temple set in a small park filled with chestnut trees.

❾ Neue Wache

The "New Guardhouse" was built in 1816 as just that—a fancy barracks for the bodyguards of the Crown Prince. (The Prince lived across the street in the Neoclassical building just ahead—it's the one with four tall columns marking the doorway.) Over the years, the Neue Wache has been transformed into a memorial for fallen warriors. Check out the pediment over the doorway: The goddess of Victory stands in the center amid the chaos of war, as soldiers fall.

The Neue Wache represents the strong, united, rising Prussian state Frederick created. It was just one of the grand new buildings built to line either side of this stretch of Unter den Linden. The style was Neoclassical—structures that looked like Greek temples, with columns and triangular pediments. Each successive German regime has used the Neue Wache to honor its soldiers. The Nazis used it as a memorial for their war dead. In 1960, the communist authorities rededicated it to the victims of fascism. Then, after the Wall fell in 1989, the structure was transformed again, into a national memorial.

Step inside. In 1993, the interior was fitted with the statue we see today—a replica of *Mother with Her Dead Son*, by Käthe Kollwitz, a Berlin artist who lived through both world wars. The statue is surrounded by thought-provoking silence. It marks the tombs of Germany's unknown soldier and an unknown concentration camp victim. The inscription reads, "To the victims of war and tyranny." The memorial, open to the sky, incorporates the elements—sunshine, rain, snow—falling on this modern-day *pietà*.

Back outside, notice the flagpoles flying the German flag and the red-and-white Berlin flag, with the city's symbol—a black bear—in the center.

• *Continue down Unter den Linden, passing by the pink-yet-formidable Zeughaus (early 1700s), the oldest building on the boulevard. Built in the Baroque style as the royal arsenal, it later became a military museum, and today houses the excellent* **German History Museum.**

When you reach the bridge, cross the Spree and step onto Museum Island.

⑩ Museum Island and Former City Palace

This island, sitting in the middle of the Spree River, is Berlin's historic birthplace. Take in the scene: the lazy river, the statues along the bridge, and the impressive buildings all around you.

Berlin was born on this island around the year 1200 as a hum-

Why Does Berlin Smell?

At some point during your visit to Berlin, it's bound to happen: You'll step into a shop, or a museum, or a restaurant...and walk into a puff of pungent air. Giving the clerk a dirty look, you'll mutter under your breath, "Jeez, open a window!"

Don't blame them. Blame the swampy soil upon which Berlin sits. Simply put, the air here can smell—particularly on a warm, moist, stale day, when swamp gas bubbles up from deep below, entering buildings through the plumbing. This phenomenon, called *Berliner Luft* ("Berlin Air"), has confused and offended visitors ever since there was a Berlin. Adolf Hitler (Austrian by birth, proudly Bavarian by choice) once sniffed that Berlin was "unfit to be German."

As for Berliners, they're used to their aromatic air...and some have even grown to love it. The unofficial city anthem is a jaunty tune called "Berliner Luft" (Berlin Air), which celebrates the sweet fragrance of Berlin.

ble, marshy burg. In fact, the name "Berlin" may be derived from an old Slavic word for "swamp." (Others theorize the city's name derives from the German word for a female bear, "Bärin," an animal found on the medieval coat of arms and today's city flag.) The location was ideal: the river brought commerce, and the island provided protection from attack.

As the city grew, this island remained the site of the ruler's castle and residence—from Brandenburg dukes and Hohenzollern prince-electors, to the kings of Prussia and the kaisers of the German Empire. Berlin was always the leading city of the northern Germanic world, even long before there was a united "Germany."

Over the centuries, the royal palace grew in magnificence to match the growing empire. At its peak under Prussian rulers (1701-1918), it was a splendid and sprawling Baroque palace called the Stadtschloss, topped at one end with a dome.

So, uh, where is this palace?

It's gone. The palace stood on the right-hand side of Unter den Linden. But after WWI, the last Prussian ruler was deposed. Then the palace was gutted in a 1945 air raid in the last days of WWII. The Soviets finished it off in 1950 by leveling the remains to the ground and replacing it with the Palace of the Republic—a massive, blocky, glass-fronted structure that held the parliament and various cultural institutions. In the early 21st century, that communist building was, in turn, demolished.

Now the site is a major construction zone. Germany is building the **Humboldt Forum,** a huge public venue that will resemble the original Baroque palace, complete with a dome on one end (you can already see it taking shape). You can drop into the big, boxy visitors center for an update, including models and plans showing the eventual goal. There's also a handy model

of the city's core, circa 1900, including the original palace that stood here (also free WCs). On the top floor is a café terrace (*Aussisctsterassen,* free entry, look for elevator up) with great views over Museum Island.

The Humboldt Forum project is controversial among Berliners (who love complaining about ambitious projects as forcefully as they pursue them). Some feel that the communist-era Palace of the Republic was still perfectly functional, and an important piece of the city's architectural heritage that should have been remodeled. The expensive new rebuild doesn't have a unified purpose—it's a loose bag of public spaces, minor museums and libraries, office space, and high-rent businesses. Whether the completed Humboldt Forum will be embraced or rejected by Berliners remains to be seen.

• *Now, turn your attention to the left side of Unter den Linden. There's a spacious garden, bordered on two sides by impressive buildings.*

⓫ Museum Island Sights

First, get oriented: The island's big, central square is called the Lustgarten. At the far end is the Altes Museum—marking the start of a cluster of Neoclassical museum buildings. And to the right is the imposing Berlin Cathedral, with its green domes.

For 300 years, the island's big central square—**Lustgarten**—has flip-flopped between being a military parade ground and a people-friendly park, depending on the political tenor of the time. In the Nazi era, Hitler enjoyed giving speeches here—from the top of the museum steps overlooking this square. In fact, he had the square landscaped to fit his symmetrical tastes and propaganda needs. (Those shrubs look kinda fascist to me...) In 1999, the Lustgarten was made into a pleasant park, one of Berlin's most enjoyable public spaces.

At the far end of the Lustgarten is a cache of grandiose **museum buildings** that represent the can-do German spirit of the 1800s. Before the 19th century, there was no "Germany"—just a collection of 39 little German-speaking countries: Bavaria, Saxony, the lands along the Rhine, and so on. The mightiest of these ministates was Prussia, with its capital right here on this island. What united the "German" people was their common language and historic roots. In the 1800s, a movement was coalescing. Its goal: to unite all those little German-speaking states into a single modern nation. Economically, German iron and coal output multiplied, and trade was booming. Finally, in 1871, Germany united, and Berlin was its capital. These buildings—in the Neoclassical style—represented German optimism, creating a New Germanic Athens.

The earliest building—the one you see from here, with the long colonnade—was the Altes Museum, which went up in the 1820s. It was designed by Karl Friedrich Schinkel, the architect who remade Berlin in the Neoclassical style. (Schinkel also designed the Concert Hall on Gendarmenmarkt, the Neue Wache, the bridge we just crossed, and even the warrior statues on the bridge.) The rest of the Museum Island complex began taking shape in the 1840s, when city leaders envisioned the island as an oasis of culture and learning. Today, the island's impressive buildings host five grand museums. The **Altes Museum** houses antiquities. Just beyond are the **Neues Museum** (with the ethereal Bust of Nefertiti), the **Pergamon Museum** (with classical antiquities), the **Old National Gallery** (German Romantic painting), and the **Bode Museum.** (For self-guided tours of each museum's highlights, see the ⌑ Museum Island Tour and the ⌑ Pergamon Museum Tour chapters.)

Dominating the island is the towering, green-domed **Berlin Cathedral** (Berliner Dom). This is only a century old, built during the reign of Kaiser Wilhelm II—that jingoistic emperor in the spiked helmet who led Europe into World War I. He considered himself not merely a king but a *kaiser*—a Caesar. The church's bombastic Wilhelmian architecture is a Protestant assertion of strength. It seems to proclaim, "A mighty fortress is our God...and he speaks German."

The years of Kaiser Wilhelm's rule, from 1888 to 1918, were a busy age of building. Germany had recently been united (in 1871), and the emperor wanted to give his capital stature and legitimacy (it was Kaiser Wilhelm who built the Reichstag). The Wilhelmian style is over-the-top: a garish mix of Neoclassical, Neo-Baroque, and Neo-Renaissance, with rippling stucco and gold-tiled mosaics. This cathedral, while Protestant, is as ornate as if it were Catholic.

The church is at its most impressive from the outside, but if you pay the pricey admission to go in, you'll see the great reformers (Luther, Calvin, and company) standing around the brilliantly restored dome like stern saints guarding their theology. King Frederick I rests in an ornate tomb. And you can pay to climb the dome for great views (270 steps with pleasant, breezy views of the city at the finish line). The crypt downstairs is not worth a look.

• *Continue down Unter den Linden past the cathedral, and pause on the bridge over the Spree.*

⓬ Spree River Sights

The Spree River is people-friendly and welcoming. A parklike promenade leads all the way from here to the Hauptbahnhof.

Along it, you'll find impromptu "beachside" beer gardens with imported sand, BBQs in pocket parks, and lots of locals walking their dogs, taking a lazy bike ride, or jogging. Spree River boat tours depart from near here.

You may notice "don't drop anchor" signs. Believe it or not, there are still unexploded WWII bombs around town, and many are in this river. Every month, several bombs are found at construction sites. Local guides explain that the bomb's triggers were set for the hard ground of Scotland, where they were tested. But Berlin sits on soft soil ("Berlin" means "swamp," remember?)—so an estimated 1 out of every 10 bombs dropped didn't explode.

• *Our Unter Den Linden stroll is finished. Now's the perfect time to carry on with your choice of other walks or tours:*

    📖 *To finish up your orientation stroll through the heart of Berlin— with a focus on the communist period—the* **Communist East Berlin Walk** *begins from right here.*

    📖 *The* **Museum Island Tour** *and* 📖 **Pergamon Museum Tour** *also begin a few steps from where you're standing.*

UNTER DEN LINDEN WALK

📖 *The* **German History Museum Tour** *requires just a short back-track across the Spree.*

If you'd like to take a **cruise along the Spree River**—*a great activity for a sunny day—my favorite dock is just up the river (behind the Humboldt Forum, on the left bank; for details, see page 27).*

📖 *The* **Scheunenviertel Walk**—*with an engaging look at a trendy neighborhood with plenty of restaurants, fun-to-explore courtyards, and artifacts of Berlin's Jewish history—beings a short walk away, at the Hackescher Markt S-Bahn station. To get there, cross the bridge behind the Berlin Cathedral, turn left, and follow the riverbank north for a couple of blocks. Bear right under the rail tracks, and you're in the heart of Hackescher Markt.*

The Hackescher Markt S-Bahn station is also a handy hub for getting to other points in the city. You can also hop on bus #100 or #200 at the Lustgarten stop (along Unter den Linden, right in the middle of Museum Island) to zip you in either direction—east to Alexanderplatz (behind the TV Tower), or back the way you came, to the Brandenburg Gate and Reichstag area. Bus #100 continues all the way through Tiergarten park to City West and the Ku'damm.

MUSEUM ISLAND TOUR

Neues Museum • Old National Gallery • Bode Museum

One of Berlin's most ambitious urban renewal projects is taking place in the cultural park of Museum Island, which sits right in the middle of the Spree. The 19th-century Prussian king Friedrich Wilhelm IV, who imagined this island as a place of art and learning, masterminded the construction of what would eventually become five separate museums. WWII bombs and communist-era neglect left the buildings and their collections in shambles. Now, each of these world-class galleries (proud home to the Greek Pergamon Altar and the exquisite Queen Nefertiti bust) is being renovated in turn. When it's finally done, a grand visitors center will link the museum campus together.

Museum lovers could spend all day here. I've provided two chapters to guide your visit: The Pergamon Museum is covered in depth in the next chapter, and the other four museums are covered here. Use this rundown to help you choose:

The **Pergamon Museum** is the most famous of the five, renowned for its treasures from ancient Babylon, Assyria, Rome, and the Islamic world. (Think of it as the "German British Museum.") Its massive-scale artifacts are thrilling, but its star attraction—the Pergamon Altar—is undergoing a years-long renovation. For complete orientation details and a self-guided tour, see the next chapter.

The **Neues Museum** rolls back in time to the prehistoric world. Among its highlights are a toothy Neanderthal skull, a remarkably crafted Golden Hat belonging to early Celtic people, and—most important—the bust of Nefertiti, arguably *the* most famous artifact from ancient Egypt. Nefertiti—a bigger crowd-pleaser than anything in the Pergamon—makes the Neues perhaps even more purely enjoyable for a casual visitor.

The **Old National Gallery** focuses on German Romantic painting from the 19th century (especially Caspar David Fried-

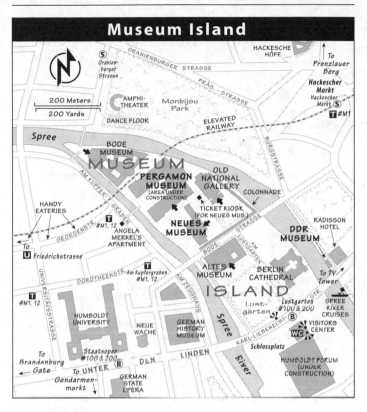

rich's moody landscapes). This is the best museum in town for *German* art.

The **Bode Museum** is, frankly, more about its striking museum building (with its grand domed entryway) than its collection of Byzantine art, sculptures, and coins. It's worth a visit for numismatists and those who appreciate Byzantine mosaics.

The **Altes (Old) Museum** is the least interesting of the bunch. Unless you're looking for more classical antiquities, skip it (I did).

Orientation to Museum Island

Cost: Individual admission to the Pergamon or the Neues is €12; it's €10 for the Old National Gallery, Bode, or Altes (audioguide included for each). If you're touring at least two of the collections—for example, the Pergamon and the Neues—invest in the €18 Museum Island Pass or the €29 Museum Pass Berlin.

Hours: Museum hours are 10:00-18:00, Thursdays until 20:00. The Pergamon and Neues museums are open daily; the Old

---

Planning Your Visit to Museum Island

Use the tours in this and the following chapter to frame your time on Museum Island. If you have a half-day, spend about an hour apiece in the Pergamon (see next chapter), Neues, and Old National Gallery—hitting only the top pieces in each one. If you have a full day, dive deeper into those three, and add a quick visit to the Bode. The Altes is skippable extra credit.

At each museum, pick up a floor plan when you enter, and use it to find the rooms I highlight on each tour.

National Gallery, Bode Museum, and Altes Museum are open Tue-Sun, closed Mon.

Information: All five museums are managed by the Staatliche Museen zu Berlin (SMB). Tel. 030/266-424-242, www.smb.museum.

When to Go: The popular Pergamon and the Neues are typically busiest in the morning, on weekends, and when it rains. Crowds aren't a problem at the Old National Gallery or the Bode.

Getting There: The nearest S-Bahn stations are Hackescher Markt and Friedrichstrasse, each about a 10-minute walk away. The Am Kupfergraben tram stop (#M1 or #12) is just across the river from the Pergamon, cutting your walk. Or ride bus #100 or #200 along Unter den Linden to the Lustgarten stop.

Getting In: A new riverside entrance pavilion called the James-Simon-Galerie is being built on the west bank of Museum Island. During construction, museum entrances could move around, but they are always well-signed. As of this writing, you'll find the entrances to the Pergamon, Neues Museum, and Old National Gallery a few steps apart, all facing a leafy courtyard behind the colonnade on Bodestrasse. To find the Bode, head to the very northern end of the island.

Tours: Each museum has its own excellent audioguide (included in admission). Ask for these when you enter, and use them to supplement the selective information given here.

Services: Each museum has free (often obligatory) coat-check desks and lockers.

Eateries: You'll find basic cafés in the Altes, Neues, and Bode (the last beautifully set in its free-to-enter domed lobby). For lunch in a nearby neighborhood, follow the elevated train tracks away from the Pergamon down Georgenstrasse (see recommendations on page 275), or cross the Friedrichsbrücke (bridge between the Old National Gallery and Berlin Cathedral), turn left, and follow signs for five minutes to Hackescher Markt, with its multitude of eateries (see page 286).

Construction Warning: A formidable renovation is under way on Museum Island. When complete (2024 at the earliest), a new visitors center will link the Pergamon Museum with the Altes Museum, the Pergamon will get a fourth wing, tunnels will lace the complex together, and this will become one of the grandest museum zones in Europe. In the meantime, pardon their dust.

Starring: The bust of Nefertiti (in the Neues Museum), German Romantic paintings (in the Old National Gallery), and sumptuous Byzantine mosaics (in the Bode Museum).

Neues (New) Museum

After being damaged in World War II and sitting in ruins for some 40 years, the Neues Museum has been gorgeously rebuilt. Oddly, this so-called "new" museum features the oldest stuff around. The star attraction is the famously beautiful bust of Egypt's Queen Nefertiti. You have permission to make a beeline for her and call it a museum. But with more time, the Neues offers much more: more ancient statues, a vivid papyrus collection, slice-of-life artifacts, and dreamy wax portraits decorating mummy cases.

SELF-GUIDED TOUR

This one-hour tour, covering the museum from top to bottom, takes you on a roughly chronological journey through time—from a 45,000-year-old skull, to a prognosticating prehistoric hat, to portraits of that ancient Egyptian power couple, Nefertiti and Akhenaton.

• *The Neues Museum ticket desk is across the courtyard from the entrance. Ticket in hand, enter and pick up the floor plan.*

*Head up the central staircase, continuing all the way to the top floor, level 3. At the top of the stairs, turn left, entering Room 311. Pass through three rooms, to **Room 309**. You run into a glass display case with a skull, a few bones, and a bust of a human head. Welcome to prehistory.*

LEVEL 3
Neanderthal Skull from Le Moustier

This skull with impressive dentition comes from a teenage Neanderthal boy who lived 45,000 years ago in central France. A bust

displayed next to the skull re-creates what archaeologists think he might have looked like. (A Neanderthal Michael Cera?)

The Neanderthal people (scholars surmise) lived alongside our Homo-sapiens ancestors. Humans and Neanderthals occasionally even interbred, but their offspring never flourished, so the two remained separate species. Around 30,000 B.C., the Neanderthals mysteriously died out. The skeleton of this teenage boy was discovered—in a fetal position, accompanied by a few crude stone-cutting tools—in 1908, in a cave in France's Dordogne River Valley. The boy's Homo-sapiens neighbors, the Cro-Magnons, would go on to create the wondrous cave paintings in nearby Lascaux.

Also displayed in Room 309 are the ancient bones of the animals these early people hunted: mammoths, moose, and so on.

• *Exit at the far end of the room and pass through a long room of early human tools, spearheads, and pottery. Crossing the landing and heading through Room 306, you'll go from the Stone Age to the Ice Age to our next stop—one of the treasures of the Bronze Age. You'll find it in the dimly-lit corner* **Room 305.**

The Golden Hat

The tall, conehead-like Golden Hat—made of paper-thin gold leaf—was likely worn by the priest of a sun cult popular among the Celtic people of central Europe around 1,000 B.C. It's stamped with symbols of the heavens—mostly sun-like circles, plus a few crescent moons, and stars on the top.

Admire the incredible workmanship of these prehistoric people. The hat, 30 inches tall, was hammered from a pound of gold into a single sheet of gold leaf less than a millimeter thick. (Originally, the gold hat probably had an inner support structure of cloth or wood.) To make the hat, these early Celtic peoples fired up a charcoal furnace stoked with a bellows that could heat things to 1500 degrees F. To strengthen the finished hat and keep it from cracking, they mixed silver and copper into the pure gold. To make the decorations, they used a dozen individual tools with sun-, moon-, and star-shaped stamps.

This weird hat could be used to predict full moons or solstices up to five years in advance. Here's how it worked: There are 21 horizontal bands, each containing a number of symbols. You'd add up the symbols within each band—e.g., a row of 20 suns, each with five concentric circles, totals up to 100 symbols. You'd add that to neighboring bands to calculate the various months, seasons, and years. Note that the fifth band from the top (with the crescent moons and eyes) is special: Its 38 symbols calculated oddities like leap years.

The hat could be used as either a solar calendar (a year of 365 sunrises) or lunar calendar (a year of 12 full moons, totaling 354 days). It could even demonstrate how those two counting methods sync up every 19 years. This "lunisolar" calendar (linking the moon and the sun) preceded the ancient Greek calendar by 500 years.

For superstitious Celtic people, this hat must have seemed supernatural. It endowed the druid who wore it with almost magical powers. He could predict upcoming events with eerie accuracy. It told the tribe when to plant and when to harvest, when to worship which gods, and when to throw the next New Year's Eve bash.

• *If you hear some strange sounds as you view the Golden Hat, they're coming from right outside the room—where you'll find a display of slinky, golden lur horns from northern Europe. Press the button to hear their haunting tone.*

Next up, ancient Egypt. Continue circling the top floor counterclockwise. You'll pass through exhibits on the Iron Age. (Europeans began forging iron around 1000 B.C.—by which time the overachieving Egyptians had already been doing it for 400 years.)

When you reach the stairwell, descend to the next floor and turn right, entering Room 208—the Egyptian Collection.

Browse through the large Room 208, full of statues in glass cases. The poses are stiff—seated or standing, with few details that mark these as individual people. Make your way through Egyptian history. There's the so-called Old Kingdom (c. 2500-2000 B.C.), when the pyramids were built. The Middle Period (c. 2000-1500 B.C.) was a turbulent time marked by foreign invasions. The New Kingdom (c. 1500-1000 B.C.) saw Egypt rise to its pinnacle of power, overseen by the husband-and-wife team we are about to meet—Akhenaton and Nefertiti.

Continue into Room 209, which features objects from the reign of the pharaoh Akhenaton.

LEVEL 2
Bust, Relief, and Stele of Akhenaton

The bust and relief on display capture the distinctive likeness of the pharaoh who transformed Egypt. Both show his narrow face, prominent chin, sensual features, and Mick Jagger lips. The bust, unfinished and badly damaged, was once painted and held a crown covered with gold leaf. Note the uraeus on Akhenaton's forehead; worn by pharaohs, this symbol of supreme authority shows a cobra rearing to strike.

When Akhenaton took the throne in 1380 B.C., he rocked conservative Egypt by promoting monotheism to his polytheistic subjects. He lumped the countless gods of the Egyptian pantheon into one all-powerful being, Aton the sun god. Akhenaton's reign was a striking exception to Egypt's 2,000 years of political, religious, and artistic rigidity.

Akhenaton married Nefertiti—a commoner, whose name meant "the beautiful one has come." They moved into a new palace

and started a family. In the small adjoining room, look for the happy couple in the carved-relief stele. Wearing their royal crowns, they relax under the shining rays of the sun god. At the tips of the rays, a few cross-shaped ankh hieroglyphs—the symbol of life—represent Akhenaton's new deity sending life to his subjects. The royal children frolic on the laps of their regal mummy and daddy. This relief, softened by its human touch, has a naturalness that's quite different from the stiffness of most traditional Egyptian art.

Postscript: Akhenaton's daughter married a teenage pharaoh, Tutankhamen—"King Tut." It was the unearthing of Tut's mummy in 1922 that helped stoke Europe's interest in Egyptology.

• *Before leaving, take a last glance at the bust of Akhenaton from the side. Notice the V-shaped tilt of the neck—we'll see it mirrored in the next room. Now let's meet Akhenaton's wife (and Tut's mother-in-law), the "beautiful one" named Nefertiti. She has a room all her own—**Room 210**. (Note that she's had it with the paparazzi—photos of Nefertiti are strictly verboten.)*

Bust of Nefertiti

The 3,000-year-old bust of Queen Nefertiti, wife of Akhenaton, is the most famous piece of Egyptian art in Europe.

Nefertiti has all the right beauty marks: long slender neck, perfect lips, almond eyes, symmetrical eyebrows, pronounced cheekbones, and a perfect spray-on tan.

Nefertiti's pose is perfectly sym-metrical from every angle—front, back and side. From the side, her V-shaped profile creates a dynamic effect: she leans forward, gazing intently, while her funnel-shaped hat swoops up and back. Her colorful hat is a geometri-cally flawless, tapered cylinder.

And yet, despite her seemingly perfect beauty, Nefertiti has a touch of humanity. Notice the fine wrinkles around the eyes—these only enhance her beauty. She has a slight Mona Lisa smile, pursed at the corners. Her eyebrows are so delicately de-tailed, you can make out each single hair. From the back, the per-fection of her neck is marked with a bump of reality—a protruding vertebra. Her look is meditative, intelligent, lost in thought. Like a movie star discreetly sipping a glass of wine at a sidewalk café, Nefertiti seems somehow more dignified in person.

In real life, Nefertiti, though born a commoner, was much honored. As the pharaoh's wife, she was also recognized as a god on earth, part of the trinity of Akhenaton, Nefertiti, and the sun god Aton. Nefertiti had six children—all daughters.

The bust is made of limestone, with a stucco surface. This bust may have been meant as a companion piece to the bust of Akhena-ton in the previous room. But this bust never left its studio. It served as a master model for all other portraits of the queen. (That's probably why the artist didn't bother putting the quartz inlay in the left eye.) Stare at her long enough, and you may get the sensation that she's winking at you.

How the queen arrived in Germany is a tale out of *Indiana Jones.* The German archaeologist Ludwig Borchardt uncovered her in the Egyptian desert in 1912. The Egyptian Department of An-tiquities had first pick of all the artifacts uncovered on their terri-tory. After the first takings, they divided the rest 50/50 with the excavators. When Borchardt presented Nefertiti to the Egyptians, they passed her over, never bothering to examine her closely. (Un-substantiated rumors persist that Borchardt misled the Egyptians in order to keep the bust for himself—prompting some Egyptians to call for Nefertiti's return, just as the Greeks are lobbying the British to return the Parthenon frieze currently housed in the Brit-ish Museum.)

Although this bust is not particularly representative of Egyp-tian art in general—and despite increasing claims that her long neck suggests she's a Neoclassical fake—Nefertiti has become a symbol of Egyptian art by popular acclaim. And since her arrival in Berlin, she's also become something of a symbol of Germany itself—Germany's "queen." Hitler promoted her as a pagan symbol of his new non-Christian Reich. When Germany was split in the Cold War, both sides fought to claim her. Today Nefertiti's timeless beauty has come to represent the aspirations of the German people.

• *The Egyptian Collection continues in* **Room 211**—*the "Library of Antiquity."*

Papyrus Collection

This large room is filled with what looks like empty display cases. Press a button to watch a 3,000-year-old document trundle out of its protective home. You'll see ancient texts in many languages—Egyptian hieroglyphs, Greek, Latin, and so on. They're written on everything from paper to cloth, wood, pottery, stone tablets, and parchment—but the most prevalent material is papyrus. The collection here contains thousands of examples of this most classically Egyptian material, made from the fibrous pith of a common marsh reed. Perusing these documents is a fascinating look at the ancient world's laws, business transactions, plays, and even early fiction.

• *Exiting Room 211, you'll pass through more rooms with exhibits on migrations, barbarians, and ancient Rome (including larger-than-life Roman statues), plaster casts of Ghiberti's famous bronze doors on the Florence Baptistery, coins, and displays about medieval times after the fall of the classical world.*

Then head downstairs to level 1, and turn left, entering **Room 111.**

LEVEL 1
More Egypt

There's much more of Egypt in this and the next rooms—statues of pharaohs, wall paintings, reliefs from tombs, even a reconstructed burial chapel. In Room 109, the glass cases of **"30 Centuries of Sculpture,"** filled with the sculpted heads of pharaohs, priests, and scribes, trace concepts of portraiture over the millennia.

In the center of Room 109, find the **Berlin Green Head,** from around 350 B.C. No one knows who this bald, smooth-skinned man was, but his knitted-brow look makes him come

MUSEUM ISLAND

to life. (Some think his shaved head indicates he was a priest.) Sculpted even as Egypt was being conquered by Greece, this combines Greek realism with timeless Egyptian features. This Green Man's determined look is a thought-provoking glimpse into Egypt's future.

If you want still more Egypt, you'll find it downstairs on level 0, where you can see small-scale statuettes and models as well as a sea of large sarcophagi.

• *But we'll finish our tour here on level 1. Backtrack the way you came, cross the stairwell, and make your way to Rooms 103-104.*

Schliemann's Troy

There's not much to see in these rooms—a few gold necklaces and old pots—but the text panels help explain the craze for antiquities that brought us the Neues Museum.

Much of it can be traced to the man featured in these rooms: Heinrich Schliemann (1822-1890) was the real-life Indiana Johann of his era. Having read Homer's accounts of the Trojan War, Schliemann set out on a quest to find the long-lost ruins of the city of Troy. He (probably) found the capital of the Trojans (in Turkey), as well as the capital of the Greeks (Mycenae, in the Greek Peloponnese). Displays in Room 103 tell the fascinating story of how Schliemann smuggled the treasures out in fruit baskets, then their long journey until they were donated to the German government. (Unfortunately, Schliemann's treasure trove was looted when the Soviets invaded Berlin during World War II, which is why so few artifacts remain here.) Schliemann's derring-do sparked the imagination of all Europe. Soon, other archaeologists were traveling to Egypt, Greece, and Rome, and returning with the artifacts that fill this grand museum. *Danke*, Herr Schliemann, for bringing the ancient world back to life.

• *Our next museum is the one that resembles a Greek temple (behind the Neues and Altes museums).*

Old National Gallery (Alte Nationalgalerie)

Dramatic, colorful, Romantic landscapes are the star of this gallery of 19th-century art. The most famous of the German Romantics is Caspar David Friedrich, and we'll see his moody painting *Monk By the Sea*. The museum also features a few choice works from well-known French Impressionists Manet, Monet, Renoir, and company. True art lovers will enjoy the German Realists, with their slice-of-life scenes from the Industrial Age. Frankly, you probably won't recognize any specific paintings in the entire museum. But it's still an enjoyable 45-minute stroll through German culture from the 1800s—the century when Germany came of age and found its cultural identity.

SELF-GUIDED TOUR

Start on the **third floor**—the main focus of the collection—and work your way down. You can take the stairs, or look for the elevator by the ticket desk.

LEVEL 3
Romantic Paintings

• *The first stop is in the small, standalone **Room 3.02** just off the landing (straight ahead as you come up the stairs; from the elevator, you'll have to backtrack to the landing).*

Casa Bartholdy Murals

Use this room's colorful paintings as an introduction to the Romantic art we'll see next. These frescoes, originally painted on the walls of a villa in Rome, tell the biblical story of Joseph. They were done by idealistic artists of the artistic brotherhood called the Nazarenes.

It was the early 1800s, and the German people were searching for their unique national identity. In art, the Nazarenes were breaking free from the Italian and French styles that had dominated Germany's academies for centuries. For inspiration, they returned to Germany's cultural roots—the Middle Ages.

As a result, the Bible story of Joseph looks strangely medieval: medieval-looking kings, peasants in tunics, rustic castles, and Germanic landscapes. The Nazarenes were seeking a purer form of expression that was uniquely German. This almost religious fervor would inspire the next generation of German artists—the Romantics.

• *Make your way through some of the smaller side-rooms to reach the large **Room 3.05**—in the very center of the building (flanked with white columns).*

Karl Friedrich Schinkel

Schinkel is best known as the architect who remade Berlin in the 1820s. He designed buildings all around the city, including the Neue Wache, the Concert Hall on Gendarmenmarkt, the Altes Museum—and even a section of the museum you're in. With Greek columns, clean lines, and mathematical symmetry, Schinkel's buildings epitomized the then-popular Neoclassical style.

But as a painter, Schinkel took a totally different path—toward Romanticism. His haunting landscapes clearly show his fascination with architecture. Gothic ca-thedrals and castles dominate his scenes. These buildings are clearly fantasies, not practical blueprints: They're impossibly tall, perched dramatically on cliffs, overlooking distant vistas, and engulfed in clouds. Foliage grows over the buildings, and animals wander through. Nature rules. Where puny humans do appear, they are dwarfed by the landscape and buildings. Scenes are lit by a dramatic, eerie light, as though the world is charged from within by the power of God. Welcome to Romanticism.

• *Head back to one of the side corridors. Next, continue to the large **Room 3.06**.*

Caspar David Friedrich Room

The greatest German artist of the Romantic era was Caspar David Friedrich (1774-1840). A quick glance around this room dedicated to his paintings gives you a sense of Friedrich's subjects: craggy mountains, twisted trees, ominous clouds, burning sunsets, and lone figures in the gloom.

Friedrich specialized in eerie landscapes. Rather than painting placid, pretty scenes as other landscape artists might, Friedrich celebrated Nature's awesome power. The few people he painted are tiny and solitary, standing with their backs to us. As they ponder the vastness of their surroundings, we're invited to see the world through their eyes, and to contemplate humankind's miniscule place in the grand scheme of things.

• *Hey, this is "Romantic" painting, so my descriptions have to be equally melodramatic. Now, let's see a few of Friedrich's paintings—in chronological order, as we trace the sometimes turbulent arc of his life.*

Monk by the Sea, 1808-1810: A lone figure stands on a sand dune, pondering a vast, turbulent expanse of sea and sky. Scholars have suggested that the monk—slender, with long blond hair—is Friedrich himself.

Romanticism

The movement known as Romanticism, popular in the early
1800s, emphasized the heart
over the head. Romantics questioned the clinical detachment
of science, industrial pollution,
and the personal restrictions of
modern life. Instead, they rev-
eled in strong emotions, personal freedom, and the beauties of
Nature.

Romantics worshipped na-
ture's awe-inspiring splendor.
Walking through forests, along
rivers, and up mountainsides, Romantics communed with their
true self: namely, the primitive, "noble savage" beneath the intellectual crust. Romantic painters tried to capture the beauty
of nature, but especially its drama. Ominous clouds, rainbows,
distant horizons, eerie lighting effects—all these suggested
not just what the eye saw but what the heart felt.

The German Romantic movement was closely tied with
German national identity. Remember, as late as the mid-
1800s, there was no German "nation." What tied the German people together was their indigenous roots, language,
folklore, and common myths. These dated back centuries, to
medieval times. So German Romantics glorified these medieval roots. The old folklore was resurrected and popularized
by the Brothers Grimm. Painters depicted unspoiled German
landscapes and dreamy German villages. Portraits of the German people showed them as rugged and proud. These were
themes that would strum the heartstrings of anyone with Teutonic blood. So inspired, the German people would unite and
form the modern nation of Germany in 1871.

This painting made Friedrich instantly famous. It was exhibited here in Berlin, in 1810,
and was bought by none
other than the king of Prussia. By then, Friedrich was in
his mid-thirties. He'd honed
his craft at a stuffy painting
academy, but his true passion
was roaming Germany's rugged countryside and sketching
with pencil and paper, directly

from nature. Then he returned to the studio to meticulously compose the final work in oils.

This beach scene is laid out in three horizontal layers: land, sea, and sky. This horizontal axis is offset by a single vertical line—the lone monk. You'll see this same horizontal/vertical technique in other Friedrich canvases.

Landscapes by Friedrich might better be called "skyscapes." In this painting, the sky taking up the majority of the canvas is a murky mix of black clouds, grey wisps, and ambiguous lighting. The scene has no obvious "frame," and seems to bleed off the edges of the canvas to infinity. This vague atmosphere mirrors the ambiguous emotions of the monk.

And what exactly is the monk thinking? Friedrich gave us a clue: When this painting was first exhibited, it had a companion piece, which we'll see next.

• *That companion piece now hangs alongside* Monk by the Sea.

Abbey Among Oak Trees, 1809-1810: It's an incredibly bleak scene—a ruined Gothic church, bare trees, and desolate tomb-stones. Almost unnoticed among the graves is a sad parade of tombstone-like monks bearing a coffin.

Death is a common theme in Friedrich's work. Between the ages of 7 and 13, Friedrich saw his mother and two sisters die, and he watched his brother drown. This dark canvas seems to hammer home the finality of death.

The one sliver of hope is the dim crescent moon. The monks carry the coffin toward the horizon and the lightening sky, lit by a new moon. Might there be some hope beyond the grave?

Hmmm...

Friedrich lets that thought drift upward above the trees, into the sky, and out the top of the canvas...where it bleeds up until it would have reached that companion painting *Monk by the Sea,* which originally hung directly above this one. There, one of the monks has wandered off, alone, to a desolate beach. He ponders the death of his fallen brother and the vast unknown that lies beyond this mortal existence.

• *You know, I think we could all use something a little cheerier. So find the next painting...*

Woman at a Window, 1822: In 1818, the renowned 44-year-old artist married 25-year-old Caroline—the woman in this painting. She leans out the window of Friedrich's studio. As with so many of Friedrich's paintings, his subject has her back to us, so we see what she sees: a blue sky and a row of colorful poplar trees.

With his marriage and the birth of three kids, Friedrich's dark life brightened. His colors get lighter and more vibrant, and he begins adding more flesh-and-blood people to his minimal landscapes.

This painting's composition is another carefully planned grid. It's strong three-dimensionality sucks you right into the scene. Notice how the floorboards direct your eye from where we stand to the woman at the window. Your attention soars out the dark studio, past the mast of a moored ship, across the river, to the distant trees and the sunny skies beyond.

• *Next up, look for...*

Man and Woman Contemplating the Moon, 1818-1825: A couple emerges from a dark forest onto a hillside. They stand and gaze into the deep night sky, lit by a hazy moon. The woman places her hand gently on the man's shoulder as they pause to contemplate. (By the way, Samuel Beckett said this painting was the inspiration for his play, "Waiting for Godot.")

• *The next two paintings were also intended as companion pieces.*

Moonrise over the Sea, 1822: It's evening, and two women and a man perch atop a rock and watch as ships return to the harbor. As the moon rises through a layer of clouds, it casts a shimmering light across the wide sea and even wider sky.

Although Friedrich rarely talked about the symbolism of his work, he often added intriguing elements that invite interpretation. To some, these ships suggest how we all "sail" through the journey of our lives like ships across the sea, hoping to return to a safe harbor where loved ones await.

The Solitary Tree, 1822: An aging but still-strong tree rises up stoically from a stark landscape. The composition of this work is classic Friedrich—a vertical tree silhouetted against a horizontal landscape, splitting a V-shaped valley in a triangular mountain range.

Notice the tiny shepherd leaning against the tree. It's as if the presence of man hardly makes a mark on the wide world of nature.
• *The biggest painting in the room is...*

The Watzmann, 1824-1825: Friedrich often painted actual locations in Germany, like this mountain in Bavaria. A strong proponent of German identity, Friedrich celebrated German topography—which he viewed as being as rugged and fierce as the German people. He was part of the rising movement that would later flower into an independent German nation.

This view looks across a craggy mountain meadow to snow-capped mountains rising beyond. Romantics like Friedrich got high on what they called the "sublime," a mystical ecstasy inspired by the power of nature. Here, we feel Friedrich's experience of having his spirit soar upward in its presence.
• *Let's see one last painting as we conclude Friedrich's life story.*

Ruins of Eldena, c. 1824-1825: Friedrich loved to wander through this ruined monastery near his home. The trees overgrowing the eroding arches suggest how nature overtakes civilization, and how time overtakes us all.

Friedrich himself was feeling the effects of time. As he aged, his already eccentric personality settled into extended bouts of depression. He spent more and more time alone, wandering the fields and woods. As a Romantic, he tried to learn the timeless spiritual truths that nature can teach. But just a few years after finishing this painting, Friedrich suffered a stroke. His health declined, and his ability to paint went downhill. At the same time, his style went out of fashion. He died poor, forgotten, and—like the solitary figures in so many of his paintings—alone.

Friedrich's work languished in obscurity for two generations. When it was finally rediscovered, it had an enormous impact. His hazy atmospherics and light effects would inspire Monet, Whistler, and Turner. His lone figures against bleak backdrops were copied by Expressionists—imagine Munch's "The Scream." His meticulously composed patterns of pure color would evolve into purely abstract art—think Mark Rothko.

More than anything, it was Friedrich's spirit that lived on. His antimaterialism inspired many others who would chose art as a spiritual path. His works celebrate the brave individuals who thumb their nose at society's expectations and forge their own path through life.

• *Whew! Let's take a break from all that drama. For a complete change of pace, check out nearby* **Rooms 3.08-3.13,** *which are arranged in a semicircle at the end of this wing.*

The Biedermeier Style

These rooms feature paintings in the so-called Biedermeier style (c. 1815-1848), the conservative flip side to Romanticism's individualism, turbulence, and political radicalism. The adjective *bieder* means "solid" and "plain," words that could describe the prosperous and morally upright middle class seen in these canvases, dressed up in their Sunday best. Eduard Gaertner's *Unter den Linden* (1852-1853) shows happy Berliners promenading down the boulevard, past the Frederick the Great statue to the Stadtschloss (the now-gone city palace). Biedermeier landscapes are pretty, not dramatic. The style is soft-focus, hypersensitive, super-sweet, and sentimental. The poor are happy, the middle class are happy, and the world they inhabit is perfectly lit.

• *Then came the democratic revolutions of 1848, the invention of the camera, Realism, and Impressionism...and all hell broke loose. For a quick look at some of the other trends in Europe of the 1800s, head downstairs to level 2. Walk straight through two big halls into* **Room 2.03.**

LEVEL 2
French Impressionists

This one big room is lined with minor works by big-name French artists. Unlike the carefully composed, turbulent, and highly symbolic paintings of the German Romantics, these scenes appear like simple unposed "snapshots" of everyday life.

Pan the room to see works that, even if not masterpieces, are typical of the Impressionist and Post-Impressionist masters. There are Renoir's pink-cheeked girls, Degas' working girls, Cézanne's fruit bowls, and Gauguin's Tahitian girls. Monet's church scene (*View of Vétheuil-sur-Seine*, 1880) uses messy blobs of paint to create the effect of shimmering sunlight. In Manet's *In the Conservatory* (1879), a woman relaxes on a park bench while a man leans in with a comment. At first, they seem to be strangers. But look at the center of the composition: their two hands, with wedding rings. They're husband and wife, secure enough in their relationship that they are intimately connected without an outward show of devotion.

• *Our tour is over. But if you still want more, it's easy to find a few other highlights on your map.*

THE REST OF THE MUSEUM

In Room 2.14 are two well-known **portraits by Franz von Lenbach** of world-changing Germans: Otto von Bismarck (Germany's

first prime minister) and the composer Richard Wagner.

Downstairs on level 1, 19th-century Realism reigns, with room after room of small brown canvases of everyday German life in the 1800s. **Adolph Menzel** made his name painting elegant (non-Realist) scenes of royal gatherings and historical events. But it's his Realist scenes that lived on. *Iron Rolling Mill* (Room 1.13) captures the gritty side of the Industrial Age with a warts-and-all look at steelworkers toiling in a hellish factory.

The **sculpture collection** (Room 1.01—at the entrance to this wing) features classical-looking works by the Danish Thorvaldsen and the Italian Canova. The highlight is the German sculptor Johann Gottfried Schadow's delightful *Die Prinzessinnen,* showing the dynamic duo of Prussian princesses, Louise and Frederike.

There. You've toured the 1800s—from spiritual Nazerenes to

emotional Romantics, from stuffy Biedermeiers to elegant Neo-classicism, from gritty Realists to the Impressionists and the dawn of the 20th century.

• *If you still have an appetite for more museums—and a combo-ticket burning a hole in your pocket—the next best stop is the Bode Museum, a 10-minute walk away at the northern tip of Museum Island.*

Bode Museum

Connoisseurs (but not most people) will love this classy, un-crowded, eclectic museum of B-list sculpture, painting, and precious objects. You can browse its

highlights—a Byzantine mosaic and one of the world's best coin collections—in 30 minutes.

The museum is perched at the "prow" of Museum Island, as if rising up from the river. Even if you're not visiting the galleries, it's free to step into the lavish lobby, under a great dome, where a statue of Frederick William of Brandenburg on horseback welcomes you. With his curly locks blowing in the wind and wielding his general's baton, Frederick put Prussia on the map in the 1600s, setting the stage for his great-grandson Frederick the Great a century later. (It's also free to climb the grand lobby staircase to the charming museum café.)

COLLECTION HIGHLIGHTS

Cross through the entry lobby, walk straight through the first hall, and step into the "Basilica" hall. From there, go through the door on the left, then work your way back (bearing left) to the corner **Room 115,** with a glittering mosaic.

Ravenna Mosaic

The Byzantine Empire was Europe's beacon of light during the dark centuries after the Fall of Rome, when barbarians roamed the land. Fortunately, the empire had secured the outpost of Ravenna, on Italy's Adriatic coast, offering a vision of strength, stability, and hope.

Imagine seeing this brilliant mosaic in a church apse back then (A.D. 550). It shows a

MUSEUM ISLAND

serene Jesus, who is the very image of youthful vigor. He stands holding a cross in one hand and a book in the other, opened to a comforting message: "Qui Vi Dit Me..." (Whoever has seen me has seen the Father, John 14:9) and "Ego et Pater..." (I and the Father are one; John 10:30).

Flanking Christ are two handsome angels, Michael and Gabriel. All three stand in a flowery meadow, suggesting that they bring a bit of heaven down to troubled mortals on earth. Notice that Christ wears the cross-shaped halo reserved for the Trinity. Above him, in the arch, are 12 doves—a joyous representation of the 12 Apostles. Above that we see Christ again, this time in the traditional pose seen in so many Byzantine churches. He's the "Pantocrator," the Ruler of All, seated on a throne, holding a book, and raising his right hand to bless the whole world. He's flanked by a heavenly host of angels, standing in a sea of fire. The angels blow their horns to announce the Apocalypse—when the old age will be destroyed so a new one can emerge.

• *To find the coin collection, retrace your steps to the "Basilica" room, cross to the far end, and take the stairs up under the "Small Dome." At the top of the stairs, take the left door and circulate around the wing, finding the smaller rooms on the outside of the building. Begin in* **Room 241**.

Coins and Medals

Browse Room 241 clockwise to get an overview of the collection, which spans 2,700 years of coinage. The "Electrum" from ancient Greece (c. 600 B.C.) is surprisingly sophisticated—a gold-silver alloy coin depicting sphinxes, Pegasuses, and masks. The chronological history starts in Room 242. There are ancient Greek drachmas (c. 500 B.C.) adorned with chariots, bulls, warriors, and rulers. The ancient Romans featured their Caesars. The medieval collection is especially strong in German coins, medals, and document seals.

Room 243 picks up the timeline, going from crude 12th-century coins all the way to 20th-century Deutsche Marks, Berlin Wall medallions, and the 21st-century euro. If you haven't had enough, hunker down at a computer terminal to explore the rest of the museum's 500,000 coins. One thing you won't see is the giant, 100-kilogram gold coin from Canada (worth $1 million Canadian)—known as the "Big Maple Leaf." It was stolen in a high-profile heist in March 2017.

Altes (Old) Museum

For museum completists, there's one more to consider—but if you're museumed out, it's definitely skippable. Back out at the south end of the complex, facing Lustgarten, is the Altes (Old Museum). Perhaps the least interesting of the five museums, this building features the rest of Berlin's Collection of Classical Antiquities—namely, Etruscan, Roman, and Greek art. It also contains Greek and Roman sculptures, vases, and some bronze figurines from the currently closed north wing of the Pergamon Museum.

PERGAMON MUSEUM TOUR

Pergamonmuseum

Of the five museums concentrated on the aptly named Museum Island, the Pergamon is most deserving of your time and attention. In the late 19th century, German archaeologists scoured the Eastern Mediterranean region, unearthing remarkable artifacts of the earliest human civilizations. Indiana Jones-like adventurers, including Heinrich Schliemann (1822-1890), Carl Humann (1839-1896), Theodor Wiegand (1864-1936), and Robert Koldewey (1855-1925), brought their oversized findings home to Berlin. The best of these are on display in the Pergamon Museum—Germany's answer to the British Museum.

The manageably sized Pergamon lets you peruse impressive treasures from four different civilizations in a couple dozen well-laid-out rooms. Although the museum's star attraction—the gigantic Pergamon Altar—is undergoing a years-long renovation, there are plenty of other jaw-dropping monuments displayed here. You can traverse a long, glazed-tiled hallway, past roaring lions, to the gargantuan Ishtar Gate. There's the hall-sized Gate of Miletus and a floor-sized mosaic from the Roman world. And there's the Islamic collection, culminating in the elaborately painted Aleppo Room, a 400-year-old testament to multiculturalism.

We'll start on the first floor with the Babylonians and their predecessors, the Assyrians. Next come several over-the-top monuments from the ancient Roman world. Finally, we'll head up to the second floor to see impressive artifacts from the Islamic world, which carried the torch of civilization through medieval darkness.

If you're planning to visit the Pergamon and one or more additional Museum Island sights, get a pass (described below) and set aside a good part of the day. For more details about Museum Island and the other sights here, see the previous chapter.

Orientation

Cost: €12, includes superb audioguide; if you'll tour at least one other Museum Island collection, invest in the €18 Museum Island Pass combo-ticket or €29 Museum Pass Berlin.

Hours: Daily 10:00-18:00, Thu until 20:00.

Information: Tel. 030/266-424-242, www.smb.museum.

Pergamon Altar Closed: The museum's namesake Pergamon Altar is undergoing conservation and won't be on view for years (see the end of this chapter). In the meantime, the rest of the museum is plenty impressive.

When to Go: Mornings are busiest, and you're likely to find long lines any time on Saturday or Sunday. Bad weather also brings crowds. The least-busy time is Thursday evening, when it's open late.

Crowd-Beating Tips: To skip ticket-buying lines, purchase a timed ticket online at the museum website; if you buy a Museum Island Pass or Museum Pass Berlin, you can book a free timed-entry reservation for the Pergamon at the same time (possible online if you read German, but easier in person at the museum or a TI).

Getting There: The nearest S-Bahn stations, Hackescher Markt and Friedrichstrasse, are a 10-minute walk away. The Am Kupfergraben tram (#M1, #12) stops are closer—just across the river from the museum. Or ride bus #100 or #200 along Under den Linden to the Lustgarten stop, and walk through Lustgarten park and around the Altes Museum to reach the Pergamon entrance.

Getting In: As part of a multi-year renovation of Museum Island, they're building a new entrance pavilion called the James-Simon-Galerie on the west bank of the island. For now, you'll enter the Pergamon from the courtyard behind the colonnade on Bodestrasse. Be prepared for changes.

Tours: The superb audioguide (included) helps broaden your experience.

Length of This Tour: Allow about 1.5 hours for the Pergamon—less if you skip the Museum of Islamic Art.

Services: Baggage check is next to the ticket desk.

Merkel Sightings: Germany's formidable leader, Angela Merkel, could live in the expansive digs at the Chancellery. But she and her husband (who's a professor at Humboldt University) have long lived in an apartment overlooking Museum Island. You'll see a couple of policemen providing modest protection in front of her place on Am Kupfergraben, directly across the bridge from the Pergamon Museum.

Eateries: Renovation has closed the museum's on-site café. For

Pergamon Museum Tour

BABYLON
1. Processional Way
2. Ishtar Gate
3. Throne Room Facade
4. Model of Babylon

ASSYRIA
5. Esarhaddon Stele

6. Statue of Hadad
7. More Assyrian Artifacts

ROME
8. Market Gate of Miletus
9. Model of Miletus
10. Orpheus Mosaic
11. Various Roman Artifacts

lunch nearby, try the cafés at the Bode or Neues museums, the restaurants down Georgenstrasse (follow the elevated train tracks; see recommendations on page 275), or Hackescher Markt (cross the Friedrichsbrücke bridge; see page 286).

Starring: Ancient wonders, from Babylon and Assyria to ancient Rome and medieval Islam.

The Tour Begins

• *From the ticket desk, head up the stairs to floor 1, turn left, and enter* ***Room 8***—*a long hallway lined with blue tiles.*

BABYLON, 609-539 B.C.
① Processional Way

You've entered the city of Babylon, circa 575 B.C., under the reign of King Nebuchadnezzar II.

Babylon (located near modern-day Baghdad) was the capital of Nebuchadnezzar's vast empire and the world's most glorious city. Rooms 8 and

9 re-create one of Babylon's architectural wonders: a ceremonial highway called the Processional Way that led into the walled city through its main entrance—the Ishtar Gate. To picture how it all may have looked, peruse the model in the center of Room 8.

Now stand at the far end of Room 8 (facing the Ishtar Gate, in the next room), look down the lion-lined hallway, and imagine walking down the Processional Way in all its glory. Trumpets blare, drums pound, and the procession begins. Following a yellow-brick road that was 200 yards long and 30 yards wide, you'd pass fierce lions depicted in colorful glazed tile on your way to the Ishtar Gate. The walls to either side rose 50 feet—if you look up, you can see the blue ramparts that once topped the gate's original height.

The roaring lions symbolize Ishtar, the fierce goddess of love (i.e., sex and fertility) and war. The lions walk against the flow, warning us of the awe-inspiring sanctuary we're approaching. Above and below the lions are rows of daisy-like flowers. The colorful tiles—arranged in bands of blue, turquoise, yellow, black, white—accentuate the horizontal flow of this impressive promenade.

The Processional Way was central to an annual 11-day festival giving thanks to the benevolent gods for the return of spring. King Nebuchadnezzar rode in his chariot down the long passageway, dressed in his finest robes. His entourage and priests carried statues of the deities from their winter hibernation back into the city. Passing through the Ishtar Gate, they would arrive at the temple dedicated to Marduk, king of the gods and patron of the city. There, the statues would be returned to their sanctuary. And Nebuchadnezzar—Marduk's mortal counterpart—would ceremonially "marry" a temple priestess who represented Ishtar, thus uniting heaven and earth and restoring harmony to the world.

• *Promenade past the gauntlet of lions, into* **Room 9,** *for a closer look at the...*

❷ Ishtar Gate

Nebuchadnezzar II made sure that all who approached his city got a grand first impression. His massive blue Ishtar Gate inspired awe and obedience. The gate stands 46 feet tall and 100 feet wide (counting its jutting facets).

This was the grandest of Babylon's gates, one of eight in the 11-mile wall that encompassed this city of 200,000. It was a double wall—the outer wall was 10 feet thick, the inner 20 feet. The Ishtar Gate we see today was the smaller gate for that smaller outer wall. Looming behind it was its counterpart—nearly twice as tall, a third wider, and much more massive. (The museum has the larger gate, but it's too big to display.) In its day, the Ishtar Gate was famous—one of the original Seven Wonders of the World.

Zero in on the decoration. Though the gate was dedicated to Ishtar, it has symbols of other gods as well. The yellow-black horned bulls (specifically the aurochs, a species now extinct) symbolize Adad, the god who brought sun and rain to provide a bountiful harvest. The skinnier animals are mythical dragons, with scaly bodies, curled horns, forked tongues, and fire breath. They combine body parts of the lion, cobra, eagle, and scorpion, and thus symbolize both Marduk and his son Nabu, god of wisdom and writing.

Check out the floor-to-ceiling inscription on the left side of the gate, which (among other things) reads: "I Nebuchadnezzar laid the cornerstone of this gate and had them built out of pure blue stone. Upon the walls are bulls and dragons—magnificently adorned with luxurious splendor for all mankind to behold and wonder."

• *On the walls to either side of the gate are two similar-looking tiled panels. These were part of the...*

❸ Facade of Nebuchadnezzar's Throne Room

Nebuchadnezzar lived near the Ishtar Gate, and these colorful panels once decorated the facade of his Royal Palace, specifically the Throne Room. This is just a slice of the original facade that once stretched 58 yards. The panels fit nicely into the whole architectural ensemble we've seen, with similar looking glazed tiles in the same colorful palette. They depict palm trees, plus lions and daisies, all framed with elaborate garlands and patterns.

All of the pieces in this hall— the Ishtar Gate, Processional Way, and Throne Room panels—are made of decorative brick, glazed and fired in the ancient Egyptian faience technique. Decorations like the lions, which project outward from the surface, were carved or molded before the painted glaze went on.

The colors—yellow, green, and blue (from rare lapis lazuli)— come from natural pigments, ground to a powder and mixed with melted silica (quartz). As the chemicals ionized, crystallized, and bonded in the kiln fires, the result was a sheen that's luminous, shiny, and even weather-resistant.

The museum's Babylonian treasures are meticulous reconstructions. After a Berlin archaeologist discovered the ruins in

The World of Nebuchadnezzar II

Nebuchadnezzar II (r. 605-562) was one of history's most notorious fiends, at least according to the Bible. He ransacked the temple of Jerusalem. He carried off many Israelites into decades of captivity in Babylon. He threw three Hebrews into a fiery furnace, forced Daniel to psychoanalyze his weird dreams, built a hubristic Tower of Babel, and became the fallen "morning star"—the metaphor for evil tyrants whom God must punish.

In fact, Nebuchadnezzar II was the ruler whose empire was—for a brief moment in the sweep of history—the queen of the civilized world. His Babylonian kingdom stretched across the Middle East, from Egypt to the Persian Gulf.

Babylonia had only recently thrown off the yoke of the Assyrians. Those wars had left the country devastated. Babylon was ransacked and burned, the temple to Marduk was desecrated, and sacred statues were stolen.

Nebuchadnezzar rebuilt. He was determined to make his capital of Babylon (50 miles from modern Baghdad) the world's richest, most sophisticated city. He reconstructed the temples and restored all the old gods. Marduk, the city's patron deity, was honored with an enormous ziggurat—a seven-story step-pyramid, 100 yards tall (the Bible's Tower of Babel). Nebuchadnezzar built a grand royal palace, faced with colorful tiles and fitted with a secret underground passageway through town. The city walls were impregnable. Most famously, he built (or maybe merely rebuilt) the awe-inspiring Hanging Gardens, a series of stone terraces landscaped with trees, vines, and waterfalls—one of the Seven Wonders of the World. And, for a ceremonial entryway into this amazing city, he built the marvelous Processional Way, lined with tiled lions, leading to the Ishtar Gate.

Babylon rose quickly, and would fall just as fast. Nebuchadnezzar reigned for 43 years—the brief Golden Age of Babylon. Two decades later, Babylonia was overrun by Persians.

PERGAMON

modern-day Iraq in 1900, the Prussian government financed their excavation. What was recovered was little more than piles of shattered shards of brick. It's since been augmented with modern tilework and pieced together like a 2,500-year-old Babylonian jigsaw puzzle.

• *You might peek into Room 6 (if it's open) to see the* ❹ *Model of Babylon, which shows the temple complex of Marduk (the end point of the Processional Way) and Nebuchadnezzar's ziggurat.*

But our tour is moving on to the next civilization. Start in **Room 3**, *with a tall artifact that marks the link between the Babylonians and their northern cousins, the Assyrians.*

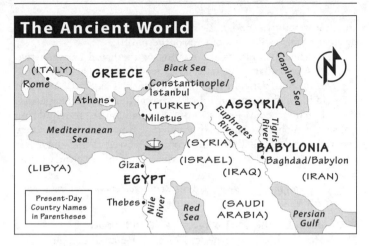

The Ancient World

ASSYRIA, 900-670 B.C.
❺ **Esarhaddon Stele**

This stele, or ceremonial column, commemorates the historical high point of Assyrian civilization, which dominated the Middle East a century before Babylon.

It's the year 670 B.C., and King Esarhaddon is celebrating his victory over Egypt. The king is huge, lording it over the two puny Egyptian captives kneeling humbly at his feet—the pharaoh's son (with crown) and another man. Esarhaddon is adorned with his royal fez crown, elaborately braided hair, and ZZ Top beard. He raises his right hand to present a thank-you offering to the gods. In his left hand he holds a scepter, as well as two leashes, to lead his two captives by the neck.

The inscription written across the entire lower half (in cuneiform script) tells of Esarhaddon's cruel conquest: "I wrought a mighty bloodbath," it says. Esarhaddon loved to boast of leveling whole villages, kidnapping the pharaoh's wife and family, plundering Egypt's wealth, and leaving behind pyramids of severed heads. Even the Bible chronicled Esarhaddon's conquest (in Isaiah 20:4): "So shall the king of Assyria lead away the Egyptian prisoners, young and old, naked and barefoot, even with their buttocks uncovered, to their everlasting shame."

With his victory over Egypt, Esarhaddon completed the conquest of the Middle East begun by his grandfather Sargon II (who invaded Palestine) and father Sennacherib (who sacked Babylon

PERGAMON

and kidnapped their gods). Esarhaddon proclaimed his dominance by erecting steles like this one in southern Turkey.

This stele also marks the passing of the baton between two great Mesopotamian powers, Assyria (in the north, near modern-day Mosul) and Babylon (in the south, near Baghdad). You see, Esarhaddon had taken control of Assyria after his brothers assassinated their father (II Kings 19:37). Esarhaddon began rebuilding Babylon, which his father had plundered. Ironically, within a few generations, a rebuilt Babylon become so powerful that the locals drove out their Assyrian overlords and soon dominated the Middle East.

• *For an even grander look at Assyria, step into* **Room 2**, *where it's not hard to locate the...*

❻ Colossal Statue of the Weather God Hadad

The 10-foot-tall basalt statue (c. 775 B.C.) depicts the popular Assyrian god Hadad (or Adad). He wears a thick beard and a helmet with curly horns (tucked close on either side), indicating his godly power. His (missing) hands likely held his symbol, the lightning bolt.

Hadad was the bringer of rain in the arid Middle East, and this statue was erected as an offering to gain the favor of this all-important god. It was Hadad's storms that fed the Tigris and Euphrates rivers, which irrigated the fields—putting the fertility in the Fertile Crescent. The inscription covering his long skirt is in Aramaic (not cuneiform), as Hadad was a popular god throughout the vast Assyrian empire.

• *Backtrack to Esarhaddon's stele and veer left to find* **Rooms 10-13** *to peruse...*

❼ More Assyrian Artifacts

Browsing through these rooms you'll get a sense of Assyrian grandeur. Assyrians were great warriors and ruthless conquerors. But they were also efficient administrators of the lands they controlled. As empire builders who dominated the Middle East for three centuries, they have been called the "Romans of the East."

You'll see artifacts from several royal palaces, as the Assyrian kings liked to make their mark by building new palaces in new capital cities along the Tigris. There are ruins from Ashur (the oldest capital, midway between modern Baghdad and Mosul), Nimrud (farther north), Nineveh (near Mosul), and Dur-Shurrakin (also near Mosul).

In Room 10, you'll see 3,500-year-old objects from the capital at Ashur, including its Temple of Ishtar. In Rooms 10-12, huge statues of winged bulls (these are casts, not originals) demonstrate the colossal scale and wealth of the Assyrians. There are also wall panels depicting the Assyrian king (with his traditional fez and beard) alongside winged spirits who spritz him with a pine-cone censer. You'll also see panels of the king in his chariot, hunting lions (the royal sport). The cuneiform inscriptions brag.

Room 12 has the basalt water basin of the Temple of Ashur. It's decorated with gods, who wear their obligatory horned crowns.

This reservoir distributed water to the priests for their sacred ablutions. It was built to celebrate the king's new system of irrigation canals.

In Room 13 you'll see examples of cuneiform script—the first system of writing. It was invented around 3,500 B.C. by the Sumerians, who predated the Assyrians and Babylonians in Iraq. The script is called cuneiform, or "wedge-shaped," because it was made not with pen on paper but with a wedge-shaped tool pressed into a soft clay tablet.

By the seventh century B.C., Assyria (in northern Iraq) was declining and Babylonia (in the south) was on the rise. When King Esarhaddon (whose stele we saw) divided his kingdom between his two feuding sons, chaos ensued, Egypt rebelled, invaders poured in, and Nineveh was sacked. Nebuchadnezzar II of Babylon became the new master of the Middle East. Then Babylon fell to Persia (539 B.C.), which in turn was conquered by the Greek Alexander the Great (c. 333 B.C.). By 150 B.C., Alexander's empire was coming under the sway of the next great civilization—Rome.

• *Return to the Ishtar Gate and pass through it, into a large hall (Rooms 1-2) with supersized monuments from ancient Rome.*

ROME, A.D. 100-200
❽ Market Gate of Miletus
After you've passed through the gate, look back, and flash-forward 700 years to the ancient Roman city of Miletus. Dominating this room is the huge Market Gate of Miletus—50 feet tall, 100 feet wide. This gate served as the entrance to the town's agora, or marketplace. Traders from across the Mediterranean and Middle East passed through the gate's three arched doorways into a football-field-sized courtyard surrounded by arcades, where business was conducted.

The gate certainly makes for a grand entryway. It's two stories tall, with niches where statues were once displayed. The sides project outward 20 feet, framing the gate. The columns are Corinthian—fluted, with capitals that sprout acanthus leaves. Overall, it's a typically Hellenistic style that mixes Greek and Roman features popular around the Mediterranean.

The gate was built around A.D. 100, likely during the reign of Trajan or Hadrian, whose statues may have stood in the upper story. The gate comes from Miletus, a wealthy and cosmopolitan Roman-ruled, Greek-speaking city on the southwest coast of Asia Minor (modern Turkey). You can peruse a ❾ **scale model of Miletus** opposite the gate, atop the balcony. Find the gate on the model: It's the small white part of the wall farthest from the harbor, standing at the entrance to the town's agora.

Miletus was destroyed by an earthquake centuries ago. Around 1900, German archaeologists unearthed the rubble, and the gate was painstakingly reconstructed here in Berlin.

• *In front of the gate, on the floor, are two large Roman mosaics.*

❿ Orpheus Mosaic

The exquisite mosaic floor of colored stone and glass comes from the dining room of a Roman villa in Miletus, c. A.D. 200. Part of

the mosaic features the mythical Greek musician Orpheus. Inside a square panel, Orpheus sits, playing his lyre, enchanting the animals who come to listen—a crow and a dog, as well as other wild beasts in the frames around him. In stark contrast, in the nearby rectangular mosaic (from an adjacent

room in the villa), the animals are wild, and winged hunters track them down. The size and workmanship of these mosaics is a testament to the wealth and sophistication of the people in Miletus, an important seaport as far back as 1900 B.C.

• *Opposite the Gate of Miletus is a mish-mosh of...*

⓫ Various Roman Artifacts

The curved marble balcony is part of the **Tomb of Cartinia,** an ancient priestess in the cult of Juno, who died near Rome around the time of Julius Caesar (c. 50 B.C.). The 4-foot-tall segment you see was part of a cylindrical tomb that rose nearly 40 feet. The facade is carved with a frieze of vines, garlands, pitchers, and bowls.

PERGAMON

Pondering Pergamon

As the collections of the museum demonstrate, each civilization topples the next. But, in the process, they also learn from and build on the previous one.

The Ishtar Gate of Babylon witnessed the rise and fall of the great Assyrians and Babylonians. Then Babylon fell to the Greco-Romans, who built the glorious Gate of Miletus. When Rome fell, the Middle East rose again under Islam, with caliphate capitals in Damascus, Baghdad, and Constantinople/Istanbul. When the Muslim Ottomans were toppled after World War I, Europe became dominant once again.

In the late 20th century, the Islamic world began to assert itself. The Iraqi dictator Saddam Hussein proclaimed himself the "son of Nebuchadnezzar" and started rebuilding the ancient Processional Way and Ishtar Gate in former Babylon. But, in 2003, Saddam's statue fell to US forces under George W. Bush—"Mission Accomplished." But as Iraq disintegrated, embittered Sunni rebels re-armed under the banner of ISIS, vowing to establish a new Islamic caliphate. To purge the land of pagan idols, ISIS thugs destroyed priceless ancient Assyrian ruins near Mosul and a Roman temple in Syria.

The systematic destruction and iconoclasm of one civilization's cultural treasures by the next wave of invaders makes the Pergamon's collection even more precious.

Also on display are **busts** of the emperors Trajan and Hadrian (with beard). These busts (c. A.D. 100) once adorned the Trajaneum—a grand temple dedicated to Trajan as a god on earth, in Pergamon. The museum takes its name (and many of its pieces) from this ancient city on the Aegean Sea (on the west coast of present-day Turkey). German archeologists excavated much of Pergamon in the early 20th century, but many more ruins still remain there today, including an amphitheater, standing columns of temples, and more.

This room also displays interesting exhibits on various places and eras of Roman history.

• *By A.D. 500, Rome's vast empire had fallen. Europe settled into 500 years of relative darkness and decline. Meanwhile, a new civilization was rising in the Middle East—Islam. Over the next centuries, the Islamic culture would take over the territories of the former Assyria and Babylonia, and many parts of the Roman Empire.*

To complete your tour of civilizations, find the stairs in front of the Ishtar Gate and head up to floor 2, which is dedicated to art and artifacts from the world of Islam. (While interesting, if you're short on time this part of the museum is skippable.)

PERGAMON

MUSEUM OF ISLAMIC ART

The Museum of Islamic Art contains ceramic tile work, bowls, jugs, carved ivory horns, metal-worked necklaces, mosque lamps, and carpets, carpets, carpets. Most of these fine objects are decorated in the distinctive Islamic style: elaborate patterns of intertwined lines, vines, and calligraphy, with only the occasional image of a person or animal. Muslim artists avoided depicting living creatures for fear of creating what the Quran and Bible call idols of false gods. The workmanship is exquisite. It demonstrates how—after Rome fell and Europe was mired in medievalism—the Islamic world carried the torch of civilization.

• *For most, a quick breeze through these rooms is enough. Some may wish to simply glance at the impressive Aleppo Room (at the start of floor 2, to the right, in Room 15, described below). But if you're up for more, here are a few highlights, placed into the sweep of Islamic history. Work clockwise through floor 2, and watch Islamic history unfold (roughly) chronologically. From the first room (with the map of the Islamic world), turn left.*

Islam's Beginnings (Room 2): Shown here are a few humble but rare objects from Islam's origins in the seventh century. After Muhammed died (A.D. 632), his teachings spread rapidly throughout the Middle East, thanks to his cousins (from the same hometown of Mecca) of the Umayyad family. At its peak (c. 700), the Umayyad empire encompassed nearly a third of the world's population and stretched into North Africa and Spain. Both secular and religious leaders, the Umayyads (661-750) ruled their caliphate from their capital in Damascus.

The rectangular stone fragment on display comes from a palace the Umayyads built in one of their holdings, Palestine. Its intertwined vines, leaves, scrolls, and stylized pomegranates are typical of Umayyad decoration.

In the year 750, the Umayyad caliph was assassinated, his surviving family members fled to Spain, and the Islamic world had a new ruling order.

PERGAMON

Abbasid Period (Room 3): The displayed art of the Abbasid period (750-1258) focuses on the palace-city of Samarra. Various ceramics, carved ivory, and ornate prayer niches (mihrabs) attest to the enlightenment of this so-called Islamic Golden Age. The Abbasids, who made their capital in Baghdad, vowed to make their rule tolerant to non-Arabs and non-Muslims, reflecting the diversity of their vast caliphate. While Europe fumbled in the darkness, the Islamic world flourished, enriched by its mathematicians, astronomers, doctors, and thinkers. Thanks to the Abbasids, we have the works of ancient philosophers such as Plato and Aristotle, whose writings were preserved in Arabic and Persian translations. The Abbasids were sensitive to the needs of their own people and the cultures on their frontiers—Egyptian, North African, European, Greek, Byzantine, and Indian.

Art of the Seljuks (Rooms 4-5): The Seljuks (c. 1050-1150) wrested temporary control of the Abbasid empire and moved the capital to Iran. In fact, the Seljuks were responsible for the conquest of Miletus, whose city gate we saw earlier. On display in Room 5 is a blue mihrab, the prayer niche found in every mosque around the world. This ceremonial alcove shows worshippers which direction to face to pray toward Mecca. This one has typical Abbasid faience tiles, decorated with vines, calligraphy of Quran verses (especially along the top), and a geometrical maze (below, with 12-pointed stars).

Alhambra Cupola (Room 6): This room is topped with an awesome domed ceiling, brought here from the Alhambra palace

in Granada, Spain. In 711 the Umayyads had expanded their caliphate as far as Spain, making that country Islamic for the next seven centuries. Moorish Muslims ruled from the glorious Alhambra palace, surrounded by lush gardens and bubbling fountains. This dome is only a tiny slice of the opulence still on display in Granada.

The cupola, carved in cedar and cottonwood, once topped a square room—as it rises, the ceiling morphs into an octagon, then a circle, which breaks up into a kaleidoscope of trapezoids and triangles, with a circular rosette in the center. The incredibly complex geometrical pattern is meant to replicate a starry sky, blended with Arabic letters boasting the Spanish Muslim motto: "There is no victor but Allah."

The Alhambra palace in Granada—the last outpost of Muslim rule in western Europe—finally fell to the Christian monarchs Ferdinand and Isabel in 1492.

Mshatta Facade (Room 9): These monumental walls and towers—120 feet long and 15 feet high—were part of an Umayyad desert castle, one of many that dotted the Middle East (especially in present-day Jordan, where this one stood). These castles were both imposing fortresses, to assert control of the locals, as well as luxury palaces.

The castle's walls are decorated in a zigzag pattern with rosettes and elaborately lacy designs. Look closely (especially in the left part) to make out a filigreed forest of intertwining trees, vines, and flowers peopled with animals both real and imagined. The design reflects elements borrowed from Sasanian art, the last great Middle Eastern empire before Islam.

Ottoman Empire (Rooms 12-14): You'll see lots of carpets, but no "ottomans"—the upholstered benches popularized by these

Turkish rulers. The Ottomans (1299-1922) rose to power after Abbasid Baghdad was sacked by Genghis Khan's followers, ending the Islamic Golden Age. The Ottomans conquered Constantinople/Istanbul and established their capital there. At their peak (c. 1650), they ruled an empire that included both the Middle East and eastern Europe—even Vienna. Under the Ottomans, carpet weaving became high art. Ottoman rulers often employed Greek (Christian) artists to craft their carpets, jewelry, and fine manuscript illustrations.

• *The grand finale is tucked off in a little glassed-in side room of its own...*

Aleppo Room (Rooms 15-16): The walls of this ornately painted room come from a 400-year-old home in today's Syria. The

owner—a Christian living in the Ottoman-dominated city of Aleppo—was a wealthy trader. He wanted his home to have an impressive entrance hall that would make his guests and clients feel at home. The man did business with people from all faiths and cultures in the cosmopolitan Aleppo, circa 1600.

That's why this room is illustrated with motifs from the Christian, Arabic, Persian, and Jewish worlds. It was a big paint job—covering almost a thousand square feet of surface area, painted

PERGAMON

on wood panels. It's impeccably preserved—a rare example of an Ottoman-era home.

The result is a happy mix that suggests diverse cultures living in harmony. The artists painted Islamic motifs, like intertwined vines, geometric designs, and calligraphic quotes from Arabic proverbs. They drew from the Jewish tradition, with scenes of Abraham sacrificing Isaac and quotes from the Psalms. There are Christian scenes—Mary with Child, Salome's Dance, the Last Supper, and St. George. There are secular scenes from Persia—of pashas with their harems or on royal hunts, and even episodes from a famous Persian love story.

• *The Aleppo Room is a good place to end this tour of the Pergamon Museum. The museum offers a once-over of many civilizations over several millennia. For me, it's a reminder that many different peoples—often at war—can also live in peace.*

AND WHAT ABOUT THE PERGAMON ALTAR?

The museum's namesake and most famous piece—the Pergamon Altar—is being carefully protected and stored out of view while the hall that houses it is slowly modernized. The altar likely won't be back until around 2025.

The "altar" is actually a temple, a masterpiece of Hellenistic art from the second century B.C. Modeled after the Acropolis in Athens, it was just one component of a spectacular hilltop ensemble of temples, sanctuaries, and theaters in the Greek city-state of Pergamon (near the west coast of today's Turkey).

When Pergamon was excavated in the late 19th century, bits and pieces of the temple were brought to Berlin and reassembled to re-create the western third of the original temple building.

Enormous and nearly intact, stairs lead up to a chamber with a small sacrificial altar where priests and priestesses sacrificed and burned animals, while toga-clad Greeks assembled in awe below. Wrapped around the entire temple was the Gigantomachy Frieze, a 269-foot-long dramatic pig pile of mythological mayhem, showing the Greek gods under Zeus and Athena doing battle with a race of giants. (Naturally, the gods win.)

While the restoration is ongoing, a nearby pavilion (on Am Kupfergraben, directly across from Museum Island) will house a **temporary exhibit** about the altar. The main attraction will be a huge, wraparound panorama painting of the Pergamon (by Berlin artist Yadegar Asisi). Some of the original sculpture from the altar will be installed in the panorama, and digital 3D

models of the entire altar frieze will let visitors virtually appreciate the statuary. For the latest, consult the Pergamon website (www.smb.museum).

GERMAN
HISTORY
MUSEUM TOUR

Deutsches Historisches Museum

While this city has more than its share of hokey "museums" that slap together WWII and Cold War bric-a-brac, then charge too much for admission, this thoughtfully presented facility is clearly the top history museum in town. With 9,000 artifacts, exhibits, documents, paintings, and photographs spread across dozens of rooms on two floors, it's a complete look at 1,500 years of German history.

That's a lot. But with this chapter as your guide, you'll sweep through it quickly and painlessly. Use it to get the big picture, then browse at will. Don't get bogged down somewhere in the Middle Ages; be sure to reserve time and energy for the fascinating 20th century.

Orientation

Cost: €8.

Hours: Daily 10:00-18:00.

Information: Tel. 030/2030-4751, www.dhm.de.

Getting There: It's at Unter den Linden 2, immediately west of Museum Island (just across the river). Buses #100, #200, and #TXL stop right in front (Staatsoper stop). By tram, the Am Kupfergraben stop (for trams #M1 and #12) is a block behind the museum. The nearest S-Bahn stop is Friedrichstrasse, a 10-minute walk away; Hackescher Markt S-Bahn station is nearly as close.

Tours: For the most informative visit, invest in the excellent €3 audioguide, with 6 hours of info to choose from.

Length of This Tour: Allow at least 2 hours for the entire museum; for a quicker visit, focus on the 20th century on the main floor (allow about 1 hour).

Baggage Check: A cloakroom and lockers are just off the main lobby, to the left of the ticket desk.

Cuisine Art/Eateries: If you need a break during your visit, there's a restful café with terrace seating. Some good restaurants are under the railroad tracks behind the museum (see recommendations on page 275).

Background: For a solid foundation for your visit, read the Germany: Past & Present chapter, at the end of this book.

Starring: The full span of German history, from the remnants of the Roman Empire to today.

The Tour Begins

The museum often has temporary exhibits, which are included in your ticket price—ask when you arrive.

From the entrance lobby, turn left and head upstairs to the first floor, then work your way down. As you tour the collection, stay on track by locating the museum's information pillars along the way (each marked with a date span—for example, "500-900"—that matches my headers below), then browse the exhibits nearby. At the top of the stairs, consider taking 45 minutes for the fairly dry but informative introductory film on German history (with English subtitles).

• *Start your tour by finding the first info pillar—"500-900."*

FIRST FLOOR
From the Beginning until 1918

500-900

"Germany" began circa A.D. 500, as the Roman Empire was falling apart. Western Europe became a land of ethnic Romans and Celts, speaking Latin and worshipping Christ. But the Germanic tribes to the East *(Ost)* remained *Deutsch*-speaking and pagan for centuries. On display from this era, you may see a medieval Saxon manuscript, and a famous portrait (by Albrecht Dürer) of the man who would finally bring Germany into the European fold: Charlemagne.

• *A few steps farther along, the collection continues with...*

900-1500

When Charlemagne was crowned "Holy Roman Emperor" in the year 800, it united much of Europe into a Kingdom of the Franks—and marked the conversion of the Germans to Christianity (see the ecclesiastical art). Charlemagne's symbol, the eagle (see the old wooden statue), became the symbol of Germany on today's coat of arms.

Charlemagne's successors as "Emperor" were essentially kings of Germany, creating the nucleus of the unified German state. The "Golden Bull of 1356" (a copy of which is on display—by the windows) made sure that the Emperors were chosen by certain "electors"—mostly Germans. The Bull also dictated that one of the electors be from far-off Brandenburg—putting Berlin on the map.

1500-1600

The most powerful Holy Roman Emperor was Charles V—see his portrait. He ruled much of Europe during the Renaissance and Age of Discovery. On display is (a copy of) the 1492 globe Columbus used to plot his voyage—round and pretty accurate, except there's no America yet.

Meanwhile, the German monk Martin Luther was shocking Europe with new and radical ideas, sparking the Protestant Reformation. Explore deeper into the adjoining rooms to find a number of Luther artifacts. There's the Edict of Worms, where Charles V condemned the Protestant heretic. There's a Bible translated by Luther into everyday German, helping to establish the "modern" German language spoken today. There are portraits by Lucas Cranach of

his good friend Martin, portraits of other Reformation players, and even of Katherina von Bora—the ex-nun that the ex-monk Luther would marry. What Luther started spiraled into a Europe-wide movement—Protestantism—that led to centuries of turmoil (for more on Luther and his life, see page 341). With Martin Luther, Germany stepped out of the medieval shadows and onto the global stage.

1600-1650

Germany's rise from feudal backwater to modern nation was swift. In the left corner of this section, find the small room with four big paintings called the "Augsburger Labours" (c. 1520s). They give a fascinating glimpse at four seasons of bustling city life in an era when German trade and industry were flourishing. It's a surprisingly cosmopolitan world of burghers and beggars, women and children, Italian dandies, Jews, and turbaned Turks. Germany was thriving, but it still remained decentralized and under the shadow of its larger neighbor, France.

1650-1740

A portrait of King Louis XIV at his peak radiates the power and sophistication of France. Meanwhile, the German-speaking peoples had to deal with an invasion from the east by the Muslim Turks (see the Ottoman tent). When Vienna was besieged in 1683, the city had to be rescued by (among others) an army from far-off northern Germany—Prussia.

1740-1789

You'll see portraits of various aristocrats who jockeyed for dominance in Germany (see Empress Maria-Theresa Habsburg in a blue dress). When Prussia's Frederick the Great reluctantly agreed to an arranged marriage with Elisabeth Christine of the Habsburg clan (see their portraits hanging side-by-side), Prussia's prestige grew. (For more about Frederick, see the sidebar on page 106).

Find Frederick the Great's military uniform—it's a few steps farther along, on the left. Though it looks dressy, this was actually the casual-Friday uniform that this man-of-the-people king usually wore instead of royal regalia. Notice the cut-fingered gloves, so he could pinch snuff. On his chest is the medallion of the Order of the Black Eagle, an honor bestowed on nobles, generals, artists, politicians, and foreign dignitaries into the 20th century.

Browse the nearby displays to understand why Frederick was so Great. He made Prussia a European power and Berlin a cultural capital. He brought the Age of Enlightenment to Germany. He met with the writer

Goethe (see his bust) and published Immanuel Kant's "Inquiry" (on display). Science flourished (see scientific instruments) as did music (see early keyboards and a picture of the Mozart family). As new ideas raced across Europe, it came to a violent eruption in France—the Revolution.

1789-1815

Spanning the next couple of rooms are scenes of the French Revolution and the rise of Napoleon. Napoleon conquered the Austrian Habsburgs (see the captured flag), leaving the German-speaking people with one great power—Prussia.

1815-1848

Find Napoleon's hat and sword. In 1815, these objects were captured when Napoleon was defeated at Waterloo by Europe's two new powers: England and Prussia.

Browsing these rooms, you can trace the rise of German nationalism. There are medallions marking Luther's 300th anniversary, a great source of national pride. You'll see machinery (thread-weavers, steam-powered contraptions) from the Industrial Revolution that was fueling Germany. Farther along you'll see a model of an early train—the invention that would soon lace the scattered German people together.

1848-1849

In 1848, revolutions broke out across Europe (you'll see turbulent scenes from cities like Paris and Berlin). Progressive Germans wanted a modern nation, ruled by the "Constitution of 1849" (on display), but the movement failed. It seemed that Germany could only be united by force, under a dominant power: Prussia.

1850-1871

These exhibits trace the rise of Prussia as it took over Germany's destiny in the 1800s. Wilhelm I and his shrewd Prime Minis-

ter, Otto von Bismarck (see their busts), used political wheeling-and-dealing and outright force to try to forge Germany's principalities and dukedoms together. They even invaded France in the Franco-Prussian War to rally the German people together in a cause. The Germans won, and you'll see paintings of their triumph and the

spiked military helmets they proudly wore. In 1871, the German people united, and they proudly waved an eagle flag (on display) of a new nation: Germany.

The Kaiser Whisperer: Otto von Bismarck (1815-1898)

The person who shaped modern Germany more than any other was not a king or a kaiser, but the walrus-mustachioed advisor whispering in the kaiser's ear: Otto von Bismarck. Bismarck held various titles over the course of 30 years (and three kaisers)—from foreign minister of Prussia to the first chancellor of Germany. But sometimes titles are meaningless; Bismarck, who never wore a crown, was one of the greatest political geniuses of all time.

In 1850, Germany was 39 little countries. But then, German industry boomed. In 20 years, German iron and coal output multiplied sixfold, surpassing that of France. German unification seemed inevitable. The big question was: Which of the two largest Germanic states—Prussia or Austria—would take the lead in a united Germany?

Otto von Bismarck, who had served as ambassador to Russia and France, had a plan. And Kaiser Wilhelm I of Prussia (r. 1861-1888) listened to him. The original master of "realpolitik," Bismarck said, "Not by speeches and majority votes are the great questions of the day decided, but by blood and iron." He united Germany as if reading from a great political recipe book.

Bismarck cozied up to Prussia's liberals to win support in parliament. He amassed Prussia's mighty army using unconstitutional taxes. He leaked classified documents to the press to twist public opinion into just the political pretzel he needed.

In his foreign policy, Bismarck mixed brutal warfare and back-slapping diplomacy. He made alliances simply to break them, thereby creating a handy excuse to fight. He started wars with Austria and Denmark to acquire more territory and knock the competition down a peg. Once victorious, he generously made them his friends. He winked at Europe's great leaders, gained their confidence, and proceeded to make them history's fools.

The final step was to acquire the small German-speaking states on the border with France. The resulting Franco-Prussian War lasted only a few weeks, with Prussia winning easily.

Bismarck's recipe for success had created the dish nobody in Europe wanted: a united Germany. By 1871, once-fragmented Germany had become a Prussian-dominated, conservative, and militaristic German empire. The balance of power had been disturbed. And the rest of Europe hoped the unification of Germany would not lead to a large war...or two.

1871-1890

A huge painting radiates the optimism and glory of the new nation. Dignitaries gather in Berlin's royal palace (which once stood on Museum Island) to announce the opening of the Reichstag. Presiding on the dais (with red robe, crown, and document) is the handsome young ruler, Wilhelm II. He wears the Order of the Black Eagle and bears the title of not merely king, but emperor *(Kaiser)*. This was, after the medieval Holy Roman Empire, the "Second German *Reich.*"

Kaiser Wilhelm II reigned over a period of unprecedented wealth and prosperity. Germany was an industrial powerhouse, was acquiring rich colonies in Africa, and was expanding its military might. Berlin's population absolutely surged, and the capital rivaled Paris and London as a cultural center. In a nearby display, the "Kaiser Panorama," you can view old photos of turn-of-the-century Berlin in its glory, as couples and carriages promenade down Unter den Linden.

By 1914, Germany was a global superpower, destined for a glorious future.

• *To see how it all played out, head downstairs to the ground floor, cross directly across the lobby, and enter the exhibit rooms.*

GROUND FLOOR
The 20th Century
1918-1925

World War I—pitting Germany against France, England, and others—was horrific. Photos show the grim reality of a war fought from defensive trenches, where a machine gun (on display) could do the killing of 500 soldiers with rifles. Posters (and a poignant woodcut by Berlin artist Käthe Kollwitz) capture the bitter and cynical mood that descended over Germany. By war's end, Germany had lost 1.7 million men, and 4 million came home wounded. Germany was defeated.

Europe's victors dealt harshly with Germany, sowing enormous resentment. The Weimar Republic was

The German National Anthem

"Deutschland, Deutschland über alles..." The song first became popular during World War I. In the 1920s it was adopted as Germany's national anthem, along with the colors of the national flag—black, red, and gold.

When Hitler took power, he loved hearing the powerful words of the song's opening verse: *"Deutschland, Deutschland über alles, über alles in der Welt."* The words proclaimed: "Germany, Germany above all, above all the world." But after Hitler's defeat, no one wanted to hear those Nazi-tinged sentiments any more. They switched the official anthem to just the third verse: *"Einigkeit und Recht und Freiheit, für das deutsche Vaterland!"* Those lyrics celebrated "Unity, justice, and freedom..."

Meanwhile, the country was divided into communist East and democratic West. East Germany had its own national anthem, a completely different song. Then in 1990 came unity, and they all sang the same song once again. A united Germany proudly sings the anthem that ends with the words "Bloom, you German Fatherland." *"Blüh' im Glanze dieses Glückes, blühe, deutsches Vaterland!"*

doomed to fail. The German economy was in shambles (see the pile of ridiculously inflated currency).

And yet, the side-room shows how, even in these tough times, booming Berlin (whose population doubled in the postwar years) flourished: the cabaret scene (flapper dresses); the development of motion pictures (Berlin was the original "Hollywood"); Bauhaus (the stripped-down architectural style that's still influential today); and impressive ocean liners.

1925-1933

Dueling displays show off propaganda and uniforms from the two poles of Germany's political spectrum: National Socialists (Nazis) and Communists.

Ultimately the Nazi Party prevailed. Their propaganda convinced the German people that they were strong and good, but had been betrayed by a rigged system. In 1933, the Nazis took control of Germany under Adolf Hitler.

1933-1939

Hitler narrowly became Chancellor. But within weeks, the Reichstag burned in a shocking fire (see photo)—giving him an opening to consolidate power.

At first, Germany seemed to prosper under the Nazis. They recruited supporters from all walks of life (see Hitler Youth posters, and the closet of Nazi uniforms). But under the surface, dissent simmered, and was brutally suppressed—find the footage of Nazis burning books on Bebelplatz, just across the street from this museum. In the smaller rooms beneath the mezzanine, view the hateful propaganda posters designed to train the German people to identify—and hate—Jews and other minorities on sight. These demonstrate how, even early in his reign, Hitler's strategy to scapegoat these groups for Germany's problems was embraced by many of his subjects.

The Nazis escalated their atrocities against Jews—the 1935 Nürnberg Laws, the 1938 destruction of synagogues (Kristallnacht)—eventually culminating in the "Final Solution" and the Holocaust. (More on that later.)

To shore up support, Hitler appealed to Germans' sense of national and ethnic pride. He preached about the *Volksgemeinschaft*—a "people's community" of purely Germanic, Aryan ideals. Back out in the main hall, find the large, wall-sized church tapestry of cutesy German-style houses and common people marching in lock-(goose)step with Nazi-uniformed troops.

The Nazis set Germany on a path of global domination. They were determined to prove Germany's might, hosting the Olympics

in 1936 (see poster). Nearby, find the model of the domed building by architect Albert Speer, and ponder Hitler's megalomania. Hitler made plans to turn Berlin into "Welthaupstadt Germania," the "world capital" of his far-reaching Third Reich. The centerpiece would be this impossibly huge domed Volkshalle—950 feet high and able to accommodate 180,000 people. It would squat over the Spree River, just north of the Reichstag, as the anchor of a grandiose north-south axis called the Avenue of Splendors. Hitler's grand plans were put on hold as Germany once again went to war.

1939-1941

At the start of World War II, Germany's Blitzkrieg ("Lightning War") demolished its enemies. But then came several devastating, watershed battles, such as Stalingrad (see the film).

1941-1943

As the tide turned against Germany, the destruction began creeping back into the Fatherland. The Allies (the US and Britain) began aerial bombardment of German cities, especially Berlin (see the bomb casings and the fragments of a downed RAF bomber, dredged from a German lake).

1943-1945

It became total war, including genocide. Exhibits document the atrocities at Hitler's concentration camps, including registration photos of prisoners. A model shows the nauseating reality of Hitler's grandiosity: a crematorium at Auschwitz (in Nazi-occupied Poland) designed to exterminate Jews. Incoming prisoners were tricked into disrobing and entering a huge, underground "shower room," only to be killed by Zyklon-B gas. Then workers (most of them inmates hoping to postpone their own demise) would pile the bodies into four huge crematoria, which blazed 24/7 to burn the evidence of Nazi crimes. (This same model appears at the Holocaust museums at Auschwitz, in Washington, DC, and at Israel's Yad Vashem.)

1945-1949

Finally, the Nazis are defeated and Hitler shoots himself. Troops from the US and USSR shake hands at the Elbe River, while newspaper headlines trumpet an Allied victory. But the cost was incalculable: More than 60 million dead worldwide, including 6 million Jews and 6 million non-Jewish Germans. A video shows how totally demolished many German cities were by war's end.

Even before the last shots were fired, Allied leaders had already met at the Potsdam Conference to divvy up a defeated Germany (see the photo of Churchill, Truman, and Stalin). Berlin and Germany were divided between the Soviet-leaning East and the US-leaning West. And essentially immediately, World War II became a protracted Cold War.

1949-1989

A border post marks the "inner German border" between West and East. Exhibits juxtapose different slices of life in the two Germanys. The West's economy recovered (see the smart VW bug), while the East's languished (the clunky Trabi). East Germany remained under the oppressive thumb of the Soviet communist government for decades. But by the 1980s, the Soviet empire was cracking, and the German people longed to reunite and be free.

1989-1994

In 1989, the Berlin Wall—the most iconic symbol of division and oppression—began crumbling. You'll see videos of the celebrations, preserved sections of the wall, and clips of US president Ronald Reagan demanding they "tear down this wall." The Wall came down, Germany was reunited, and the homemade banners of freedom were raised.

THE REST OF THE MUSEUM

For architecture buffs, the big attraction is the modern annex behind the history museum, designed by American architect I.M. Pei. (To get there from the old building, cross through the courtyard, admiring the Pei glass canopy overhead.) This annex complements the museum with often-fascinating temporary exhibits. A striking glassed-in spiral staircase unites four floors with surprising views and lots of light. It's here that you'll experience why Pei—famous for his glass pyramid at Paris' Louvre—is called the "perfector of classical modernism," "master of light," and a magician at uniting historical buildings with new ones.

COMMUNIST EAST BERLIN WALK

From Museum Island to Alexanderplatz

From 1949 to 1990, East Germans had it tough. On this nearly mile-long walk, we'll focus on sights associated with communist East Germany—also known as the DDR *(Deutsche Demokratische Republik)*.

We'll see statues of Marx and Engels, the founders of communism, who had roots here in Berlin. We'll see the Marien Church, which carried the Christian torch through the atheistic communist era. We'll learn how the people of the DDR coped with their unfortunate lot—so at odds with the lives of West Berliners, a literal stone's throw away, just over the Wall. And we'll pass by the skyscraping TV Tower, built by the communists as an exclamation point for their way of life. This walk ends at Alexanderplatz—once the symbol of communist modernity, now a thriving people zone—and offers a peek at the very Soviet-style boulevard called Karl-Marx-Allee (formerly Stalinallee).

Let's embark on a stroll through what was the showcase "downtown" of communist East Berlin.

Orientation

Length of This Walk: Allow about 45 minutes.

When to Go: This walk picks up right where the Unter den Linden Walk drops off (see the 📖 Unter den Linden Walk chapter). Because this walk has no sights that are important to enter, it can be done anytime—perhaps if you have energy left after your Museum Island sightseeing.

Getting There: This walk begins at Museum Island—easy to reach on bus #100 or #200 (Lustgarten stop). These buses—and, for some stops, also bus #TXL—basically follow the course of this walk, making it easy to skip ahead or backtrack. You

Communist East Berlin Walk

1. DDR Museum
2. Radisson Hotel
3. Ampelmann Store
4. Marx & Engels Statues
5. Spree River Cruises
6. Nikolai Quarter
7. City Hall
8. Plattenbau
9. Marien Church
10. Women's Protest Memorial
11. TV Tower
12. Alexanderplatz
13. World Time Clock
14. Karl-Marx-Allee

can also take the S-Bahn to Hackescher Markt and walk 10 minutes to the start of the walk.

DDR Museum: €9.50, daily 10:00-20:00, Sat until 22:00, Karl-Liebknecht-Strasse 1, tel. 030/847-123-731, www.ddr-museum.de.

Marien Church: Free, daily 10:00-16:00, Karl-Liebknecht-Strasse 8, www.marienkirche-berlin.de.

TV Tower: €13, more expensive skip-the-line "fast track" tickets available online, daily 9:00-24:00, Nov-Feb from 10:00, Panoramastrasse 1A, www.tv-turm.de.

Services: The visitors center at Humboldt Forum—on Museum Island, at the start of this walk—has free WCs.

Eateries: You'll pass plenty of tourist-oriented fast-food joints along this walk. A couple of recommended breweries—Brauhaus Georgbräu (in the Nikolai Quarter) and Brauhaus Lemke (across the street from the TV Tower)—are a short detour.

And the walk ends at Alexanderplatz, with plenty of bratwurst vendors and other casual eateries.

Starring: Landmarks, legacies, and the severe communist aesthetic of East Berlin.

The Walk Begins

• *We'll begin at Museum Island, and head (fittingly) east. From the massive Berlin Cathedral, take Unter den Linden across the bridge toward the TV Tower. As you cross the bridge, the road changes names and suddenly you're walking along...*

Karl-Liebknecht-Strasse

From here eastward this street is named for a founder of Germany's communist party: Karl Liebknecht, a martyr to the Marxist cause, and reminder of the communist regime.

At the end of the bridge, look down on your left to see the ❶ **DDR Museum.** A visit to this museum—where everyday artifacts paint a vivid picture of life in Cold War-era East Germany—can

whet your appetite for the outdoor landmarks we're about to see. (For details, see page 41.)

Continue down Karl-Liebknecht-Strasse toward the TV Tower. A half-block down on the left, step into the lobby of the ❷ **Radisson Hotel.** The lobby's centerpiece is a stunning aquarium—a huge glass cylinder with an elevator zipping up through its middle. It seems that right here in the center of the old communist city, capitalism has settled in with a spirited vengeance.

Just past the Radisson, also on the left, is the ❸ **Ampelmann store**—part of a local chain that

features all manner of products emblazoned with jaunty green-and-red pedestrian stoplight figures that date from the old East Berlin days. All over the city, keep an eye out for these—called, affectionately, *Ampelmännchen* ("little traffic-light man"). Even after the fall of the Wall, the figures proved

so popular that residents waged a 10-year court battle to keep them from being replaced. And now, they're even beginning to show up in the former West Berlin—perhaps the only East German symbol to gain popularity. The mania for *Ampelmännchen* is a good example of what's known as "Ost-algia"—a play-on-words describing nostalgia towards the "Ost," or East.

• *Unfortunately, there's no Herr Ampelmännchen here to tell us when it's safe to cross—but our next stop is the big park directly across Karl-Liebknecht-Strasse. If you dare, wait for a lull in traffic and carefully cross the busy street to the park. (If you'd rather stay strictly legal, backtrack to the bridge by the DDR Museum, cross underneath the street, and ascend at the corner of the park.)*

Once in the park, head through the trees and look for two big statues.

Marx-Engels-Forum

The ❹ **statues of Karl Marx and Friedrich Engels** within this park recall the economists who studied at Berlin's Humboldt Univer-

sity in the early 1800s (though they didn't meet until later). They went on to co-author the landmark *Communist Manifesto*, which ends with the famous closing line, "Workers of the world, unite!"

The statues don't look particularly fierce. Locals have nicknamed these two grandfatherly guys "The Old Pensioners." Young people enjoy ironically posing with this duo (notice Marx's shiny lap, and Engels' well-worn finger). Surrounding them are stainless-steel monoliths with evocative photos illustrating the struggles of workers all around the world.

The *Communist Manifesto* came out in 1848. Preoccupied with the "class struggle" through history—between the haves (bourgeoisie) and the have-nots (proletariat)—Marx and Engels believed that everyday working people should take control of the means of production. Over the next decades, Marx and Engels' ideas proved enormously influential. They caught on—among other places—with a Russian named Vladimir Lenin. In 1917, Lenin led the Bolshevik Revolution that toppled the Russian czar and established the Soviet Union. Their motto? "Workers of the world, unite!"

Three decades later, Lenin's successor Josef Stalin sent the Red Army into Germany to defeat Hitler and the Nazis. After the war, they stayed. They occupied the eastern half of Germany, and established a communist state: the DDR.

As you face Marx and Engels, a handy ❺ **boat dock for Spree River cruises** is immediately behind you (see page 27). And to your right—behind a row of modern buildings, but not quite visible

Life in the DDR

Throughout the Cold War, East Germans had basic security but no freedom. When the DDR was established in 1949, the So-cialist Unity Party of Germany (SED) held all the power. East Germany had no president, chancellor, or prime minister—just the SED general secretary, who reigned supreme.

The DDR economy be-came increasingly centralized. The government produced all goods, forcing East Germans to lead cookie-cutter lives: wearing identical wardrobes while eating off identical dishes in identical apartments. The best goods were made in the West—and were smuggled in and sold on the black market. Things that couldn't be smuggled in were usually cheap knock-offs.

Travel was severely restricted. If you were lucky, your family had a *Datsche*—a humble, shack-like holiday house in the countryside. Trips to Hungary's Lake Balaton or Baltic Sea beaches were as exotic as you could hope for.

Movies and TV shows were more propaganda than enter-tainment, though most East Germans could (illegally) receive Western broadcasts. They'd watch with the volume turned down, and hope nobody was listening.

But someone *was* always listening. The DDR had spies everywhere, including tens of thousands of everyday people induced to inform on their neighbors. The Stasi security force read people's mail and observed the most intimate details of their lives using hidden cameras. Public life was filled with sus-picion, fear, and paranoia. (For more on the Stasi, see page 69.)

All of this amounted to a life of constant contradiction: A system claiming to be "for the common person" actually did everything it could to make people's lives more difficult.

And yet, when communism ended, the transition wasn't easy. For years, many former East Germans remained "Ost-algic"—nostalgic for the *Ost*, or East. What they missed was the relaxed pace of life: With no real advancement opportuni-ties, people had ample time to spend with family and friends. Some also pined for the security of knowing they'd always be provided for...albeit humbly.

Today's thirtysomethings and fortysomethings—who were too young to really suffer under communism—embrace symbols of the era, like the *Ampelmann* traffic lights, more out of nostalgia than a desire to return to life behind the Iron Cur-tain. For most Berliners, the East-West stuff is a distant mem-ory. It may be big business among tourists, but locals tend to think about communism or the Berlin Wall only when visitors bring it up.

from here—is the small district called ❻ **Nikolai Quarter** (Nikolaiviertel). In 1987, both East and West Berlin celebrated the 750th anniversary of their city's founding. For the occasion, East Berlin re-created a cobbled "old town" around the spire of its oldest church. While it feels very much like the on-the-cheap communist rebuild that it is, if you're curious, it's an easy detour from this walk: Simply follow the river in that direction, and look left after the next bridge for the twin church spires. (For more on the Nikolai Quarter, see page 44.)

Continue your walk heading east through the park, in the direction of the TV Tower. Where Karl-Liebknecht-Strasse intersects with Spandauer Strasse, look right to see the red-brick ❼ **city hall,** where Berlin's mayor has an office. It was built after the revolutions of 1848 and was arguably the first democratic building in the city. Later it became the city hall of communist East Berlin—giving its nickname, Rotes Rathaus (Red City Hall), a dual meaning.

As you continue toward the TV Tower, glance around at the ❽ **high-rise concrete** *Plattenbau* ("panel buildings"), mostly on the left side of Karl-Liebknecht-Strasse. For more on these practical (but eyesore) buildings—where so many East Berliners lived—see the sidebar.

• *Cross Spandauer Strasse and angle left through the plaza, toward the spire of the...*

❾ Marien Church

The Marien Church, with its prominent steeple, dates from 1270. Under communist rule, religion was frowned upon, as the state was officially atheist. (Many Berlin churches, miraculously spared destruction by Allied bombs, were unceremoniously torn down by the new regime.) East Berliners could still worship at the Marien Church, but being openly Christian was never a good career move.

Inside the church, an artist's rendering helps you follow the interesting but very faded old "Dance of Death" mural that wraps around the entry narthex (c. 1470). Farther in, the church's whitewashed interior is austere, with heavy oak pews. To learn more, buy the little pamphlet for an interesting self-guided tour.

• *Immediately across the street from the church, detour a half-block down little Rosenstrasse to find a beautiful memorial set in a park. We'll take a break from communist East Berlin to ponder this poignant monument from Nazi times.*

❿ Women's Protest Memorial

This is a reminder of a courageous—and unusually successful—protest against Nazi policies. In 1943, when "privileged Jews" (men

married to Gentile women) were arrested, their wives demonstrated en masse on this street—the famous "Rosenstrasse Protest." The location was fitting, as this was also the site of Berlin's oldest synagogue (you can see the faint footprint of that old building in the field just beyond the monument).

Remarkably, these brave women actually won their husbands' freedom. Note the Berliner on the bench nearby. As most Berliners did, he looks the other way, even when these bold women demonstrated that you could speak up and be heard under the Nazis.

• *Back on Karl-Liebknecht-Strasse, gaze up at the 1,200-foot-tall...*

⓫ TV Tower (Fernsehturm)

The communist regime is long gone, but it left an enduring legacy: the TV Tower. This tower was built in 1969 to celebrate the 20th anniversary of communist East Germany.

The tower was meant to show the power of the atheistic state at the very time when DDR leaders were removing the crosses from the country's church domes and spires. But when the sun hit the tower, the reflected light happened to create a huge cross on the mirrored ball. Cynics called it "God's Revenge." East Berliners dubbed their tower the "Tele-Asparagus." They also joked that if it fell over, they'd have an elevator to freedom in the West.

For a hefty fee, you can go up the tower for a fine view, and lunch at the retro-style revolving restaurant. From the top, you can look out at the flat, red-roofed sprawl of Berlin and peek inside the city's many courtyards *(Höfe)*.

Plattenbau: Communist Concrete Apartment Blocks

While the DDR government maintained a few token historic landmarks (like the Nikolai Quarter and the Rotes Rathaus),

their real architectural forte was pre-fabricated, high-capacity, low-aesthetics housing—called *Plattenbau* ("panel buildings").

These apartment blocks may seem undesirable, but they were fairly popular places to live. Although cheaply constructed, they came with modern amenities like central heating and real plumbing (for example, each unit had its own bathroom), and many even had elevators that actually worked...sometimes. For many, this was far preferable to the much older, more primitive flats in historic districts like Prenzlauer Berg (today renovated and so trendy).

While the buildings' exteriors and public spaces are frightfully gloomy, residents prided themselves on creating cozy and welcoming little nests inside. Being invited to dinner at one of these apartments in DDR times showed you the stark contrast between cold, paranoid public life and colorful, gregarious private life. In their own homes, people could pursue hobbies and spend time with family.

• *Continue walking east down Karl-Liebknecht-Strasse, passing the TV Tower's base on your right. You'll cross under a big railway overpass, then walk alongside a mall called Galeria Kaufhof. Just past the mall, turn right onto a broad pedestrian street. It leads through a low tunnel and into a big square, surrounded by modern buildings. The blue U-Bahn station signs announce you've arrived at*

⓬ Alexanderplatz

Alexanderplatz was built in 1805, during the Prussian Golden Age. Because this was a gateway for trade to Eastern Europe, it was

named for a Russian czar, Alexander. In the Industrial Age, it became a transportation hub. In the roaring 1920s, it was a center of cabaret nightlife to rival Friedrichstrasse. And under the DDR, it was transformed into a commercial center. This was the pride and joy of East Berlin shoppers. The Kaufhof department store (now Galeria Kaufhof) was the ultimate shopping mecca...which wasn't saying much.

And then, on November 4, 1989, more than a half-million East Berliners gathered on Alexanderplatz to demand their freedom. Protesters chanted, *Wir wollen raus! We want out!* The winds of change were in the air; less than a week later, the Berlin Wall was history (see sidebar).

Today's square is a mix of old and new. Stand roughly between the two U-Bahn entrances, in the middle of the square, and take a 360-degree, clockwise spin-tour—starting with the TV Tower. It rises above the C&A store—a typical blocky-grey building from the communist era. To the right is the Galeria Kaufhof store—a slightly sleeker form of concrete bunker (c. 1967). In front is an abstract-sculpture fountain ringed with a colorful base that attracts sitters. Further right is a glassy skyscraper, the Park Inn. Next is a popular snack bar and a summertime biergarten, with tropical plants. Keep spinning to the Alexa building, with its colorful Kandinsky-esque facade.

Next is another bunker-like building, with the once-futuristic ⓭ **World Time Clock,** a nostalgic favorite installed in 1969 that remains a popular meeting point. The

clock—topped with a slowly spinning model of the solar system—can tell you the time anywhere in the world (though it might be an hour off thanks to daylight savings). You may see **human hot-dog stands.** These hot-dog hawkers wear ingenious harnesses that let them walk around while they cook and sell tasty, cheap German sausages.

Today, Alexanderplatz is a popular landmark—locals call it "Alex-platz." Trams go one way, trains go another, dueling drummers and buskers vie for attention, and people crisscross the square on their way to wherever. Alexanderplatz is a people place.

• *If you've had enough of the DDR, you can finish your walk now (see your transportation options at the end of the next section). But if you'd like to see one more communist-era artifact, carry on to the next stop.*

From the World Time Clock, follow the tram tracks (away from the station), walking out the far end of Alexanderplatz past the Saturn electronics store. Then hook right, pausing at the busy intersection of Alexanderstrasse and...

⓮ Karl-Marx-Allee

This socialist-style boulevard was designed after the original buildings here were leveled by the Red Army in 1945. As an expres-

The Wall Comes Down

The collapse of the Soviet Union and the DDR was less about pressure from the West and more about the internal failings within the communist system. The world was rapidly global-izing. Isolation was no longer an option. By the mid-1980s, Moscow was warming to the West. Soviet leader Mikhail Gor-bachev declared that he would no longer employ force to keep Eastern European satellite states under Soviet rule.

In the summer of 1989, Hungary opened its borders to the West—making it impossible for DDR authorities to keep their people in. In October, a series of anti-regime protests swept the East German city of Leipzig, attracting hundreds of thousands of supporters. Then, on November 4, East Berliners held a rally on Alexanderplatz, with more than a half-million protesters.

All of this persuaded the East German Politbüro to begin a gradual process of relaxing travel restrictions. In back-room meetings early on Thursday, November 9, officials decided they would allow a few more Easterners to cross into the West. The Politbüro members then left town early for a long week-end.

The announcement of the new policy was left to a spokes-man, Günter Schabowski, who knew only what was on a piece of paper handed to him moments before he went on TV for a routine press conference. At 18:54, Schabowski read the statement dutifully, with little emotion: "exit via border cross-ings...possible for every citizen." Reporters, unable to believe what they were hearing, prodded him about when the borders would open. Schabowski looked with puzzlement at the brief statement, shrugged, and offered his best guess: *"Ab sofort, unverzüglich."* ("Immediately, without delay.")

Schabowski's words spread like wildfire through the streets of both Berlins, its flames fanned by West German TV broadcasts. East Berliners began to show up at Wall check-points in droves, demanding that border guards let them pass. But the guards could not reach anyone who could issue of-ficial orders. (It later became clear that Politbüro members, who had also seen the announcement, were effectively hiding out.)

Finally, around 23:30, a border guard named Harald Jäger at the Bornholmer Strasse crossing decided to simply open the gates. In a giddy pandemonium, East Berliners rushed into the West, reuniting with family and friends. Once open, the Wall could never be closed again.

sion of their adoration to the "great Socialist Father" (Stalin), the DDR government decided to rebuild the street better than ever (the USSR provided generous subsidies). They intentionally made it one meter wider than the Champs-Élysées, named it Stalinallee, and lined it with "workers' palaces" built in the bold "Stalin Gothic" style so common in Moscow in the 1950s. Now renamed after Karl Marx, the street and its restored buildings provide a rare look at Berlin's communist days. The pillars in the distance mark Strausberger Platz, the centerpiece of this socialist paradise.

On the tall, glassy building overlooking the intersection, notice the colorful tile-mosaic **mural** decorating the communist-era Ministry of Education. The mural trumpets the accomplishments of the DDR's education system. East Germany—like all communist states—believed strongly in a well-educated populace... at least, about topics it deemed appropriate.

On October 7, 1989, the DDR celebrated its 40th anniversary with a massive military parade along this route. At the podium, below bright-red *40 Jahre DDR* banners, Mikhail Gorbachev stood alongside East German premier Erich Honecker and watched an endless stream of soldiers goose-step by. Surveying the pageantry, Honecker declared, "The Wall will be standing in 50 and even in 100 years."

As we now know, he was only off by 99 years and 11 months. In the following weeks, Honecker was removed from power; the Wall opened, then crumbled; and the stage was set for the reunification of a fully democratic and capitalistic Germany—leaving communist artifacts like this boulevard as something of a white elephant.

• *Our walk is over. Alexanderplatz is a convenient transportation hub to the rest of Berlin. The U-Bahn stops are in the middle of the square, and the S-Bahn station is just beyond it (in the direction of the TV Tower): Track 3 trains go east, and track 4 trains go west. Or you can take bus #100, #200, or #TXL back along Karl-Liebknecht-Strasse and on to Unter den Linden.*

Alternately, if you're really enjoying this walk down communist memory lane, consider this...

Optional Extension for Communist Architecture Fans

Distances are a bit long for convenient walking, but if you're intrigued to see more of Karl-Marx-Allee, taxi or ride the U-Bahn to Strausberger Platz, which was built to resemble an Italian promenade (about a mile down the boulevard). From Strausberger Platz, you can take a mile-long long hike east to Frankfurter Tor, reading the good information posts along the way. Notice the Social Realist reliefs on the buildings and the lampposts, which incorporate the wings of a phoenix (rising from the ashes) in their design. Once a "workers' paradise," the street now hosts a two-mile-long capitalist beer festival the first weekend in August...and not much else the rest of the year.

The **Café Sibylle,** two long blocks beyond Strausberger Platz (at the intersection with Koppenstrasse), is a fun spot for a coffee, traditional DDR ice-cream treats, and a look at its free informal museum that tells the story of the most destroyed street in Berlin. While the exhibit is humble, it's fun to see the ear (or buy a plaster replica) and half a moustache from what was the largest statue of Stalin in Germany (the street's centerpiece until 1961). The museum also provides a few intimate insights into apartment life in a DDR flat. The café is known for its good coffee and *Schwedeneisbecher mit Eierlikor*—an ice-cream sundae with a shot of egg liqueur, about as fancy as things got under communism (Karl-Marx-Allee 72, tel. 030/2935-2203).

SCHEUNENVIERTEL WALK

From Hackescher Markt to the New Synagogue

Despite its tongue-twisting name, Berlin's Scheunenviertel (SHOY-nen-feer-tel, "Barn Quarter") is one of the most accessible places to enjoy the city's thriving foodie, culture, and arts scene. It's also at the heart of Berlin's former Jewish quarter, with a big synagogue and several smaller, easy-to-miss landmarks that evoke a complicated history.

This walk combines these two themes—trendy Berlin and Jewish history. We'll also duck into several quintessentially Berliner *Höfe*—interconnected courtyards that burrow deep into city blocks, where much of Berlin life plays out. Perhaps most of all, I enjoy the Scheunenviertel as an opportunity to connect with a real-life Berlin neighborhood that's conveniently close to—yet apart from—the touristy historic core.

Orientation

Name Game: In addition to "Scheunenviertel," locals use various other names for this part of town—including Spandauer Vorstadt, the Former Jewish Quarter, North Mitte, or simply "Hackescher Markt Area."

Length of This Walk: Allow about 45 minutes (a bit more if lingering in the New Synagogue).

When to Go: This walk works well anytime—and may be even better in the evening, after you've wrapped up your Museum Island sightseeing, and when restaurants and bars are lively (but if you want to enter the New Synagogue, note the closing time—listed below).

Getting There: It's simple—just ride the S-Bahn (or tram #M1) to Hackescher Markt. If you're walking from Museum Island, follow the riverbank behind and across from the Berlin Cathedral, then angle right under the train tracks (takes less than 10 minutes).

Hackesche Höfe: Free, open 24 hours daily.

Haus Schwarzenberg Museums: Free, daily 10:00-20:00.

New Synagogue: Main exhibit-€5, dome-€3, combo-ticket for both-€6, temporary exhibits-€3; April-Sept Mon-Fri 10:00-18:00, Sun until 19:00; Oct-March dome closed, exhibit open Sun-Thu 10:00-18:00, Fri until 15:00; closed Sat year-round.

Bonbonmacherei (in Heckmann Höfe): Wed-Sat 12:00-19:00, closed Sun-Tue.

Services: Otto Weidt's Workshop for the Blind—in the Haus Schwarzenberg—has a free WC, as do area cafés and fast-food restaurants.

Eateries: You'll pass plenty of options; for recommendations, see the Eating in Berlin chapter.

Starring: Bustling local life, characteristic courtyards *(Höfe)*, and poignant reminders of Berlin's Jewish heritage.

The Walk Begins

• *Begin in the bustling square next to the Hackescher Markt S-Bahn station.*

❶ Hackescher Markt

This delightful people zone—tucked up against the train station trestle—is a lively place to simply hang out. It has ample al fresco cafés and restaurants, and on Thursday and Saturday mornings, it's further enlivened by a modest open-air market, with food stalls, clothes, and touristy items.

The handsome old S-Bahn station is a classic example of the city's Brandenburg Neo-Gothic brickwork, called *Back-stein* ("baked stone"). It frames off a beautiful space, with artful iron window frames and benches with built-in chessboards—inviting Berliners to linger. Most of the brick archways are filled with hip shops, which have official—and trendy—addresses such as "S-Bahn Arch #9, Hackescher Markt."

Hackescher Markt marks the boundary between the touristy hotels-and-museums zone of the historic core and the more characteristic neighborhoods of residential Berlin. This is the gateway to the Scheunenviertel, which sits just across the river from the city center, to the northeast. In German cities (with prevailing

1 Hackescher Markt
2 Hackesche Höfe
3 Haus Schwarzenberg
4 Oranienburger Strasse
5 Grosse Hamburger Strasse
6 Sophienkirche
7 The Barn Coffee Shop
8 Auguststrasse
9 Kennedys Museum
10 Heckmann Höfe
11 Central Post Office
12 New Synagogue
13 Monbijoupark

southerly and westerly winds), the northern and eastern parts of town—downwind of industry—were historically considered undesirable. In the olden days, the Scheunenviertel had barns full of gassy cows—which would have been a fire hazard in the city center, thanks to all that methane (a lesson learned the worst possible way in the Great London Fire). This part of town was also a logical place for warehouses, allowing merchants to store goods near the river that transported them.

Starting in the late 1600s, the Scheunenviertel became home to the core of Berlin's Jewish community, after Berlin was hit particularly hard by the devastating Thirty Years' War (1618-1648)—sometimes called the "first world war" because of its high number of casualties. The Prussian rulers needed help rebuilding and repopulating. Their pragmatic brainstorm was to import wealthy minorities, who were unwanted in other countries. They invited 50 wealthy Jewish families from Vienna—escaping pogroms in Austria—to resettle in this relatively undesirable part of town. Beliefs at the time forbade Christians from engaging in certain monetary tasks; tasks that Jews were allowed to do. Based in the Scheunenviertel, the Jews were close to the city's commercial center.

At the time, Jews found a relatively tolerant home in Berlin—they were even permitted to build their synagogue in the city center. (The scant footprint of that original Jewish synagogue, from 1714, is just a couple of blocks away, under the S-Bahn tracks and down Rosenstrasse. It's in a park with a monument to Christian women, married to Jewish men, who stood up to the Nazis—see page 174.)

Hackescher Markt got its current shape thanks to Hans Christoph Friedrich Graf von Hacke, a military hero who was promoted to Berlin City Commandant under Frederick the Great. In 1750, Hacke turned the smelly barns and swamplands of this area into a fine market square, similar to what you see today. The king was so pleased, he named the new space after Hacke.

From Hackescher Markt, walk with the train station on your righthand side to the busy cross-street with **tram tracks.** In Berlin, it's easy to lose track of whether you're in the "former West" or the "former East." Here's a tip: Trams were abundant in the East, while the West favored buses and subway lines. It's not always the case, but usually if you see tram tracks, you're in the former East Berlin.

• *Cross the street, turn left, and carry on straight across Rosenthaler*

Strasse, past the tram stop. You're headed for the entrance to that stately yellow-and-blue building (at Rosenthaler Strasse 40), the...

❷ Hackesche Höfe

Step inside and explore this series of eight courtyards bunny-hopping through a wonderfully restored *Jugendstil* (German Art Nouveau) building. Many of Berlin's apartment buildings are organized like this: courtyard after courtyard leading off the main road. However, the Hackesche Höfe is an unusually pristine—and unusually commercialized—example of a *Höfe* complex. This genteel space was built during a genteel age

(1907), with artful details and spacious courtyards that were a reaction against the overcrowded, hastily built apartment blocks of nearby Prenzlauer Berg. We'll see other, starkly different examples of Berlin *Höfe* on this walk, revealing that much of Berlin's charm hides off the street-front.

The Hackesche Höfe is a fun place to browse. Wander, explore, and do a little window-shopping (for tips, see the Shopping in Berlin chapter). Courtyard #3 is a tranquil garden, while courtyard #5 is particularly charming, with outdoor benches. Throughout, information plaques explain the building's history. The Hackesche Höfe links into yet another string of shop-lined courtyards, the Rosenhöfe.

When you're done exploring, backtrack to the entrance. Standing in the doorway, pause and look down at your feet, where you'll find four brass plaques embedded in the cobbles. These are **Stolpersteine** ("stumbling stones"): small monuments to everyday people who were murdered in the Holocaust. Each little plaque tells a story—in this case, of the Salinger family, who lived at this address. In 1942, daughter Ursula was deported to Riga, where she was killed. In 1943, dad Georg, mom Rosa, and son Gerd were deported to Auschwitz, where they were executed. If you keep an eye on the ground, you'll see many *Stolpersteine* around Berlin—but particularly in this neighborhood, the former Jewish quarter.

• *With your back to the Hackesche Höfe entrance, turn left. Just two doors down (at Rosenthaler Strasse 39) is the funky, ramshackle entrance to another courtyard, with a totally different feel.*

❸ Haus Schwarzenberg

Owned by an artists' collective, this *Hof* comes with a bar, cinema, graffiti-slathered open-air art space (reminiscent of mid-1990s

Stolpersteine (Stumbling Stones)

As you wander through the Scheunenviertel—and throughout Europe—you might stumble over small brass plaques in the sidewalk called *Stolpersteine*. *Stolpern* means "to stumble," which is what you are meant to do. These plaques mark the former homes of Jewish and other WWII victims of the Nazis. The *Stolpersteine* are meant not only to honor and personalize the victims, but also to stimulate thought and discussion. In addition, they're a meaningful rebuke to a prewar slur: When non-Jews tripped on a protruding rock or cobble, it was the custom among some Germans to say, "A Jew must be buried here." The *Stolpersteine* turn this idiom around, creating individual monuments to those who have no graves to mark their unjust deaths.

More than 50,000 of these plaques have been installed across Europe, mostly in Germany. They're made of brass so they stay polished as you walk over them. On each plaque is the name of the victim who lived in that spot, and how and where that person died. While some Holocaust memorials formerly used neutral terminology like "perished," now they use words like "murdered" (*ermordet*)—part of the very honest way in which today's Germany deals with its past. (The word *versteckete* means the person hid for a time.) Installation of a *Stolperstein* can be sponsored for €120 and has become popular in schools, where students research the memorialized person's life as a class project. You can learn even more about each person's story at www.stolpersteine-berlin.de.

Berlin), and the basement-level Monsterkabinett gallery (with far-out hydro-powered art). Its Café Cinema is one of the last remaining '90s bohemian-chic bars. In keeping with its anarchistic spirit, the courtyard is named after the self-proclaimed "Free Republic of Schwarzenberg," which tried to carve out its own

little statelet between the US and Soviet sectors at the end of World War II. (It lasted about six weeks.)

This courtyard holds a pair of inspirational museums.

The **Museum of Otto Weidt's Workshop for the Blind** (Museum Blindenwerkstatt Otto Weidt) vividly tells the amazing story of a Berliner who heroically protected blind and deaf Jews during World War II. Otto Weidt employed them to produce brooms and brushes, and because that was useful for

the Nazi war machine, he managed to finagle a special status for his workers. You can see the actual brush factory with pedal-powered machines still lined up. The exhibits are described well (in English and Braille), and there's a good intro video and free audioguide.

Right at the courtyard's entrance, the **Silent Heroes Memorial Center** (Gedenkstätte Stille Helden) is a well-presented exhibit celebrating the quietly courageous individuals who resisted the persecution of the Jews from 1933 to 1945. Take some time to learn the stories of a few of them.

A third museum here, the pricey Anne Frank Center, is geared toward visiting school groups and offers almost no history on Berlin itself.

• *Exiting Haus Schwarzenberg, backtrack past the entrance to Hackesche Höfe and hook right around the corner, then keep right at the fork to walk along...*

❹ Oranienburger Strasse

This street once held merchant warehouses, and later—under the military-minded Prussians—was widened to more easily move armaments around the city. If you're in a hurry, this street leads straight to the New Synagogue—where this walk ends—but we're taking a more roundabout route, to uncover some hidden gems.

Oranienburger Strasse is an eclectic mix of local and touristy. You'll pass (on the left) a Beata Uhse sex shop, part of a German chain owned by a Luftwaffe pilot-turned-businesswoman who opened what's considered "the world's first sex shop" in 1962—helping to normalize a healthy attitude about sexuality in postwar Germany. You'll see popular street-food stands slinging Berlin's two favorite handheld meals: *Gemüse Kebab* and *Currywurst*. And you'll pass a variety of other everyday shops, including a costume superstore.

• *After just one block, turn right up...*

❺ Grosse Hamburger Strasse

For 200 years, Grosse Hamburger Strasse was known as the "street of tolerance" because the Jewish community donated land to Protestants so they could build a church. Hitler turned it into the "street of death" *(Todesstrasse),* bulldozing 12,000 graves in the city's oldest Jewish cemetery and turning a Jewish nursing home into a deportation center.

Just a few steps up Grosse Hamburger Strasse, on the right, pause at the small park that marks the entrance to a **Jewish Cemetery.** Defiled by the Nazis, today it's carefully fenced off, with little to see inside. Through the gate, you can see two large tombstones with Hebrew carvings. If it's open, you can find a few more examples deeper in the cemetery (men should cover their heads when entering).

In front of the fence is a small but evocative **memorial,** honoring the 55,000 Berlin Jews who were murdered in the Holocaust.

The monument is piled with small stones, following the Jewish tradition of placing a stone on a grave as a sign of remembrance, and to prevent the body from being disturbed. The memorial dates from DDR times. In the waning years of communist East Germany, the failing government grew desperate for international support. Following the USSR's lead, the DDR made overtures to Israel, including the creation of this monument (which originally was intended for the Ravensbrück Concentration Camp Memorial, but was installed in this more high-profile location instead). Berlin still has a sizeable Jewish population, though only a few local Jews are descended from those original Viennese settlers. Other groups include Polish Jews who passed through here after World War II and decided to stay, and Russian Jews who came during DDR times. Because each group brought their own traditions, there's no single, unified "Berlin Jewish community." And because Jewish citizens are understandably wary of being counted by the German government, it's difficult to know their exact numbers; around 30,000 is a likely estimate.

Just beyond the cemetery, on the right, is a **Jewish high school** (you can still faintly read its original, prewar inscription over the door: *Knabenschule für Jüdischen Gemeinde).* This school—like all important Jewish locations in Berlin—is heavily fortified and carefully guarded by police. While fringe factions in German society (Neo-Nazis, Islamic extremists) do pose a small risk to Jewish institutions, the stout protection is also symbolic: Germany, ashamed of its history, is determined to make today's Jewish people feel safe and cared for.

Nearby, across the street, notice the big gap between the two yellow buildings. **"Missing buildings"**—bombed out in World War II and never rebuilt—are not rare in Berlin, but this one has been turned into a thought-provoking memorial: High up on the white walls facing into the courtyard, notice the names of the people who once lived here.

A few steps farther, on the right, a courtyard leads to the ❻ **Sophienkirche**—a Protestant church built on land that the Jewish community voluntarily donated for that purpose in the 1890s, giving this "Street of Tolerance" its nickname. See the photo of Martin Luther King, Jr., who delivered a sermon here in 1964, possibly at the invitation of East German authorities (who, in keeping with their "people's party" politics, may have wanted to exploit the poor history of race relations in the US for propaganda reasons).

Keep going up Grosse Hamburger Strasse. At the intersection with Krausnickstrasse, look left to see the gilded dome of the New Synagogue, where this walk ends. But for now, continue straight one more block, passing the St. Hedwig Catholic Hospital (the huge red-brick complex) on your left—further showing this street's historic intermingling of faiths (Jewish, Protestant, Catholic).

• At the end of the block, you reach the intersection with Auguststrasse. We'll turn left here to continue the walk, but first consider a couple of optional detours: Straight ahead up Grosse Hamburger Strasse, on the right, is ❼ **The Barn**, a gourmet coffee shop that impresses coffee snobs. If you keep going past that, you'll reach the pleasant park called **Koppenplatz**. At the far end of the park is a subtle but affecting Holocaust memorial called "The Room Left Behind" (by Nelly Sachs, a Berlin Jew who fled to Sweden): A table and two empty chairs, one tipped over.

To resume the walk, head west down...

➑ Auguststrasse

While outwardly nondescript, Auguststrasse hides beautiful little pockets of Berlin's uniquely artistic sensibility. This is *the* place in town to go gallery-hopping. Head down the street, passing the fun Do You Read Me? bookstore (on the left at #28) and the first of many galleries (on the right at #61).

A few doors down, the crumbling building set back from the street on your left (at #24) is **Clärchens Ballhaus.** This old-slash-

new, traditionalist-slash-hipster venue has been a Berlin institution since 1913 (and is government-listed as a protected building). In the evenings, it hosts ballroom dancing, dance lessons, and a lively courtyard restaurant under twinkly lights. If it's a weekday lunchtime, head upstairs for a peek into the Spiegelsaal—the Mirror Room—a grand-but-faded tearoom with dingy-chic decor and crystal chandeliers (and a popular location for movies; only open to the public Mon-Fri 11:00-15:00). For a fun and accessible taste of Berlin nightlife, swing back here in the evening.

Continue down Auguststrasse, dipping into the galleries and enjoying the quiet, untouristy pace of life. After passing a couple of crumbling facades on your left, you reach a big, red-brick building that once housed a Jewish girls' school; today it hosts some trendy restaurants (including the recommended Mogg Deli, the best place in Berlin for a Brooklyn-style Rueben) and—upstairs—the ➒ **Kennedys Museum,** with exhibits on the American president who uttered his most famous quote here in Berlin (for more on the museum, see page 46).

• *Just after the former Jewish girls' school, also on the left, is the entrance to the...*

➓ Heckmann Höfe

This classic Berlin courtyard complex is a pleasing mix of residential and commercial. As you cut through the complex— enter through the door marked *Zur Oranienburger Strasse,* then keep going all the way to the opposite end of the block—think about how these *Höfe* were organized, socially. Notice that not all apartments were created equal: The units at the back of the complex (where you entered) are small, with relatively small windows and not much natural light. As you move through the courtyards to the main entrance at the far end, the apartments get bigger and more light-filled. Clearly, these *Höfe* were designed to house different socioeconomic classes in the same residential complex. It was believed that by mingling with wealthy and cultured people from the front, the poorer people at the back would be inspired and empowered to improve their lot in life. The idea was for a family to gradually work their way ever closer to the apartments in the front as they became more educated and found more lucrative work.

This unusually progressive attitude—which was fundamental to Prussian society—originated with Frederick the Great, the ultimate "enlightened despot." Unlike his contemporary, the French King Louis XVI, Frederick realized that he had a duty to better his commoners' lot in life. Perhaps not coincidentally, Prussia managed to avoid the ugliness of a homegrown, barricades-and-guillotines revolution. (For more on Frederick, see page 106.)

Enough history. It's time for candy. Working your way through the courtyard, you'll pass a fine inner square (with leafy trees, public seating, a sweet teahouse, and a small theater). From here, you can see the back of the New Synagogue—its dome, and the glass structure that stands where part of the original building stood. Keep going, pausing (just before reaching Oranienburger Strasse) at the **Bonbonmacherei,** where you can watch traditional candy being made the old-fashioned way.

Exit the Heckmann Höfe onto Oranienburger Strasse. To your right is a striking building, the former ⓫ **Central Post Office** (Postfuhramt, from 1881). In the building's heyday, mail was delivered by horse—so this consisted mostly of stables. On the gorgeous red-brick facade, pick out the portraits of famous scientists (including Benjamin Franklin and Samuel Morse).

• *Our next stop is in the opposite direction from the post office, a few doors up Oranienburger Strasse. You can't miss the glittering dome of the...*

⓬ New Synagogue (Neue Synagogue)

Consecrated in 1866, the original synagogue that stood here was the biggest and finest in Germany, with seating for 3,200 worshippers and a sumptuous Moorish-style interior modeled after the Alhambra in Granada, Spain. It was desecrated by Nazis on Kristallnacht ("Crystal Night," for the broken glass littering the streets) in 1938, bombed in 1943, and partially rebuilt in 1990. Only the dome and facade have been restored—a window overlooks the vast vacant field marking what used to be the sanctuary. On its facade, a small plaque—added by East Berlin Jews in 1966—reads "Never forget" *(Vergesst es nie)*. Today the former synagogue is a museum and cultural center. The interior is only worth seeing if you have a strong interest in Berlin's Jewish story. (For more on what you'll see inside, see page 45.)

• *The main part of our walk is finished. But if you'd like to unwind, a fine park is just a few minutes away. With the New Synagogue at your back, turn left and walk along Oranienburger Strasse (toward the TV Tower). After a long block, veer right to reach...*

⓯ Monbijoupark

Convivial spaces like this one—busy with locals on a warm summer day—are the essence of today's Berlin. Everybody's out, meet-

ing up with friends and enjoying a green space in a busy city: sunbathing, grilling, splashing in the children's swimming pool (near the river), shooting hoops, or nursing a drink at the bar along the balustrade facing the Spree River.

Back when the Scheunenviertel really was the Barn Quarter, this was one of the pastures. Later it was the site of the opulent, Rococo-style Monbijou Palace, which was battered by World War II, demolished in 1959, and replaced by this park in the 1960s. Notice the suspiciously symmetrical bulge in the park (at the corner nearest the synagogue)—in Berlin, a likely sign that wartime rubble is buried beneath.

Also deep in the park is a popular amphitheater for summer performances. Monbijoupark is the centerpiece of Berlin's thriving tango scene. In keeping with its youthful and international bent, Berlin brags it has the world's second-best tango culture after Buenos Aires.

Take a seat. Relax. Grab a drink and settle in to enjoy it—like a real Berliner—looking out over the Spree and Museum Island. And think about all we've seen on this walk: trendy hangouts, fun-to-explore courtyards, and thought-provoking echoes of Berlin's Jewish past. In a city like Berlin—and a neighborhood like the Scheunenviertel—it just makes sense that all those things can coexist so naturally.

• *From Monbijoupark, you're about a 5-minute walk from two handy*

S-Bahn stations along Oranienburger Strasse: You can head east, back the way we started, to the Hackescher Markt station; or you can head west, past the synagogue, to the Oranienburger Strasse station.

From Hackescher Markt, you can hop on tram #M1 and zip up to the Prenzlauer Berg hotel, eating, shopping, and nightlife zone (and my ▢ Prenzlauer Berg Walk). Or, from Monbijoupark, you can cross the bridge to the Bode Museum and start exploring Museum Island (see my ▢ Museum Island Tour and ▢ Pergamon Museum Tour chapters); the ▢ German History Museum is also not far away.

PRENZLAUER BERG WALK

You can't just see the big sights and say you've been to Berlin. This is a city of neighborhoods—of fierce local pride and funky one-off businesses. And to experience that essence of Berlin, one of the best neighborhoods to visit is Prenzlauer Berg (PRENTS-low-er behrk), just north of the historic core.

Prenzlauer Berg is Berlin's Brooklyn. It has its own proud identity as a huge and fascinating city within-a-city (pop. 160,000). It grew like crazy in the late 19th century, when newly unified Germany was on the rise, Berlin was industrializing, and housing was needed for the influx of labor from the countryside. It was spared the worst of WWII devastation, but grew dilapidated under the communists. After the fall of the Wall, many locals fled to a better life in the West—vacating their flats and opening the door (literally) to a generation of squatters, students, artists, tree huggers, and alternative-lifestyle idealists who remade the neighborhood in their own image. Years of rent control kept things affordable for its bohemian inhabitants and its remaining working-class residents.

And more recently, Prenzlauer Berg has continued to evolve. Landlords are now free to charge what the market will bear, and the vibe is changing. As hipsters grow up and get real jobs, many are staying put—happy to push their designer baby carriages through Prenzlauer Berg's inviting parks. Other longtime residents, who cling to their bohemian ways, are finding themselves priced out.

This walk isn't about sightseeing. There's barely a museum or a landmark here worth going out of your way for. Rather, it's about the past, present, and future of this quintessentially Berlin neighborhood. Prenzlauer Berg is a great place to spend the night, to have a meal, to go shopping, or simply to explore.

Prenzlauer Berg Walk

1 Senefelderplatz
2 Wasserturm (Water Tower)
3 Rykestrasse Synagogue
4 Kollwitzplatz
5 Husemannstrasse
6 Kulturbrauerei
7 Konnopke's Imbiss
8 Kastanienallee
9 Oderberger Strasse
10 Schwedter Strasse
11 Mauerpark

Orientation

Length of This Walk: Allow 1.5 hours, or more if you plan to visit the Everyday Life in the DDR museum.

When to Go: This walk works anytime. It could be especially pleasant on a warm evening, when locals are out enjoying their neighborhood.

Getting There: Ride the U2 to Senefelderplatz.

Everyday Life in the DDR: Free, Tue-Sun 10:00-18:00, Thu until 20:00, closed Mon.

Eateries: Prenzlauer Berg is packed with eateries; for my recommendations—most of which are on or near this walk—see the Eating in Berlin chapter.

Starring: Historic apartment blocks, leafy squares, pierced and tattooed parents, and hipster boutiques in Berlin's most inviting residential neighborhood.

The Walk Begins

• *Our walk begins near the boundary between Prenzlauer Berg and the central Mitte district, at the Senefelderplatz U-Bahn stop. Exit the U-Bahn toward* Schönhauser Allee/Schwedter Strasse/Metzer Strasse. *At the top of the stairs, turn right, cross the street, walk toward the TV Tower, and pause at the corner. You're in the area called...*

❶ Senefelderplatz

Welcome to Prenzlauer Berg. This sprawling neighborhood has several smaller sub-areas (like Senefelderplatz), each with its own character. On this walk, we'll hopscotch around Prenzlauer Berg, checking out landmarks and sampling various slices of Berlin life.

Looking downhill, it's clear that Prenzlauer Berg really is a *Berg* ("mountain"—er, maybe just a hill). While the city center of Berlin is flat, Prenzlauer Berg was a forested hill on the outskirts. Today, part of Prenzlauer Berg's appeal is how well-preserved it is—just beyond the core, and therefore largely untouched by WWII bombs or heavy-handed DDR developers. That means that any random street corner can hide echoes of a complex history.

For example, turn around to face the big Meininger Hotel, and find the small metal gate immediately to its right. Peer through the Star of David cutouts in the gate to see an open space that runs through the middle of the block. This lane is the *Judengang* ("Jews' Way"), which led unobtrusively to a large **Jewish Cemetery.** The cemetery was founded in 1827—back when this area was just forests, mills, breweries, and graveyards— after Berlin's first Jewish cemetery (on Grosse Hamburger Strasse, described on page 186) filled up. The main entrance to the cemetery, around the corner and up the street from here, faces the busy road called Schönhauser Allee—which leads to Schönhausen Palace. Some believe that the king grew impatient with Jewish funeral processions impeding his progress to his weekend home—so he had the *Judengang* built.

As we explore this neighborhood, keep an eye out for the red-painted bike lanes—which are heavily used. Be warned: Pedestrians reading their guidebooks who absentmindedly wander into these lanes are given no quarter.

• *Turn with your back to busy Schönhauser Allee and walk two blocks along Metzer Strasse through a sleepy residential area. At Strassburger Strasse, turn left and walk toward the park with a big mound in the middle. As you walk, notice the original Prenzlauer Berg homes on the right side of the street, and the modern-style building on the left.*

Soon you'll reach the park known as...

❷ Wasserturm (Water Tower)

This mound covers a series of large reservoirs that provided water to the fast-growing district of Prenzlauer Berg in the late 19th century. Jog left to find the staircase that takes you all the way to the top of the mound. Up top, the red-brick structure in the middle of the mound is the cupola of a huge, earthenware dome that covers the subterranean reservoirs. This waterworks intentionally sits on the highest spot in the city—and water could be pumped up into the two big towers nearby, creating even more water pressure. The taller, skinnier water tower was built first, and later came the fatter one—which also housed workers at this water plant. Later, the Wasserturm cellars took on a sinister tinge, as one of the earliest sites of Hitler's *"Wildes-KZ"* (improvised concentration camps for political enemies)—before the Nazis established their more ambitious and organized concentration camp network.

Stand with the cupola at your back and walk to the edge of the hill, surveying the neighborhood (with the TV Tower on the horizon). Consider the history of Prenzlauer Berg:

This forested area was originally called Windmühlen-berg—"Windmill Hill." Later, it was the location for many breweries, since it was easier to dig cellars into the solid ground here than in the shallow and mucky Mitte district. From here, barrels of beer would be loaded onto the Nordbahn train line (in today's Mauerpark, where this walk ends).

By the late 19th century, as the capital of the newly unified, modern state of Germany (1871), Berlin was an industrial engine. Factories and railroads were being built, and peasants from the countryside flocked here for work. From 1860 to 1910, Berlin's population quadrupled from a half-million to over two million. For a time, Berlin was the third-largest city in the world, and the most densely populated in Europe. In Germany, most cities' version of "the other side of the tracks" is on the north and east side of town—downwind of heavy industry. And here in Berlin, Prenzlauer Berg quickly grew as a low-rent residential quarter.

Apartment buildings sprouted like dandelions. Property owners were in a hurry to take on tenants—often renting apartments at a discount even though the extremely slow-drying mortar was still damp. The tenants were glad to get a price break, and their body heat helped speed up the drying process (this was called *Trockenwohnen*—"dry living"). Unfortunately, the mortar fumes caused severe health problems.

Prenzlauer Berg quickly became congested. People lived in almost Dickensian conditions, with many residents crowded into each apartment. At that time, London typically had eight residents per building, New York had 17, Berlin overall had 76, while Prenzlauer Berg had a staggering 110 people per building. To save money, tenants might take on a *Schlafbursche*—someone who worked the night shift and would sublet your bed to sleep in during the day ("the sharing economy," Airbnb-style, well before its time).

With so many people living in such close quarters, fire was a big threat. Looking out over the skyline, notice the uniformity of building heights—they rarely exceed 70 feet, because that's how high the fire department's ladders could reach (the Berlin government decreed this *Traufhöhe*, or "eave height," in the 1860s).

• *Now that you have the big picture, head down the stairs next to the taller, skinnier water tower, passing a playground where you may see children from a nearby kindergarten. Then bear left and carry on past the big water tower, to the far end of the park. Across the way, take a few steps up the pretty, broad street called Rykestrasse. On the left side of this street is the...*

❸ Rykestrasse Synagogue

Notice the substantial barriers jutting out in front of a red-brick building. This is a synagogue—built in 1904, and one of a handful that still exists in Berlin.
While it looks small from the outside, this is Germany's largest surviving synagogue—with an original capacity for 2,000 worshippers. It's typical for synagogues to be set back from the street like this—hiding in a big courtyard, and camouflaged to blend in with the other houses

on the street. As it turns out, this is what helped save this synagogue. On Kristallnacht ("Crystal Night," November 9, 1938), in a modern-day pogrom, anti-Semitic government agents and civilians smashed and set fire to synagogues all over Germany. In most cases, fire departments simply let them burn to the ground. But here at Rykestrasse, the burning synagogue put the surrounding non-Jewish homes in jeopardy, so the fires were extinguished. The synagogue remains a place for worship, an active cultural center, and school. Like all Jewish sites in Berlin, it has a strong police presence.

• *Head back out toward the Wasserturm and turn right, passing Pasternak Restaurant. Continue straight along Knaackstrasse. After one short block, you emerge at...*

❹ Kollwitzplatz

This square is named for the artist **Käthe Kollwitz** (1867-1945), who lived in a building that stood on your right (currently #56A, with the wide blue stripe). Kollwitz—a printer and sculptor—lived through tumultuous times. She lost a son in World War I and a grandson in World War II. Her husband ran a medical office, where Käthe witnessed an almost constant wartime stream of sick and downtrodden citizens. Her work is, understandably, reflective of the trauma of her era. Kollwitz's most famous work is the *pietà* she sculpted for the Neue Wache on Unter den Linden, Germany's primary monument to lives lost to fascism (see page 113). For a more intimate look at Kollwitz's work and life, visit the small but excellent museum devoted to her near the Ku'damm, in Western Berlin (see page 78).

A few doors down from Kollwitz's former house, at **#60,** you can read some of this building's history into its current state. First, notice the two little doors flanking the main entrance—still marked with the names of the businesses that once occupied them (*H. Weigand* and *Restauration*). Finely crafted medallions are still visible over those doors. At the base of the arch, notice the bulbous barriers protecting the corners—designed to prevent horse carriages from scuffing the walls when they came and went out of the courtyard. But like much of Prenzlauer Berg, this house has clearly been renovated quite recently. Looking up, you can see the date *9 Nov 1989* and the word *Freiheit* (freedom), commemorating the fall of the Berlin Wall. Despite its cramped heyday in the late 19th and early 20th centuries, and its post-DDR stint as the domain of squatters (more on that later), Prenzlauer Berg has become one of Berlin's poshest neighborhoods.

Cross the street into the park and hang out for a moment by the big, seated sculpture of Käthe Kollwitz and (just to the right) the lively playground. Berlin is a city of small sub-neighborhoods

called *Kieze*. Each *Kiez* ("keets") is just a few square blocks, named for a nearby landmark (for more on *Kieze*, see the sidebar on page 58). In this case, you're in the heart of the Kollwitzkiez—the poster child for the pros and cons of gentrification. Look around. Do you see lots of designer strollers? Well-
coiffed, latte-sipping young parents? Dapperly dressed toddlers? Kollwitzplatz is the epicenter of Prenzlauer Berg's über-wealthy yuppie scene. A popular satirical cartoon strip—*Die Mütter vom Kollwitzplatz*—lampoons exactly this scene. (Prenzlauer Berg is also ground zero for a major baby boom. Count how many strollers you see on the rest of this walk—I'm betting on double digits.)

Class stratification is a huge preoccupation among Berliners. Over the last decade, several neighborhoods—like the Kollwitzkiez—have swung from seedy-but-affordable to gentrified-and-overpriced...sometimes in a matter of mere months. Today, a small, 600-square-foot apartment in this area runs about €1,000 per month. While that may seem cheap by London or Paris standards, keep in mind that a decade ago, Prenzlauer Berg was a bohemian paradise, where creative free spirits could afford to live dirt cheap while pursuing their interests, and maybe working a little on the side. Now these people are being priced out by *die Mütter vom Kollwitzplatz*, and being forced to move farther and farther into the suburbs—bringing with them lots of resentment about the changing face of Berlin.

• *With the Kollwitz statue at your back, exit the park past the playground. Continue straight across the street, down...*

❺ Husemannstrasse

While Prenzlauer Berg largely survived World War II, it fell into disrepair under the communists. (Cynical East Berliners would joke, "The DDR is really civilized—they create ruins without using weapons.") In 1987, East and West Berlin both celebrated the 750th anniversary of the city's founding, and the DDR government had the street spruced up—restoring it to its original, circa-1900 glory.

Stroll along the left side of the street, enjoying the fine little details: At #1, notice the frilly horse-cart guardrails at the base of the arch. Farther down at #9, decorative heads look down—facing a green wellhead. Look for flagpole holders by some doors—dating from a time when you were required to fly the communist DDR flag for holidays like the First of May.

Also along here, notice the typical arrangement of Prenzlauer

Berg homes: The ground floor was generally for shops and workshops (often tucked far back in courtyards—we'll see good examples of these later). Notice that the first floor up has much higher ceilings and bigger windows—this *belle-etage* (also called *piano nobile*—"beautiful" or "noble" floor) was by far the most desirable and expensive. The higher up, and the farther back in the building, the smaller the windows—servants often lived in the top-back parts of the courtyards, with the most stairs and lowest ceilings.

Near the end of the block (at #15, on the left), you'll see where those 1987 DDR restorers cheaped out. Looking up, notice that only the first story was painted, while the rest was left dilapidated.

At the intersection with Sredzkistrasse, notice the old-timey street signs, with the Berlin bear—also dating from that 1987 remodel. On the round poster kiosk (invented in Berlin), notice the emergency telephone number: *Volkspolizei 110*. While that was true in DDR times, today the "People's Police" are long gone.

• *Turn left on Sredzkistrasse and walk to the big, yellow, castle-like building.*

❻ Kulturbrauerei

Remember that Prenzlauer Berg was once a wooded hill with dozens of breweries—including this one, the Schultheiss-Brauerei. By the 1920s, this was one of the largest breweries in the world. World War II put an end to that, as Nazis confiscated the brewery, turned it into a factory for the Wehrmacht (armed forces), and, in the closing days of war, barricaded themselves within the brewery grounds. Today the entire site has been renovated to maintain its historic buildings, and to provide a venue for the cultural transformation of Prenzlauer Berg.

Head up the stairs just past the smokestack, step through a round gate into the main courtyard, and stroll all the way through

to the far end. You'll see a cinema, several small theater and music venues (Frannz Club and Alte Kantine are local favorites; the Haus für Poesie has poetry readings), and various shops, cafés, and restaurants—all wrapped in a 19th-century, brick-industrial shell, with much of the original signage intact. On Sundays, you'll find a trendy street-food market here (12:00-18:00), and in December, it plays host to a Christmas market. On the left, notice the Ramba Zamba theater—an acclaimed venue, with productions (in German) performed by people with and without disabilities.

At the far end of the courtyard, in the passage, is the entrance to the **Everyday Life in the DDR** museum—a concise look at East German lifestyles. For more on this museum, see page 49.

• *Continue through the passage past the museum, emerging at a busy street. Turn left, then left again around the corner onto Danziger Strasse, toward the green rail bridge. Cross the street, go under the bridge, and hook left to reach...*

❼ Konnopke's Imbiss

If you have yet to try Berlin's most famous dish—*Currywurst* (sausage smothered in curry ketchup)—now's your chance. For more on this dish, see page 278. Konnopke's is a local favorite, not just because they grill up a mean *Currywurst,* but also because of their long heritage. Konnopke's has been around since 1930, and remained family-operated even through DDR times...a rare feat. Back then, opportunities to eat out were rare, so people would enjoy gathering here, under the railroad tracks, to down a sausage and meet up with friends. And they still do. In fact, after the stand was demolished in 2010 during roadwork, Berliners rioted—and Konnopke's was rebuilt in this slick, glass-and-steel hut.

Their window display offers a handy visual orientation to a variety of German meats: *Krautwurst, Knacker, Bockwurst,* and *Bratwurst* (subtle variations on grilled sausages); *Paar Wiener* (a pair of weenies); *Chili Krakauer* (spicy sausage); *Geflügelspiess* (chicken skewers); and *Bulette* (a classic Berlin dish—basically a huge meatball, like a round hamburger). They even have a vegan *Currywurst...* this *is* Prenzlauer Berg, after all.

• *With your back to Konnopke's, cross the street and proceed to the smaller street, which angles to the left. This is...*

❽ Kastanienallee

This delightful drag is the essence of today's Prenzlauer Berg—with a fun and lively variety of restaurants, shops, and residences. Locals have nicknamed this "Casting Alley"—this is where Prenzlauer Berg's fashionable residents go to see and be seen. We'll stroll the most colorful stretch of Kastanienallee, then double back to another fine street that leads to the end of our walk.

Along here, notice the abundance of tempting eateries, dishing up every type of cuisine. While I've recommended some spe-

cific restaurants in the Eating in Berlin chapter, you almost can't go wrong getting a bite or drink along this stretch.

A few steps down Kastanienallee on the right, notice **Prater Biergarten**—Berlin's oldest beer garden. Step under the gate and explore, passing a huge bicycle parking lot (a must in this bike-happy city). Deep in the beer garden, amid the trees and the tables, you get the feeling of what this place must have been like when it opened in 1837—back when it was in the middle of a forest. Workers, soldiers, and servants would escape the city to drink, hang out, and fool around in the woods. Prater Biergarten is such a treasured landmark that the surrounding apartment blocks were built around it rather than disturb it.

Back out on Kastanienallee, keep heading down the street. At #12, on the right, see if **Galerie Kurt im Hirsch** is open (it has very short hours—usually Sat-Sun 14:00-17:00). This is the most venerable of Prenzlauer Berg's funky art collectives—taking you back to the bohemian vibe of the 1990s.

Cross to the left side of Kastanienalle. At Oderberger Strasse, look left to see a fine old Neo-Renaissance building with pretty gables. This was built in 1902 as a **public bathhouse** (*Volksbadeanstalt*). Remember how crowded Prenzlauer Berg apartments were back then? On top of the tight conditions, most people didn't even have private bathrooms. Buildings came equipped with an *Etagenklo*—a shared toilet on the stairwell connecting floors. And if you wanted to bathe, you had to go to a public bathhouse, such as this one. Like much of Prenzlauer Berg, it fell into disrepair, and for decades it was used only as an occasional venue for concerts. But the building was recently completely restored, and now houses the recommended Hotel Oderberger, a restaurant, and—as in the old days—a shallow swimming pool in a beautiful hall (you can step into the reception and peek into the pool).

Continue down Kastanienallee. A half-block farther, on the left at #86, you can't miss the **Tuntenhaus** ("Drag Queen House")—with a ramshackle exterior and provocative, old-school-Prenzlauer Berg messages spelled out in big silver letters: *Kapitalismus zerstört tötet* ("Capitalism destroys and kills"). During the post-DDR but pregentrification period—in the 1990s—Prenzlauer

Berg was a hotbed for squatters, including the drag queens *(Tunten)* who lived at this address. (For more on the squatting lifestyle, see page 205.) Now legal, the Tuntenhaus maintains its creative and collective vibe. Next door, the **Café Morgenrot** ("Red Dawn") is also operated by an artists' collective, with coffee, cocktails, vegan goodies, and weekend punk concerts in the cellar.

Continuing down Kastanienallee, you'll pass GLS (a language school), and then, at #79, **Dock 11**—a renowned modern-dance school and studio, which attracts performers from all over Germany. They're very active in the community (offering, for example, children's dance classes) and often present high-quality, cutting-edge dance performances (look for these advertised at the entrance, or check www. dock11-berlin.de). Step into the graffitied, ramshackle courtyard, and watch parents drop off their kids.

Next door, at #77, is a green building marked **Farben.** Its short stature (just three stories) is a sign that this is one of Prenzlauer Berg's oldest surviving buildings (dating from the 1850s). Today it houses the tiny Lichtblick art house cinema. Being discreet—people live here—walk deep back into this building's courtyard to

see how Prenzlauer Berg housing complexes are designed: a series of courtyards broken up by high-density housing. At the far end is a little *Keramik Werkstatt*—evocative of the busy little workshops that would traditionally be buried far from the street.

In the late 1980s, these courtyards became a cradle of anti-DDR sentiment. Prenzlauer Berg was run down, and the authorities proposed tearing the neighborhood down and replacing it with more efficient and modern concrete block housing instead. But locals had a respect for this area's history, and fought to keep the original architecture. They'd take ownership of courtyards like this one,

Squatters

When the Wall came down in 1989, many East Berliners packed up and set out to create a new life in the West—leaving behind deserted apartments. Meanwhile, students and artistic types flocked the other way, coming from all over Germany to live in an exciting and creative city in transition.

For a year or two after 1989, it was pretty much anything goes in East Berlin. People would arrive in Prenzlauer Berg, choose a building, go door to door, find an apartment that appeared empty, move in, change the locks...and it was theirs. If you wanted to make it official (rather than be a "squatter"), after a certain time had passed you could offer to pay rent at the local housing authority. They'd write up a contract and you'd be legal.

This wasn't easy living: Prenzlauer Berg was a shamble, and the apartments were old. For heat, you'd have to haul coal up several flights of stairs, passing the building's shared toilet on the stairwell. It was rare to have a telephone—most people waited in line to use the corner pay phone. (One Prenzlauer Berg resident from that time told me his apartment not only had a phone, but one that allowed free long-distance calls to anywhere in the world. He never got a bill, so he just kept on calling—until the day the phone simply stopped working.)

Over time, you could make small improvements to "your" property and really make it your own. There's even a special expression in German—*instand besetzen*—that means, essentially, "squatting in a house while you repair it." To further incentivize people to fix up these desperately dilapidated buildings, for a brief period in the early 1990s the city offered *Selbsthilfe* ("self-help"). That is, if you did the work yourself, the city would pay about half for the materials.

And so, while squatting is conventionally thought of as a social evil, in post-DDR Berlin, it was an essential component of the city's recovery. It's one of those "social ills"—like graffiti—that just seem to fit Berlin to a T.

chipping away at the concrete and planting grass and gardens—a process called *Hofbegrünung* ("courtyard greening-up"...urban gardening before it was hip). It was a literal "grassroots movement" of opposition to the centrally planned communist aesthetic (which hated the idea of people making their own decisions)—people were reclaiming their "shared property" from a government they didn't trust. As the DDR's grip slipped, courtyards became gathering places for artists, musicians, and rabble-rousing neighbors. (Another such gathering place were churches. For more on the role of churches—especially the nearby Zionskirche—in providing a haven for free speech under a dictatorship, see the sidebar on page 207.)

• *Exiting the Farben courtyard, cross the street to the Künstler Magazin art-supply store (at #33), turn right, and head back up the other side of Kastanienallee. Enjoy browsing the businesses on this side of the street, and when you get back to Oderberger Strasse, turn left.*

❾ Oderberger Strasse

This unusually wide and inviting street is a favorite of Prenzlauer Berg residents. Its width suggests that, during the neighborhood's

industrial heyday, this was a main artery for deliveries to the Nordbahn (where we're headed now).

Window-shop the funky bars and cafés along here. But choose wisely. You'll spot many tacky, interchangeable "tropical cocktail" bars, with hanging lanterns out front and menus of forgettable Asian dishes, falafel, and Mexican food. These places—mostly catering to tourists—are disdained by many locals as not being authentically Berlin.

Instead, as you stroll, keep an eye out for these favorites: **Kiezkantine** (on the left at #50) is a cheap lunch spot run as a charity

for the mentally disabled. **Entweder Oder** ("Either Or," on the right at #15) is a sentimental favorite—it's been in business since around the time the Wall came down. On the left at #44, **Kauf dich Glücklich** ("Shop Yourself Happy") is another neighborhood classic—a ramshackle bar known for its tasty waffles and ice cream.

Across the street from Kauf dich Glücklich (just past #18), notice the big gap in the buildings—a sure sign that one of Prenzlauer Berg's few random casualties from WWII bombs once stood here. This gap in particular leads to a historic courtyard: the **Hirschhof** ("Deer Courtyard"), which was the main location of those grassroots, urban-beautification movements in the late-communist period. You could say that the Hirschhof was the birthplace of East Berlin's "Green" movement. This courtyard is now private property, but you can see kids playing nearby...under the gaze of a graffiti deer *(Hirsch)*.

Continue along Oderberger Strasse. You'll pass the recommended **Engelberg** café (on the right at #21, with Bavarian food in

"Church from Below": Church-Based Resistance and the Zionskirche

A couple of blocks from this walk (down Kastanienallee) stands the Zionskirche. While there's little to see there, inside

or out, it's an important landmark of the neighborhood—and Prenzlauer Berg's history of resistance.

In the Depression-era 1930s, a wealthy young man named Dietrich Bonhoeffer (1906-1945) chose the simple life of a priest, and worked with disadvantaged children here at the Zionskirche. Later he spoke out boldly against the rise of Nazism, conspired against the Hitler regime, was sent to a concentration camp, and was hanged just weeks before the end of the war.

In the 1980s, the Zionskirche hosted the "Environmental Library" (*Umweltbibliothek*)—an underground resource for the anti-DDR, pro-environment crew that took root in dilapidated Prenzlauer Berg courtyards. In a sign of the DDR's waning power, the government's attempts to shut down the library failed.

This is a good example of the role that the Church played throughout DDR times: While the atheistic regime formally stripped the Church of its power, individual churches provided a safe place for like-minded people to gather and organize. This phenomenon—called *Kirche von unten* ("Church from below")—was one of the most significant footholds of anti-DDR resistance. To attract participants, many DDR churches had *Bluesmesse*—church services combined with popular musical acts. In October of 1987, the Zionskirche famously hosted a rock concert by a West Berlin band, who screamed into their microphones from the pulpit. Later that night, concertgoers were attacked by East Berlin skinheads—a PR black eye for the proudly "antifascist" DDR government, just when it least needed one.

And it wasn't just in East Berlin. In nearby Leipzig, Monday evening "prayer for peace" gatherings began in 1982, and later became the nucleus of citywide protests in September and October of 1989—which proved instrumental in the collapse of the DDR.

These days, churches are considered conservative and old-fashioned. The Zionskirche offers an intriguing lesson that, back in DDR times, it was exactly the opposite.

a trendy Berlin setting), then Berlin's oldest red-brick fire station, and then another gap (WWII-destroyed building).

Just past the gap, peruse the window displays at **VEB Orange** (#29, with the East German hammer-and-compass insignia)—a tongue-in-cheek antique store specializing in DDR-era items. If it's cheaply made of bright-colored plastic, you'll find it here. The little cups shaped like chickens—for eating a hard-boiled egg—were standard-issue throughout the DDR, and remain a kitschy symbol of those times. The name *VEB (Volkseigener Betrieb)* means "people's own company"—the main way of doing business in communist times, when private property was frowned upon (as opposed to West Germany's standard, the GmbH—a privately owned "business with limited liability").

Across the street at #35, **Bonanza Coffee Heroes** is a favorite of coffee snobs.

• *Soon you'll reach a point where the road takes a dramatic bend to the left—as if to avoid the busier road (Bernauer Strasse) just beyond. This bend curls into...*

⓾ Schwedter Strasse

The Berlin Wall came over the hill on the horizon, then took a sharp left turn along Bernauer Strasse. This was the East. Just across Bernauer Strasse was the West. That's why, rather than flowing logically into the main road, Schwedter Strasse has last-minute second thoughts and retreats from it. This street was so close to the Wall that locals had to show their ID to even be allowed to walk here. Meanwhile, a platform on the other side of Bernauer Strasse allowed Westerners to peer down into the mysterious East—and even shout across to loved ones who were still trapped there. In 1964, Martin Luther King, Jr. stood here to survey the Wall.

Facing away from the busy street, notice the blown-up photograph on the side of the building: Hundreds of people gathered right here. It's 1989, and the Berlin Wall has just (finally) cracked open. You come here, with everyone else in the neighborhood, and wait for your turn to cross...to set foot in West Berlin for the first time since 1961. And then—unbelievably—it actually happens.

By the way, that giant photograph—and the rust-colored pillars just below it—are the last stop of the more than one-mile-long **Berlin Wall Memorial.** You could follow informational pillars like this one all the way to the beginning—or, at the end of this walk, you can hop on a tram to Nordbahnhof and follow those sights in order. (More on that in a moment.)

• *Cross busy Bernauer Strasse and head into the...*

⓫ Mauerpark

This "Wall Park" fills an area that used to be the deadly no-man's-land between East and West. Today it's a lively gathering place.

Head up the hill to the graffitied wall of the sports stadium to get the big picture. Have a seat (or go for a swing) and survey the valley below you.

The brick path is where the wall once ran. The vast field beyond (now under development) was, before that, the site of the Nordbahn train line—once the economic lifeline of Prenzlauer Berg. The big wall behind you—now a favorite canvas for local graffiti artists—strategically blocked the view of the West for people attending an event at the DDR soccer stadium, the Friedrich-Ludwig-Jahn-Sportpark. This was built to host the World Youth Festival in 1951 and is still marked by its original bombastic light towers (even light towers were designed to stir young communist souls).

While this park is usually quiet, it's packed on Sundays, when it hosts a lively outdoor market and a big karaoke sing-off on the outdoor stage...a celebration of life, as Berliners literally dance on the grave of the Wall that divided their city. In Prenzlauer Berg, the future is very bright indeed.

• *Our walk is finished. If you head back to Bernauer Strasse, you'll find a stop for tram #M10. If you'd like to see more of the Berlin Wall, you can take this to the right, to the Berlin Nordbahnhof stop, at the start of the* ▢ *Berlin Wall Memorial Tour.*

Alternatively, you can take tram #M10 to the left one stop (or simply walk a few minutes) to reach the Eberswalder Strasse U-Bahn station—with Konnopke's (if you're ready for a Currywurst) and several other great restaurants; the start of Kastanienallee (for more browsing); tram #M1 back down along Kastanienallee, and eventually to Hackescher Markt and the Scheunenviertel; and the U2 subway line to anywhere in Berlin. The Kulturbrauerei and Everyday Life in the DDR museum are a short walk just beyond the U-Bahn station.

PRENZLAUER BERG WALK

BERLIN WALL MEMORIAL TOUR

Gedenkstätte Berliner Mauer

Nowhere in Berlin is the Cold War division between East and West clearer than at the Berlin Wall Memorial. The Memorial is located along the former "death strip"—the no-man's-land between East and West. For decades, it was strewn with barbed wire and patrolled by guards with itchy trigger fingers. Today it's a long, narrow, poignant park, running for nearly a mile alongside the most complete surviving stretch of the Wall in Berlin. The park is dotted with thought-provoking memorials and information-packed displays. There's even a small stretch of Wall that's been preserved with its original double-walled construction, heavy fortifications, and an intimidating guard tower. Along the way, you can visit two different museums with excellent films, photos, and exhibits on this turbulent chapter of human history.

Orientation

Cost: Free.

Hours: Outdoor areas accessible 24 hours daily; Visitors Center and Documentation Center open Tue-Sun 10:00-18:00, closed Mon, memorial chapel closes at 17:00.

Information: Tel. 030/4679-86666, www.berliner-mauer-gedenkstaette.de.

When to Go: To really pack your day with sightseeing, this tour could be done in the evening, after other museum visits. But if you'd like to enter the two indoor exhibits, be mindful of the 18:00 closing time.

Getting There: Our tour begins right next to the Nordbahnhof S-Bahn station. In fact, the station itself is a Cold War sight (see the sidebar on page 217). Take the S-Bahn (line S1, S2, or S25) to Nordbahnhof. Exit by following signs for *Bernauer*

Berlin Wall Memorial Area

- Berlin Wall Memorial
- ...... Former Course of the Wall

500 Meters
500 Yards

Strasse—you'll pop out across the street from a long chunk of Wall and kitty-corner from the Visitors Center. You can also get there on tram #12 or #M10 (from near Prenzlauer Berg hotels).

Getting Oriented: The Visitors Center hands out free brochures with maps and information on the Memorial. These point out many "incident markers" of events that occurred here, such as escape attempts. Note that there are four different brochures for the four sections of the park (A, B, C, D), so be sure to pick up all you'll need. My tour covers Sections A and B in depth, with a basic overview of the rest.

Length of This Tour: Allow about one hour for a quick visit. Add another 30 minutes to watch both movies at the Visitors Center, and another 30-45 minutes to walk the entire length of the memorial (Sections C and D) to Mauerpark.

Services: The Visitors Center and Documentation Center both have free WCs.

Cuisine Art/Eateries: There's a small bakery/café at the Documentation Center.

Starring: The Berlin Wall, the "death strip," and the irrepressible human spirit.

BACKGROUND

This particular stretch of the Wall (running right along Bernauer Strasse) was long the focus of the world's attention—something of

The Berlin Wall: The Basics

West Berlin was a 185-square-mile island of capitalism entirely surrounded by East Germany. Between establishment of the DDR (East Germany) in 1949 and construction of the Berlin Wall in 1961, an estimated three million East Germans emigrated (fled) to freedom. To stanch their population loss, the DDR erected the 96-mile-long "Anti-Fascist Protective Rampart" almost overnight, beginning on August 13, 1961. They claimed the Wall was to keep bourgeois West Berliners safely at bay. Of course, its real purpose was the opposite: to keep East Berliners from leaving.

The Berlin Wall (Berliner Mauer) was actually two walls. The outer was a 12-foot-high concrete barrier topped with barbed wire and a rounded, pipe-like surface to discourage grappling hooks. The inner wall was lower-profile. Sandwiched between the walls was a no-man's-land (or "death strip") between 30 and 160 feet wide.

The boundaries of West Berlin—and the outline of the Berlin Wall—were anything but a straight line. Because the Soviet sector included the historic core of the city (Mitte), East Berlin took a big bite out of the West. Train tracks between West Berlin stations cut underneath the East, creating "ghost stations" where trains would pass through but never stop—their passengers seeing only cobwebs and DDR border guards.

There were eight points where you could legally cross between West and East Berlin, the most famous of which were Checkpoint Charlie (see page 225) and the Friedrichstrasse train station, with its so-called "Palace of Tears" (see page 47). In general, Westerners could temporarily enter the East, but not vice-versa.

Even after the Wall went up, people didn't stop trying to es-

a poster-child for Berlin's division, and for the Cold War in general. That's because, in a grotesquely literal symbol for a divided city, apartment buildings were incorporated into the structure of the Wall itself. Film footage and photographs from the early 1960s show Berliners worriedly watching workmen seal off these buildings from the West, brick by brick. Some people attempted to leap to freedom from upper-story windows, with mixed results. It was here that international news crews came to document the dramatic escape attempts, the bleak no-man's-land, the anti-Soviet protests, and the makeshift memorials to fallen victims. As you visit the park, you'll learn about how the Wall went up, the brutal methods used to keep Easterners in, and the brave stories of people who risked everything to be free.

cape. On their way into the death strip, would-be escapees would trip a silent alarm, which alerted sharpshooters. According to documents, border guards fired a total of nearly 1,700 times and made more than 3,000 arrests. During the Wall's 28 years, there were about 5,000 documented successful escapes—and 565 of those were East German guards. An estimated 136 people were killed at the Wall while trying to escape.

Meanwhile, living in West Berlin—surrounded by concrete, barbed wire, and enemy soldiers armed to the teeth—was no picnic. The West German government offered generous tax incentives to encourage people to live here. It also waived compulsory military service for men—which is partly why West Berlin attracted many draft-dodging, alternative-lifestyle punks and hippies.

The Berlin Wall came to symbolize the larger Cold War between East and West. President John F. Kennedy gave a speech of solidarity in West Berlin, declaring, *"Ich bin ein Berliner"*—I am a Berliner. A generation later, President Ronald Reagan stood directly in front of the Brandenburg Gate and demanded of his Soviet counterpart, "Mr. Gorbachev, tear down this wall."

Finally, one November night in 1989, the Berlin Wall came down, as suddenly as it went up. For that story, see page 177.

The Tour Begins

Our walk laces together several scattered sights associated with the Memorial. First stop: the Visitors Center, with its introductory films. Then comes the Memorial park. Along the way, we'll stop into the Documentation Center, a museum about the Wall's history.

• *Start your visit at the Visitors Center, the rust-colored, blocky building located kitty-corner from the Nordbahnhof (at the far west end of the long Memorial park, at Bernauer Strasse 119).*

❶ Visitors Center (Bezucherzentrum)

At this modern, cube-shaped building, you'll find a helpful staff, a number of maps and info brochures, a handy WC, and a few vending machines. Check the next showtimes for the two 15-

minute introductory films. (If you're in a hurry, don't wait for the English versions—the German ones have subtitles and easy-to-follow graphics.)

The film entitled *The Berlin Wall* covers the four-decade history of the Wall. First, it shows the events leading up to the Wall, as the Cold War gradually turned Berlin into a flashpoint between communism and the West. It chronicles the postwar division into Allied and Soviet sectors (1945), the Soviet Blockade and Allied Airlift (1949), and the democratic uprising crushed by Soviet tanks (1953). Then, in 1961, the Soviets told the East Germans to close the border entirely and erect the Wall. You'll hear about frantic escape attempts. Finally, there's the gradual thawing of the Cold War, and the eventual tearing down of the Wall in 1989.

The other film, *Walled In!*, is even more helpful. With computer graphics, it makes a 3-D re-creation of the former death strip, helping you visualize what it is you're about to walk through.

Now, exit the Visitors Center, cross Bernauer Strasse, and enter the Memorial park. You're leaving former West Berlin and entering the no-man's-land that stood between East and West Berlin.

• *Once in the park, find the rusty rectangular monument with a 3-D map.*

❷ 3-D Map of the Former Neighborhood

The map shows what this neighborhood looked like back in the Wall's heyday. Find where you are on the map: the shiny metal dot. If you were standing here 50 years ago, you'd be right at the

division between East and West Berlin—specifically, in the narrow no-man's-land between two sets of walls. One of those Walls is still standing—there it is, stretching along Bernauer Strasse. As you gaze down the long park, West Berlin would be to your left (on the north side of Bernauer Strasse), and East Berlin to your right.

Now find the Nordbahnhof, both on the map and in real life—the entrance is directly across Gartenstrasse street. While the Wall

Berlin Wall Memorial

To Sections C & D,
🇺 Bernauer Strasse,
🇹 #M10 to Prenzlauer Berg
& Mauerpark

▢ Berlin Wall Memorial
⋯⋯ Former Course of the Wall

TOUR ENDS ⑨

STRELITZER STR.

HUSSITENSTRASSE

BERNAUER STRASSE

TUNNEL 57

OPEN-AIR DISPLAY

ACKERSTRASSE

ESCAPE ATTEMPTS

#M10 🇹

CHAPEL OF RECONCILIATION

⑦

⑧

SECTION B

DOCUMENTATION CENTER

⑥

GUARD TOWER

PRESERVED PART OF WALL

⑤

100 Meters

100 Yards

✝ CEMETERY CROSS

WALL OF REMEMBRANCE

⚑ TOUR BEGINS

④

ACKERSTRASSE

WALL FRAGMENTS

VISITORS CENTER

①

③ "DEATH STRIP"

②

3-D MAP

SECTION A

Sophien Parish Cemetery

#M10 🇹

NORDBAHNHOF EXIT

GARTENSTRASSE

BERGSTRASSE

INVALIDENSTRASSE

🇸 Nordbahnhof

BERLIN WALL

① Visitors Center
② 3-D Map of the Former Neighborhood
③ "Death Strip"
④ Wall of Remembrance
⑤ The Wall

⑥ Documentation Center
⑦ Escapes from Border Strip Buildings
⑧ Chapel of Reconciliation
⑨ Tunnel 57

stood, the Nordbahnhof station straddled both East and West. (For more on its curious predicament, see the sidebar.)

• *Stroll slowly along the path through this first section of the park ("Section A"). Along the way are a number of small sights, remembrances, and exhibits you could stop at, either now or later. As you stroll, you're walking through…*

❸ The "Death Strip" (Section A)

Today's grassy park with a pleasant path through it was once the notorious "death strip" *(Todesstreifen)*. If someone was trying to es-

cape from the East, they'd have to scale one wall (a smaller one, to your right), cross this narrow strip of land, and climb the main Wall (to your left, along Bernauer Strasse). The death strip was an obstacle course of barbed wire, tire-spike strips to stop cars, and other diabolical devices. It was continually patrolled by East German soldiers leading German Shepherds. Armed guards looked down from watchtowers, with orders to shoot to kill. At night, the area was harshly lit by streetlamps—four originals remain standing (just up ahead). Before it was the no-man's-land between the walls, this area was the parish graveyard for a nearby church; ironically, DDR officials had to move a thousand graves from here to create a "death strip."

• *About midway through this section of the park, find the freestanding rusted-iron wall filled with photos of people.*

❹ Wall of Remembrance

The semitransparent photos are of people who died trying to escape East Berlin. You'll see their faces, names, and dates of death (displayed chronologically).

Find **Otfried Reck,** just 17 years old (first panel, top row). On November 27, 1962, he and a friend pried open a ventilation shaft at the boarded-up Nordbahnhof, and descended to the tracks, where they hoped to flag down a passing westbound train. The police discovered them, and Reck was shot in the back. There's a memorial to him now directly across from the Visitors Center.

Ernst Mundt (just left of Otfried) died directly behind you, at the cemetery wall. On September 4, 1962, he rode his bike to the cemetery, which—because of its location near the Wall—was constantly patrolled by guards. He climbed the death strip's inner wall and ran across the top, headed in the direction of the Nordbahnhof and freedom. He was shot in the head, and his hat (the one in the picture) flew off. He died, age 40.

Across the path from the Wall of Remembrance is a row of

The Nordbahnhof "Ghost" Station

This S-Bahn station was one of the "ghost stations" of Cold War Berlin. It was built in 1926, closed in 1961 (although trains kept passing through), and opened again in 1989. When the Wall went up, the station was boarded up by East Germany. West Berlin subway trains had permission to zip through on the underground tracks, but they couldn't stop here, and no one was allowed to get on or off.

Today, the station keeps reminders of its haunted past. Inside, photos posted on the walls compare 1989 with 2009.

As the displays explain, East German border guards, who were stationed here to ensure that nobody got on or off those trains, were themselves locked into their surveillance rooms to prevent their escape. (But one subway employee and his family used the tunnels to walk to the West and freedom.)

At the station's exit to Bernauer Strasse, note the plaques (at the top and bottom of the stairs) that say *Sperrmauer 1961-1989*—"Barrier wall." Back in the 20th century, this exit was blocked—a bricked-off no-man's-land.

overgrown, graffiti-covered, discarded Wall panels. We'll see an intact version soon.

Continue walking through Section A. You're now walking along the original, preserved asphalt patrol path. You pass by those four original streetlamps. You'll also pass a cross marking the Sophien Parish Cemetery. The church cemetery still exists (it's to your right), but the cross marks a section of graves they had to dig up in 1961 to build the death strip.

• *Now, walk across the grass and find a place to get a good close-up look at...*

❺ The Wall

The Wall here is typical of the whole system: about 12 feet tall, made of concrete and rebar, and capped by a rounded pipe that made it tough for escapees to get a grip. The top would have been further adorned with coils of barbed wire.

This was part of a 96-mile-long Wall that encircled West Berlin, making it an island of democracy in communist East Germany. The West Berlin side of the Wall was typically covered with colorful graffiti by free-spirited West Berliners. A few bits of graffiti remain here.

Reach out and touch the Wall...go ahead. Fondle an exposed bit of rebar. Think of the lives lost. Lives wasted. You're touching history.

• *Now, exit the park through the hole in the Wall, turn right along Bernauer Strasse, and make your way a short distance to the crosswalk. Across Bernauer Strasse is a modern grey building with a view terrace, located at #119 (labeled* Gedenkstätte Berliner Mauer*). This is the Berlin Wall Memorial's...*

❻ Documentation Center (Dokumentationszentrum Berliner Mauer)

This excellent museum is geared to a new generation of Berliners who can hardly imagine their hometown split so brutally in two.

The **ground floor** (1961-1988) has photos and displays to explain the logistics of the city's division and its effects. Have a seat and listen to the riveting personal accounts of escapees—and of the border guards armed with machine guns and tasked with stopping them. The next floor up gives the historical and political context behind the Wall's construction and eventual destruction. Immediately, there was a push to preserve that history with a memorial like this. Photos let you track the changes here from 1965 to 1990 (look for the photo of a church being toppled by DDR dynamite—we'll see its successor soon).

At the back of the room, take seven minutes to watch the powerful film *Peaceful Revolution,* which traces the process that led to the Wall's collapse: the 1989 protests in Hungary, Leipzig, Prague, Berlin, and Dresden; the press conference where a bumbling bureaucrat accidentally announced the opening of the Wall "immediately"; the massing of desperate East Berliners at the Bornholmer Strasse crossing of the Wall that very night—and the guards finally shrugging at each other and simply opening the checkpoint; crowds rushing through the Wall, embracing loved ones, climbing up top, and chipping off a chunk; and an awe-filled, wide-eyed East Berliner wandering along the Ku'damm, saying, "Me! In West Berlin!"

Now climb the stairs or take the elevator to the top floor, the **Tower** *(Turm).* From this high viewpoint, you can look across Bernauer Strasse, and down at Berlin's last preserved stretch of the death strip with the original guard tower. More than 100 sentry towers like this one kept a close eye on the Wall. (Full disclosure:

This particular guard tower came from a different part of the Wall. It was actually purchased on that great capitalist invention, eBay. Somewhere, Stalin spins in his grave.) In the far distance, the communist-built TV Tower overlooks the scene like Big Brother.

• *The Documentation Center has a simple café and WCs. Exit and continue on. Cross Bernauer Strasse (where it intersects with Ackerstrasse) and enter the next section of the Memorial park...*

❼ Escapes from Border Strip Buildings (Section B)

At the intersection of cobbled Ackerstrasse and Bernauer Strasse, notice the rectangular markings in the ground (a thin, double strip of metal). These trace the footprint of buildings that stood here along the south side of Bernauer Strasse as the Wall began to go up.

Nearby you'll see a group of information panels—some with text and photos, other with audio and video clips. These are the first of many such information points, which stretch the entire length of the Memorial.

The panels tell the story of what happened right here: On August 13, 1961, the East German government officially closed the border. A sense of dread spread among East Germans, as they feared being permanently trapped under Soviet control. People began fleeing to the parts of Berlin controlled by other European powers—like the French, who held the neighborhood on the north side of Bernauer Strasse.

Over the next few weeks and months, bit by bit, the border hardened. Ackerstrasse was closed to traffic, as East German soldiers laid down rows of barbed wire. They began to evacuate the residents living on the border strip. They bricked up the buildings' street-side entrances so no one could flee. People were suddenly separated from their West Berlin neighbors just across the street.

During this brief window of time (summer of '61 to early '62), there were many escape attempts. (For more on these events and exactly where they happened, read your free Visitors Center brochure on Section B.)

A man stepped out his upper-story window and slid down a rope to Bernauer Strasse, fleeing across the street to freedom (see #B333 in the Visitors Center brochure). In another case, the rope broke, and the escapee was injured...but limped away a free man (#B366). Another man drove his VW bug up Ackerstrasse at high speed. The barbed wire barriers snared the car, but it skidded to a stop in West Berlin territory, and he was free (#B340). Others tried to climb down a manhole on Ackerstrasse and escape through the sewer tunnel, but were caught by border guards (#B376).

After the border-strip buildings were completely evacuated, they were used as escape routes. Two men leap-frogged across several adjoining rooftops and lowered themselves down to Bernauer Strasse (#B354). An East German border guard slipped away from his post, broke into a boarded-up building, and escaped through the window (#B358).

The people of West Berlin did all they could to help people escape. West German first responders were at the ready. A woman called out of the window for the fire department, which came with a ladder to bring her down to freedom (#B377). A man jumped down into the waiting rescue net of firefighters (#B365). A desperate man simply fell three stories from the rooftop onto the pavement of Bernauer Strasse. He was badly injured, but a West Berlin ambulance was there to whisk him to the hospital...and freedom (#B363). Another man slid down a rope to safety as West Berlin police blinded the East German guards with their floodlights. More people escaped as the West Berlin police brandished their weapons while the fire department raised their ladders (#B357).

Most of these escape attempts were in those first few months. By 1962, the residents had been evicted, the buildings demolished, and the formidable Wall was going up. People kept trying to flee, but most later attempts from here ended in arrests (#B383 and #B343). Not everyone survived. On August 22, 1961, Ida Siekmann fell to her death as she jumped from her third-floor apartment at Bernauer Strasse 48, and became the first casualty of the Berlin Wall.

· *Keep going up the path through Section B, to the round building up ahead.*

❽ The Chapel of Reconciliation (Kapelle der Versöhnung)

This modern "Chapel of Reconciliation" stands on the site of the old Church of Reconciliation. Built in 1894, that old Gothic-style church served the neighborhood parish. When the Wall went up, it found itself stranded in the death strip. The congregation had to find another place to worship, and the church was abandoned. Border guards used the steeple as a watchtower. The church became famous in the West as a symbol of how the godless commies had driven out religion and turned a once-great culture into a bleak wasteland. The church itself was finally blown up by the East Germans in 1985, ostensibly because it got in the way of the border guards' sight lines. (In fact, it was one of several churches demolished around this time, to send a message to troublesome Christian protestors.) Little remains of the original church. You can see its footprint traced in the ground around the chapel. The church bells and twisted iron cross are displayed a few paces away. The church was gone, but people on both sides of the Wall continued hoping that someday there'd be a "reconciliation" between East and West.

After the Wall came down, this chapel was built to remember the troubled past and try to heal the memory. Inside the church, the carved wooden altarpiece was saved from the original structure. The chapel hosts daily prayer services for the victims of the Wall.

• *Continue past the chapel into the second portion of Section B.*

Tunnels and More

Walk up the mild incline, then bear left to a large **open-air display** under a canopy (amid the ruins of a destroyed Bernauer Strasse home). Photos, info boards, and press-the-button audio clips explain what it was like to live here, so close to the front line of the Cold War. They paint a stark picture of daily life under oppressive communist rule.

History is all around you. Just steps from where you stand, a man who was attempting to escape was arrested (#B364). Nearby, a family slid down a makeshift rope to safety (#B335). Two more families jumped into fire department nets (#B351 and #B371). Another family barely escaped in the nick of time, fleeing their home just before it was to be bricked up (#B344).

There's also history under your feet: Two escape tunnels were dug near here. Tunnels were one of the many ingenious ways people tried to escape. During the Wall's existence, about 300 people escaped via tunnel.

Head back up to the main path, turn left, and continue. You'll pass two parallel rows of metal slabs, labeled *Fluchttunnel 1964.* This marks the route of the most famous tunnel of all: **❾ Tunnel 57** (named after the 57

people who escaped through it). Its location is marked by rows of metal plates embedded in the ground.

In the spring of 1963, a group of grad students in West Berlin hatched a wild plot to free their friends in the East. They set up their operation in an abandoned West Berlin bakery north of Bernauer Strasse. There they cut a hole in the floor and started tunneling toward the East. They went down 35 feet, then across—under Bernauer Strasse, under the Wall, and under the death strip. After five months of hard labor, they'd hollowed out a tunnel stretching more than 150 yards. Fortunately, when they surfaced, they found themselves safely behind a nondescript building on Streitzler Strasse—about 75 yards south of today's park. The students alerted their friends to get ready to escape.

On Sunday evening, October 3, 1964, the East Berliners began making their way as nonchalantly as possible to the address they'd been given. They gave the password—"Tokyo"—and were ushered inside by the West Berliners, who led them to the tunnel entrance. One by one they went into the narrow, pitch-dark tunnel, crawling on their hands and knees. As the night wore on, suspicions were aroused. East German police descended on Streitzler Strasse. Shots were fired. An East German guard was killed. The West German helpers beat a hasty retreat through the tunnel to safety.

The tunnel was immediately destroyed by the communist authorities. But it had served its purpose—saving 57 lives. Years later, one of the helpers, Reinhard Furrer, look back and reflected on the whole experience. He could view it from a unique perspective—200 miles up, as he orbited the earth on Spacelab (he'd survived the Wall to become an astronaut).

Before you move on, check out the row of modern apartment buildings that abut the south edge of the park. With their bright colors and kids' bikes parked out front, it's clear that the bleak past is fading, and regeneration is well underway.

• *The main part of our walk is done. To experience more of the Memorial, you could continue through Sections C and D, where you'll find more open-air exhibits similar to what we've already seen (explained next).*

But if you're ready to leave the area, the Bernauer Strasse U-Bahn station is just a block further up Bernauer Strasse. Or you can backtrack to the Nordbahnhof. And tram #M10 follows Bernauer Strasse all the way to Eberswalder Strasse, in the heart of Prenzlauer Berg.

The Rest of the Memorial

The last two sections of the Berlin Wall Memorial—with periodic information points—stretch along Bernauer Strasse another four blocks (about two-thirds of a mile) all the way to the Mauerpark. You can easily skip ahead to the Mauerpark—or other sections of the memorial—by hopping on tram #M10 (which runs along Bernauer Strasse, tracing the path of the Memorial; the Friedrich-Ludwig-Jahn-Sportpark stop is right at the Mauerpark).

If you walk, here's what you'll see:

Section C focuses on the building of the Wall: the gradual beefing up of the fortifications; surveillance over the death strip; and metal markings showing the path of two additional escape tunnels.

At the end of this section (at the intersection with Brunnenstrasse, and the Bernauer Strasse U-Bahn stop), one of the most iconic Berlin Wall escape photographs fills the entire wall of a building: teenaged DDR border guard Conrad Schumann, in full uniform and carrying his weapon, running full-tilt and leaping over barbed wire to freedom in the West. He dropped his gun, hopped into a waiting car, and was whisked to safety. This was taken on August 14, 1961—the day after the Wall officially went up—during a narrow window of time when an improvised escape like this was possible. Schumann became a minor celebrity and moved to Bavaria, but always felt conflicted about leaving his parents and siblings behind in East Germany. He committed suicide in 1998.

Finally, **Section D** is nearly as long as the first three sections combined. Here the path cuts a half-block inland, to a strip between buildings that mostly follows an old patrol road (jog right as you cross Brunnenstrasse and look for signs). The theme of this area is everyday life in the shadow of the Berlin Wall, including exhibits about how West Berlin was affected; those who dug tunnels and carried out other activities to help escapees; the soldiers who guarded the Wall; the politics of the Wall (look for the photo of Martin Luther King, Jr. at Bernauer Strasse in 1964); and how the media were used as a tool and a weapon during the Cold War. You'll emerge at Schwedter Strasse, where a building-size photograph shows the people who amassed here on the night of November 9, 1989, eagerly anticipating the opening of the Wall.

The story of **Schwedter Strasse**—and the **Mauerpark** across the street—is explained at the end of the ☐ Prenzlauer Berg Walk (see page 208).

• *From Mauerpark, you can walk two blocks (or ride tram #M10 one stop) to the Eberswalder Strasse U-Bahn stop. In the opposite direction, tram #M10 goes all the way back the way you came, to the Nordbahnhof S-Bahn station.*

FASCISM & COLD WAR WALK

From Checkpoint Charlie to Potsdamer Platz

A variety of fascinating sites relating to Germany's tumultuous 20th century are south of Unter den Linden, clustering in three areas a few blocks apart: Checkpoint Charlie, the most famous Cold War border crossing; the Topography of Terror and former Air Ministry, rare surviving Nazi artifacts; and Potsdamer Platz, a skyscraper jungle representing Berlin's late-20th-century reconciliation, reunification, and rejuvenation. This area is beloved by armchair historians, including people who never cared about history before coming to Berlin (a common affliction).

These sites don't really align chronologically, so as you stroll, keep in mind that we're hopping back and forth between two distinct periods of Germany history: First, the 1930s and early 1940s, when fascism was on the rise—ultimately resulting in Adolf Hitler taking power as Führer, his National Socialism (Nazism) becoming the law of the land, and his brutal SS fighting force being widely feared by Germans and enemies alike. And second, the Cold War that kicked off as Hitler was defeated, dividing a battle-wracked Berlin down the middle into capitalist West and communist East, from the mid-1940s through 1989. (For background on the Berlin Wall, see page 212.)

Orientation

Length of This Walk: Allow about an hour for the walk itself; if also entering the Museum of the Wall or the Topography of Terror, add at least an hour apiece.

When to Go: The walk can be done at any time. If you're pressed for time, you can squeeze this walk in later in the day (the Topography of Terror is open until 20:00, and the Museum of the Wall until 22:00).

Getting There: Ride the U-Bahn to Kochstrasse/Checkpoint Charlie (U6); exit toward *Haus am Checkpoint Charlie*. You'll emerge across the street from the Museum of the Wall, a block south of this walk's starting point. It's also a short walk from Stadtmitte (U2 or U6), or about a 15-minute walk south of Unter den Linden (just head down Friedrichstrasse).

Checkpoint Charlie: The replica checkpoint is free to view and always open (but you'll pay to take photos with the "guards").

Museum of the Wall at Checkpoint Charlie: €12.50, daily 9:00-22:00, last entry one hour before closing.

Topography of Terror: Free, included audioguide explains the outdoor site (ID required), daily 10:00-20:00, outdoor exhibit closes at dusk and closed entirely mid-Oct-mid-April, Niederkirchnerstrasse 8, tel. 030/254-5090, www.topographie.de.

DDR Watchtower: €3.50, open sporadically (though officially daily 11:00-15:00, longer in summer).

Services: There are free WCs at both the Museum of the Wall and the Topography of Terror.

Eateries: Several tourist-oriented eateries (e.g., sausage stands, American fast-food chains) cluster around Checkpoint Charlie and along Zimmerstrasse.

Starring: The Berlin Wall (intact fragments, and a reconstruction of its most famous crossing) and Hitler's crimes (documented on the site where they took place).

The Walk Begins

PART 1: COLD WAR SIGHTS (NEAR CHECKPOINT CHARLIE)

• *Find a spot on a corner at the crowded intersection facing "Checkpoint Charlie." Ideally, stand under the* "You are leaving the American sector" *sign (by the KFC).*

❶ Checkpoint Charlie

For nearly three decades (1961-1989), this was a border crossing between East and West Berlin. It became known worldwide and stood as a symbol of the Cold War itself. Today, the checkpoint and associated buildings are long gone, but a re-creation gives you a sense of what it was like.

The name "Charlie" came about because it was the third checkpoint in a series. Checkpoint A (Alpha) was at the East-

Fascism & Cold War Walk

1. Checkpoint Charlie
2. Museum of the Wall
3. Zimmerstrasse
4. Fragment of the Wall
5. Air Ministry
6. Communist Art
7. Topography of Terror
8. Stresemannstrasse
9. Potsdamer Platz
10. Sony Center

West German border, a hundred miles west of here. Checkpoint B (Bravo) was where people left East Germany and entered the Allied sector of Berlin. This was Checkpoint C (Charlie). Its roots lie in the days immediately after World War II, when this intersection was the border between the US-occupied neighborhood and the Soviet zone. In 1952, the Soviets officially closed the border between East and West Germany, and blocked East Germans from leaving with a fence. But West Berlin was still open until the Wall went up here in 1961. Afterwards, Friedrichstrasse was one of the few places where people could legally pass between East and West—provided they had the proper documents, of course. That generally meant foreigners and officials from the Allies—not East Germans.

The East Germans fortified their side of the checkpoint heavily. There was the Wall, a watchtower, concrete barriers to prevent cars from speeding through, barbed-wire fences, and even a garage where vehicles could be checked for smuggled goods or people. (None of these structures stand today.)

On the US side, there was...Checkpoint Charlie. This was a

humble shack for the document-checking GIs. It sat on a traffic island in the middle of Friedrichstrasse, fortified with a few piles of sandbags. While the actual checkpoint has long since been dismantled, you can see a **mock-up,** with a guard station, sandbags, and a US flag.

There's a replica of the original sign, which warned ominously in several languages: "You are leaving the American sector." Larger-than-life posters show an American soldier facing east and a young Soviet soldier facing west. A couple of actors posing as GIs will take a selfie with you for a fee.

Imagine crossing this checkpoint as a Western visitor. Any friends you have in West Berlin desperately load you up with care packages (and possibly contraband) to deliver to their loved ones in the East. While you know you're not the target of the machine gun-toting guards on watchtowers, approaching the border is still a frightening experience. Upon crossing, you're required to change a certain amount of Deutschmarks into Ostmarks (the East German equivalent), at a ridiculous rate—winding up with far more money than you could possibly spend (since there's very little to buy in the East). You enter a room where the guards might search you if they think you're hiding contraband or foreign currency. At last, your passport gets stamped, and you're allowed to go.

Stepping from West to East is the opposite of Dorothy opening the door to Oz: From a world of color, vibrancy, and freedom, you're plunged into a monochromatic, soot-stained scene, with beaten-down people always looking over their shoulders. You keep an eye on the clock, since there is a strict limit to how much time you can be here. Finally, after spending or giving away your last Ostmarks (you're forbidden to take any back), you retreat at day's end to the safety of the West.

Lots of dramatic history has happened on this spot. In 1961, a car came speeding up Friedrichstrasse, crashed through the East German barriers, and made it to freedom. In 1962, Peter Fechter tried running to the West through no-man's-land, but got tangled in barbed wire, was shot, and was left there, where he bled to death with the whole world watching—the first high-profile casualty of the Berlin Wall. Numerous brave escapees snuck their way through this checkpoint with forged documents, or hidden inside cars, or other ingenious schemes.

Checkpoint Charlie was a flashpoint in the Cold War. Here, US and East German soldiers could stare each other down, separated by only a few dozen yards of barbed wire. In 1961, 10 US tanks faced off here against 10 Soviet tanks...before cooler heads (and negotiations by Robert F. Kennedy) prevailed, thankfully averting a possible World War III. In 1963, President John F. Kennedy came to this spot to show solidarity with the embattled West Berliners.

Today, the area around Checkpoint Charlie has become a kind of Cold War freak show and kitschy tourist trap. Sidewalk vendors nearby sell Cold War-era memorabilia—chunks of the Wall, Soviet and US medals, DDR-era soft-serve ice cream, and so on. Be-

FASCISM WALK

ware: Hustlers charge an exorbitant €10 for a Cold War-era stamp in your passport. Be warned: Technically, this invalidates your passport—which has caused some tourists big problems.

As if celebrating the final victory of crass capitalism, a McDonald's now defiantly overlooks the scene. Even the larger-than-life posters are fake: the so-called "Soviet" soldier is actually a Dutch model, photographed years after the fall of the USSR, wearing a nonsensical uniform of random medals, with a Russian (not Soviet) flag on his shoulder.

But the history here is real. For a more sober look at the checkpoint's history, the Wall, and the many daring escape attempts, visit the Museum of the Wall at Checkpoint Charlie (listed next).

• *A half-block past Checkpoint Charlie, on the left, is the entrance to the...*

❷ Museum of the Wall at Checkpoint Charlie

The museum traces the history of the famous border crossing, with a focus on the many brave and clever escape attempts over, under, and through the Wall.

More than that, the museum itself is a piece of Cold War history. Since 1962, this exhibit has stood here defiantly—within spitting distance of the border guards—showing the whole world the tragedy of the Wall. During the years of the Cold War, many famous people came here just to show their solidarity with West Berliners and lovers of freedom.

Today, the yellowed descriptions, which have scarcely changed since that time, tinge the museum with nostalgia. Hunks of the Wall stand like trophies at its door. The mazelike museum itself feels like an artifact: cluttered, cramped, dusty, disorganized, and overpriced, with lots of reading involved. While the museum is not for everyone (and serious historians will prefer the more thoughtful 📖 Berlin Wall Memorial Tour), the Museum of the Wall has retro charm and tells its escape stories well. If you'd like to visit, you'll find more information on page 52.

• *Outside the museum, at the giant "You are leaving" sign, you're at the cross street called Zimmerstrasse. We'll turn left and follow Zimmerstrasse a couple of blocks. Along the way are several Cold War sightseeing options.*

The Trabi

Communist East Germany (a.k.a. the DDR) is forever linked to its trademark automobile—the Trabant, or, affectionately, the Trabi (TRAH-bee). Built in Zwickau, Saxony, starting in 1957, the Trabi was the DDR's big play to compete with the popular West German Volkswagen Beetle. But its design and engineering (limited by a centrally planned economy) were nowhere near VW standards.

A ride in a Trabi was cramped, bumpy, and smelly. To gas up your Trabi, you'd open the hood and pour a gas-oil mix into a tank above the two-cylinder, two-stroke engine, which used gravity instead of a fuel pump. The body was made of a re-cycled, cloth-reinforced plastic resin called Duroplast. (So the body was as "green" as the engine was polluting.) On the upside, the construction was so simple that handy East Germans (who, out of necessity, were excellent do-it-yourselfers) could fix just about any problem with a hammer, a screwdriver, and a wrench. Production was limited, so the privilege of owning a Trabi required you to sign up on a waiting list and be prepared to wait many, many years.

In the summer of 1989, when Hungary suddenly opened its borders, whole fleets of Trabis were left behind by East Germans who went to vacation on Lake Balaton...and decided to flee West, never to come home. The Trabi remained in production until 1991, totaling more than three million cardboard boxes with lawnmower engines on Eastern Europe's roads.

The best thing about the Trabi were the jokes it generated:

• Why is the Trabi the world's quietest car? Because your knees cover your ears.

• How do you double a Trabi's value? Fill the tank.

• "I'd like two windshield wipers for my Trabi." "Sounds like a fair trade."

• How many workers does it take to build a Trabi? Three: One to cut, one to fold, and one to paste.

• Why is the Trabi's back window heated? To keep your hands warm while pushing.

• When does a Trabi reach top speed? When it's being towed.

• What's the longest car on the market? The Trabi, of course, at 60 feet long—6 feet of car and 54 feet of smoke.

Who says Germans don't have a sense of humor?

Like the *Ampelmann* (traffic-light man), the Trabi is enjoying a renaissance as a bit of "Ost-algic" communist kitsch. Old Trabis are being rehabilitated and souped up for tourist trips. Just be ready to get out and push.

❸ Zimmerstrasse—A Cold War Carnival

Zimmerstrasse—connecting Checkpoint Charlie to the Topography of Terror area—has lots of touristy attractions. These range from thoughtful to tacky, and from free to overpriced...but all of them are skippable. Note that this area continues to be developed, so most of these attractions are, to some degree, temporary.

Radiating out from the corner of Zimmerstrasse and Friedrichstrasse, you'll see several **information posters** that offer a helpful visualization of Checkpoint Charlie history—with illustrations, maps, and descriptions of the history here. While you could get this information from a book, seeing it here helps bring meaning to this place.

At the same corner, facing the Checkpoint Charlie action, are two paid exhibits: **Black Box Cold War** displays a few artifacts

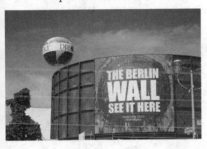

and documents on Checkpoint Charlie and the Wall, but essentially repeats information in better museums around town. Across the street, **The Wall: The Asisi Panorama** is an oversized, 360-degree panorama illustration (by local artist Yadegar Asisi) that immerses you in a re-creation of the Kreuzberg neighborhood in the shadow of the Wall. While impressive, it's outrageously overpriced.

From here, head west down Zimmerstrasse (past the panorama building). You're walking along the former "death strip," the no-man's-land between the inner and outer layers of the Wall. Along the left side of the street, you can see the **double row of cobbles** marking the exact route of the Berlin Wall. Cobbles like this trace a route of 25 miles through the city (of the 96 miles total).

We'll follow Zimmerstrasse (and its cobbles) two blocks, passing more temptations: The **Trabi Museum,** on the left at #14

(about the oft ridiculed East-German tin-can car); **Trabi World,** farther along on the right (where you can book a Berlin tour in a Trabi, or even rent one); and the "Die Welt" **balloon ride,** offering aerial views over Berlin.

Notice that many of these attractions fill vacant lots—undeveloped prime real estate in the very heart of Berlin. Thanks to such a complicated history, it can still be difficult to establish ownership. Under the Nazis, Jews were forced to sell their property. After the war, the Soviets occupied it. Then the DDR government seized private property, which was occupied (but not technically "owned") by private citizens. And after the fall of the Wall, many East Berliners flocked west, while adventurous young West Germans came here to squat in abandoned property and claim it as their own. So who owns it today? While Germany has made great progress in fairly redistributing property, some question marks remain.

• *Soon, where the road becomes Niederkirchnerstrasse, those sidewalk cobbles dead-end at an actual, surviving...*

❹ Fragment of the Berlin Wall

Intact segments of the Berlin Wall are rare in this high-rent downtown area. This block-long section survived because it abuts the ruins of a Nazi building (the

SS and Gestapo headquarters) that was intentionally left as a memorial, while the rest of the death strip was razed and rebuilt. This stretch of the Wall is especially evocative because, with its holes, you can see its rebar innards. This fit the DDR mantra of "cheap but efficient" for constructing the 96 miles of Wall that surrounded West Berlin. The tube-shaped top made it difficult for escapees to get a grip or attach a grappling hook. The heavy L-shaped slab bases both supported the weight of the Wall and prevented easily tunneling underneath.

But that didn't stop people from going over the Wall—*high* over. Notice the tall, blocky office building across the street from the Wall—the former Air Ministry building. In July of 1965, a young, seemingly "model DDR" couple climbed to the roof, tied tennis racket strings to a hammer, and threw it across the wall. Their West Berlin relatives on the other side secured the line, and the couple zipped to freedom.

• *This Berlin Wall section stands near the heart of Hitler's political and military administration. The next two sites are on either side of the Wall.*

PART 2: FASCISM SITES (NEAR THE TOPOGRAPHY OF TERROR)

We'll begin our look at Nazi sites with the huge Air Ministry building—on your right as you face the fragment of the Wall. (This is fitting, since this same building was used by both the Nazis and the communists—bridging this tour's two historic themes.)

• *Turn right and head down Wilhelmstrasse (with the massive building on your left, and the vacant lot on your right). Pause when you reach the main courtyard of that building, set back behind a heavy fence.*

❺ Former Air Ministry (Reichsluftfahrtministerium)

The only major Hitler-era government building that survived the war's bombs, this once housed the headquarters of the Nazi Luftwaffe (Air Force). The building—completed in 1936 and designed by Ernst Sagebiel—exemplifies Hitler's bigger-is-better, fascist aesthetic. It's designed to intimidate...to make the average person feel small and powerless. This is what much of Berlin looked like back when Germany occupied nearly all of Europe. (The courtyard is often used by modern film producers needing a Nazi backdrop.)

Large as it is, this building was constructed mostly in secret. Imagine: It's the mid-1930s in Berlin. Hitler has just come to power as chancellor, then grabs even more (with the Reichstag fire) to become Führer. But Germany—just 15 years removed from its loss in World War I—is still subject to the Treaty of Versailles. One of the treaty's provisions is that Germany is not allowed to have an air force. But Hitler and his military leader, Hermann Göring, have a secret "Four Year Plan" to re-arm Germany, including the re-creation of the Luftwaffe. In the summer of 1936, the world comes to Berlin for the Olympics...and sees that Germany now has an Air Ministry. Hitler is probing, provoking, testing...will anyone put a stop to it? They do not. Later that same year, Hitler remilitarizes the Rhineland—another illegal act. And again, nobody has the will to push back. Historians cite that pivotal year—1936—as the moment when Hitler realized how much he could get away with, emboldening him to build an empire. While all-out war was still years away, 1936 was the turning point when Hitler went on the offensive. And it all began with the Air Ministry.

After the war, this building became the headquarters for the Soviet occupation. And it was right here, on October 7, 1949, that the German Democratic Republic (a.k.a. communist East Germany) was officially founded. The DDR used the building to house their—no joke—Ministry of Ministries. In this building, on June 15, 1961, East German Premier Walter Ulbricht reassured nervous East Berliners, "Nobody has any intention of building a wall." Less than two months later, the first bricks were laid. (Today, the building houses the German Finance Ministry.)

Across the street from the main courtyard, look for the information kiosk with a series of **video screens.** It can be hard to envision the weighty history at a monumental site like this, but these screens help—showing original footage of historic moments for 1914 through 2014 (that's World War I to Angela Merkel).

• *Continue to the far end of the giant building. There, at the corner with Leipziger Strasse, you'll find a small plaza cut into the structure.*

Look under the Air Ministry's portico to find a wonderful (and unusually well-preserved) example of ❻ **communist art.** The

mural, Max Lingner's *Aufbau der Republik* (*Building the Republic*, 1953), is classic Socialist Realism, showing the entire society—industrial laborers, farm workers, women, and children—all happily singing the same patriotic song. Its subtitle: "The importance of peace for the cultural development of humanity and the necessity of struggle to achieve this goal."

This was the communist ideal. The reality was quite different. When the DDR barricaded its borders with West Germany in 1952, the economy floundered—and it quickly became clear that the West was better off. After Josef Stalin died in March of 1953, people across the Eastern Bloc hoped for change. On June 16 of that year, workers who were busy constructing the ambitious Soviet-style boulevard "Stalinallee" (now Karl-Marx-Allee) laid down their tools, went on strike, and marched to this square to demand change. (Look at the ground in the courtyard in front of the mural to see an enlarged photograph from that demonstration—a stark contrast with the idealized mural.) The next day—June 17—a general strike went into effect across East Germany. But the uprising never had a chance to gain momentum—it was shut down by Soviet tanks. Today the square is officially named the "Square of the Popular Uprising of 1953."

• *Now backtrack all the way along the former Air Ministry, to the fragment of Wall we saw earlier. Just beyond it is a modern building that stands in a vast, gravel-filled lot.*

❼ Topography of Terror (Topographie des Terrors)

This museum stands on what was once the most feared address in Berlin: the Gestapo and SS headquarters. This is where Hit-

ler's reign of terror was hatched, where prisoners were detained and tortured, and where Heinrich Himmler plotted the Final Solution. (Today, virtually nothing survives from that time. The stark, gray, boxy museum building before you is completely new.)

Heinrich Himmler's SS State

Hitler's right-hand man was Heinrich Himmler (1900-1945). Among Hitler's inner circle, Hermann Göring was the military mastermind, Martin Bormann was the chief of staff concerned with domestic matters, and Joseph Goebbels was the propagandist. But the close-cropped, bespectacled Himmler—who looked more like a meek accountant than a war criminal—was responsible for the most despicable legacy of the Nazis: He controlled both the SS and the Gestapo and was the primary architect of the Holocaust. And all of this took place right here, on the site of today's Topography of Terror.

This was the headquarters of the Reich Main Security Office, or *Reichssicherheitshauptamt* (RSHA), under Himmler's command. Their mission was to fight "enemies of the state" both inside and outside Germany—a terrifyingly broad authority that Himmler wielded unrelentingly.

Himmler oversaw three interrelated organizations: The Gestapo *(Geheime Staatspolizei)* was a secret state police force. The SS *(Schutzstaffel)* began as Hitler's personal bodyguards and evolved into a dreaded paramilitary force (the *Waffen-SS*). The less-well-known SD *(Sicherheitsdienst)* was the Nazi intelligence agency, which spied on foreign governments but also on their own German people to root out spies and traitors. Together, they amounted to a state-within-a-state, with talons in every corner of German society. The Gestapo, SS, and SD were considered omnipotent, omnipresent, and omniscient. The threat of *Schutzhaft* ("protective custody") was enough to terrify civilians into compliance.

The Nazi worldview was rooted in the idealistic notion of a *Volksgemeinschaft* ("people's community") of a purely Germanic culture and race—which empowered Hitler to create a pervasive illusion that "we're all in this together." Anyone who was not an Aryan was *Untermensch*—subhuman—and must be treated as such.

It was from these headquarters that Himmler administered the concentration camps, where enemies of the state were rounded up, imprisoned, and worked to death. And later, it was from here that the Nazis firmed up plans for their genocide of Jews. Himmler and his SS were specifically tasked with the "racial purification" of German-held lands, especially Eastern Europe: the "Final Solution to the Jewish Question." Special concentration camps were set up specifically to murder Jews by the thousands—super-efficient factories for the mass production of death.

Himmler oversaw everything from his giant office building, where bureaucrats clocked in and dispassionately documented it all in triplicate. The cold-blooded paper-pushing at this site is what philosopher Hannah Arendt had in mind when she originated the phrase "the banality of evil."

FASCISM WALK

The Topography of Terror is one of the few memorial sites that focuses on the perpetrators rather than the victims of the Nazis. It's chilling to see just how seamlessly and bureaucratically the Nazi institutions and state structures merged to become a well-oiled terror machine. There are few actual artifacts displayed, but the site itself is powerful, and the exhibits are excellent. Photos and good English descriptions take you chronologically through the rise of Nazism, and the repression of all dissent through the organizations headquartered here.

Visiting the Museum: The museum has displays both inside and outdoors. Start inside, in the entrance lobby, with a **model** of the neighborhood. (We're standing at #20.) Back in the 1930s and '40s, this was just one of many governmental office buildings along Wilhelmstrasse. Seeing this sprawling bureaucratic quarter gives you a sense of how much mundane paperwork was involved in administering Hitler's reign of terror in an efficient, rational way. (Nearby, the dry introductory film is skippable.)

Stepping into the **main room,** you begin a chronological journey (with a timeline of events, old photographs, documents, and newspaper clippings) through the rise of Nazism, the reign of terror, the start of World War II, and the Holocaust. The displays illustrate how Hitler, Himmler, and their team expertly manipulated the German people to build a broadly supported "dictatorship of consent." You'll learn about the web of intersecting organizations whose duties were run from here. And you'll learn about the Gestapo, SS *(Schutzstaffel),* and SD *(Sicherheitsdienst),* and about their brutal methods—including their chillingly systematic implementation of the Holocaust.

Some images here are indelible. Gleeful SS soldiers, stationed at Auschwitz, yuk it up on a retreat in the countryside (as their helpless prisoners were being gassed and burned a few miles away). A German woman, head shaved, is publicly humiliated for fraternizing with a Polish prisoner. On a street corner, jeering SS troops cut off the beard of an elderly Jewish man. A Roma woman's eye color is carefully analyzed by a doctor performing "racial evaluation." Graphic images show executions—by hanging, firing squad, and so on.

The exhibits end, mercifully, with the end of the war in 1945. A photo shows this former building in total ruins. The finale is a wall of colored cards used in collecting data for the postwar trials of the people who worked here. While the Nazi leadership was captured and prosecuted at the Nürnberg trials, the vast majority of midlevel bureaucrats who worked in this building—and who routinely facilitated genocide with the flick of a pen—were never brought to justice.

Before heading outside, ask at the information desk for the free audioguide. Also downstairs is a WC and a library with research books on these topics.

Outside, in the trench that runs along the surviving stretch of Wall, you'll find the exhibit called **Berlin 1933-1945: Between Propaganda and Terror** (occasionally replaced by special exhibits). The photos and placards (which overlap slightly with the indoor exhibit) focus on Berlin, from the post-WWI Weimar Republic through the ragged days just after World War II. One display explains how Nazis invented holidays (or injected new Aryan meaning into existing ones) as a means of winning over the public. Another section covers the "Aryanization" of Jewish businesses: They were simply taken over by the state and handed over to new Aryan owners. You'll read about Hitler's plans for converting Berlin into a World Capital of gigantic buildings—the "Welthauptstadt Germania." The exhibit even covers some of postwar Berlin, including the Berlin Airlift, which brought provisions to some 2.2 million West Berliners whose supply lines were cut off by the Soviets (for more on the airlift, see page 63). With more time, use the audioguide and posted signs to explore the grounds around the blocky building.

On one part of the grounds you'll find the excavated (and pretty scant) remains of the **basement prison cells.** The building was equipped with dungeons, where the Gestapo detained and tortured thousands of prisoners. The general public knew what went on here, and it sent a message.

• *Exit the Topography of Terror out the far end from where you entered—just past the end of the Wall fragment. You'll pop out on Niederkirchner-strasse. Turn left and walk about a block, passing some important buildings. On the left, at #7, is the fanciful **Martin-Gropius-Bau**—designed by a relative of Walter Gropius of Bauhaus-style fame. On the right is the*

FASCISM WALK

Berlin House of Representatives—*the government for the "city-state" of Berlin. Notice the three flags flying out front: the EU, Germany, and Berlin (a black bear on a red-and-white background).*

After a long block, you'll end at Stresemannstrasse. Turn right and walk toward the DB Tower.

❽ Berlin Wall Sights Along Stresemannstrasse

Once the course of the Wall (notice the cobbles running under parked cars across the street), and long since renovated, this otherwise boring street hides a few interesting Berlin Wall-era landmarks.

A half-block down the street, look left (across the street) to see Köthener Strasse. This is home to the famous **"Studio at the Wall"** (Honsa Tonstudio). Just barely inside West Berlin, the haunting acoustics and historic vibe of this music studio attracted artists the likes of David Bowie (*Low*, "Heroes"), Iggy Pop *(Lust for Life)*, Depeche Mode *(Some Great Reward),* and U2 *(Achtung Baby)* to record here...while watching the eerie sight of heavily armed East German border guards on patrol, just up the street.

Continue almost all the way to the end of the block. The second building on your right (at #128) is the Ministry of the Environment (Bundesministerium für Umwelt). At the far end of the building—almost to the corner—look through the modern building's glass walls to see a graffitied stretch of the **inner Wall,** which worked in concert with the larger outer wall (across the street) to create an impenetrable death strip.

If you're a Wall aficionado, consider a five-minute detour to see a rare surviving watchtower: Just past the inner wall fragment, turn right up Erna-Berger-Strasse. After a long block, on the left side of the street, you'll see a lonely concrete **DDR watchtower**—one of many such towers built in 1966 for panoramic surveillance and deterrence. Note the rifle windows, allowing shots to be fired in 360 degrees. It was constantly manned by two guards. The guards were forbidden to get to know each other (no casual chatting), so they could effectively guard each other from escaping. This is one of only a few such towers still standing. You can pay to enter the tower's tiny interior and peek out its windows.

Back on Stresemannstrasse, continue a few steps farther, then pause and look left (across the street) to spot a large **stone block** in the middle of the sidewalk, in front of Potsdamer Platz 10. This was placed in 1951 as the base for a planned statue of German communist pioneer Karl Liebknecht. But when the Berlin Wall went up, this was in the middle of the death strip—halting all further plans. (The block is still engraved with Liebknecht's name.)

PART 3: THE TRIUMPH OF DEMOCRACY AND CAPITALISM

• *On Stresemannstrasse, keep going toward all those skyscrapers. At the big intersection, use the crosswalk (or the pedestrian underpass) to cross over to the big plaza at the base of the towers. Position yourself by the small clock tower, near the big glass tubes, midway between the two cubical S-Bahn entrances marked* Bahnhof Potsdamer Platz. *This is...*

⓿ Potsdamer Platz

Before World War II, Potsdamer Platz was the "Times Square of Berlin," and possibly the busiest square in all Europe. But it was pulverized in World War II, and stood at the intersection of the American, British, and Soviet postwar sectors. When the Wall went up, the platz was cut in two and left a deserted no-man's land for 40 years. As throughout Berlin, two subtle lines in the pavement indicate where the Wall once stood. With reunification, a redevelopment campaign was immediately begun (christened by a 1990 concert of Pink Floyd's *The Wall*). Since then, Sony, Daimler, and other major corporations have turned the square once again into a city center. Like great

Christian churches built upon pagan holy grounds, Potsdamer Platz—with its corporate logos flying high and shiny above what was the Wall—trumpets the triumph of capitalism.

The green hexagonal **clock tower** is a replica of the first electronic traffic light in Europe, which once stood at the six-street intersection of Potsdamer Platz. The traffic cops who stood with flag and trumpet in the middle of the intersection were getting hit by cars too routinely, so this perch was built for them.

Take in the **skyscrapers** around you—representing the rousing recovery of Berlin from its miserable 20th century. Start with the easy-to-spot DB Tower—a curved, green-glass, crescent-shaped building. This is the corporate headquarters for Deutsche Bahn, the national train system. Jutting out behind the DB building is the (much lower) tent-like roofline of the Sony Center—more on that later.

To the right of the DB Tower is the Beisheim Center. Its twin, blocky-grey buildings are meant to recall the early skyscrapers of 1920s-era Chicago. The Beishem Center hosts ritzy hotels, offices, and a shopping mall beneath (accessed via the *Bahnhof* entrances).

To the left of the DB Tower is the 25-story, red-brick Potsdamer Platz 1 building. It's better known as the Kollhoff Tower, named for the architect who built it. Though it looks like a retro Art Deco building from 1920s New York, it was built in 1999. This plays host to Daimler-Benz and big-name law firms. You can go up the tower to the Panorampunkt for great views (see page 73).

The next skyscraper to the left is the glass-wedge, 18-story Forum Tower. It's by Renzo Piano, the renowned Italian architect who created the master plan for the entire Potsdamer Platz renovation. (Architecture students who want more could walk a few steps south of Potsdamer Platz to Linkstrasse 2 to find Richard Rogers' practical-yet-elegant buildings housing more Daimler offices.)

Now turn your attention to the **street level** of Potsdamer Platz. The slanted glass cylinders sticking out of the ground help light the underground train station. Mirrors on the tops of the tubes move with the sun to collect light and send it underground, saving piles of euros in energy costs. Futuristic as it is today, the Potsdamer Platz station was once one of the Cold War-era "ghost stations"—West Berlin trains passed through, but nobody was allowed on or off.

The street running between the red-brick Kollhoff Tower and the glass-wedge Forum Tower is **Alte Potsdamer Strasse.** This tree-lined boulevard tries to re-create some of the charm of the prewar Potsdamer Platz...with venerable establishments like McDonald's, Tony Roma's, and Starbucks. The Haus-Huth (on the left, at #5) is a hundred-year-old wine merchant shop that's one of the few structures to survive the bombs of WWII. Today it's a classy place for a coffee and sandwich (operated by respected local restaurant chain Lutter & Wegner). At the far end of the street is a theater dedicated to Berlin's homegrown siren of the silver screen, Marlene Dietrich.

• *For the grand (capitalist) finale of our walk, we'll continue to a shopping mall and entertainment complex that embody the last generation's changes in Berlin. It's tucked behind the towering Deutsche Bahn skyscraper—cross the street, head back behind the tower, and enter...*

❿ Sony Center

The complex sits under a grand canopy, designed to evoke Mount Fuji. At night, multicolored floodlights play on the underside of this tent. There's a Lego-land and other touristy attractions. Office workers and tourists eat here by the fountain, enjoying the parade of people. The modern Bavarian Lindenbräu beer hall—the Sony boss wanted a *Brauhaus*—serves traditional food. Across the plaza, Josty Bar is built around a surviving bit of a venerable hotel that was a meeting place for Berlin's rich and famous before the bombs (preserved in the glass box to the right of the entrance).

The Sony Center is a hub for Berlin's thriving cinema scene. It hosts red-carpet events, where major stars come to greet fans and promote their latest movie. Berlin has a major film festival ("Berlinale") each February. And there are several movie theaters here, along with the **Deutsche Kinemathek Film and TV Museum** (described on page 72). A huge screen shows big sporting events on special occasions. (Otherwise it runs historic video clips of Potsdamer Platz through the decades.)

For all the attempts to make Potsdamer Platz a "city center" like it once was...it isn't. The corporate-sponsored buildings feel pretty soulless. But then, Berlin has never had a single "main square" the way, say, Munich has its Marienplatz. Berlin is more a collection of former towns that now comprise dozens of distinct neighborhoods—Prenzlauer Berg, Charlottenburg, Savignyplatz, Kreuzberg, and so on. Potsdamer Platz may not be Berlin's "center," but it is a major hub for transportation and shopping. The place remains lively after dark—a sure sign something must be happening here. Locals are unimpressed by the grandeur and the overpriced tourist restaurants, but they do admit, it's a good place to catch a movie.

• *You've survived this historical minefield of terrible topography and jarring architecture, representing the full span of Berlin's 20th century.*

Potsdamer Platz is a major transportation hub, with S-Bahn, U-Bahn, and bus connections all over the city. Art lovers are a short stroll away from the **Kulturforum**—boasting some of Berlin's best museum collections, from Old Masters (the Gemäldegalerie) and decorative arts to musical instruments. It's about a 10-minute walk from here, just past the far end of Sony Center; 📖 see the Gemäldegalerie and Kulturforum Tour chapter.

FASCISM WALK

GEMÄLDEGALERIE & KULTURFORUM TOUR

The Kulturforum, with its collection of various museums, libraries, and concert halls, rivals Museum Island as Berlin's cultural heart. Established after many of the city's artistic treasures were lost behind the Wall, the Kulturforum's modernist buildings were mostly erected in the 1960s. Today, its collections pick up where those of Museum Island leave off, covering art from the late Middle Ages to the present.

The main sight here is the **Gemäldegalerie**—a world-class collection of European paintings that ranks alongside great museums anywhere. Here you'll see works by Rembrandt, Dürer, Vermeer, Rubens, and others. There aren't a lot of "must-see" iconic paintings, but visitors with some background in art will find many that are instantly recognizable.

The Kulturforum's next-best sight is the **Decorative Arts Museum,** a breezy look at an assortment of beautiful objects through the ages. You'll see jeweled medieval reliquaries, elegant Louis XIV furniture, and a parade of ladies' dresses that even lowbrow tourists find interesting.

The complex is also home to the **Musical Instruments Museum,** the **Berlin Philharmonic's concert hall,** and the Mies van der Rohe-designed **New National Gallery** (closed for renovation).

Orientation

Combo-Ticket: Each Kulturforum museum has a separate ticket (listed below). If you're visiting at least two of the museums, get the €12 combo-ticket, which covers all the museums listed here (can cost more if a special exhibit is on, www. kulturforum-berlin.de).

Planning Your Visit to the Kulturforum

To hit the main highlights of the Kulturforum's collections, start by orienting yourself to the various buildings of the sprawling campus. Start at the Gemäldegalerie with its collection of world-class paintings (allow an hour). When you're done there, head next door to the Museum of Decorative Arts or to the Musical Instruments Museum, just a block away (allow 30-45 minutes each).

Supplement my descriptions in this chapter with the maps and audioguides available at each museum.

When to Go: The museums are rarely crowded—anytime works well.

Getting There: The Kulturforum is a 10-minute walk from Potsdamer Platz: Ride the S-Bahn or U-Bahn to Potsdamer Platz, walk west along Potsdamer Strasse, then turn right on Scharounstrasse to enter the heart of the complex. (On your way from Potsdamer Platz to the Kulturforum, consider detouring into the Sony Center—it's right on the way.) It's efficient to combine your Kulturforum visit with my 📖 Fascism and Cold War Walk).

From Zoologischer Garten or Alexanderplatz, take bus #200 to the Philharmonie stop (a very slow trip during rush hour.)

Gemäldegalerie: €10, Tue-Fri 10:00-18:00, Thu until 20:00, Sat-Sun 11:00-18:00, closed Mon, Matthäikirchplatz 4, tel. 030/266-424-242, www.smb.museum.

Museum of Decorative Arts: €8, Tue-Fri 10:00-18:00, Sat-Sun 11:00-18:00, closed Mon, Herbert-von-Karajan-Strasse 10, tel. 030/266-424-242, www.smb.museum/kgm.

Musical Instruments Museum: €6, Tue-Fri 9:00-17:00, Thu until 20:00, Sat-Sun 10:00-17:00, closed Mon, low-profile white building east of the big yellow Berlin Philharmonic concert hall (easy to miss entrance is down Ben-Gurion-Strasse, facing the back of the Sony Center), tel. 030/2548-1178, www.sim.spk-berlin.de.

New National Gallery: Closed for years-long renovation; for the latest, consult www.smb.museum.

Berlin Philharmonic: You can visit the concert hall with a guided one-hour **tour** in English (€5, daily at 13:30 except none July-Aug, same-day tickets sold at 12:00 at the artists' entrance—facing the busy road and the park). Popular, free **lunch concerts** are held in the lobby most Tuesdays at 13:00 (none July-Aug; tickets available same-day only—try to arrive by 12:00). Box office open Mon-Fri 15:00-18:00, Sat-Sun

Potsdamer Platz & Kulturforum Area

11:00-14:00 except closed July-Aug, tel. 030/2548-8999—answered daily 9:00-18:00, July-Aug until 16:00, www.berliner-philharmoniker.de).

Getting Oriented: Locate the Kulturforum's various buildings by first finding the green steeple of the St. Matthaus Church. Just to the left and beyond the church is the glass-walled New National Gallery. Panning to the right of the church, you find the low-lying, sprawling Gemäldegalerie—this area's highlight. Further right is the cubical Museum of Decorative Arts. Then comes the golden, angular Philharmonic concert hall. Behind the concert hall (not really visible from here) is the Musical Instruments Museum (entered from Ben-Gurion-Strasse).

Tours: Each museum has a good, free audioguide; for insights beyond my tour, pick one up as you enter.

Services: You'll find free lockers and a cloakroom at the Gemäldegalerie.

Cuisine Art/Eateries: The Gemäldegalerie has a decent $$ cafeteria/salad bar (upstairs, cash only); otherwise, you'll find touristy eateries a 10-minute walk away, around Potsdamer Platz and the Sony Center.

Starring: European masters, musical instruments, glittering treasury items, and women's fashion through the ages.

Gemäldegalerie

The Gemäldegalerie—literally the "Painting Gallery"—is Germany's top collection of 13th- to 18th-century European paintings (more than 1,400 canvases). They're beautifully displayed on one

Gemäldegalerie Tour

① **HOLBEIN** - Merchant Georg Gisze

② **DURER** - Holzschuher & Muffel

③ **CRANACH** - Fountain of Youth

④ **VAN DER WEYDEN** - Portrait of a Young Woman

⑤ **RUBENS** - Various Paintings

⑥ **HALS** - Catharina Hooft & Malle Babbe

⑦ **REMBRANDT** - Various Paintings

⑧ **VERMEER** - Girl with a Pearl Necklace & The Glass of Wine

⑨ **CARAVAGGIO** - Amore Vincit Omnia & **BAGLIONE** - Sacred and Profane Love

vast floor in a building that's a work of art in itself. Virtually every major European artist has at least one quality work, and connoisseurs could spend days here. The focus here is on Northern art, especially German (Holbein, Cranach, and Dürer) and Dutch (Rembrandt and Vermeer), with a few Italians and others thrown in.

SELF-GUIDED TOUR

This "top dozen-or-so highlights tour" will get you started. I've selected artists and paintings that are famous, unique, and fairly easy to find in this sprawling museum. But you'll walk past many more fine paintings in the Gemäldegalerie's extensive collection. To go beyond my choices, make ample use of the excellent included audioguide.

When you buy your ticket, pick up the current museum map to help you locate specific paintings (which can move around; be flexible). Northern Art is on one side (where we'll begin) and Italian art is on the other (where we'll end).

Note that inner rooms have Roman numerals (I, II, III), while adjacent outer rooms use Arabic numerals (1, 2, 3). We'll work counterclockwise (and roughly chronologically) through the collection.

• *From the entrance, turn right through Rooms I and II, then turn right again into* **Room 1** *(not Room I—got it?).*

Northern Art

The German paintings that fill Rooms 1-4 and I-III are a snapshot of Germany in the early 1500s. The many portraits of middle-class businessmen and town burghers are a testament to Germany's booming trade and craftsmanship. In those days, the austere Protestant Reformation was brewing, and there are few bubbly paintings of Madonnas and saints. Artistically, the style is realistic and down to earth. Colors are dark, and there's a meticulous attention to detail. Many depicted items are symbolic, with meanings passed down since medieval times.

❶ Hans Holbein the Younger, 1497-1543

Typical of German painting of the period is work by Hans Holbein. Holbein's sober, unvarnished portraits chronicle the movers and shakers of the early 1500s, from Martin Luther to Erasmus to Henry VIII.

Holbein's portrait *Merchant Georg Gisze* (*Der Kaufmann Georg Gisze*, 1532) depicts a wealthy 34-year-old German businessman. Gisze glances up from his work in his Hanseatic branch office in London. His black beret and immaculate clothes mark him as a successful dealer in cloth. Around him are the tools of his trade—logbooks, business letters with wax seals, signet rings, scales, and coins. The Turkish tablecloth and Venetian-glass vase remind us of Gisze's cosmopolitan tastes.

Holbein adds another layer of complexity to this seemingly straightforward portrait. Typical of detail-rich Northern European art, the canvas is bursting with highly symbolic tidbits. To the left, on the wall, is the motto *Nulla sine merore voluptas* ("No joy without sorrow"), a hint that Gisze's success has been hard-won. The clock (on the table, inside the small gold canister) reminds the viewer that time passes and worldly success fades. The unbalanced scales over his shoulder suggest that wealth is fleeting. Those negative symbols are counterbalanced by the hopeful image of the carnations and herbs in the vase, representing Gisze's upcoming marriage and his eternal devotion to his betrothed bride.

But the overwhelming impression Holbein leaves is not of medieval symbolism but of a flesh-and-blood human being. Renaissance humanism was alive in Europe, and Holbein was celebrating the glory and intrinsic beauty of an individual human being. As the artist himself wrote (in the white plaque above Gisze's head): "What you see here—this picture—shows Georg's features and figure. These are his eyes, this is his profile, just as they are in real life."

• *In* **Room 2** *are works by...*

❷ Albrecht Dürer, 1471-1528

In 1494, the young Dürer traveled from Germany to Italy, where he soaked up the technique and spirit of the burgeoning Renaissance movement. Dürer returned home and melded Italian harmony and classical grandeur with a Northern European attention to detail.

In his portrait *Hieronymus Holzschuher* (1526), Dürer captured the personality of a white-bearded friend from Nürnberg, right down to the sly twinkle in his sidelong glance. Technically the portrait is perfection: Look closely and see each individual hair of the man's beard and fur coat. Dürer does not gloss over the 57-year-old's unflattering features like the wrinkles or receding hairline (with the clever comb-over). Dürer, trained as a meticulous engraver, could even capture the tiny reflection of the studio's windows in the man's eyes. Also notice Dürer's little pyramid-shaped, D-inside-A signature. Signing one's work was a revolutionary assertion of Dürer's renown at a time when German artists were considered anonymous craftsmen.

Painted the same year and the same size, the portrait *Jakob Muffel* may be a companion piece. It depicts the mayor of Nürnberg (another friend of Dürer's) in a straightforward way, against a neutral background. We see the man's wrinkles, duck-billed nose, and prominent cranial bones. Muffel has a blank, calm expression, as though lost in thought. His high forehead reinforces the "high-mindedness" of this incorruptible public servant.

• *To get to our next stop, head through Rooms 3 and 4, turn left into Room IV, then left again into Room III. (Confused yet?)* **Room III** *has some large-scale works by...*

➌ Lucas Cranach the Elder, 1472-1553

Cranach was a court painter for the prince electors of Saxony and a close friend of Martin Luther. He painted solemn portraits of

these men. But Cranach also painted religious and mythological subjects.

His *Fountain of Youth* (*Der Jungbrunnen*, 1546) depicts the perennial human pursuit of eternal youth. Ladies flock to bathe in the swimming pool of youth. They arrive (on the left) as old women—by wagon,

on horseback, carried by men, even in a wheelbarrow. They strip and enter with sagging breasts, frolic awhile in the pool, rinse and repeat, then emerge (on the right) young again. Newly nubile, the women go into a tent to dress up, snog with noblemen in the bushes (right foreground), dance merrily beneath the trees, and dine grandly beneath a landscape of mountains and towers.

• *Head back into* **Room IV** *to see some masterworks by ...*

➍ Rogier van der Weyden, 1400-1464

Netherlandish painters—represented in the next several rooms—were early adopters of oil paint (as opposed to older egg tempera). Its relative ease of handling allowed them to brush the super-fine details for which they became famous.

Rogier van der Weyden was a virtuoso of the new medium. In *Portrait of a Young Woman* (*Bildnis einer jungen Frau*, 1440-1445), the subject wears a typical winged bonnet, addressing the viewer directly with her fetching blue eyes. The subjects (especially women) of most portraits of the time look off to one side; some art historians guess that the confident woman shown here is Van der Weyden's wife.

In the same room is a remarkable, rare trio of three-panel altarpieces by Van der Weyden: The *Marienaltar* shows the life of the Virgin Mary; the *Johannesaltar* narrates the life of John the Baptist—his birth, baptizing of Christ (with God and the Holy Spirit hovering overhead), and gruesome death by decapitation; and the *Middelburger* altar tells the story of the Nativity. Savor the fine details in each panel of these altarpieces.

• *Browse through the next several rooms (V-VII, and the adjoining 5-8), with early Flemish artists. Ignore several undeniable masterpieces—by the likes of Van Eyck, Bruegel, and Bosch—as you keep going to our next stop,* **Room VIII.**

❺ Peter Paul Rubens, 1577-1640

Here in Room VIII (and adjoining rooms) are works by Rubens. We've fast-forwarded a hundred years, and it's apparent how much

the Protestant Reformation changed the tenor of Northern European art. Rubens' paintings represent the Catholic response, the Counter-Reformation.

You'll see huge, brightly colored canvases of Mary, alongside angels, bishops, and venerated saints (like the arrow-pierced martyr, St. Sebastian). This exuberant Baroque style trumpeted the greatness of the Catholic Church. The Church had serious competition for the hearts and minds of its congregants. Exciting art like this became a way to keep people in the pews. Notice the quivering brushstrokes and almost too-bright colors.

You'll also see fleshy nudes and mythological scenes in the Italian tradition, such as *Perseus Freeing Andromeda* (*Perseus befreit Andromeda*, c. 1622, next to St. Sebastian). Rubens painted for wealthy Catholic nobles who were schooled in the classical imagery and sensual nudes of Renaissance art.

Finally, find a portrait of Rubens' first wife, the noble-looking Isabella Brandt. You may also see glimpses of Rubens' second wife, Helene Fourment, in mythological scenes such as *Andromeda* (1638). Helene, the amply-figured nymph with a sweetly smiling face, came to define the phrase "Ruben-esque."

• *Continue through a few more rooms to the museum's far-right corner,* **Room 13.** *You'll have to refocus your eyes from Rubens' huge colorful canvases to the tiny, dark slices-of-life of Dutch art.*

❻ Frans Hals, c. 1582-1666

Dutch painters captured convivial portraits of everyday folk during Holland's Golden Age of sea-trading prosperity.

Hals' *Portrait of Catharina Hooft with Her Nurse* (*Bildnis der Catharina Hooft mit ihrer Amme*, 1619-1620) presents a startlingly self-possessed baby (the newest member of a wealthy merchant family), dressed in the lacy, jeweled finery of a queen and clutching a golden rattle. The smiling nurse supporting the tyke offers her a piece of fruit, whose blush of red perfectly matches the nanny's apple-fresh cheeks. By the way, baby Catharina would grow up to marry the mayor of Amsterdam.

At the other end of the social spectrum is Hals' *Malle Babbe* (1633-1635). The subject, a notorious barfly nicknamed "Crazy" Babbe, was well known in Hals' hometown. Hals captures her in a snapshot from the local pub, hefting her pewter beer stein and turning to laugh at a joke. The messy brushstrokes that define her collar and cap are as wild and lively as her over-the-top personality. The bird perched on Babbe's shoulder was a sign to everyone that she was (as they used to say) "drunk as an owl."

• *Continue counterclockwise to Room 16 and the large, adjoining* **Room X.**

❼ Rembrandt van Rijn, 1606-1669

The ultimate Dutch master, Rembrandt was propelled to fame in his lifetime by his powers of perception and invention. His style—dark brown canvases highlighted by a few brightly lit details—is moody and dramatic.

Browse these rooms to get a taste of the range of Rembrandt's work. There are storytelling scenes, taut with pulse-racing emotion. In *The Rape of Persephone* (1631, Room 16), Pluto grabs Persephone from his chariot and races toward the underworld, while other goddesses cling to her robe, trying to save her. Cast against a nearly black background, the almost overexposed, action-packed scene is shockingly expressive.

There are Bible scenes: In *Samson and Delilah* (1628-1629, Room 16), Delilah cradles Samson's head in her lap while silently signaling to a goon to shear Samson's hair, the secret to his strength. The larger-scale *Samson Threatens His Father-in-Law* (*Samson bedroht seinen Schwiegervater*, 1635, Room X) captures the moment just after the mighty Samson (with his flowing hair, elegant robes, and shak-

GEMÄLDEGALERIE & KULTURFORUM

ing fist) has been told by his wife's father to take a hike. I wouldn't want to cross this guy.

You may see the famous *Man with the Golden Helmet* (*Der Mann mit dem Goldhelm,* 1650-1655, Room 16). This is probably *not* by Rembrandt, but it shows how his style was so mimicked by followers that it's sprouted a cottage industry of art scholars trying to authenticate Rembrandt paintings.

In Room X, a *Self-Portrait* (1634) shows Rembrandt wearing a beret. The 28-year-old genius was already famous. He soon married the beautiful Saskia (*Portrait of Saskia,* 1643, Room 16), and seemed to have it all. But then Saskia died, Rembrandt declared bankruptcy, his painting style went out of fashion, and he moved in with his young housekeeper, Hendrickje Stoffels (depicted in *Young Girl in an Open Door/Junge Frau am geöffneter Tür,* 1656-1657)...all of which contributed to his brooding, dark canvases.

• *Continue counterclockwise a couple of rooms, to **Room 18.***

❽ Johannes Vermeer, 1632-1675

Today, Vermeer is just as admired as Rembrandt, though he was little known in his day, probably because he painted relatively few works for a small circle of Delft collectors. Vermeer was a master at conveying a complicated story through a deceptively simple scene with a few significant details—whether a woman reading a letter at a window, a milkmaid pouring milk from a pitcher into a bowl, or a woman with a pearl necklace.

Though not as famous as *Girl with the Pearl Earring* (which inspired a novel), *Young Woman with a Pearl Necklace* (*Junge Dame mit*

Perlenhalsband, 1664) is classic Vermeer. He lets us glimpse an intimate, unguarded moment in the life of an everyday woman. She wears a beautiful yellow coat with an ermine fur lining, ribbons in her hair, and pearl earrings. As she completes her *toilette,* adjusting her necklace with the ribbon ties, she pauses for a moment. What catches her attention? It's as though a thought bubble hangs in the empty space between her and the mirror—the center of the composition.

This painting has many signature elements of Vermeer's style. Two colors dominate: the yellow of her jacket and the ultramarine blue of the bunched-up tablecloth (Vermeer liberally used this blue pigment, despite its being made from incredibly expensive powdered lapis lazuli). The scene is lit from a window at left, creating a soft, diffuse atmosphere. Vermeer tells us a bit about the woman with objects on the table: her comb, make-up brush, and water bowl.

Who is this young woman? Vermeer painted her on other occasions, and she may be the woman who became his wife.

Vermeer's *The Glass of Wine* (*Das Glas Wein*, 1661) lets us glimpse a racier subject. A young man offers a drink to a young

lady. Her elegantly dressed seducer has been playing his lute (which now sits, discarded, on a chair) and is hoping to seal the deal with some alcohol. The woman is finishing one glass of wine, and her suitor stands ready—almost *too* ready— to pour her another. His sly smirk hints at his hopes for what will come next. Vermeer has perfectly captured the exact moment of "Will she or won't she?" The painter offers some clues—the coat of arms in the window depicts a woman holding onto the reins of a horse, staying in control—but ultimately, only he (and the couple) know how this scene will end.

• *Continuing counterclockwise, turn the corner into the South Wing, and skip ahead to* **Room XIV,** *where our tour concludes.*

Italian Art

The South Wing is dedicated primarily to art from Italy (with a smattering from France and Spain). We'll focus on just one artist, whose sensational originality turned the Italian art world on its head.

❾ Caravaggio, 1573–1610

In the year 1600, living in Rome, Caravaggio burst onto the scene with a new and shocking art style. He populated his canvases with everyday people drawn directly from life, set in a dark background and lit by a harsh, dramatic, unflattering light. (Remember Rembrandt? Well, Rembrandt sure remembered Caravaggio.)

Even religious and allegorical subjects got his uncompromising, gritty, ultrarealistic treatment.

In Caravaggio's *Amor Vincit Omnia* (*Amor als Sieger,* 1601-1602), "Love Conquers All." Cupid stands victorious over all the vain accomplishments of ambitious men: Military triumphs (symbolized by the fallen armor), Art (the discarded musical instruments), Literature (paper and pen), Science (a globe), Grand Architecture (compass and square), and Power (the crown). Cupid—a young, naked boy—mocks those grown-up ambitions. He laughs derisively and splays his genitals over the fallen symbols. This Cupid was Caravaggio's favorite male model, fitted with obviously fake stage-prop wings. The photorealistic style broke the fourth wall of illusion in what should be a high-falutin' allegorical painting. A secular-minded noble bought the painting and made it the showpiece of his collection.

For the next phase of Caravaggio's story, turn your attention to a painting in Room XIV by a different artist—**Giovanni Baglione**'s *Sacred and Profane Love* (*Der himmlische Amor besiegt den irdischen Amor*, 1602-1603).

Baglione was hired by the secular noble's brother—a conservative cardinal—to paint a moralizing response. Here, the main figure is a more upright incarnation of love—Sacred Love—embodied by a radiant angel. He corners his rascally counterpart, the cowering and "Profane" little Cupid (lower right). This breaks up the illicit tryst between Profane Love and the Devil (lower left). Baglione was satirizing Caravaggio's rude painting and also satirizing Caravaggio's groundbreaking style of dark/light contrasts.

The plot thickens. When Caravaggio saw Baglione's satire, he was furious. Baglione began spreading rumors that Caravaggio was sodomizing young boys. Baglione even painted a second version of this painting, with Caravaggio himself as the Devil. Caravaggio responded with dirty limericks about Baglione's own sex life, charged that he'd plagiarized his unique style (true), and harshly critiqued Baglione's "clumsy" work. Baglione successfully sued Caravaggio for libel, sending the young genius to jail for a few weeks.

Caravaggio's star began to fall. He became increasingly quick-tempered, killed a man in a street fight, spent years as an outlaw, and eventually died of a knife wound. After Caravaggio's death, his bad-boy reputation was cemented by his first biographer—none other than Baglione.

• *The rest of the South Wing features lesser-known works by great Italian Renaissance painters. Check out several Raphael Madonnas (Room 29), Titian's* Venus and the Organ Player *(Room XVI), and much, much more.*

Museum of Decorative Arts

With displays covering a thousand years of applied arts—porcelain, fine *Jugendstil* furniture, Art Deco, and reliquaries—the huge space of the Museum of Decorative Arts (Kunstgewerbemuseum) will delight some and bore others. But everyone will love one display: an impressive collection of clothing (mostly women's) through the ages.

COLLECTION HIGHLIGHTS

Entering the museum, pick up the free map and get oriented—you're on the "Mode/Foyer/Entrance" level. Go downstairs to the "Alte Kunst/Ground Floor" level, do a U-turn, and head for the door marked Mittelalter. You'll step into Room I.

Guelph Treasure

The more than 40 gleaming gold, silver, and bejeweled objects in Room I are known as the Guelph Treasure. Ranging in date from the 8th to 15th centuries, most are reliquaries, which once held reminders of long-dead saints—a piece of bone, a bicuspid, a shred of clothing, or a sliver of their walking stick. By standing in the presence of such remains, housed in gloriously decorated reliquaries, medieval Christians experienced awe and a closer connection to their saints. For centuries, they were venerated by medieval pilgrims in the Cathedral of Braunschweig, a town 150 miles west of Berlin, ruled by the Guelph family.

Start (in the center of the room) with the most treasured of the Treasure, the **Dome Reliquary** (Kuppelreliquar). It's shaped like

a tiny jeweled church (18 inches tall), topped with a dome. This magnificent container, created c. 1175 by artists in Cologne, once housed the skull of brainy St. Gregory the Theologian (c. 329-390), whose writings helped define the mystery of the Trinity. The saint's remains were brought from his resting spot in Constantinople to Germany by a Guelph Crusader. The domed reliquary may have been modeled after Jerusalem's famed Dome of the Rock Church, which the Crusaders were bent on liberating from Muslim control.

Admire the beauty and workmanship of the Dome Reliquary. Its wood core is covered with gilded copper, and the dome is plated with colorful enamels of blue, green, and red, traced with intertwining vines. The church rests on four crouching griffins of gilt bronze, and is topped with a globe of gold filigree. Ringing the base of the dome are 13 majestic figures on thrones carved from walrus-tusk ivory—the 12 Apostles plus Christ. Each has a different hairstyle, beard, and robe, and each holds an identifying attribute: Peter, for example (at Christ's right hand), holds his keys to the kingdom of heaven. The lower part of the reliquary has more carved ivory saints and four intricately carved scenes of the Crucifixion, the women at Christ's tomb, the Holy Family, and the Three

The Guelph Treasure through History

The precious ecclesiastical objects of the Guelph Treasure were made in medieval times and for centuries belonged to the Braunschweig Cathedral. In 1671, the town's ruling noble family, the Guelphs, acquired the Treasure from the cathedral. Some 350 years later, in 1928, the cash-strapped descendants of the Guelphs sold the entire collection to a consortium of Jewish art dealers. They in turn took the Treasure on tour through America, offering it for sale (they sold off about half of the 82 pieces, many to museums). In 1935, with the Nazis now in power, the German state (under the art-loving Hermann Göring) "bought" the remaining bits of the Treasure from the art dealers. The timing of the sale begged the question—was it a fair bargain, or were the dealers pressured by the Nazis because of their Jewish heritage? After the war, the dealers' heirs sued the German government, asserting that the sale had been made under duress for less than true market value. In 2015, after years of legal wrangling, a German court declared the Guelph Treasure to be the property of the German state and a national treasure. But the legal maneuvering is not over, though, as the heirs are pursuing their claim in a still-pending civil suit.

Magi. Though small and stiff, these scenes are the infancy of what would grow into Renaissance realism.

Browse **other reliquaries of the Guelph Treasure** in this room. Some are shaped like arms (to hold the arm bone of a saint); others are busts, crosses, or boxes. Some have a transparent rock-crystal receptacle where you can actually see the relic inside. All are magnificently gilded, silvered, enameled, jeweled, and pearled. Is the security guard eyeing you a little too closely? Well, the total value of the Guelph collection in this room has been estimated at €250 million.

• *To see more treasure, face the Dome Reliquary, turn right and follow Rundgang signs on a counterclockwise loop.*

First up, in Room II, are Renaissance **tapestries and porcelain** from southern Europe. Then comes Room III, with still more finely crafted Renaissance wonders from northern Europe, including a cache of **silver** from the civic treasury in Lüneburg. Look for two charming hand-washing pots—one in the shape of a lion, the other an elephant. They're both marvels of beauty and function.

Lift either by the tail, and water pours out its mouth. These were prized pieces of tableware in the messy days before silverware was introduced.

• *Circle back to the foyer and head upstairs to the "Mode/ Entrance" level. Enter the series of rooms devoted to...*

Fashion

These rooms trace ladies' fashions from 1845 to 2000. (Earlier fashions, from 1700-1845, are found on the upper floor.) Altogeth-

er about 130 costumes (and nearly as many accessories) are presented in chronological order and accompanied by bits of historical context that make fashion seem more fascinating than fickle, even to the style-challenged (we know who we are). In a long, dark hallway, you'll walk past Victorian-era dresses with narrow waists and floor-length hemlines, including elegant ballgowns. There's a peek at ladies' undergarments—hoop skirts, corsets, padded bras, and bustles (for the bootylicious Victorian)—that accentuated the shape of the dress in order to reflect the era's ideal body type. Continuing through history, you'll see slinky and shapeless 1920s-era flapper dresses, 1940s business suits, 1960s miniskirts and hot pants, 1970s women's-libber pantsuits and short skirts, and late-century designer labels such as Yves Saint Laurent, Chanel, and Versace.

• *Continue upstairs to the Neue Kunst/Upper Floor level and turn left through the door marked* Renaissance bis Barock *for a look at...*

Renaissance to Baroque, 1500-1800

Heaven's garage sale might look like this: room after room of exquisitely beautiful handmade objects. Browse through elegant Delftware porcelain, Versailles-era furniture, "Kunstkammer" curiosity chests, ceremonial beer steins, and Tiffany lamps and carved-wood furniture from the Art Nouveau (Jugendstil) era.

The Rest of the Kulturforum

The **Musical Instruments Museum** (Musikinstrumenten Museum) fills a striking hall with 600 exhibits, spanning the 16th century to modern times. This place is fascinating if you're into pianos. Highlights include a pre-piano keyboard (the Bach Cembalo), Stradivarius violins, venerable church organs, Frederick the Great's flute, a silent-movie-era Wurlitzer organ, electric guitars, and 20th-century synthesizers—once cutting-edge,

now museum pieces. Wander among old keyboard instruments and funny-looking tubas. Pick up the included audioguide and free English brochure at the entry. In addition to the English commentary, the audioguide lets you listen to various instruments being played; while the musical snippets are beautiful, there are too few of them.

The **New National Gallery** (Neue Nationalgalerie)—currently closed for a lengthy renovation—features 20th-century art, with ever-changing special exhibits. The building, which opened in 1968, was the last commission completed by esteemed architect Ludwig Mies van der Rohe.

Poke into the lobby of the yellow, pentagonal-shaped **Berlin Philharmonic** concert hall and see if there are tickets available for performances during your stay (for more on ticketing, see page 301). The hall is famous for its extraordinary acoustics. Even from the outside, this is a remarkable building, designed by a nautical engineer to look like a ship—notice how different it appears from each angle.

Immediately north of the Philharmonic, facing the park, was the building where the Nazis administered a campaign of what they called "euthanasia" against mentally and physically disabled people. The long blue wall between the parking lot and Tiergartenstrasse is the **Memorial to the Victims of Nazi "Euthanasia."** (For details, see page 92.)

SLEEPING IN BERLIN

Choosing the right neighborhood in Berlin is as important as choosing the right hotel. I've focused my recommendations in safe, colorful areas convenient to sightseeing. Two of my top districts are in northern Berlin: Prenzlauer Berg, my favorite area to sleep, offers a local neighborhood vibe, easy transit connections, and an excellent selection of eateries; Scheunenviertel, also with good restaurants, is closer to the sights but more impersonal than Prenzlauer Berg. Farther out, City West—the heart of the former West Berlin—is an upscale residential neighborhood. I recommend the best accommodations values for each, from €20 bunks to deluxe €300 doubles. Most of my listings cluster around the €100-150 range.

Berlin lacks the characteristic, traditional, family-run hotels that I favor in other German cities. Outside of a few small hotels in Prenzlauer Berg and near Savignyplatz in City West, most of my listings are larger, business-oriented hotels—often part of a chain. I've also listed a handful of business-class hotels in the historic core and a few budget chains. Pricing at these big hotels fluctuates with demand; since the hotels themselves are fairly standard, I recommend picking a few places and comparing prices for your travel dates.

A few notes about hotels in Berlin:

- Most hotels offer an optional **breakfast** buffet for about €10-15 per person, though it's often not included in their quoted rates (you can choose whether to add breakfast when booking). Light eaters and budget travelers can opt out of the hotel breakfast and get coffee and a pastry at a neighborhood café for about half the cost.

- **Air-conditioning** is relatively rare (I've noted hotels that have it in all rooms). If it's important to you, ask about it when you book.
- Many hotels offer **bike rentals** to guests (usually €8-12/day)— again, ask when you reserve.

For some travelers, short-term, Airbnb-type rentals can be a good alternative to hotels; search for places in my recommended hotel neighborhoods.

Book any accommodations well in advance, especially if you'll be traveling during peak season or if your trip coincides with a major holiday or festival, when Berlin can be packed and prices go up (see page 437). Rooms can be especially short supply when big trade shows are in town (including Green Week in mid-January and the ITB travel show in mid-March).

For information and tips on pricing, getting deals, making reservations, and finding a short-term rental, see page 396.

PRENZLAUER BERG

My favorite Berlin neighborhood to call home, Prenzlauer Berg offers easy transit connections to sightseeing; diverse eateries, coffee houses, and nightspots; and a welcoming personality that's just the right mix of urban yet residential, local yet tourist-friendly. A onetime hipster mecca, this area is now gentrified and more sedate—yet it still retains a bit of its alternative edge (think of all that graffiti as just some people's way of saying they care). If staying here, orient yourself with my 📖 Prenzlauer Berg Walk. For eating, shopping, and nightlife options, see my recommendations in those chapters.

Most of my recommended hotels are between Kastanienallee and Prenzlauer Alle. The area's transit hub is the Eberswalder Strasse U-Bahn station (U2 line). Trams also serve this neighborhood: The #M1 and #12 run up and down Kastanienallee, connecting to the Rosenthaler Platz U-Bahn (#M1 continues all the way to the Hackescher Markt S-Bahn station), while the #M10 heads west from Eberswalder Strasse along Bernauer Strasse to the Berlin Wall Memorial, and eventually to the Hauptbahnhof.

$$$ Hotel Oderberger has 70 modern rooms filling part of a Neo-Renaissance bathhouse complex (originally opened in 1902, renovated and reopened in 2016). From the reception, you can peek into the elegant old swimming pool area. It's a fine choice, with its understated elegance, historic aura, and good location, tucked away on a quiet side street near the most happening stretch of Kastanienallee (elevator, guest discount for swimming pool, Oderberger

Strasse 57, tel. 030/780-089-760, www.hotel-oderberger.de, info@hotel-oderberger.berlin).

$$$ Linnen rents five rooms above a cozy and characteristic café, along a busy street between the Eberswalder Strasse U-Bahn station and Mauerpark. Linnen stays true to its motto, "more home, less hotel"—the vibe is casual, and the spacious, stylishly decorated rooms feel homey. This place pleases well-heeled hipsters (breakfast extra at downstairs café, Eberswalder Strasse 35, tel. 030/4737-2440, www.linnenberlin.com, booking@linnenberlin.com).

$$$ Myer's Hotel rents 50 comfortable rooms that are decorated with a heavy hand (lots of bold colors and gold accents). Located on a tranquil, tree-lined street, and overlooking a sleepy courtyard, Myer's is closer to charming Kollwitzplatz than to the Kastanienallee action. Staying at this peaceful hub, you'll find it hard to believe you're in the heart of a capital city. The gorgeous public spaces, including an art-filled patio and garden, host frequent cultural events (air-con, elevator, sauna, Metzer Strasse 26—midway between U2: Senefelderplatz and #M2 tram: Prenzlauer Allee/Metzer Strasse, #M2 goes to/from Alexanderplatz, tel. 030/440-140, www.myershotel.de, info@myershotel.de).

$$$ Hotel Kastanienhof feels less urban-classy and more like a traditional small-town German hotel. It's wonderfully lo-

cated on the Kastanienallee #M1 tram line, with easy access to the Prenzlauer Berg bustle (but since trams run all night, ask for a room in the back). Its 44 rooms come with helpful service (breakfast extra, some top-floor rooms with air-con and/or balcony, elevator, wheelchair-accessible room, pay parking, 20 yards from #M1: Zionskirchplatz at Kastanienallee 65, tel. 030/443-050, www.kastanienhof.berlin, info@kastanienhof.berlin). The hotel's recommended Ausspanne restaurant serves excellent German dishes with a modern twist (see listing on page 281).

$$$ Hotel Jurine (zhoo-REEN—the family name) is a pleasant 53-room business-style hotel with a friendly staff that aims to please. Though a bit old-school and slightly overpriced, it's comfy and well-located. In good weather, you can enjoy the (optional) breakfast buffet on the peaceful backyard patio and garden (breakfast extra, RS%, elevator, pay parking—reserve ahead, Schwedter Strasse 15, #M1: Zionskirchplatz, or 10-minute walk to U2: Senefelderplatz, tel. 030/443-2990, www.hotel-jurine.de, mail@hotel-jurine.de).

Prenzlauer Berg Hotels & Restaurants

Accommodations
1. Hotel Oderberger
2. Linnen Rooms
3. Myer's Hotel
4. Hotel Kastanienhof
5. Hotel Jurine
6. Meininger Hotel Alexanderplatz
7. EastSeven Hostel

Eateries
8. Prater Garten
9. Zum Schusterjungen
10. Konnopke's Imbiss
11. Ausspanne
12. Der Hahn Ist Tot!
13. Altberliner
14. Restaurant Die Schule
15. Les Valseuses
16. To Osmans Töchter
17. La Bodeguita del Medio
18. Maria Bonita
19. Engelberg Café
20. Kauf Dich Glücklich
21. Bonanza Coffee
22. Café Morgenrot
23. Gugelhof
24. Imbiss 204
25. Chutnify
26. Zula
27. Metzer Eck Pub
28. Leibhaftig Pub

Entertainment,
Shopping & Services

29 Theater RambaZamba
30 Frannz Club
31 To Kookaburra Comedy Club
32 Bassy Club

33 Mauerpark Flea Market
34 Arkonaplatz Flea Market
35 Brandenburgerie Shop
36 Launderettes (2)
37 Bike Rental

¢ **Hostels:** A convenient branch of the hostel/budget hotel **Meininger** is at Senefelderplatz; for details, see page 273. **East-Seven Hostel** rents 60 of the best cheap beds in Prenzlauer Berg. Modern and conscientiously run, it offers all the hostel services, and more: inviting lounge, guest kitchen, backyard terrace, and bike rental. Children are welcome. Easygoing people of any age are comfortable here (private rooms available, no curfew, 100 yards from U2: Senefelderplatz at Schwedter Strasse 7, tel. 030/9362-2240, www.eastseven.de, info@eastseven.de).

SCHEUNENVIERTEL

Scheunenviertel ("Barn Quarter"), south of Prenzlauer Berg, makes for a fine home base thanks to its good location (close to public transportation and easy walking distance to the center) and traveler-friendly offerings, including cozy restaurants, independent shops, delightful Monbijou Park, and a few interesting sights (especially those relating to the former Jewish quarter that once stood here). It's closer to the historic core than Prenzlauer Berg, but feels less residential, and the hotels here are bigger and less personable. To get your bearings, take my 📖 Scheunenviertel Walk; you can find recommendations for eateries, shopping, and entertainment in those chapters.

Near Rosenthaler Platz

Rosenthaler Platz is halfway between Hackescher Markt and the heart of the Prenzlauer Berg scene (on Kastanienallee). Though bustling and congested, it makes a good base for getting around the city because of its U-Bahn stop (U8: Rosenthaler Platz) and tram service (#M1 heads north to Kastanienallee/Eberswalder Strasse and south to the Hackescher Markt S-Bahn hub; #M8 connects to the Hauptbahnhof).

$$ The Circus Hotel is fun, entirely comfortable, and a great value. The achingly hip lobby has a café serving delicious (optional) breakfasts, and the 60 rooms are straightforward and colorful. Run by the same folks who manage the popular Circus Hostel (listed below), it's service-oriented, with a very "green" attitude and special events for guests. As the hotel overlooks a busy intersection, ask for a quieter back room (breakfast extra, elevator, Rosenthaler Strasse 1, tel. 030/2000-3939, www.circus-berlin.de, info@circus-berlin.de). The Circus also offers spacious, modern **$$$ apartments** within the hotel and two blocks away at Choriner Strasse 84.

$$ Amano Hotel, while big (163 rooms) and impersonal, is well-priced for what you get: chic contemporary design and all the little amenities you don't need, but appreciate nonetheless (breakfast extra, air-con, elevator, pay parking, Auguststrasse 43, tel. 030/809-4150, www.amanogroup.de, amano@amanogroup.de).

$ EasyHotel Berlin Hackescher Markt is part of an un-apologetically cheap, Europe-wide chain where you pay for exactly what you use—nothing more, nothing less. You are charged a low base rate, then pay à la carte for each service you add (Wi-Fi, TV, etc.). The 125 orange-and-gray rooms are very small, basic, and feel popped out of a plastic mold (no breakfast, elevator, call to request a quieter back room after booking online, Rosenthaler Strasse 69, tel. 030/4000-6550, www.easyhotel-berlin.de, enquiries@berlinhm.easyhotel.com).

¢ The Circus Hostel is a brightly colored, well-run place with 250 beds, plenty of social networking, and a trendy lounge and microbrewery. It has typical hostel dorms as well as some hotel-like private rooms; for a few big steps up in comfort, consider the Circus Hotel, listed earlier (no curfew, elevator, Weinbergsweg 1A, U8: Rosenthaler Platz, tel. 030/2000-3939, www.circus-berlin.de, info@circus-berlin.de).

By Hackescher Markt

Lively Hackescher Markt, just north of the river and the gateway to Scheunenviertel, is brimming with people, eateries, and on some days, an open-air market. It's also home to an S-Bahn station and is connected to Prenzlauer Berg by tram #M1.

Of the following listings, the first two (Adina and Hotel Alexander Plaza) are in a characterless glass-and-concrete zone just south of Hackescher Markt. The others face each other across the tracks of a tram depot (ask for a quieter room). All of these hotels are bigger than they are charming.

$$$ Adina Apartment Hotel Berlin Hackescher Markt has 134 studio apartments with kitchenettes, though a breakfast option is available for an extra fee (air-con, elevator, pay parking, An der Spandauer Brücke 11, tel. 030/209-6980, www.tfehotels.com, berlinhm@adina.eu).

$$$ Hotel Alexander Plaza offers 94 brightly appointed, business-style rooms (breakfast extra, elevator, pay parking, Rosenstrasse 1, tel. 030/240-010, www.hotel-alexander-plaza.de, frontoffice@hotel-alexander-plaza.de).

$$$ Monbijou Hotel's 101 rooms are small, but they make up for it with pleasing public spaces, a postcard-worthy rooftop terrace (with views of the cathedral and TV Tower), and a flair for design—from reclaimed wood and antique furnishings to plenty

Scheunenviertel Hotels & Restaurants

<u>Accommodations</u>

1 The Circus Hotel
2 Amano Hotel
3 EasyHotel Berlin Hackescher Markt
4 The Circus Hostel
5 Adina Apartment Hotel Berlin Hackescher Markt
6 Hotel Alexander Plaza
7 Monbijou Hotel
8 Hotel Hackescher Markt

9 Hotel Zoe by Amano
10 Hotel Augustinenhof
11 Calma Berlin Mitte
12 NH Collection Berlin Mitte Friedrichstrasse
13 Hotel Eurostars Berlin
14 Leonardo Hotel Berlin Mitte
15 To Hotel Albrechtshof
16 To Motel One Hackescher Markt
17 Meininger Hotel & Aufsturz Pub

SLEEPING

Eateries
- 18 Mogg Deli
- 19 Gipsy Restaurant & Spiegelsaal
- 20 Schwarzwaldstuben
- 21 Cordobar
- 22 The Barn Coffee Shop
- 23 Princess Cheesecake
- 24 Transit
- 25 St. Oberholz Café
- 26 Weinbergsweg Eateries
- 27 Hasir Turkish Restaurant
- 28 Weihenstephaner Bavarian Restaurant

Entertainment, Shopping & Services
- 29 To Kunstfabrik Schlot Music Venue
- 30 Galerie Eigen+Art
- 31 Do You Read Me? Bookstore
- 32 Schee Shop
- 33 Kauf dich Glücklich
- 34 Launderettes (2)

SLEEPING

of natural light (family rooms, no breakfast, elevator, pay parking, Monbijouplatz 1, tel. 030/6162-0300, www.monbijouhotel.com, info@monbijouhotel.com).

$$ Hotel Hackescher Markt, with 32 rooms, offers an inviting lounge and modern decor without being predictable or pretentious (breakfast extra, family rooms, air-con, elevator, Grosse Präsidentenstrasse 8, tel. 030/280 030, www.hotel-hackescher-markt.com, reservierung@hotel-hackescher-markt.com).

$$ Hotel Zoe by Amano is a trendy and slightly more upscale branch of the Amano Hotel group, listed earlier (breakfast extra, air-con, elevator, Grosse Präsidentenstrasse 6, tel. 030/2130-0150, www.amanogroup.de, zoe@amanogroup.de).

On or near Auguststrasse

These good-value hotels are on or close to fun, art gallery-lined Auguststrasse, in an area that feels more characteristic than my other Scheunenviertel listings. They're located between the Oranienburger Strasse S-Bahn and Oranienburger Tor U-Bahn (U6), and tram #M1 is nearby.

$$ Hotel Augustinenhof has 66 spacious rooms, nice woody floors, and comfortable beds. Rooms in front overlook the courtyard of the old Imperial Post Office, rooms in back are a bit quieter, and some rooms have older, thin windows (breakfast extra, elevator, Auguststrasse 82, tel. 030/3088-6710, www.hotel-augustinenhof.de, augustinenhof@albrechtshof-hotels.de).

$$ Calma Berlin Mitte, part of a small local chain, is a good budget bet. Its 46 straightforward but comfortable, modern rooms are tucked away on a tranquil courtyard, just steps from the lively Oranienburger Strasse scene (breakfast extra, elevator, Linienstrasse 139, tel. 030/9153-9333, www.lindemannhotels.de, calma@lindemannhotels.de).

Near Friedrichstrasse Station

Straddling the Spree River, this area—between the transit stations Oranienburger Tor (U6) and Friedrichstrasse (U6 and several S-Bahn lines)—feels big and sterile, with little personality. But hotels here have plenty of beds and are easy walking distance to both Unter den Linden and Scheunenviertel. The first two hotels (NH Collection and Eurostars) are south of the river and closer to Friedrichstrasse Station; both are plush, high-end, and belong to international Spanish chains. The last two listings (Leonardo and Albrechtshof) are north of the river and a bit simpler, but still comfortable.

$$$ NH Collection Berlin Mitte Friedrichstrasse feels upscale and professional. Its 268 rooms come with sleek hardwood floors, high ceilings, and red accents (breakfast extra, air-con, el-

evator, gym, sauna, Friedrichstrasse 96, tel. 030/206-2660, www.
nh-collection.com, nhcollectionberlinfriedrich@nh-hotels.com).

$$$ Hotel Eurostars Berlin is a classy hotel with 221 spa-
cious, rich wood rooms towering over the everyday hustle and
bustle. As it faces train tracks, ask for a quieter room—several face
into the lobby atrium (breakfast extra, air-con, elevator, spa, Fried-
richstrasse 99, tel. 030/701-7360, www.eurostarsberlin.com, info@
eurostarsberlin.com).

$$$ Leonardo Hotel Berlin Mitte occupies a modern build-
ing set back on a little park overlooking the river. It features retro
public spaces and a mazelike floor plan leading to 309 tight, tidy,
stylish rooms (breakfast extra, air-con, elevator, spa, gym, limited
pay parking, Bertolt-Brecht-Platz 4, tel. 030/374-405-000, www.
leonardo-hotels.com, info.berlinmitte@leonardo-hotels.com).

$$ Hotel Albrechtshof is a bit scruffier than its sister hotel,
the Augustinenhof (described earlier), but still a good choice. It
has the most personality of the hotels in this area. The 98 rooms
come with a similar design, friendly staff, peaceful courtyard,
and weekly chapel services. Martin Luther King Jr. once stayed
here and attended one (breakfast extra, elevator, Albrechtstrasse
8, tel. 030/308-860, www.hotel-albrechtshof.de, albrechtshof@
albrechtshof-hotel.de).

CITY WEST

City West—the heart of the former West Berlin—is a pleasant, up-
scale, low-impact residential neighborhood. While most travelers
prefer to sleep closer to the center, City West can be an ideal home
base if you don't mind a longer commute to sightseeing. The area
retains an artsy aura, going back to the cabaret days of the 1920s,
when it was the center of Berlin's gay scene. Today, City West feels
sedate and posh (if quite touristy along Ku'damm)—lacking the
edginess of Prenzlauer Berg or the gritty urban feel of Scheunenvi-
ertel. Travelers sleeping in City West have several transit options:
Bus #100 is slow but scenic (see my "Do It Yourself Bus #100 Tour"
on page 23), while the S-Bahn zips much faster from Savignyplatz
or Zoologischer Garten to the center.

Near Europaplatz

$$$$ 25hours Hotel Bikini Berlin is your trendy hotel option
overlooking Europaplatz in the busiest and buzziest part of City
West. Filling a high rise adjacent to the Berlin Zoo and the Bi-
kini Berlin shopping mall, it has 149 plywood-and-concrete rooms
and public spaces with an industrial-zoo ambience. This is where
trendsetters sleep in City West (breakfast extra, air-con, elevator,
Budapester Strasse 40, tel. 030/120-2210, www.25hours-hotels.
com, bikini@25hours-hotels.com).

City West Hotels & Restaurants

Accommodations
1. 25hours Hotel Bikini Berlin
2. Hecker's Hotel
3. Hommage à Magritte B&B
4. Hotel-Pension Funk
5. Pension Peters
6. Motel One Ku'damm

Eateries & Other
7. Restaurant Marjellchen
8. Dicke Wirtin Pub
9. Café im Literaturhaus
10. Heno Heno
11. Diener Tattersall Pub
12. To Weyers
13. Bleibtreustrasse Eateries
14. Curry 36
15. Schleusenkrug Beer Garden
16. Winter Garden Buffet
17. A Trane Jazz Club
18. Bar Jeder Vernunft
19. Bike Rental

Around Savignyplatz

These listings huddle around the delightful, tree-lined Savigny-platz, which has a neighborhood charm and an abundance of simple, small, friendly, good-value places to sleep and eat. To get here, ride the S-Bahn directly to Savignyplatz—or get off at Zoologischer Garten (with more connections) and walk about 10 minutes.

$$ Hecker's Hotel is an excellent value, with 69 big, fresh, well-maintained rooms and all the Euro-comforts. Herr Kiesel's "superior" rooms have air-conditioning and more-modern furnishings—and cost a bit more—than his "comfort" rooms (a few rooms with kitchenettes, free breakfast for Rick Steves readers, elevator, pay parking, between Savignyplatz and Ku'damm at Grolmanstrasse 35, tel. 030/88900, www.heckers-hotel.com, info@heckers-hotel.com).

$$ Hommage à Magritte is a spiffy, tidy B&B in a classic old apartment building on a quiet street between Ku'damm and

Savignyplatz. Its 18 rooms come with an artistic touch, inspired by its namesake, the Belgian Surrealist painter René Magritte (Grolmanstrasse 32, tel. 030/8956-7087, www.hommage-a-magritte. com, info@hommage-a-magritte.com).

$$ Hotel-Pension Funk, the former home of a 1920s silent-movie star, is a delightfully quirky, only-in-Berlin time warp. Kind manager Herr Michael Pfundt and his right-hand man, Ding, offer 15 elegant old rooms with rich Art Nouveau furnishings and hardly any modern trappings. Most guests adore it; some are put off by its old-fashioned feel. Figure out which you'll be before you book (cheaper rooms with shared bath, cash preferred, no TVs, a long block south of Ku'damm at Fasanenstrasse 69, tel. 030/882-7193, www.hotel-pensionfunk.de, berlin@hotel-pensionfunk.de).

$ Pension Peters, run by a German-Swedish couple, is sunny and central, with a cheery breakfast room and a super-friendly staff who go out of their way to help guests. With sleek Scandinavian decor and 33 rooms, it's a good choice. Some ground-floor rooms facing the back courtyard are a bit dark—and cheaper. If street noise bothers you, request a quiet room. Annika and Christoph (with help from his sister, Daisy, as well as Uwe and others) have been welcoming my readers for decades (breakfast extra, RS%, family rooms, cash preferred, 10 yards off Savignyplatz at Kant-strasse 146, tel. 030/312-2278, www.pension-peters-berlin.de, info@pension-peters-berlin.de).

OTHER SLEEPING OPTIONS
Business Hotels in the Historic Core

Berlin's historic core is handy to sightseeing, but—frankly—pretty dull. Locals who don't work in this area rarely venture here, making it sleepy at night. But these large, business-oriented hotels are worth considering if you're looking to sleep in the very center of town and can score a deal. Breakfasts here are expensive add-ons. For locations see the map on page 276.

$$$$ Hotel de Rome, holding court on Frederick the Great's showpiece Bebelplatz and facing Unter den Linden, is *the* Berlin splurge, with 108 rooms and all the luxurious little extras. If money is no object, this is a tempting choice for your Berlin address (breakfast extra, air-con, elevator, Behrenstrasse 37, tel. 030/460-6090, www.roccofortehotels.com, info.derome@roccofortehotels.com).

$$ Hotel Gendarm Nouveau, just steps off Gendarmen-markt, has a modern, impersonal lobby and 47 Goldilocks rooms with just enough color and comfort. While the area lacks energy after dark, it's lively at lunchtime, classy, and central (breakfast extra, air-con on upper floors, elevator, Charlottenstrasse 61, U2: Stadtmitte, tel. 030/206-0660, www.hotel-gendarm-berlin.de, info@hotel-gendarm-berlin.de).

$$ NH Berlin Mitte Leipziger Strasse is a midrange chain hotel on a busy street a short walk from Gendarmenmarkt, with nearly 400 fresh, interchangeable rooms at affordable rates (breakfast extra, air-con, elevator, Leipziger Strasse 106, U2: Stadtmitte, tel. 030/203-760, www.nh-hotels.com, mailto:nhberlinmitte@nh-hotels.com).

In Eastern Berlin's Friedrichshain

$$ Michelberger Hotel, right across from the Warschauer Strasse S-Bahn station (the gateway to gritty, quickly gentrifying Fried-richshain), is so artsy and self-consciously hip that it'd all be just too much...if it weren't for its helpful staff. Its 111 bright rooms are reasonably priced, and its common spaces—a bar/lounge and a breezy courtyard restaurant—are welcoming (breakfast extra, family rooms, elevator, sauna in courtyard; from atop Warschauer Strasse S-Bahn station, turn left to cross the bridge—it's across from the U-Bahn station and #M10 tram stop at Warschauer Strasse 39; tel. 030/2977-8590, www.michelbergerhotel.com, reservations@michelbergerhotel.com).

Good-Value Chain Hotels

$ Motel One has multiple locations across Berlin; all have the same aqua-and-brown decor and posh-feeling but small rooms. The four most convenient locations are between Hackescher Markt and Alexanderplatz (Dircksenstrasse 36—see map on page 266, tel. 030/2005-4080, berlin-hackeschermarkt@motel-one.com); near the Zoologischer Garten station (Kantstrasse 10—see map on page 270, tel. 030/3151-7360, berlin-kudamm@motel-one.com); just behind the Hauptbahnhof (Invalidenstrasse 54, tel. 030/3641-0050, berlin-hauptbahnhof@motel-one.com); and a few blocks east of Gendarmenmarkt (Leipziger Strasse 50, U2: Spittelmarkt, tel. 030/2014-3630, berlin-spittelmarkt@motel-one.com). For the last two locations, see the map on page 276. All four branches tend to charge the same prices; less central locations are a bit cheaper (air-con, elevator, limited pay parking, www.motel-one.com).

Meininger is a Europe-wide budget-hotel chain with several locations in Berlin. With both ¢ cheap dorm beds and **$$** comfortable, hotelesque private rooms, Meininger is basic but lively, modern, and generally a solid budget option, even for nonhostelers. They have three well-located branches: in Prenzlauer Berg ("Alexanderplatz" branch, actually at Schönhauser Allee 19 on Senefelderplatz—see map on page 262); in Scheunenviertel (Mitte "Humboldthaus" branch, next to the recommended Aufsturz pub at Oranienburger Strasse 67—see map on page 266); and near the Hauptbahnhof at Ella-Trebe-Strasse 9—see map on page 276 (all locations have elevator and 24-hour reception, pay parking at some, tel. 030/666-36100, www.meininger-hostels.com, welcome@meininger-hostels.com).

Apartment Rentals

Consider this option if you're traveling as a family, in a group, or staying four nights or longer. Websites such as Airbnb and VRBO let you correspond directly with European property owners or managers. For more information on renting apartments, see page 396 in the Practicalities chapter.

EATING IN BERLIN

Berlin has a world of ever-changing restaurants from which to choose. While the city abounds with traditional German eateries, Berliners consider this cuisine old-school; when they go out to eat, they're not usually looking for traditional local fare. Nouveau German is California cuisine with scant memories of wurst, kraut, and pumpernickel.

Berlin is also a place to venture beyond German cuisine. As one of Europe's primary melting pots, Berlin has a wide range of restaurants from around the world. You'll find sushi, Turkish, Italian, Peruvian, Cuban, Thai, Georgian, Vietnamese, Indian, Argentinian—usually done quite well.

EATING TIPS

For general advice on eating in Germany, including details on dining and tipping in restaurants, where to find budget meals, and descriptions of popular German dishes and beverages, see page 399.

Choosing Restaurants: Berlin has far more quality restaurants than could fit in any guidebook. It's hard to go wrong by just browsing the neighborhood you're in until you find something that strikes your fancy. Lunches are especially easy, as the city is crammed with places selling fresh, affordable sandwiches and salads. Consider picking up the annual *Zitty Essen Gehen*, with reviews and photographs of the city's hottest eateries, produced by a local culture magazine (German only, sold at newsstands, www. zitty.de/gastro).

Smoking in Restaurants: Berlin does not have a universal smoking ban. Bars that don't serve food may permit smoking, while restaurants over a certain size can choose to have both smoking and nonsmoking areas. If you are a strict nonsmoker, ask the restaurant about their smoking policy.

Berlin Specialties: Don't be too determined to eat "Berlinstyle." The city is best known for its street food—*Currywurst* and kebabs (see the "Berliner Street Fare" sidebar).

But if you do eat German food in Berlin, popular dishes include *Buletten* and *Königsberger Klopse* (both meatball dishes), plus other meaty plates, such as *Schnitzel Holstein* (veal cutlet with egg), *Eisbein* (boiled ham hock), *Leber Berliner Art* (veal liver), *Kassler* (or *Kasseler;* smoked pork), and *Mett* (or *Hackepeter;* minced pork). Also popular are *Aal grün* (boiled eel), and *Rollmops* (pickled herring), and *Senfeier* (hard-boiled eggs with potatoes). As for sweets, *Berliner Pfannkuchen* is the local jelly doughnut, and *Berliner Luft* is a popular dessert. All of these dishes are described in more detail in the Practicalities chapter (under "Traditional German Fare," starting on page 403).

HISTORIC CORE

While this government/commercial area is hardly a hotspot for eateries, I've listed a few places handy for your sightseeing, all a short walk from Unter den Linden.

Near Museum Island

Georgenstrasse, a block behind the Pergamon Museum and under the S-Bahn tracks, is lined with fun places (bars, sit-down eateries, frozen yogurt, designer coffee, etc.) filling the arcade of the train trestle. This strip is close to the sightseeing action, but largely undiscovered by tourists—its main clientele consists of students (and professors) from nearby Humboldt University.

$$ Deponie No. 3 is a reliable, rustic, but sophisticated Berlin *Kneipe* (pub). Garden seating in the back is nice if you don't mind the noise of the S-Bahn passing directly above you. The bar interior is a cozy, wooden wonderland with several inviting spaces. They serve basic salads, traditional Berlin dishes, and hearty daily specials (daily 10:00-24:00, S-Bahn arch #187 at Georgenstrasse 5, tel. 030/2016-5740).

$$ Die Zwölf Apostel ("The Twelve Apostles") serves up Italian dishes in a vast, romantic, dimly lit interior under frescoed arches (daily 11:00-23:00, S-Bahn arch #177 at Georgenstrasse 2, tel. 030/201-0222).

Historic Core Hotels & Restaurants

Accommodations

1. Hotel de Rome
2. Hotel Gendarm Nouveau
3. NH Berlin Mitte Leipziger Strasse
4. To Motel One Hauptbahnhof & Meininger Hauptbahnhof
5. Motel One Spittelmarkt

Eateries

6. Deponie No. 3
7. Die Zwölf Apostel
8. Brauhaus Lemke
9. Brauhaus Georgbräu
10. Lutter & Wegner Restaurant
11. Dom Curry Stand
12. Galeries Lafayette Food Circus

Near the TV Tower

$$ Brauhaus Lemke is a big, modern, lively beer hall that makes its own brews and offers a menu of Berliner specialties and Bavarian dishes. They have decent salads and serve a six-beer sampler board (daily 12:00-24:00, across from the TV Tower and tucked a bit back from the street at Karl-Liebknecht-Strasse 13, tel. 030/3087-8989).

In the Nikolai Quarter

A short walk from Museum Island and Karl-Liebknecht-Strasse, Berlin's rebuilt "old town" (the Nikolai Quarter) is pretty soulless by day but a popular restaurant zone at night.

$$ Brauhaus Georgbräu is a thriving beer hall serving homemade suds on a picturesque courtyard overlooking the Spree River. Eat in the lively and woody but mod-feeling, hops-infused interior, or outdoors with fun riverside seating—teeming with German

EATING

Berliner Street Food

In Berlin, it's easy to eat cheap, with a glut of *Imbiss* snack stands, bakeries (for sandwiches), and falafel/kebab counters. Train stations have grocery stores, as well as bright and modern fruit-and-sandwich bars.

Sausage stands are everywhere—including the reigning local favorites, Konnopke's Imbiss (see page 281) and Curry 36 (see pages 289 and 291). You may even see portable human hot-dog stands—two companies, Grillrunner and Grillwalker, outfit their cooks in clever harnesses that let them grill and sell hot dogs from under an umbrella.

Most sausage stands specialize in **Currywurst,** created in Berlin after World War II, when a fast-food cook got her hands on some curry and Worcestershire sauce from British troops stationed here. It's basically a grilled pork sausage smothered with curry sauce. *Currywurst* comes either *mit Darm* (with casing) or *ohne Darm* (without casing). If the casing is left on to grill, it gives the sausage a smokier flavor. (*Berliner Art*— "Berlin-style"—means that the sausage is boiled *ohne Darm,* then grilled.)

Either way, the grilled sausage is then chopped into small pieces or cut in half (East Berlin style) and topped with sauce. While some places simply use ketchup and sprinkle on some curry powder, real *Currywurst* joints use a proper *Currysauce:* tomato paste, Worcestershire sauce, and curry. With your wurst comes either a toothpick or small wooden fork; you'll usually get a plate of fries as well, but rarely a roll. You'll see *Currywurst* on the menu at some sit-down restaurants, but purists say that misses the point: You'll get a more authentic dish (and pay a third less) at a street stand under elevated S-Bahn tracks.

Other (less popular) meaty street foods include *Bulette* (a big meatball) and *Ketwurst* (a sausage stuffed into the ketchup-filled hole of a long bun).

The other big Berlin street food is the kebab—either **döner kebab** (Turkish-style skewered meat slow-roasted and served in pita bread) or the recently trendy, healthier, vegetarian alternative, **Gemüse kebab** (with lots of veggies, and sometimes falafel). Other variations include the *döner teller* (on a plate instead of in bread) and *döner dürüm* (in a thin flatbread wrap, also called *dürüm kebab* or *yufka*). Just as Americans drop by a taco truck for a quick bite, Germans find a kebab stand.

tourists. It's a good place to try one of the few typical Berlin dishes: *Eisbein* (boiled ham hock) with sauerkraut and mashed peas with bacon. The statue of St. George once stood in the courtyard of Berlin's old castle—until the Nazis deemed it too decadent and not "German" enough, and removed it (daily 12:00-24:00, 2 blocks south of Berlin Cathedral and across the river at Spreeufer 4, tel. 030/242-4244).

Near Gendarmenmarkt

South of Unter den Linden, Gendarmenmarkt, with its twin churches, is a delightful place for an al fresco meal. Here you'll find several business-lunch-type places that are handy but pricey (given the high-rent location). In addition to these options, you can also browse the eateries along Charlottenstrasse.

$$$ Lutter & Wegner Restaurant is a Berlin institution respected for its Austrian cuisine (*Schnitzel* and *Sauerbraten*). Popular with businesspeople, it's dressy, with fun sidewalk seating or a dark and elegant interior. Lunch specials are an affordable way to sample their cooking (daily 11:00-24:00, Charlottenstrasse 56, tel. 030/202-9540, www.l-w-berlin.de).

The **$ Dom Curry** *Currywurst* stand, behind the German Cathedral, works for a quick bite out on the square (daily 11:00-18:00, closed in winter, operated by the nearby Hilton).

$$ Galeries Lafayette Food Circus is a French festival of fun eateries in the basement of the landmark department store—ideal for a quality lunch. You'll find a variety of prices and food, including sandwiches, savory crêpes, quiches, sushi bar, oyster bar, *les macarons*, and so on (Mon-Sat 10:00-20:00, closed Sun, Friedrichstrasse 76, U-Bahn: Französische Strasse, tel. 030/209-480).

PRENZLAUER BERG

Prenzlauer Berg is overstuffed with excellent restaurants, serving up every cuisine imaginable. Even if you're not staying in this area, it's worth venturing here for dinner (consider combining it with my ☐ Prenzlauer Berg Walk). Before choosing a restaurant, I'd spend at least a half-hour strolling and browsing through this bohemian wonderland of creative eateries. Or consider one of my recommendations (for locations, see the map on page 262).

Heart of Prenzlauer Berg

The epicenter of this neighborhood is Kastanienallee (between the Eberswalder Strasse U-Bahn station and Zionskirche), and surrounding streets. It's a youthful and trendy place to eat and drink. I've organized my recommendations in three categories: German cuisine (both traditional and modern), international options, and cafés.

Berlin's Brew and Beverage Scene

Berlin is the epicenter of Germany's growing small-batch craft beer scene. Specialty craft-beer bars and microbreweries are popping up all around the city, such as the recommended Hopfenreich, in Kreuzberg.

The city does have its own mass-produced beers, too. Most famous are the fizzy Berliner Weisse and the basic Berliner Kindl pilsner. Berliner Weisse is commonly served *mit Schuss*—with a shot of fruity syrup in your suds. Choose either *rot* (red) or *grün* (green) syrup. These beers are— locals readily admit—uninspired at best. (Maybe that's why they need to add syrup.) Berliners leave it to Bavarian brewers to be the masters of traditional brews.

A good place to sample the local brew is at a beer hall, beer garden, or one of the city's *Kneipen*. These traditional, colorful pubs, offering a fine old- Berlin ambience, not only serve drinks, but also light, quick, and easy meals. Classic Berlin *Kneipen* listed in this chapter in- clude Metzer Eck and Zum Schusterjungen (Prenzlauer Berg), Deponie No. 3 (near Museum Island), Aufsturz (in Scheunen- viertel), and Dicke Wirtin (City West, near Savignyplatz).

For all its other hallmarks of a great foodie city, Berlin does not have a particularly good craft cocktail scene, though all of the standards are available. Nonalcoholic specialties to look for include Fritz-Cola, a high-end soft-drink brand, and Club-Mate (MAH-tay), a carbonated iced-tea drink made of yerba mate leaves, with as much caffeine as a cup of coffee. It comes in several varieties, and is sometimes mixed into a cocktail (which helps keep the party going).

German Food

Prater Garten, Berlin's oldest beer garden, has been in business since 1837—back when Prenzlauer Berg was a forested hill. The rustic indoor **$$ restaurant** serves well-executed German classics and good salads (table service). But for most, the big draw is the mellow, shaded, super-cheap **$ beer garden,** with a family-friendly outdoor area, including a playground (order at the counter). Both sections proudly pour Prater's own microbrew (restaurant open Mon-Sat 18:00-24:00, Sun from 12:00; beer garden open daily in good weather 12:00-24:00, closed in winter; cash only, Kastanien- allee 7, tel. 030/448-5688).

$$ Zum Schusterjungen ("The Cobbler's Apprentice") is a classic, old-school, German-with-attitude eatery that retains its circa-1986 DDR decor. Famous for its filling meals (including vari- ous types of schnitzel and Berlin specialties such as pork knuckle), it's a no-frills place with quality ingredients and a strong local fol-

EATING

lowing. It serves the needs of those Berliners lamenting the disappearance of solid, traditional German cooking amid the flood of ethnic eateries (small 40-seat dining hall plus outdoor tables, daily 12:00-24:00, corner of Lychener Strasse and Danziger Strasse 9, tel. 030/442-7654).

$ Konnopke's Imbiss, a super-cheap German-style sausage stand underneath the U2 train tracks, has been a Berlin institu-

tion since 1930—it was family-owned even during DDR times. Loyal Berliners say Konnopke's cooks up some of the city's best *Currywurst;* they also serve a wide variety of other wurst specialties (Mon-Fri 10:00-20:00, Sat from 11:30, closed Sun; Schönhauser Allee 44A—underneath elevated train tracks where Kastanienallee dead-ends, tel. 030/442-7765).

$$ Ausspanne, right along Kastanienallee, looks like a traditional, uninspired hotel restaurant. But the menu boldly elevates German classics with surprising flourishes—such as a puff of habanero foam with duck breast and red cabbage. It's an interesting and reasonably priced take on modern German cooking (Tue-Sun 18:00-22:00, closed Mon, in recommended Hotel Kastanienhof at Kastanienallee 65, tel. 030/4430-5199).

$$$ Der Hahn Ist Tot! ("The Chicken Is Dead!") has whimsical style and cozy outdoor tables facing the Zionskirche, on a pleasant Prenzlauer Berg square. They serve only four-course, fixed-price dinners. Prices are decent, and the cuisine is a thoughtful combination of rustic German and French dishes. The name refers to a popular French children's song. It's as tiny as it is popular—book ahead (Tue-Sun 18:30-24:00, closed Mon, Zionskirchstrasse 40, tel. 030/6570-6756, www.der-hahn-ist-tot.de).

$$$ Altberliner ("Old Berliner") serves hearty but refined traditional Berlin cooking in an uncluttered, upscale-bistro ambience or outside, where you're immersed in modern Berlin. Claiming to be the oldest bar in the city, they brought the original paneling along when they relocated here from the original location in Mitte (daily 12:00-23:00, Fürstenberger Strasse 1—near the Zionskirche, facing the park at Arkonaplatz, tel. 030/449-5151, www.altberliner-restaurant.de). Note: Several Berlin eateries call themselves "Altberliner," but this is the original.

$$ Restaurant Die Schule is a modern, no-frills eatery where you can sample traditional German dishes tapas-style. Assemble a collection of cheap little plates of old-fashioned German food you might not try otherwise. They have several varieties of *Flammkuchen* (German pizza—a flatbread dish from the French borderlands). The nondescript interior is perfectly fine, but I prefer their outdoor tables—along the most colorful stretch of Kastanienallee (daily 11:00-22:00, Kastanienallee 82, tel. 030/780-089-550).

International Eateries

$$$ Les Valseuses is a hole-in-the-wall French bistro. Everything is simple and unpretentious, from the subway tile-clad exterior to the cozy, stripped-down interior to the short menu. Reserve ahead (daily 18:30-23:00, Eberswalder Strasse 28, tel. 030/7552-2032).

$$$ Osmans Töchter ("Ottoman Daughters"), run by sisters from Istanbul, is a fun mash-up of industrial-mod interior and modern Turkish cuisine. Although the service can be a bit full of itself, this popular restaurant is the most appealing place in Prenzlauer Berg to sample well-executed Turkish dishes. Reservations are smart (daily 17:30-24:00, Pappelallee 15, tel. 030/3266-3388, www.osmanstoechter.de).

$$ La Bodeguita del Medio is purely fun-loving Cuba—graffiti-caked walls, Che Guevara posters, animated staff, and an ambience that makes you want to dance. Come early to eat or late to drink. This restaurant has been here since 1994—and in fast-changing Prenzlauer Berg, that's an eternity. The German-Cuban couple who run it take pride in their food, and the main dishes are big enough to split. You can even puff a Cuban cigar at the sidewalk tables (Tue-Sun 18:00-24:00, closed Mon, cash only, a block from U2: Eberswalder Strasse at Lychener Strasse 6, tel. 030/4050-0601).

$ Maria Bonita is an American-run Mexican bistro on a busy street offering some of the most authentic tacos in Berlin (daily 12:00-23:00, equidistant from Kollwitzplatz and Eberswalder Strasse U-Bahn at Danziger Strasse 33, tel. 030/2025-5338).

Browsing Kastanienallee: For other ethnic options, simply wander down Kastanienallee from the Eberswalder Strasse trestle. In just a few blocks, you'll see Italian, Vietnamese, falafel, *Gemüse kebab,* and other cuisines, along with burgers, funky cafés, colorful *Kneipe,* and much more (plus the recommended Prater Garten, Die Schule, Ausspanne, and Café Morgenrot).

Cafés

The following places are good for lingering over a drink and/or snack, ideally at an outdoor table where you can soak up the essence of Prenzlauer Berg (Engelberg also works well for a full meal). Most of these are on Oderberger Strasse, a wide street branching off from Kastanienallee (and seemingly every Berliner's favorite street).

$$ Engelberg is a delightful little café serving authentic southern German fare imported from Bavaria, including sausages, spätzle, and streusel. Stop by here for breakfast, lunch, or coffee and cake in a relaxed, convivial atmosphere (Tue-Sun 10:00-18:00, closed Mon, Oderberger Strasse 21, tel. 030/4403-0637).

Kauf Dich Glücklich makes a great capper to a Prenzlauer Berg dinner. It serves an enticing array of sweet Belgian waffles and homemade ice cream in a candy-sprinkled, bohemian lounge on a great street (daily 11:00-24:00, indoor and outdoor seating—or get your dessert to go, Oderberger Strasse 44, tel. 030/4862-3292).

Bonanza Coffee is one of Berlin's most respected artisanal coffeehouses (Mon-Fri 8:30-18:00, Sat-Sun from 10:00, Oderberger Strasse 35, tel. 030/208-488-020).

Café Morgenrot ("Red Dawn") is a Prenzlauer Berg classic—a holdover from the neighborhood's squatter days, and still run by an artists' collective (closed Mon, vegan options, 85 Kastanienallee, tel. 030/4431-7844).

Kollwitzkiez Area

This small neighborhood, a few blocks east of Kastanienallee, is Prenzlauer Berg's gentrified heart—quieter and more residential. Hip parents bring their hip kids to the leafy playground park at its center, Kollwitzplatz. The first listing (Gugelhof) is a pricier sit-down option right on the park; the others allow you to enjoy great food and this area on the cheap. Some of these (and many others in the neighborhood) offer take-away; grab something to go, and find a bench on this prime square.

$$$ Gugelhof, right on Kollwitzplatz, is an institution famous for its Alsatian German cuisine—French quality with German proportions. An enthusiastic local crowd fills its minimalist yet classy interior. In good weather, outdoor seating sprawls along its sidewalk. Their fixed-price meals are fun, and they welcome swapping (Mon-Fri 17:00-23:00, Sat-Sun from 12:00, reservations smart, where Knaackstrasse meets Kollwitzplatz, tel. 030/442-9229, www.gugelhof.de).

$ Imbiss 204 is a bit farther from the core of Prenzlauer Berg, but worth the trek for huge portions of traditional German dishes. Highlights include wiener schnitzel and *Buletten*. This place—popular with food-loving tourists who've done their homework—is tiny and crowded, and they don't take reservations. Come at an off time or expect to wait outside. Be ready to share a table and make new friends (Mon-Fri 12:00-22:00, closed Sat-Sun, Prenzlauer Allee 204, tel. 030/2403-8543).

$ Chutnify offers a modern take on Indian street food. You can get a *dosa* (southern India's version of a burrito, with various fillings), a *thali* (mixed platter), or a curry, either to eat in the

EATING

Food Tours

A variety of Berlin companies offer culinary tours. Most either focus on traditional German fare or the trendier foodie scene, some do a combination of both, and virtually all of them include a *Currywurst*. Some well-established tour operators—including **Original Berlin Walks, Fat Tire Bike Tours,** and **Brewer's Berlin** (which does a craft beer tour)—have added food tours to their lineup (see page 24). Meanwhile, an array of specialty companies focus on doing only food tours. As this is a quickly evolving scene, it's difficult to recommend a specific company. But for starters, consider the following: **Fork and Walk Tours** (higher-end, combines sightseeing with food stops, www.forkandwalktoursberlin.com), **Bite Berlin** (a smaller operation with thoughtful tours, www.biteberlin.com), and **The German Food Tour** (brief and affordable, www.thegermanfoodtour.de). Check their websites (and online reviews) to find a tour that suits your interests and travel philosophy.

cozy interior or to go (daily 12:00-23:00, Sredzkistrasse 43, tel. 030/4401-0795).

$ Zula is handy for cheap hummus wraps. The main draw here is the location: You can either sit at an outside table on one of Prenzlauer Berg's finest streets, or enjoy your food at Kollwitzplatz, just down the street (daily 11:00-23:00, Husemannstrasse 10, tel. 030/4171-5100).

Pubs near Senefelderplatz: These two options—a few blocks south of Kollwitzplatz, handy to the Senefelderplatz U-Bahn—are good choices for beer with grub. The first is old-school, the other modern. **$ Metzer Eck** is a time-warp *Kneipe* with cozy charm and a family tradition dating to 1913. It serves cheap, basic, typical Berlin food with five beers on tap, including the Czech Budvar (Mon-Fri 16:00-24:00, Sat from 18:00, closed Sun, Metzer Strasse 33, on the corner with Strassburger Strasse, tel. 030/442-7656). **$$ Leibhaftig** is the modern yin to Metzer's yang, serving their own brews and small plates of nouveau German cuisine. The cellar setting is tight but convivial (Mon-Sat 18:00-24:00, closed Sun, Metzer Strasse 30, tel. 030/5481-5039).

SCHEUNENVIERTEL

Of Berlin's trendy dining zones, this is the closest from the main sightseeing core. Most of these places are a reasonable walk from Unter den Linden and within 10 minutes of the Hackescher Markt S-Bahn station. For locations, see the map on page 266.

On or near Auguststrasse

The best place to find good eateries in Scheunenviertel is along or near Auguststrasse, Berlin's "art gallery row" (close to the New Synagogue and my 🕮 Scheunenviertel Walk). Though the other areas I cover (Rosenthaler Platz and Hackescher Markt) are easier to reach, Auguststrasse is worth the short detour, as it's attracted a fun cross-section of creative chefs that make it your best choice for a good meal.

Note: The nearby and much bigger Oranienburger Strasse is jammed with dime-a-dozen Indian, Cuban, and Singapore-themed restaurants serving tropical cocktails. While this street is trendy (and not a terrible choice for a practical meal), the places I recommend here are more interesting and more respected by locals.

$$ Mogg Deli, run by an expat Brooklynite, is a foodie favorite, serving a short but thoughtful menu of soups, salads, and sandwiches. They're known for their home-cured pastrami, especially their monster, easily splittable Reuben (daily 11:00-22:00, inside the huge red-brick former Jewish girls school at Auguststrasse 11, tel. 030/330-060-770).

$$ Gipsy Restaurant fills the courtyard in front of Clärchens Ballhaus (a classic old Berlin ballroom) with twinkle lights, ram-

shackle furniture, and a bohemian-chic atmosphere—especially nice on a balmy evening. They serve good, reasonably priced German and Italian dishes, including brats, pizza, and homemade cakes (daily 12:30-23:00, Auguststrasse 24, tel. 030/282-9295). At lunch, climb the stairs to the delightful old **$$ Spiegelsaal** dining hall, with faded-elegant decor and flickering chandeliers that take you back to Berlin's Weimar-era glory days (lunch only, Mon-Fri 11:00-15:00, closed Sat-Sun).

$$ Schwarzwaldstuben is a Black Forest-themed pub—which explains the antlers, cuckoo clocks, and painting of a thick forest on the wall. It's friendly, with good service, food, and prices. The staff chooses the music (often rock or jazz), and the ambience is warm and welcoming. If they're full, you can eat at the long bar or at one of the sidewalk tables (daily 12:00-23:00, Tucholskystrasse 48, tel. 030/2809-8084).

$$$ Cordobar is a cozy wine bar with a clean, trendy vibe and an appealing range of both German and international wines by the glass, paired with upscale small plates. Come here not for a filling meal, but to enjoy a posh local scene and try some interesting wines. It's quite popular, so reserve ahead (Tue-Sat 19:00-24:00, closed Sun-Mon, Grosse Hamburger Strasse 32, tel. 030/2758-1215).

EATING

$$ Aufsturz is a lively pub that's more for serious drinkers than serious eaters. It has a huge selection of beer and whisky and dishes up traditional Berliner pub grub to a young crowd (daily 12:00-24:00, Oranienburger Strasse 67, tel. 030/2804-7407).

Coffee: At **The Barn,** curt baristas serve up some of Berlin's best gourmet coffee with an extra shot of pretense. Hipster coffee snobs will be satisfied (Mon-Fri 8:30-18:00, Sat-Sun 10:00-18:00, Auguststrasse 58). Another branch is near Senefelderplatz in Prenzlauer Berg (Schönhauser Allee 8).

Dessert: For your afternoon *Kaffee und Küchen,* stop at **Princess Cheesecake,** beloved by locals and selling several varieties of cheesecake (daily 10:00-19:00, Tucholskystrasse 37, tel. 030/2809-2760).

Rosenthaler Platz Area

This busy neighborhood with some enticing options is roughly between Scheunenviertel and Prenzlauer Berg (near the U8: Rosenthaler Platz station, and on the tram #M1 line that runs between Kastanienallee and the Hackescher Markt S-Bahn station).

$$ Transit is a popular, tight, affordable eatery that cranks out Thai/Indonesian/pan-Asian small plates. Sit at one of the long shared tables and dig into the creative menu. Two people can make a filling meal out of three or four dishes. This place can be crowded, and they don't take reservations, so come at an off time or expect to line up on the street (daily 11:00-24:00, cash only, Rosenthaler Strasse 68, tel. 030/2478-1645).

St. Oberholz Café, filling a fine old two-story space overlooking the busy Rosenthaler Platz intersection, epitomizes today's Berlin: a hipster coffee shop where startup types sip lattes waiting for inspiration. Customers can rent tables to work at, and everyone seems to have the latest MacBook. The owner even wrote a how-to book on building a Berlin startup (daily 8:00-24:00, Rosenthaler Strasse 72A).

Eclectic Eats on Weinbergsweg: If you're sniffing around for a meal in this area, don't miss the first block of Weinbergsweg, the narrower, tram track-lined lane that heads north to Prenzlauer Berg. In just one block, you'll find cafés, bakeries, superfoods and organic juice, *Gemüse kebab, döner kebab,* an Italian deli, Mexican street food, Russian, Korean barbecue, a French bistro, Chinese dumplings, gelato, and more.

Hackescher Markt Area

$$$ Hasir Turkish Restaurant is a popular, upscale, somewhat stuffy opportunity to splurge on Anatolian specialties amid candles and hardwood floors. While a bit past its prime and with hit-or-miss service, Hasir remains fairly respected, and enjoys a handy

EATING

location in a courtyard next to the Hackesche Höfe shopping complex (large and splittable portions, daily 11:00-24:00, a block from the Hackescher Markt S-Bahn station at Oranienburger Strasse 4, tel. 030/2804-1616).

\$\$ Weihenstephaner Bavarian Restaurant serves upmarket traditional Bavarian food in an atmospheric cellar, on an inner courtyard, or on a busy people-watching terrace facing the delightful Hackescher Markt square; and, of course, it has excellent beer (daily 11:00-24:00, Neue Promenade 5 at Hackescher Markt, tel. 030/8471-0760).

KREUZBERG

To dig into Berlin's up-and-coming food scene, head to Kreuzberg. This southern Berlin neighborhood—historically known for its large immigrant community and counterculture squatter types— has taken off as *the* place for upwardly mobile young Berliners to eat out. I list a few options in some of the most appealing areas. As this is a very trendy destination, it's smart to reserve ahead at most of these—especially on weekends—or avoid prime meal times. For more on Kreuzberg and its various *Kieze* (smaller sub-neighborhoods), see page 58.

Cozy Hangouts in Graefekiez: In addition to its fascinating **Turkish Street Market** (see page 294), the area just south of the Landwehr Canal is home to the delightful Graefekiez neighborhood (U8: Schönleinstrasse). On its main drag, Graefestrasse, you'll find several tempting options, such as the inviting **\$ Kaffeebar,** serving drinks, breakfast, and sandwiches (Mon-Fri 7:30-19:00, Sat-Sun 9:30-19:00, Graefestrasse 8). Closer to the river—near the bridge (Admiralbrücke)—locals flock to the **Isabel** ice-cream parlor (daily 10:00-18:00, Böckhstrasse 1) and the cheap-and-cheery **\$ Il Casolare** pizzeria (daily 12:00-24:00, Grimmstrasse 30).

High-End Foodie Splurges on Paul-Lincke-Ufer: This strip—along the north bank of the Landwehr Canal (across from the Turkish market)—is home to several top-tier Berlin eateries (U8: Schönleinstrasse). Close to the bridge (Kottbusser Brücke) are **\$\$\$\$ Horváth,** a Michelin-star restaurant featuring elevated Austrian/international-fusion fare (Wed-Sun 18:30-22:30, closed Mon-Tue, #44a, tel. 030/6128-9992, www.restaurant-horvath.de) and **\$\$ Cocolo Ramen X-berg,** an outpost of a high-end Japanese restaurant, serving slurpy noodle bowls (Mon-Sat 12:00-23:00, Sun 18:00-23:00, #39, tel. 030/9833-9073, www.kuchi.de). Farther east along the canal are **\$\$\$\$ Lode & Stijn,** featuring the eclectic high-end cooking (without pretense) of two talented Dutch-transplant chefs (Tue-Sat 18:00-22:30, closed Sun-Mon, Lausitzer Strasse 25, tel. 030/6521-4507, www.lode-stijn.de) and **\$\$\$\$ Restaurant Volt,** with upscale international dishes in a for-

EATING

mer power station (Tue-Sat 18:00-24:00, closed Sun-Mon, #21, tel. 030/338-402-320, www.restaurant-volt.de).

Kebabs and Fried Chicken near Oranienstrasse: At the scruffy Kottbusser Tor U-Bahn station (U1/U8), you'll find several hole-in-the wall **$ kebab stands** (good choices include Konak Grill at Reichenberger Strasse 10 and Doyum Restaurant at Admiralstrasse 36). A block north of Kottbusser Tor runs the east-west thoroughfare Oranienstrasse. At the intersection with Adalbertstrasse is an outpost of **$$$ Hasir,** the high-end Turkish restaurant based at Hackescher Markt—see listing on page 286 (daily 12:00-24:00, Adalbertstrasse 12). A couple of blocks north is the old-school local favorite **$ Henne,** which serves just one thing: fried chicken (Tue-Sun 18:00-24:00, closed Mon, Leuschnerdamm 25). East on Oranienstrasse—on Heinrichplatz—is the funky **$ Angry Chicken,** selling spicy Korean fried chicken (daily 12:00-22:00, Oranienstrasse 16).

Markthalle Neun: Kreuzberg's best foodie destination is this beautifully renovated 19th-century market hall, filled with local producers and fun food stalls (U1: Görlitzer Bahnhof). You'll find gourmet butchers, wine shops, tapas, Berlin meatballs *(Buletten),* tofu sandwiches, fair trade spices, Turkish dishes, and an Aldi supermarket. This is Berlin's answer to London's Borough Market or New York's Chelsea Market (on a much smaller scale; most vendors open Mon-Sat 10:00-18:00, closed Sun, busiest on Tue and Fri-Sat; for location see map on page 52). It's most worthwhile on "Street Food Thursdays," when extra eateries open up (weekly 17:00-22:00); Eisenbahnstrasse 42, event schedule at www.markthalleneun.de). Note: The Görlitzer Bahnhof area can feel seedy; on arrival, head straight for Lausitzer Platz, marked by the big church, then cut up to the top of the park and keep going 1.5 blocks to the market. Attached to the market are a good gourmet coffee shop (Café 9) and **$$$ Weltrestaurant Markthalle,** with classic *Kneipe* decor and big portions of traditional German dishes (daily 12:00-24:00, Pücklerstrasse 34).

Wrangelkiez: This area is loaded with restaurants (U1: Schlesisches Tor). Beer pilgrims appreciate **Hopfenreich,** with 22 good microbrews on tap, but no food (daily 16:00-24:00, Sorauer Strasse 31, tel. 030/8806-1080). For a delicious and authentic Georgian meal, make your way to **$$ Schwiliko**—with owners (and ingredients) imported from the Republic of Georgia (daily 17:00-24:00, Schlesische Strasse 29, tel. 030/6162-3588, www.schwiliko-berlin.

de). **$$ Freischwimmer,** serving a range of European dishes, is a great place to break on a sunny day thanks to its peaceful spot right on the river (daily 12:00-22:00, Vor dem Schlesischen Tor 2a, tel. 030/6107-4309).

Bergmannkiez: Another fine market hall is located in this upscale Kreuzberg neighborhood (U7: Gneisenaustrasse). **$ Marheineke Markthalle** is filled with appealing food counters serving Greek, Asian, Spanish tapas, French crêpes and galettes, grilled fish, pizza, Berlin specialties, and so on (Mon-Fri 8:00-20:00, Sat until 18:00, closed Sun, Marheinekeplatz 15; for location see map on page 52). Facing the same square are a pair of related restaurants that Berliners swear by for traditional Austrian cuisine: the aptly named **$$$ Austria Restaurant,** in business since 1858 (Tue-Sun 12:00-23:00, Mon from 18:00, cash only, Bergmannstrasse 30, tel. 030/694-4440), and their smaller, trendier-feeling annex, **$$ Felix Austria** (daily 10:00-24:00, just a half-block away toward the market hall at Bergmannstrasse 26, tel. 030/6167-5451). Nearby, the wine bar **Not Only Riesling** has an array of German vintages (Mon-Thu 12:00-22:00, Fri-Sat 10:00-24:00, closed Sun, Schleiermacherstrasse 25, tel. 030/6953-8866).

At the opposite (west) end of Bergmannkiez, the thriving **$$ Golgatha Gaststätten** beer garden sits at the base of Viktoriapark's Kreuzberg monument (daily in good weather 9:00-18:00, Dudenstrasse 40, tel. 030/785-2453).

Famous Street Food at Mehringdamm: Two beloved-by-Berliners street food joints stand a few steps apart along the west side of Mehringdamm street, near the U-Bahn stop of the same name (U6/U7). **$ Mustafa's Gemüse Kebab** is famous for its top-quality kebabs (both meat and vegetarian versions)...and its extremely long lines. Nearby, **$ Curry 36** is a local favorite for *Currywurst* and generally has a shorter/faster-moving line (both places open long hours daily).

CITY WEST

These eateries are of interest primarily to travelers sleeping here. For locations, see the map on page 270.

Near Savignyplatz

While not worth a special trip, many good restaurants are on or within 100 yards of Savignyplatz, near my recommended hotels. Savignyplatz is lined with attractive, relaxed, mostly Mediterranean-style places. Take a walk and survey the places I list here; continue your stroll along Bleibtreustrasse to discover many trendier, creative little eateries.

$$$ Restaurant Marjellchen is a trip to East Prussia, with big portions of hearty, delicious German/Polish cuisine. Dine in cozily cluttered elegance in one of two six-table rooms. While it doesn't have to be expensive, plan to go the whole nine yards here, as this can be a great experience, with caring service. The menu is inviting, and the place family-run—all the recipes were brought to Berlin by the owner's East Prussian mother after World War II. Reservations are smart (daily 17:00-22:30, Mommsenstrasse 9, tel. 030/883-2676, www.marjellchen-berlin.de).

$$ Dicke Wirtin ("Fat Landlady") has a traditional old-Berlin *Kneipe* atmosphere, seven good beers on tap (including Andechs from Bavaria), and solid home cooking at reasonable prices—such as their famously cheap *Gulaschsuppe*. Their interior is fun and pubby, with soccer on the TV; their streetside tables are also inviting. Pickled eggs are on the bar—ask about how these can help you avoid a hangover (daily 11:00-23:00, dinner served from 18:00, just off Savignyplatz at Carmerstrasse 9, tel. 030/312-4952).

$$$$ Café im Literaturhaus sits above a rare-books shop on a delightfully tranquil garden courtyard, facing the Käthe Kollwitz Museum. It has the ambience of an Old World villa, with classy gold Art Deco accents—perfect for their evening poetry and other literary readings. While the full menu is quite pricey, you can enjoy the place far more affordably with a sandwich or coffee and cake (daily 9:30-24:00, smart to reserve for dinner if eating inside, Fasanenstrasse 23, tel. 030/882-5414).

$ Heno Heno is a very popular Japanese hole-in-the-wall, serving a variety of rice bowls, noodle dishes, and soups (but no sushi) in a long, sleek, minimalist space (Mon-Sat 12:00-22:00, closed Sun, Wielandstrasse 37, tel. 030/6630-7370).

$ Diener Tattersall is a neighborhood favorite *Kneipe* with a complicated history. The building started as a horse riding school, later became a casino, and was eventually bought by the German heavyweight champion Franz Diener, who attracted an eclectic clientele of boxers and artists to his *Kneipe*. Today it's known for the affordable menu, specializing in homemade liver sausage (daily from 18:00, Grolmanstrasse 47, tel. 030/881-5329).

$$ Weyers offers modern German cuisine in a simple, elegant setting, with dining tables in the summer spilling out into the idyllic neighborhood park in front (daily 8:00-24:00, Pariser Strasse 16—facing Ludwigkirchplatz at intersection with Pfalzburger Strasse, tel. 030/881-9378).

On Bleibtreustrasse: On the stretch just south of the Savignyplatz S-Bahn tracks, Bleibtreustrasse is lined with an eclectic array of dining options—wander and take your pick: **$$ Zillemarkt,** an old-time beer hall with nice atmosphere and uninspired service (#48A); **$$$ Die Zwölf Apostel,** with Italian dishes and sophisticated ambience (#49); neighborhood budget favorite **$ Ali Baba,** with pizzas and outdoor seating (#45); plus **$ Repke**

Spätzlerei (Spanish tapas, including buttery dumplings) and **Nibs Cacao** (churros and chocolate; both at #46).

Near the Berlin Zoological Garden
In addition to a beer garden and department-store cafeteria, there's plenty of fast food near the Zoologischer Garten station and on Ku'damm.

$ Curry 36—the locally beloved *Currywurst* vendor from Kreuzberg (see page 289)—has a handy outpost just outside of the Zoologischer Garten station.

$$ Schleusenkrug beer garden is hidden in the park over-looking a canal between the Zoologischer Garten and Tiergarten stations. Choose from an ever-changing self-service menu of huge salads, pasta, and some German dishes (daily 10:00-24:00, food served 12:00-22:00, shorter hours and more basic menu off-season, cash only; from Zoologischer Garten station it's a 5-minute walk following the path into the park between the zoo and train tracks; tel. 030/313-9909).

KaDeWe: The top floor of this famous department store holds the **$$ Winter Garden Buffet** cafeteria, while its sixth-floor **deli/food department** is a picnicker's nirvana. Its arterials are clogged with more than 1,000 kinds of sausage and 1,500 types of cheese (Mon-Sat 10:00-20:00, closed Sun, U-Bahn: Wittenbergplatz).

SHOPPING IN BERLIN

Berlin is a good shopping city—if not quite a great one. Those who enjoy browsing design boutiques with clever hipster housewares are on cloud nine in Berlin. However, you can do that kind of shopping in many other cities, and Berlin isn't known for any one must-buy item. And, while there's not much "destination" shopping in this city, you can find fun areas to window-shop anywhere you go. This chapter focuses mainly on markets, neighborhoods, and streets where browsing is its own reward...even if you don't buy anything.

Most Berlin shops keep similar hours: Monday through Friday from about 9:00 or 10:00 to somewhere between 18:00 and 20:00, often somewhat shorter hours on Saturday, and typically closed on Sunday.

For information on VAT refunds and customs regulations, see page 389.

WHAT TO BUY

Shops all over town stock the typical array of **souvenirs** (T-shirts, posters, bottle openers, etc.) emblazoned with icons of Berlin: Brandenburg Gate, TV Tower, Berlin Wall, bears (the namesake and official mascot of "Bear-lin"), and so on.

One big draw is **communist kitsch.** Stories about life behind

the Berlin Wall have a way of capturing visitors' imaginations. Gift shops at museums (such as the DDR Museum or the Museum of the Wall at Checkpoint Charlie) sell a variety of "East Berlin" paraphernalia: circa-1968 city maps that mysteriously leave out West Berlin, postcards and posters of DDR propaganda or famous Wall escapes, miniature Trabis, old DDR military armbands and medals, defunct communist currency, and little plastic chicken-shaped cups that every East German family had on their breakfast table. While you can get modern replicas all over town, if you're looking for authentic communist artifacts, head to VEB Orange (in Prenzlauer Berg, described on page 208) or the flea market by the Ostbahnhof (Sun mornings, described later).

Maybe *the* top communist-kitsch souvenir is something—anything—with the image of the **Ampelmann** (traffic-light man),

the DDR-era crossing-guard symbol that's become Berlin's unofficial mascot. The best selection is at the local chain of Ampelmann shops, with locations all over the city. The flagship store—with a hunk of Berlin Wall autographed by David Hasselhoff (no joke)—is along Unter den Linden at #35 (at the corner with Friedrichstrasse). Others are near Gendarmenmarkt (Markgrafenstrasse 37), between Museum Island and the TV Tower (Karl-Liebknecht-Strasse 5), in the Hackesche Höfe (described later), at Potsdamer Platz, in the Hauptbahnhof, and on City West's Kurfürstendamm (at #20).

One communist-era souvenir to avoid is an **"authentic" chunk of the Berlin Wall**—enough of which have been sold since 1989 to encircle all of Germany. Don't trust any vendor who swears they chipped it off the Wall themselves. (And, because the few remaining stretches of Wall are now protected monuments, it's not appropriate to chisel off your own souvenir.)

Berlin's true forte is **design.** In this city of stylish young urbanites, the streets are lined with hipster gift shops that sell ironic T-shirts, clever kitchen or desk gadgets, snarky books and postcards, twee "put a bird on it" knickknacks, and so on. Stroll through home decor, housewares, and furniture shops: Even if what they sell is too big to pack home, you'll get an eye-opening look at how locals furnish their lives.

Other shopping options to consider include Berlin's many appealing **bookstores** (consider Do You Read Me? at Auguststrasse 28 in the Scheunenviertel; or Ocelot, near Rosenthaler Platz at Brunnenstrasse 181); CDs of quality **music,** perhaps performed by the renowned Berlin Philharmonic (shop at the Philharmonic building itself, also check out the big Dussmann book-and-record store at Friedrichstrasse 90; for something more recent, Hard Wax in Kreuzberg at Paul-Lincke-Ufer 44A is *the* seminal record shop in town); or **museum gift shops,** which stock books and prints of artwork that you enjoyed seeing in person.

FLEA MARKETS AND FARMERS MARKETS

In such an outdoorsy city, some of the most enjoyable "shopping" experiences aren't in shopping malls or hole-in-the-wall boutiques, but at sprawling outdoor flea markets and farmers markets. In good weather, Berliners have a knack for turning these into opportunities to enjoy their city.

Flea Markets *(Flomarkt)*

Virtually every Berlin neighborhood hosts a regular flea market.

Prenzlauer Berg: The Sunday rummage market in the **Mauerpark** isn't just about buying and selling—it's an excuse for a big, weekly, community-wide party. If it's nice out, people come here simply to chill, drink, barbecue, and socialize. You'll find lots of inventive snack stalls and, in the afternoon, karaoke in the park's amphitheater (Sun 9:00-18:00, U2: Eberswalder Strasse, www.flohmarktimmauerpark.de). Sunday is also the time for a lively "junk market" *(Trödelmarkt)* several blocks south on **Arkonaplatz** (10:00-16:00, U8: Bernauer Strasse or a 10-minute walk from Mauerpark).

Scheunenviertel: Just across the Spree from Monbijoupark, the riverbank facing the **Bode Museum** hosts a weekend antique-and-book market (Sat-Sun 10:00-17:00, tram #M1 or #12 to Am Kupfergraben or a 10-minute walk from Hackescher Markt or Friedrichstrasse S-Bahn stations, www.antik-buchmarkt.de). Closer to the heart of the Scheunenviertel, **Hackescher Markt** hosts a twice-weekly market with an odd variety of produce, clothes, trinkets, jewelry, hats, and food stalls; while smaller, more touristy, and less funky than the best Berlin markets, it's conveniently located (Thu 9:00-18:00, Sat from 10:00).

Kreuzberg: Along the south bank of Landwehr Canal, the twice-weekly **Turkish street market** is a very local place to shop for everything from clothes and fabrics to basic housewares to produce and meat. The clientele is a mix of Turkish and Middle Eastern immigrants, Kreuzberg punks, and a smattering of tourists. While you can pick up some tasty Turkish-style snacks (such as mint tea and dried fruits and nuts), I'd come here more for the people-watching than for souvenirs (Tue and Fri

11:00-18:30, U8: Schönleinstrasse, for location see map on page 52). Also in Kreuzberg—in the ritzier Bergmannkiez—the leafy and delightful **Marheinekeplatz** hosts a weekend flea market (Sat-Sun 10:00-17:00, U7: Gneisenaustrasse, for more on this area see page 61).

Friedrichshain: The swiftly gentrifying square **Boxhagener Platz** (affectionately called "Boxi" by locals) hosts a lively flea market on Sundays (10:00-18:00, U5: Samariterstrasse or U1/S5/S7: Warschauer Strasse plus a lengthy walk, www.troedelmarkt-arkonaplatz.de; also a Sat farmers market—see later). On Sunday mornings, the **Antikmarkt Ostbahnhof** (on the north side of the Ostbahnhof S-Bahn station) is the place to pick through the Cold War knickknacks that keep turning up in the basements of former East Berliners.

Near Tiergarten Park: One of Berlin's largest flea markets is right next to the Tiergarten park on **Strasse des 17 Juni,** with great antiques, more than 200 stalls, collector-savvy merchants, and fun German fast-food stands (Sat-Sun 10:00-17:00, S-Bahn: Tiergarten, www.berlinertroedelmarkt.com).

City West: Consider the big flea market on **Fehrbelliner Platz** in Charlottenburg (Sat-Sun 10:00-16:00, U2/U3/U7: Fehrbelliner Platz), or the smaller one in front of the **Schöneberg City Hall** (Sat-Sun 8:00-16:00, U4: Rathaus Schöneberg, for more on this area see page 80).

Food and Farmers Markets

Weekly farmers markets are huge in this city of foodies, and the biggest include stalls proffering fresh snacks of all kinds.

The city's best food market is Kreuzberg's **Markthalle Neun,** with a variety of vendors and even more activity during the thrice-weekly farmers market (Tue and Fri 12:00-20:00, Sat 10:00-18:00) and on "Street Food Thursdays." For more, see page 61.

Another local favorite is on **Boxhagener Platz** in Friedrichshain (farmers market Sat 9:00-15:30, see also Sunday flea market, listed earlier). Prenzlauer Berg also has options: **Kollwitzplatz** (Thu 12:00-19:00 and Sat 9:00-16:00) and in the courtyard of the **Kulturbrauerei** (Sun 12:00-18:00). In City West, head for **Wittenbergplatz** (near KaDeWe, Thu 10:00-18:00).

BROWSING AREAS
Prenzlauer Berg

My favorite hotel and dining neighborhood is also an enjoyable place to window-shop. It's a delight to simply wander colorful Kastanienallee between Eberswalder Strasse (with a U-Bahn station) and Weinbergspark, but I've also mentioned some other options here.

On Kastanienallee: Perhaps the most satisfying place to browse in Berlin—with so many shops in such a small area—Kastanienallee is made-to-order for a shopping stroll. Here's just some of what you'll see as you work your way downhill from Eberswalder Strasse: **Stoffbruch** (#99, set back on a modern plaza) is a concept store with stylish clothes "designed in Berlin, fair-produced in Europe." **Da Capo** (#96) is a funky, classic Prenzlauer Berg vintage record-and-book shop. **Heimat Berlin** (#13) is part of a small chain of fun-to-explore hipster gift shops (as is #41 and the **Luxus International** shop at #84).

After crossing Oderberger Strasse, you're near two fashion outposts: **Fein und Ripp** (#91) has hip, made-in-Germany clothes, while **Thatchers Fashion Berlin** (across the street at #21) is a bit more upscale. Farther down, **Uhranus** (#31) is perhaps the most enjoyably eclectic Kastanienallee design shop, with tea towels, bags, and prints that celebrate Berlin. In the next block, **Musik Department** (#41) is an appealingly grungy basement record store; **Kleine Fabriek** (#63) has high-end artisanal stuff for kids; and **Grünbein** (#47) sells fashionable, Swiss-made shoes and boots. Near the bottom of Kastanienallee, facing Weinbergspark, is **Glücklich am Park**—a branch of the popular Oderberger Strasse waffle café, Kauf dich Glücklich, with its own little fashion boutique upstairs.

Elsewhere in Prenzlauer Berg: The **Kulturbrauerei** brewery-turned-cultural center (described on page 201) has a smattering of little shops, including Green Living (with environmentally friendly housewares and home decor). The Kollwitzkiez (a few blocks east) is mostly residential, but you'll also find some pleasant shops here. For locally produced goods, stop by **Brandenburgerie,** with a variety of mostly edible products (meat, cheese, chocolate, juices, schnapps) made in the Brandenburg region that surrounds Berlin (closed Mon-Sun, Sredzkistrasse 36).

Clothing Boutiques and Pop-Ups Along Rosenthaler Strasse

The otherwise nondescript street that connects the Hackescher Markt and Rosenthaler Platz areas (along the handy tram #M1 route) attracts those interested in Berlin's fashion and design scene. Most shops along here are **pop-up** spaces, giving you a glimpse at what local designers are up to right now. A couple of permanent fixtures are worth checking out: **Kauf dich Glücklich,** a ramshackle Berlin café famous for its waffles (see page 283), but which has since moved into fashion (at #17, www.kaufdichgluecklich-shop.de); and **Schee,** with appealing handmade items, including prints and textiles (at #15, www.schee.net).

Hackesche Höfe

This delightfully restored old series of eight interlocking shopping courtyards sits in the heart of the Scheunenviertel (and is described on page 184 of the Scheunenviertel Walk). While not cheap, it's a convenient and tempting place to window-shop. Your options include Auerbach (top-end leather goods and men's fashion), Königliche Porzellan-Manufaktur (locally made porcelain), Sawade (gourmet chocolates), Hoffnung Berlin (handmade belts), Home on Earth (products made of natural materials—felt, cork, wicker, and so on), Eat Berlin (artisanal local foods), Golem (decorative *Jugendstil* tiles), Ampelmann (goods featuring the kitschy DDR-era traffic-light man), and many other boutiques selling shoes, jewelry, handbags, and more (shops typically open Mon-Sat from 10:00 or 11:00 until 19:00, closed Sun, Rosenthaler Strasse 40, www.hackesche-hoefe.com).

The Hackesche Höfe connects directly into another series of shopping courtyards called the **Rosenhöfe.** Though this space has a nice, slinky *Jugendstil* flair, its shops are less characteristic (with more international chains, like H&M and MAC).

Kreuzberg's Bergmannkiez

While a bit less colorful than the areas described above, Kreuzberg's classy Bergmannkiez can be fun to browse for designer boutiques and plenty of antiques. While most are concentrated along Bergmannstrasse, you'll find more options on the side streets. For more on exploring this area, see page 61.

Chocolate Shops on Gendarmenmarkt

The delightful square called Gendarmenmarkt—a short detour south of Unter den Linden—has two very different chocolate shops that are fun to browse: one bourgeois, and the other proletarian. For locations see the map on page 276.

Fassbender & Rausch claims to be Europe's biggest chocolate store. After 150 years of chocolate-making, this family-owned business proudly displays its sweet delights—250 different kinds—on a 55-foot-long buffet. Truffles are sold for about €1 each; it's fun to compose a fancy little eight-piece box of your own. Upstairs is an elegant café with fine views. The window displays feature giant chocolate models of Berlin landmarks—Reichstag, Brandenburg Gate, Kaiser Wilhelm Memorial Church, TV Tower, a chunk of the Wall, and so on. If all this isn't enough to entice you, I have three words: erupting chocolate volcano (Mon-Sat 10:00-20:00, Sun from 11:00, corner of Mohrenstrasse at Charlottenstrasse 60—look for green awnings directly behind German Cathedral, tel. 030/757-882-440).

If you're a choco-populist, head to the opposite end of Gendarmenmarkt, near the French Cathedral, for the Volkswagen of candy. **Rittersport Bunte Schokowelt** is home to the flagship store of Rittersport, the famous chocolate company—*"quadratisch, praktisch, gut"* ("square, practical, good"). This is basically Germany's answer to the M&M's store. While you can find Rittersport in any grocery store, it's fun to see floor-to-ceiling walls of chocolate, stop at their café, and create a make-your-own chocolate-bar souvenir: select milk, dark, or white chocolate; add three "mix-ins"; wait 30 minutes (browsing the attached retail shop) while it cools, and *voilà* (Mon-Wed 10:00-19:00, Thu-Sat until 20:00, Sun until 18:00, Französische Strasse 24, tel. 030/200-950-810).

BIG, GLITZY DEPARTMENT STORES

Consumerism—the Cold War victor—has taken root with a vengeance in Berlin, where super-modern malls and department stores abound.

Central Berlin

Unter den Linden is lined with some high-end shops, but for a wider selection, head a few blocks south.

The stretch of **Friedrichstrasse** near Gendarmenmarkt was slated to become Berlin's "Fifth Avenue" shopping district after the fall of the Wall. While it hasn't quite taken off the way developers had hoped, the French department store **Galeries Lafayette** has a large outpost here with several floors of high-end goods under a glass dome (top-quality basement food court; Mon-Sat 10:00-20:00, closed Sun, Französische Strasse 23).

Several blocks west is the massive, recently opened, state-of-the-art **Mall of Berlin,** with 270 shops surrounding a cavernous, glass-covered passageway (Mon-Sat 10:00-21:00, closed Sun, Vossstrasse 35, www.mallofberlin.de). Nearby, **Potsdamer Platz** and **Sony Center** have additional shops.

City West
Several swanky shops line **Kurfürstendamm,** the area's main boulevard (and the place to go if you're in the market for another Rolex).

The trendy **Bikinihaus** shopping center faces Europaplatz on one side and the Berlin Zoo on the other. This "concept mall" has

a mix of international chains, local artisan boutiques, a few food stalls, a small Kaiser's supermarket, and "pop-up boxes" highlighting a changing variety of Berlin vendors (plus a free glimpse of the zoo's monkeys; Mon-Sat 10:00-20:00, closed Sun, Budapester Strasse 38, www.bikiniberlin.de).

City West's most venerable shopping is a couple blocks east (near the Wittenbergplatz U-Bahn), at **KaDeWe**—one of Europe's fanciest department stores, in business since 1907 and a worthwhile sight in itself (for more, see page 79).

Farther west, the Charlottenburg neighborhood's **"Antique Mile"** stretches along Suarezstrasse (between Kantstrasse and the Sophie-Charlotte-Platz U-Bahn stop).

ENTERTAINMENT IN BERLIN

In the 18th century, Frederick the Great transformed Berlin into a cultural capital. In the early 20th century, the city emerged as Europe's counterculture capital—with a flourishing of edgy performing arts, from Marlene Dietrich's cabaret-singer origins to Bertolt Brecht's intentionally alienating theatrical staging. And today, Berlin remains a hub of both mainstream and alternative arts. This city has three opera companies, multiple symphonies and chamber orchestras, and organ concerts in churches nearly every day of the week. But you'll also find wild dance clubs, hipster ballrooms, dilapidated techno beach bars, and smoky jazz cellars.

This chapter focuses on two big facets of Berlin's entertainment scene: live music and how to spend your time after hours. In this sprawling city, options are many; I've focused on an (admittedly narrow) selection of ideas, with an emphasis on my favorite neighborhoods. Use these resources as a starting point to find entertainment and nightlife to meet your interests.

Entertainment Info: The TI can provide basic information about what's on; for classical music, look for the free, monthly *Concerti* magazine. But to really understand your options, go beyond the TI. For good listings of live music, see www.askhelmut.com. If you're serious about tracking down the local scene, shell out a few euros for a Berlin magazine (€4-5, sold at kiosks): For the young and determined sophisticate, *Zitty* (www.zitty.de) and *Tip* (www.tip-berlin.de) are the top guides to alternative culture (mostly in German); *Exberliner Magazine* has fewer hard details, but is colorfully written in English (www.exberliner.com). Also pick up the free *030* schedule in bars and clubs (www.berlin030.de).

Half-Price Tickets: Hekticket, Berlin's ticket clearinghouse, offers advance tickets to concerts, cabaret, theater, etc. And every day after 14:00, they sell deeply discounted last-minute tickets (up to half off, ticket prices usually range from €10 to €40). You can either call or check online (tel. 030/230-9930, www.hekticket.de, pay by credit card), or visit one of their locations (cash only) to see what's on the push list for that evening. Booths are near Alexanderplatz (Mon-Fri 10:30-19:00, closed Sat-Sun, Alexanderstrasse 1 across from Hotel Park Inn) and in City West (Mon-Sat 12:00-20:00, Sun 14:00-18:00, across from Zoologischer Garten train station at Hardenbergstrasse 29).

Smoking: Berlin bars that don't sell food can allow smoking (unlike in much of Europe). Locals who are sensitive to smoke should check in advance that their chosen bar is nonsmoking.

Late-Hours Sightseeing: Berlin's museums typically close at 18:00, but many stay open later at least one day a week, allowing smart planners to stretch their sightseeing day. Four of the biggies are open late every day: the Reichstag (until midnight, last entry at 22:00), the Museum of the Wall at Checkpoint Charlie (until 22:00), the Topography of Terror (until 20:00), and the Jewish Museum (Tue-Sun until 20:00, 22:00 on Mon). All the Museum Island museums are open until 20:00 on Thursdays. Outdoor monuments such as the Berlin Wall Memorial and the Memorial to the Murdered Jews of Europe are accessible, safe, and pleasantly lit late into the night, though their visitor centers close earlier.

CLASSICAL MUSIC
Serious Performances at World-Class Venues

Housed in a striking, modern building at the Kulturforum cultural complex, the **Berlin Philharmonic** is a perennial Top Ten orchestra in the world rankings.

It's under the direction of Simon Rattle until 2018 or so, when the baton will be passed to Kirill Petrenko. Inexpensive and legitimate tickets are often sold on the street an hour before performances. You can also buy tickets at the box office, by phone, or online (ticket office open Mon-Fri 15:00-18:00, Sat-Sun 11:00-14:00 except closed July-Aug, tel. 030/2548-8999—answered daily 9:00-18:00, July-Aug until 16:00, www.berliner-philharmoniker.de). The philharmonic also presents a popular series of free lunch concerts (most Tue at 13:00 except in July-Aug, tickets handed out in person the same day—try to arrive by 12:00). For guest performances, you must buy tickets through the organizer (see website for details). For more on the building, see the end of the Gemäldegalerie & Kulturforum Tour chapter.

Other important classical-music venues in the historic core include the gorgeous, Schinkel-designed **Konzerthaus Berlin** on Gendarmenmarkt (home of the Konzerthausorchester symphony orchestra, popular 45-minute "espresso concert" series Wed at 14:00, tel. 030/203-092-101, www.konzerthaus.de) and the cutting-edge, Frank Gehry-designed **Pierre Boulez Saal** (theater-in-the-round for chamber music, not far from Bebelplatz at Französische Strasse 33D, tel. 030/4799-7411, www.boulezsaal. de). To enjoy an affordable (sometimes free) recital by talented students, consider the **Hochschule für Musik Hanns Eisler,** with two venues in the historical center (facing Gendarmenmarkt at Charlottenstrasse 55, and on Museum Island at Schlossplatz 7, tel. 030/203-092-101, www.hfm-berlin.de).

Berlin also has multiple opera venues. The most historic is the stately **Staatsoper,** on Bebelplatz overlooking Unter den Linden. While that building is being renovated, the Berlin State Opera is performing at the Schiller Theater (in City West, just north of the Savignyplatz hotel and restaurant neighborhood, U2: Ernst-Reuter-Platz, box office tel. 030/2035-4555, www.staatsoper-berlin.de). Quite different is Berlin's famous **Komische Oper,** with a long tradition for avant-garde, adventurous performances of operas and operettas (near Unter den Linden and Friedrichstrasse at Behrenstrasse 55, tel. 030/4799-7400, www.komische-oper-berlin. de). And finally, the modern **Deutsche Oper** building (in Charlottenburg, near City West, just northwest of the Savignyplatz area) houses both its own opera company and the Berlin State Ballet (Bismarckstrasse 35, U2: Deutsche Oper, tel. 030/3438-4343, www.deutscheoperberlin.de).

Daytime Concerts in Churches

Several Berlin churches and other venues offer frequent daytime and early evening concerts. Note that each of these is a historic

building described in the Sights in Berlin chapter (and often in one of my walks or tour chapters). Even "free" concerts request a donation. Any of these can cancel unexpectedly, so confirm before making a special trip.

Marien Church, along Karl-Liebknecht-Strasse near the TV Tower, hosts free organ concerts twice weekly (Thu and Fri at 13:30, www. marienkirche-berlin.de), as well as a variety of other concerts.

Nikolaikirche, in the Nikolai Quarter, hosts 30-minute organ concerts on Friday afternoons (at 17:00, €8, www.en.stadtmuseum.de/nikolaikirche).

French Cathedral, on Gendarmenmarkt, hosts 30-minute organ concerts on Tuesdays (at 15:00, €3, www.franzoesische-friedrichstadtkirche.de), as well as a variety of other organ and choral worship services.

St. Hedwig's Catholic Cathedral, on Bebelplatz, has free 30-minute organ concerts on Wednesdays (at 15:00, www.hedwigs-kathedrale.de).

Berlin Cathedral, on Museum Island, hosts evening concerts, ranging from organ to choral (often on weekends, starting between 18:00-20:00, tickets at the door—prices vary from free to €50, but often €10, www.berlinerdom.de).

Kaiser Wilhelm Memorial Church, the modern annex next to the WWII-ruined church in City West, hosts a series of quality concerts (sporadic schedule, often choral, some are free and others charge, www.gedaechtniskirche-berlin.de).

Clärchens Ballhaus—not a church but the Scheunenviertel's beloved classic ballroom—hosts concerts most Sunday evenings in its twinkling upstairs Mirror Room, the Spiegelsaal (often piano or small ensembles, €12—or €8 if you buy ahead, usually begins at 19:00 or 19:30, www.sonntagskonzerte.de).

MODERN MUSIC AND THEATER
Jazz
Berlin has a lively jazz scene (for schedules, see www.jazzclubsinberlin.com). Here are some favorites that are close to my recommended accommodations. Each has live music nightly from 21:00 (doors open at 20:00).

In City West (near Savignyplatz), consider **A Trane Jazz Club** (great stage and intimate seating, €10-25 cover depending on act, Bleibtreustrasse 1—see map on page 270, tel. 030/313-2550, www.a-trane.de).

Near the TV Tower, **B-Flat Acoustic Music and Jazz Club** has live shows and jam sessions (from free to €10-14, in Alexanderplatz at Dircksenstrasse 40—see map on page 276, tel. 030/283-3123, www.b-flat-berlin.de).

Kunstfabrik Schlot, in a cellar between the Nordbahnhof and the Natural History Museum (northwest of Scheunenviertel), is another respected venue (from free to €12-15, tucked back in a courtyard at Invalidenstrasse 117, see map on page 266, U6: Naturkundemuseum, tel. 030/448-2160, www.kunstfabrik-schlot.de).

Theater and Variety Shows

Since the cabaret days, Berlin has had a flair for the dramatic. Most of these offerings are in German only. If you're adventurous or speak some German, this can be a plus; if not, confirm the language carefully before you book. For the big spectacles, the language matters less.

Bar Jeder Vernunft, in City West, offers modern-day cabaret a short walk from my recommended Savignyplatz hotels. This variety show—under a classic old tent perched atop the modern parking lot of the Berliner Festspiele theater—is a hit with German speakers and can be worthwhile for those who don't speak the language (as some of the music shows are in a sort of *Deutsch*-English hybrid). Some Americans even perform here periodically. Tickets run about €25-30, and shows change regularly (performances generally Tue-Sat at 20:00, Sun at 19:00, seating can be cramped, south of Ku'damm at Schaperstrasse 24—see map on page 270, U3 or U9: Spichernstrasse, tel. 030/883-1582, www.bar-jeder-vernunft.de).

Just north of Unter den Linden, the **Friedrichstadtpalast** stages glitzy spectacles—going for Las Vegas-style bombast

(Friedrichstrasse 107, www.palast.berlin). Nearby, a bit closer in to Unter den Linden, the historic **Admiralspalast Theater** features lower-key concerts, plays, and musicals (including the Distel Cabaret Theater company; Friedrichstrasse 101, www.mehr.de/en/venues/admiralspalast-berlin).

Other venues to consider: **Theater RambaZamba,** in Prenzlauer Berg's Kulturbrauerei, highlights performers who are disabled and creatively transforms those "disabilities" into assets (www.theater-rambazamba.org). **Chamäleon,** inside Hackesche Höfe and handy to many recommended accommodations, is an intimate venue that tries to channel the creative spirit of 1920s Berlin (www.chamaeleonberlin.com). **Kookaburra,** between my Scheunenviertel and Prenzlauer Berg hotels, is a comedy club that regularly presents acts in English (usually Tue at 20:00, Schönhauserallee 184, www.comedyclub.de). And the **Berliner Festspiele** hosts a variety of performances, often Off-Broadway-type fringe theater (check their website to see what they're up to lately: www.berlinerfestspiele.de).

Live Music

Berlin has a staggering array of smaller music venues. Equip yourself with good information (see sources at the start of this chapter) and cast a wide net. In addition to the classical and jazz venues described earlier, here's a sampling worth consideration: **Frannz Club,** in Prenzlauer Berg's Kulturbrauerei, has been around since

1970 and was a DDR-era hotspot; today it attracts talented rock and alternative bands (www. frannz.com). **Bassy Club,** near Senefelder Platz in Prenzlauer Berg, is a surreal cowboy-themed club boasting "wild music before 1969," with a loyal

local following (www.bassyclub.com). Though it's a dance hall, **Clärchens Ballhaus** also has live music Friday and Saturday nights; **Ballhaus Berlin** is another good option (see descriptions for both later, under "Dancing"). **Aufsturz** pub, the recommended pub in the Scheunenviertel, hosts jazz and other music (see page 286, www.aufsturz.de). And **SO36,** on Oranienstrasse in Kreuzberg, is Berlin's most venerable punk venue (www.so36.de).

Big concerts are often held at **Olympic Stadium, Mercedes-Benz Arena** in Friedrichshain, the **Spandau Citadel,** and the outdoor **Waldbühne** ("Forest Stage").

NIGHTLIFE

Al Fresco Summer Fun

Berliners have a knack for enjoying life without spending a lot of money. On a warm summer evening, it seems everyone's out, simply enjoying their city. Here are some ideas for how to join them.

Great places to **stroll** while people-watching Berliners include the Spree riverbank (especially around Monbijoupark and Museum Island); Prenzlauer Berg's Kastanienallee, Oderberger Strasse, and Helmholtzplatz; and Kreuzberg's Paul-Lincke-Ufer, a leafy embankment on the Landwehr Canal with upscale homes and a lively *boules* court (see page 57). The Scheunenviertel's Oranienburger Strasse (near the New Synagogue) and City West's

Europaplatz/Kurfürstendamm boulevard are packed, but are more tourist-oriented.

To nurse a drink, stop by a *Biergarten*. Big, beloved, and lively choices include Prater Biergarten, in Prenzlauer Berg (page 203); Schleusenkrug in City West, tucked back in the park near the Zoologischer Garten train station (page 291); and Golgatha Gaststätten in Kreuzberg's Viktoriapark (page 62).

An even more summery variation is Berlin's emerging **beach bar** scene—where people grab a drink along the riverfront and watch the excursion boats go by. The classic spot is the **Strandbar Mitte** in Monbijoupark, with a breezy and scenic setting overlooking the Bode Museum on Museum Island. Others are farther afield, in the Friedrichshain and Kreuzberg neighborhoods: **Yaam** is funky, with playgrounds, real sand, an African theme, and often live music (near the Ostbahnhof and Radialsystem—described later, www.yaam.de). Two more are farther east (close to U1: Schlesisches Tor): **Badeschiff,** a floating swimming pool with a bar (May-Sept daily, www.arena.berlin/en/location/badeschiff); and **Club der Visionaere,** a very cramped wooden pier with DJs spinning throbbing electronic music (Mon-Fri 15:00-late, Sat-Sun 12:00-later, www.clubdervisionaere.com).

Gallery Hopping

Berlin, a magnet for new artists, is a great city for gallery browsing. Many galleries stay open late and welcome visitors who are "just looking." The most famous gallery district is in the Scheunenviertel, along **Auguststrasse** (branches off from Oranienburger Strasse). Check out the Berlin outpost of the edgy-yet-accessible art of the New Leipzig movement at Galerie Eigen+Art (Tue-Sat 11:00-18:00, closed Sun-Mon, Auguststrasse 26, tel. 030/280-6605, www.eigen-art.com). The other gallery area is in City West, along **Fasanenstrasse** (near the Käthe Kollwitz Museum).

Dancing

The old ballroom **Clärchens Ballhaus** has been a Berlin institution since 1913 (described on page 189 of the Scheunenviertel Walk). At some point, everyone in Berlin comes through here, as the dance hall attracts an eclectic Berlin-in-a-nutshell crowd of grannies, elegant women in evening dresses, yuppies, scenesters, and hippies. The music changes every day—swing, waltz, tango, or cha-cha—with live music on Friday and Saturday (from 23:15, €7-9 cover; dance hall open daily from 11:00 until the last person goes home, in the heart of the Auguststrasse gallery district at Auguststrasse 24—see map on page 266, S-Bahn: Oranienburger Strasse, tel. 030/282-9295, www.ballhaus.de). Dancing lessons are also available (€9, beginner lessons Thu at 19:30 and

Sun at 12:00, 1.5 hours). The **$$** Gipsy Restaurant, which fills a huge courtyard out front, serves reasonably priced German and Italian food. If you enjoy the *Ballhaus* scene, consider the campy (and less venerable) **Ballhaus Berlin,** just west of Prenzlauer Berg (Chausseestrasse 102, U6: Naturkundemuseum, www.ballhaus-berlin.de).

Berlin boasts the largest **tango** scene outside Buenos Aires (well-described at www.tangoberlin.de). In summer, it's easy to get a taste of tango on any balmy night in the riverside **Monbijoupark,** between Museum Island and Hackescher Markt. Most nights also include sessions with one or two other dance styles (€7 beginner classes often available; www.monbijou-theater.de). Also check out **Tangoloft** in Wedding, northwest of Prenzlauer Berg (Gerichtstrasse 2, take S-Bahn to Wedding station, www.tangoloft-berlin.de).

Pub Crawls

The "free" tour companies that cater to students offer wildly popular pub crawls, promising "four cool bars and one hot club" for about €12. Just imagine what kind of bar lets in a tour of 70 college kids. It can be fun...if you want to get drunk with a bunch of American students in a foreign country.

Friedrichshain Nightlife

Prenzlauer Berg and Kreuzberg both have pockets of excitement. But these days, the most happening scene is a few tram stops or U-Bahn stops farther from the center, in the neighborhood of Friedrichshain (just east of Prenzlauer Berg). While this area is famous for its rowdy and exclusive dance clubs, here are some more accessible options.

One particularly striking Friedrichshain venue is **Radialsystem,** a red-brick industrial building right by the water and near the East Side Gallery. Priding itself on being a "space for arts and ideas," they host everything from classical music to electronica (and good €5 meals to boot, Holzmarktstrasse 33, take S-Bahn to Ostbahnhof station, www.radialsystem.de).

The edgier **RAW-Tempel,** just north of the Warschauerstrasse S-Bahn station, is a huge complex of industrial buildings that have been renovated by a community group dedicated to hosting low-cost arts events, including club nights, concerts, a bar, and even a circus. It's a ramshackle wonderland of twinkle lights and graffiti (www.raw-tempel.de).

Across from the Warschauerstrasse S-Bahn station is the iconic **Monster Ronson's** karaoke bar, complete with private cabins and live music (daily 24 hours, Warschauerstrasse 34, www.karaokemonster.de).

BERLIN CONNECTIONS

This chapter covers Berlin's airports; its main train station (Berlin Hauptbahnhof), including train connections to other German destinations and beyond; its bus depot; and the cruise port at Warnemünde.

By Plane

Berlin's airport situation is in flux. The completion of Willy Brandt Airport has been delayed for years; in the meantime, two older airports—Tegel and Schönefeld—do their best to handle Berlin's heavy flight load. When heading to the airport, be very clear on which one you're flying from.

In addition to being well-served by Lufthansa and other big, traditional airlines, Berlin is also a destination for many budget airlines. These include **EasyJet** (www.easyjet.com), **Air Berlin** (www.airberlin.com), **Eurowings** (www.eurowings.com), **Condor** (with several long-haul routes, www.condor.com), **WizzAir** (with a handful of direct flights to southeastern Europe, www.wizzair. com), TUIfly (www.tuifly.com), and **Ryanair** (www.ryanair.com). For more on cheap flights, see page 433.

Willy Brandt Berlin-Brandenburg International Airport

This state-of-the-art airport (airport code: BER), 11 miles south of central Berlin, has been under construction since 2006. Overdue and over budget, the airport may open sometime in late 2018...but, as cynical locals say, "If you believe that, you still believe in Santa Claus."

In case it's open for your visit, here's the scoop (subject to change, of course): The airport is planned to connect to the city center by fast and frequent Airport Express trains (ignore the S-Bahn, which doesn't go directly to the city center). The airport station (Flughafen Berlin Brandenburg Bahnhof) sits directly under the terminal. A train (2/hour, 25 minutes, direction: Dessau or Nauen) will likely run to Alexanderplatz (for Prenzlauer Berg and Scheunenviertel hotels, 25 minutes), then continue to Zoologischer Garten (for City West hotels, 40 minutes). Additional trains are planned to connect the airport to the main train station, via Potsdamer Platz (2/hour, 30 minutes). Any train into the city center costs €3.40 (ABC zone ticket, buy at machine and validate it before boarding). A taxi to the city center costs about €35.

Tegel Airport

Tegel (airport code: TXL), just four miles northwest of the center, serves as Berlin's "main airport" until Willy Brandt finally opens. Smaller and older than you'd expect for the airport of a huge city, it's limping along as well as it can. The easiest way to get downtown is by bus (follow the little bus icons to exit D).

To reach my **Prenzlauer Berg** or **Scheunenviertel** hotels, hop on bus #TXL, which stops at the Hauptbahnhof, then heads south down Friedrichstrasse before turning east on Unter den Linden, which it follows all the way to Alexanderplatz. Hop off just before Alexanderplatz—at the Spandauer Strasse/Marienkirche stop—then walk about five minutes north up Spandauer Strasse to Hackescher Markt. This is close to most Scheunenviertel hotels, and an easy ride on tram #M1 to most Prenzlauer Berg hotels.

To reach **City West** hotels, take bus #X9 directly to Zoologischer Garten (a.k.a. Zoo Station), or slower bus #109 by way of Ku'damm to Zoologischer Garten.

Any bus is covered by an AB zone transit ticket (€2.80 single ticket, buy from machine, validate before boarding). A taxi from Tegel Airport costs about €30 to Alexanderplatz or €20 to City West.

Schönefeld Airport

Most flights from the east and many discount airlines arrive at Schönefeld (airport code: SXF), 11 miles south of downtown and next to the under-construction Willy Brandt Airport. From the arrivals hall, it's a three-minute walk to the train station, where you can catch a regional express train or S-Bahn into the city. The S9 line is especially handy for Prenzlauer Berg and Scheunenviertel hotels: From the Schönhauser Allee stop, tram #M1 runs south along Kastanienallee, then all the way to Hackescher Markt. You can also take Airport Express RE and RB trains directly to Ostbahnhof, Alexanderplatz, Friedrichstrasse (near some Scheunenviertel hotels), Hauptbahnhof, and Zoologischer Garten (handy for

City West hotels; train runs 2/hour, direction: Nauen or Dessau). Either train is covered by an ABC transit ticket (€3.40, buy at machine and validate before boarding). A taxi to the city center costs about €40.

By Train

Virtually all long-distance trains pass through the Berlin Hauptbahnhof ("Berlin Hbf" on schedules)—a massive, state-of-the-art temple of railroad travel in the heart of the city. Below are tips on how to make your way from the station to your

hotel, and a partial list of the many destinations you can reach from here.

Arrival at the Hauptbahnhof

Europe's biggest, mostly underground train station is where the national train system meets Berlin's S-Bahn—unique for the way its major lines come in at right angles. Note that many arriving trains (especially regional ones) stop at multiple Berlin stations, one of which may be more convenient to your hotel than the Hauptbahnhof. Before you arrive, figure out which station is best for you.

Orientation: The gigantic station has five floors, but its open layout makes it easy to navigate...once you understand the signage.

The main floor, at street level, is labeled "EG" (for *Erdgeschoss*), or level 0. Below that are UG1 (level -1) and UG2 (level -2), while above it are OG1 (level +1) and OG2 (level +2). Tracks 1-8 are on UG2, while tracks 11-16 and the S-Bahn are on OG2. Shops and services are on the three middle levels. Enter

and exit the station on level EG: The Washingtonplatz entrance faces south (toward the Reichstag and downtown, with a taxi stand). The north entrance is marked *Europaplatz*.

Services: On the main floor (EG), you'll find the **TI** (just inside the north/Europaplatz entrance) and the **"Rail & Fresh WC"** facility (public pay toilets, near the Burger King and food court).

Up one level (OG1) are a 24-hour **pharmacy** and **lockers** (directly under track 14).

Train Information and Tickets: The Deutsche Bahn *Reisezentrum* information center is up one level (OG1), between tracks 12 and 13, (open long hours daily). For those staying in western Berlin, the info center at the Zoologischer Garten station is just as good—and much less crowded.

EurAide is an English-speaking information desk with answers to your questions about train travel around Europe. It's located at counter 12 inside the *Reisezentrum* on the first upper level (OG1). It's American-run, so communication is simple. This is an especially good place to make fast-train and *couchette* reservations (generally open Mon-Fri 11:10-18:50, until 20:00 May-July and Sept, check website for specific hours, closed Jan-Feb and Sat-Sun year-round; www.euraide.com).

Shopping: The Hauptbahnhof is home to 80 shops with long hours—some locals call the station a "shopping mall with trains" (many stores open Sun). The Kaiser's supermarket (UG1, follow signs for tracks 1-2) is handy for assembling a picnic for your train ride.

Getting into Town: Taxis and buses wait outside the station, but the S-Bahn is probably your best bet for connecting to most hotels. It's simple: S-Bahn trains are on tracks 15 and 16 at the top of the station (level OG2). Trains on track 15 go east, stopping at Friedrichstrasse, Hackescher Markt, Alexanderplatz, and Ostbahnhof; trains on track 16 go west, toward Zoologischer Garten and Savignyplatz (best for City West hotels). Your train ticket to Berlin covers any connecting S-Bahn ride (but for the U-Bahn, trams, or buses, you'll need an additional ticket).

To reach most hotels in northern Berlin's **Prenzlauer Berg** neighborhood, it's fastest to take any train on track 15 two stops to Hackescher Markt, exit to Spandauer Strasse, go left, and cross the tracks to the tram stop. Here you'll catch tram #M1 north (direction: Schillerstrasse), which trundles north through Rosenthaler Platz and up Kastanienallee to Eberswalder Strasse. (For Rosenthaler Platz hotels, it's even more direct to hop on tram #M8, which leaves from in front of the Hauptbahnhof's Europaplatz entrance.)

For **Scheunenviertel** hotels, you'll also take the S-Bahn from track 15. Some of these hotels are closer to the Friedrichstrasse station (first stop), while others are closer to Hackescher Markt (second stop).

To reach **City West** hotels, catch any train on track 16 to Savignyplatz, where you're within a five-minute walk of most recommended hotels.

Bus #TXL to **Tegel Airport** leaves from in front of the Europaplatz exit.

The Berlin Hauptbahnhof is not well-connected to the city's U-Bahn (subway) system—yet. The station's sole U-Bahn line—U55—goes only two stops, to the Brandenburger Tor station, and doesn't really connect to the rest of the system. It's part of the extension of the U5 line beneath Unter den Linden to Alexanderplatz, which is scheduled to be finished in 2020. For now, transit junkies find the U55 an interesting ride on Europe's shortest subway line.

Destinations

For help buying tickets, stop by the EurAide office in the Hauptbahnhof (described earlier). Before buying a ticket for any long train ride from Berlin (over 7 hours), consider taking a cheap flight instead (buy it well in advance to get a super fare). Train info: Toll tel. 0180-699-6633, www.bahn.com.

From Berlin by Train to: Potsdam (2/hour, 30 minutes on RE1 train; or take S-Bahn from other points in Berlin, S7 direct, S1 with a change at Wannsee, 6/hour, 30-50 minutes—see page 316 for details), **Oranienburg** and Sachsenhausen Memorial and Museum (hourly, 25 minutes; or take the S1 line from Friedrichstrasse or other stops in town, 2/hour, 50 minutes), **Wittenberg** (a.k.a. *Lutherstadt Wittenberg,* hourly on ICE, 40 minutes; also every 2 hours on slower regional train, 1.5 hours), **Dresden** (every 2 hours, more with a transfer in Leipzig, 2-3 hours), **Leipzig** (hourly direct, 1.5 hours), **Erfurt** (every 2 hours direct, 2 hours; more with transfer in Leipzig or Naumburg/Saale), **Eisenach** and Wartburg Castle (3/day direct, 2.5 hours; more with transfer in Leipzig or Erfurt), **Hamburg** (1-2/hour direct, 2 hours), **Frankfurt** (hourly, 4.5 hours), **Bacharach** (hourly, 5-6.5 hours, 1-3 changes), **Würzburg** (hourly, 4 hours, change in Göttingen or Fulda), **Rothenburg** (2-3/hour, 5.5-7 hours, 2-3 changes), **Nürnberg** (direct train hourly, 5 hours, more with changes, 6 hours), **Munich** (1-2/hour, 6.5 hours, direct train hourly, otherwise change in Nürnberg or Hannover), **Cologne** (hourly, 4.5 hours, night train possible), **Amsterdam** (3/day direct, 6.5 hours; wise to reserve in advance), **Budapest** (1 direct train/day, others with 1 change, 11.5 hours, some go via Czech Republic and Slovakia; if your rail pass doesn't cover these countries, save money on a longer route via Vienna), **Copenhagen** (2/day, 8 hours, reservation required, change in Hamburg, 1/day direct departs at 11:30), **London** (4/day, 10.5 hours, 2-4 changes—you're better off flying cheap, even if you have a rail pass), **Paris** (9/day, 8 hours), **Zürich** (1-2/hour, 9 hours, transfer in Hannover or Basel; 1 direct 11-hour night train), **Prague** (6/day direct, 4.5 hours, wise to reserve in advance), **Warsaw** (6/day direct, 6.5 hours; 3 more with 1-2 changes, reservations required on all Warsaw-bound trains), **Kraków** (1/day direct, 8 hours; more with transfer in Warsaw, 8.5 hours), **Vienna** (10/day, most with 1-2 changes, 1/

night direct, 12 hours; some via Czech Republic, but trains with a change in Nürnberg, Munich, or Würzburg avoid that country—useful if it's not covered by your rail pass).

Night trains run from Berlin to these cities: Cologne, Vienna, Budapest, Basel, and Zürich. A *Liegeplatz*, a.k.a. *couchette* berth (€15-36), is a great deal; inquire at EurAide at the Hauptbahnhof for details. Beds generally cost the same whether you have a first- or second-class ticket or rail pass. Trains are often full, so reserve your *couchette* a few days in advance from any travel agency or major train station in Europe.

By Bus

CONNECTIONS

The city's bus station, **ZOB** (Zentraler Omnibusbahnhof), is west of Zoologischer Garten (Zoo Station), in Charlottenburg (Masurenallee 4-6, U2: Kaiserdamm or S41/S42: Messe Nord). **FlixBus, Berlin Linien,** and **Eurolines** all operate from here to locations around Germany and Europe (see page 425).

By Cruise Ship at the Port of Warnemünde

Many cruise lines advertise a stop in "Berlin," but ships actually put in at the Baltic seaside town of Warnemünde—a whopping 150 miles north of downtown Berlin. By train, by tour bus, or by Porsche on the autobahn, plan on at least six hours of travel time round-trip between Warnemünde and Berlin. The easiest option is to book a package excursion from your cruise line. You can also book a tour with a local Berlin-based operator such as Original Berlin Walks; see contact information on page 24). Otherwise, several train connections run each day from Warnemünde's train station to Berlin (roughly every 2 hours, 3 hours, transfer in Rostock).

For more details on visiting Berlin while on a cruise, pick up the *Rick Steves Northern European Cruise Ports* guidebook.

DAY TRIPS FROM BERLIN

Potsdam • Sachsenhausen Memorial and Museum • Wittenberg

While you could spend days in Berlin and not run out of things to do, a few worthwhile side-trips are within an hour of downtown. Frederick the Great's opulent palace playground at Potsdam is a hit with those who enjoy ornate interiors and pretty parks; the town also has a fun-to-explore center and some interesting Cold War sights. On the opposite side of Berlin—and the sightseeing spectrum—the Sachsenhausen Memorial and Museum commemorates the tens of thousands of prisoners who died at this concentration camp during the Holocaust. And for a small-town experience—in a pleasant village that packs a huge historical wallop—head 45 minutes to Wittenberg, where Martin Luther famously nailed his 95 Theses to the church door.

Potsdam

Squeezed between the Wannsee and a lush park strewn with the escapist whimsies of Frederick the Great, the sleepy town of Potsdam has long been Berlin's holiday retreat. While Potsdam's palaces are impressive, they don't quite crack Europe's top 10. But they are your best opportunity to get a taste of Prussia's Hohenzollern royalty (though Charlottenburg Palace, in Berlin proper, is easier to reach—see page 81).

Beyond these royal retreats, Potsdam is simply enjoyable—a swanky bedroom community, where, thanks to its aristocratic heritage, everything seems bigger and better than it needs to be. Cold War buffs might skip Frederick's palaces entirely, and focus on Cecilienhof (site of the famous post-WWII Potsdam Conference) and nearby KGB Prison Memorial. And anyone can enjoy prowl-

Near Berlin

ing Potsdam's well-manicured town center. Don't come here just for the palaces—come here to escape the city, and to spend a sunny day exploring a stately burg and its picnic-friendly park.

GETTING TO POTSDAM

Potsdam is about 15 miles southwest of Berlin, about an hour away by train. You have two easy train options for zipping from the city to Potsdam's Hauptbahnhof, both covered by a Berlin transit day pass (€7.40, with zones ABC; if you have a pass for just zones AB, buy a €1.60 *Anschlussfahrausweis*/extension ticket to get here—valid for 2 hours).

Direct **Regional Express/RE1 trains** depart twice hourly from three different Berlin stations: Zoologischer Garten (20 minutes to Potsdam), Hauptbahnhof (30 minutes), and Friedrichstrasse (35 minutes; any train to Brandenburg or Magdeburg stops in Potsdam). Note: Some RE1 trains continue past the Potsdam Hauptbahnhof to a stop called Park Sanssouci, which is closer to the New Palace.

The **S-Bahn** is slightly slower (30-50 minutes depending on starting point), but more frequent (6/hour) and handier from some areas of Berlin. The S7 line goes directly to Potsdam from Alexanderplatz, Hackescher Markt, Friedrichstrasse, Berlin Hauptbahnhof, Zoologischer Garten, Savignyplatz, and other city-center stations. Additional stations—Oranienburger Strasse, Brandenburger Tor, and Potsdamer Platz—are served by the S1 line, which you can ride to the end of the line at Wannsee, cross the platform to an S7 train, and ride it three more stops to Potsdam.

Avid cyclists can rent a bike in Berlin, take it on the train (€1.90 extra), and combine a visit to Potsdam with an enjoyable ride along skinny lakes and through green parklands back into the city.

PLANNING YOUR TIME

Potsdam's main draw are its **palaces**—particularly Sanssouci, which takes about an hour to visit (plus a potential wait for your entry time). Try to arrive at the palace by 10:00 to avoid a long line. Regardless of when you get to Potsdam, make a beeline to Sanssouci to secure your entry time so you can plan the rest of your day. If you'd like to see more, you can add on the New Palace (another hour, usually little or no wait). The two palaces are connected by a huge park—it's a pleasant 30-minute walk or a 10-minute bus ride between them. If you arrive early enough to get in right away, you can visit both palaces in as little as 3-4 hours.

Potsdam may inspire you to stretch your visit to a full day. In good weather, consider simply hanging out and exploring Sanssouci Park. Cold War enthusiasts can head to Cecilienhof and the KGB Prison Memorial. And the town center warrants a wander—ogle the Alter Markt, consider dipping into the Museum Barberini, or prowl the cobbles of the Dutch Quarter. On your way back to Berlin, you could hop off the train at the Wannsee station and take a boat ride on the lake.

Here are a few other scheduling considerations:

Weekends are particularly busy; consider saving Potsdam for a weekday (noting that Sanssouci Palace is closed on Monday, and the New Palace is closed on Tuesday).

For many, touring both Sanssouci and the New Palace is overkill. Consider doing only the better of the two (Sanssouci), and using the rest of your time for the park or other Potsdam sights. The New Palace's only advantage is that it's easier to get into—if you arrive late and Sanssouci is booked solid, the New Palace is a suitable replacement.

Orientation to Potsdam

Potsdam (pop. 160,000) sits just outside of Berlin's city limits, on the southern edge of the lake called Wannsee. (During the Cold War, Potsdam was just outside West Berlin—the Wall ran right

DAY TRIPS

along the lakeshore.) The main train station (Potsdam Hauptbahnhof) is at the southeastern corner of the city center. Sights cluster in three areas, each a long walk or a short bus ride apart: the city center, just across the bridge from the train station; Park Sanssouci, a vast royal park at the western edge of town, peppered with grand Hohenzollern

palaces (Sanssouci and New Palace are best); and, to the north, the park called Neuer Garten, where Cecilienhof Palace looks out over Wannsee.

TOURIST INFORMATION

A handy TI is inside Potsdam's **main train station** (near track 7, Mon-Sat 9:30-18:00, closed Sun, tel. 0331/2755-8899, www. potsdamtourismus.de). The next handiest location faces the old main square, **Alter Markt,** just across the bridge from the station—below the giant church dome (Mon-Sat 9:30-19:00, Sun 10:00-16:00, Humboldtstrasse 1). The third location—at **Luisenplatz,** on the eastern end of Sanssouci Park—is less convenient (Mon-Sat 9:30-18:00, Sun 10:00-16:00, closed Sun Nov-March, Brandenburger Strasse 3).

ARRIVAL IN POTSDAM

At the Main Station (Potsdam Hauptbahnhof): This station has ample shops and services. On arrival, to take the **bus or tram** to the palaces (easiest) head out the exit past track 4, labeled *Friedrich-Engels-Strasse;* here you'll find the tram stops, then the bus stops.

To **walk** into town—or rent a **bike**—use the opposite door, past track 7, labeled *Babelsberger Strasse.* Exiting, turn left to find the bike-rental office. To walk, just keep going, then turn right at the next traffic light. You'll cross a bridge and head straight for Alter Markt (with the huge dome).

At Sanssouci Park Station: From this smaller station, simply walk straight out and head up the boulevard called Am Neuen Palais, with the big park on your right. In about 10 minutes, you'll reach the New Palace.

GETTING AROUND POTSDAM

By Bike: Flat Potsdam is ideal by bike, and from the station it's a pleasant and well-signed 20-minute ride to Sanssouci Palace. There's one caveat: Within Sanssouci Park you're restricted to a bike path between the palaces; you can't even walk with a bike anywhere else in the park. At the main train station, **Radstation/**

Pedales rents bikes and provides a map showing recommended routes (Mon-Fri 7:00-19:00, Sat 9:30-18:00, closed Sun, out the Babelsberg Strasse exit and on the left, tel. 0331/7480-057). On Sundays in summer (April-Oct), they may

have another location under tracks 6/7.

By Bus or Tram: Potsdam's public transit is well-designed for connecting most points of interest. Remember that Potsdam is covered by a Berlin ticket with zones ABC, but not by one with just zones AB. You can either buy an *Anschlussfahrausweis*/extension ticket (€1.60, each one valid 2 hours), or buy individual tickets covering Potsdam transit: €2.10 per ride, €4.20 all day (buy tickets from machine on board). These are the buses you're most likely to take and the lane from which they depart at the main train station:

Bus **#695**—essentially made for tourists (and therefore packed)—cruises through Potsdam's appealing town center, stopping first at Sanssouci, then at the New Palace (3/hour, 15-20 minutes, leaves from lane 4).

Bus **#X15,** which runs only on summer weekends, makes a beeline to Sanssouci Palace (3/hour, mid-April-Oct Sat-Sun only, 10 minutes, leaves from lane 4).

Buses **#606** and **#605** work only if you're going directly to the New Palace (3/hour, 10-15 minutes, from lane 4).

Bus **#603** goes up to Cecilienhof Palace, then loops back down past the KGB Prison Memorial (Persiusstrasse stop) and the Dutch Quarter (Hebbelstrasse) before returning to the station (3/hour, 15 minutes to Cecilienhof, from lane 6).

Tram **#91** is worth considering if you're up for a scenic walk through the terraced palace gardens: Get off at Luisenplatz, then walk 20 minutes through the park, which lets you enjoy a classic view of Sanssouci Palace (3/hour, 8 minutes, leaves from lane 1).

By Foot: It's a long (but scenic) 45-minute walk from the station to Sanssouci Palace (get directions and pick up a map at the TI; exit the station on the opposite side from the bus/tram stops). Tram #91, described above, shaves off the least interesting part.

By Taxi: A taxi can help link up otherwise difficult-to-connect sights (for example, €15 between the New Palace and Cecilienhof—otherwise a complex bus connection).

Tours in Potsdam

Local Tours

Various bus tours (including hop-on, hop-off options) conveniently connect this town's spread-out sights. Pick up brochures at the TI or check their website (www.potsdamtourismus.de).

Tours from Berlin

Original Berlin Walks and Brewer's Berlin Tours offer inexpensive all-day tours from Berlin to Potsdam—focusing on the park and the palace exteriors, but not actually going inside the palaces as a group (€15-17, admissions and public transportation not included; for contact info see page 24).

Sights in Potsdam

Potsdam's sights cluster in three areas: Sanssouci Park; the city center; and Neuer Garten, with Cecilienhof.

FREDERICK THE GREAT'S PALACES AT SANSSOUCI PARK

The dynamic Frederick the Great put Prussia on the map in the 18th century with his merciless military prowess. Yet he also had

tender affection for the finer things in life: art, architecture, gardens, literature, and other distinguished pursuits. During his reign, Frederick built an impressive ensemble of palaces and other grand buildings around Sanssouci Park, with the two top palaces located at either end. Frederick's small, super-Rococo Sanssouci Palace is dazzling, and his massive New Palace was built to wow guests and disprove rumors that Prussia was running out of money after the costly Seven Years' War.

Background: While the palaces are impressive, the included audioguides do a terrible job of bringing them to life (focusing more on the opulent furnishings of each room than on the dynamic rulers who lived in them). It's essential to read the "Prussian King Frederick the Great" sidebar (on page 106) before your visit to better understand the historical context.

Getting Between the Palaces: It's about a 30-minute walk between Sanssouci and the New Palace, and about 10 minutes by bike. Otherwise you can hop on bus #695, which takes you between the palaces in either direction (covered by a cheap €1.50 *Kurzstrecke* ticket, as well as by a Berlin transit pass with zones ABC). If you

DAY TRIPS

do walk, you'll find the park wilder, more forested, and less carefully manicured than those in other big-league European palace complexes (such as Versailles or Vienna's Schönbrunn). The park's €2 suggested donation gets you a helpful map.

Combo-Ticket: The €19 combo-ticket covers nearly all the royal buildings in the park. It's worthwhile only if you're visiting Sanssouci, the New Palace, and at least one other sight (for most visitors, those two are more than enough). The combo-ticket is sold online and at the ticket offices at Sanssouci Palace and the New Palace. Buying online costs a few euros extra (€21 total), but allows you to reserve a coveted time slot for Sanssouci, saving you time and stress—since it's the only way to book ahead.

Touring the Palaces: There are no English guided tours. You'll visit both palaces with an (included but inferior) audioguide. During the summer season (April-Oct), visitors are allowed to see each palace at their own pace. Off-season, you'll be accompanied either by an escort or by a German-speaking guide, who will herd your group from room to room.

Information: Tel. 0331/969-4200, www.spsg.de.

DAY TRIPS

▲▲Sanssouci Palace

Sans souci means "without a care," and this was the carefree summer home of Frederick the Great (built 1745-1747). Of all the palatial buildings scattered around

Potsdam, this was his actual residence. While the palace is small and the audioguide does little to capture the personality of its former resident, it's worth seeing for its opulence.

Cost and Hours: €12, €19 combo-ticket includes New Palace and other sights, Tue-Sun 10:00-18:00, Nov-March until 17:00, closed Mon year-round.

Crowd-Beating Tips: Your ticket comes with an appointed entry time for the main living quarters. Tickets are sold for the same day only, and only in person; an electronic board above the ticket desk counts down the number of available tickets per time slot. (The only way to get a reserved entry time in advance is to buy a combo-ticket online, explained earlier). To get right in, arrive by 10:00, when the ticket office opens. After 11:00, plan to stand in line to buy your ticket. You'll probably have to wait for your entry time, too—usually an hour or two later. Pass this time visiting the Ladies' Wing (open only on weekends in summer) and the Palace Kitchen or by exploring the sprawling gardens. If you have a very long wait, zip over to visit the New Palace, then circle back to Sanssouci.

Visiting the Palace: Your ticket covers three parts—the Ladies' Wing (to the left as you face the palace from the front/garden side); the Palace Kitchen (to the right); and the living quarters and festival halls (the main, central part). You can visit the first two sights anytime, but you must report to the main part of the palace

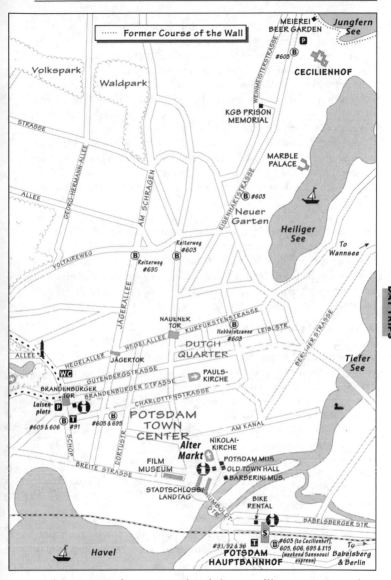

at the time noted on your ticket (where you'll receive your audio-guide; tour takes about 40 minutes).

The **Ladies' Wing** (Damenflügel), worth a visit only if you have time to kill (and maybe not even then), contains cluttered apartments with cutesy decor for ladies-in-waiting and servants. The servants' quarters upstairs have been turned into a painting gallery.

At the **Palace Kitchen** (Schlossküche), see well-preserved mid-19th-century cooking equipment. Hike down the tight spiral staircase to the wine cellar, which features an exhibit about the grapes that were grown on the terraced vineyards out front.

The **Main Palace** was where Frederick the Great spent his summers. You'll stroll through the classic Rococo interior, where golden grapevines climb the walls and frame the windows. First explore the Royal Apartments, containing one of Frederick's three libraries (he found it easier to buy extra copies of books rather than move them around), the "study bedroom" where he lived and worked, and the chair where he died. The domed, central Marble Hall resembles the Pantheon in Rome (on a smaller scale), with an oblong oculus, inlaid marble floors, and Corinthian columns made of Carrara marble.

Finally, you'll visit the guest rooms, most of which exit straight out onto the delightful terrace. Each room is decorated differently: Chinese, Italian, and so on; the niche at the back was for a bed. The happiest is the yellow Voltaire Room, where realistic animals and flowers dangle from the walls and ceiling. As you exit (through the servants' quarters), keep an eye out for the giant portrait of Frederick by Andy Warhol.

▲▲New Palace (Neues Palais)

This gigantic showpiece palace (with more than 200 rooms) is, in some ways, more impressive than the intimate Sanssouci. Frederick the Great built the New Palace (1763-1769), but he rarely stayed here—it was mostly used to host guests and dazzle visiting dignitaries. The palace has close to 1,000 rooms, but its big attractions are the recently restored, lavishly decorated Grotto Hall and Marble Hall—you'll see these, and several other fine apartments, on the one-hour "Grand Tour." Unlike at Sanssouci, there's rarely a long wait to buy tickets or enter. The palace is putting the finishing touches on a long-term renovation, so you may find a few rooms closed when you visit.

Cost and Hours: €8, €19 combo-ticket includes Sanssouci and other sights; Wed-Mon 10:00-18:00, Nov-March until 17:00, closed Tue year-round. Buy your ticket at the visitors center/ticket office near the bus stop—where you can also use the WC (none at the palace itself) and watch an eight-minute introductory film (alternating in German and English)—then head to the palace at the appointed time to meet your escort and pick up your audioguide.

Visiting the Palace: The one-hour "Grand Tour" takes you through the palace's ornate halls. On the main floor, the highlight is the Grotto Hall, whose marble walls are encrusted with a quarter of a million seashells, semiprecious stones, and fossils. From there, continue on through the eight suites of the Lower Princes' Apartments, which accommodated guests and royal family members. In the 19th and early 20th century, German emperors Frederick III (different from the earlier Frederick II, who built the place) and Wilhelm II (the last kaiser) resided here. The Gentlemen's Bedchamber holds the red-canopy bed where Kaiser Frederick III died in 1888. The Ladies' Bedchamber is a reminder that noblemen and their wives slept separately.

Upstairs, the Upper Princes' Quarters include a small blue-tiled bathroom that was installed for Kaiser Wilhelm II, and a bedchamber shared by a married couple—my, how times have changed. You'll also find Wilhelm's bedroom, as well as a small painting gallery with portraits of Frederick the Great and Russia's Catherine the Great (who was actually a German princess). The grand finale is the sumptuous, 52-foot-high Marble Hall, with its dramatic ceiling painting (of the Greek myth of Ganymede) and floors inlaid with Silesian marble. Through the windows, enjoy views of the gardens.

The King's Apartments: The "Grand Tour" described above is enough for most. But Frederick completists can ask about the King's Apartments, which can be seen only on a guided tour in German (and may be closed for renovation).

Other Palaces

The two main palaces (Sanssouci and the New Palace) are just the beginning. Sprawling Sanssouci Park contains a variety of other palaces and royal buildings, many of which you can enter. Popular options include the Italian-style **Orangery** (the last and largest palace in the park, may be closed for renovation; when open, its five royal rooms can be toured only with a German guide, plus a view tower); the **New Chambers** (a royal guesthouse); the **Chinese House;** and other viewpoints, such as the **Klausberg Belvedere** and the **Norman Tower.**

Cost and Hours: Each has its own entry fee (€2-4; all but Belvedere covered by €19 combo-ticket) and hours, some open weekends only (get a complete list from Potsdam TI or palace ticket office).

DAY TRIPS

Bornstedt Royal Estate (Krongut Bornstedt)

Designed to look like an Italian village, this warehouse-like complex once provided the royal palaces with food and other supplies. Today the estate houses the Hof Brauerei (brewery and distillery), which delivers fine brews and (sometimes) schnapps, as it has since 1689. The brewpub's **$$ restaurant** is a good place for lunch, serving local specialties. The kid-friendly grounds also house a wood-fired bakery with fresh bread and pastries. You can watch hatmakers, candlemakers, coopers, potters, and glassmakers produce (and sell) their wares using traditional techniques.

Cost and Hours: Free to enter except during special events, Mon-Fri 12:00-18:00, Sat-Sun from 11:00, restaurant serves food until 22:00, Ribbeckstrasse 6, tel. 0331/550-650, www.krongut-bornstedt.de.

Getting There: From Sanssouci, walk toward the windmill, then follow the street to the right (An der Orangerie) about 500 yards.

POTSDAM'S TOWN CENTER

The easy-to-stroll town center has pedestrianized shopping streets lined with boutiques and eateries. For a small town, this was once a cosmopolitan place: Frederick the Great imported some very talented people.

▲Alter Markt

Potsdam's "Old Market Square" is marked by the massive dome of the Nikolaikirche—visible from all over town. This square, always pleasant, has been further rejuvenated by the opening of the new Museum Barberini. It's worth a quick stroll through here to ogle the striking Hohenzollern architecture and consider your sightseeing options.

Stand in the middle of the square, facing the giant church (and the obelisk in front of it). Do a clockwise spin-tour to get oriented:

The oversized **Nikolaikirche,** designed by Frederick the Great's favorite architect, Karl Friedrich Schinkel, is an icon of Potsdam. Step inside to see its austere, very Protestant, Neoclassical interior—a world of perfectly formed domes and Corinthian columns.

To the right sits the **Old Town Hall** (Altes Rathaus), with its frilly cupola. Immediately next door is the **Potsdam Museum,** showcasing local history.

Farther to the right, the **Museum Barberini** opened to acclaim in early 2017. This state-of-the-art museum, filling a beautifully restored old building, shows off temporary exhibits of world-class artists. Now Berlin art snobs have even more reason to zip out to Potsdam. Check what's on—for art lovers, a good exhibit here could be worth ▲▲ (€14, Wed-Mon 11:00-19:00, first Thu until 21:00, closed Tue, audioguide-€2, www.museum-barberini.com).

Farther to the right is **Humboldtstrasse,** with the TI (and the quickest route to the train station).

Next is the **Stadtschloss/Ladtag.** You're just barely outside of "Land Berlin," a city-state that constitutes one of Germany's 16 states *(Länder).* Potsdam is the capital of Brandenburg, the *Land* that completely surrounds Berlin—and this fine courtyard is Brandenburg's "state capitol."

And finally, spinning back toward the church, you see...ugh. Eyesore **communist concrete.** Remember, Potsdam was part of East Germany. And, like all DDR cities, it mingles its historic beauty with communist-era blight. This unfortunate complex is slated to be redeveloped—and may already be torn down by the time you read this.

Dutch Quarter (Holländisches Viertel)

For a quick visit to the Low Countries, walk about 10 minutes north of the Alter Markt until you see pretty brick gables. Frederick the

Great imported Dutch merchants and architects to build this gingerbread-cute little swath of town, radiating out from the intersection of Leiblstrasse and Benkertstrasse. It's very touristy today, with lots of boutiques, restaurants, and cafés (some selling Dutch pancakes and *poffertjes*).

Other Sights

Potsdam seems to have a museum for every interest, including a good film museum and a museum of Prussian history (both near Breite Strasse). Skip Potsdam's much-promoted Wannsee boat rides, which are exceedingly dull. (If you're in a mood to relax on a lake, consider stopping off at Wannsee for some beach time on your way home to Berlin—see "Near Potsdam," later).

CECILIENHOF PALACE AND THE NEUER GARTEN

At the north end of town, another (more modest but still pleasant) park, called Neuer Garten, faces Wannsee. This is where you'll find two stirring sights for those interested in Cold War history, and a fine brewery.

Getting There: This area is connected to the center by bus #603, which departs from the main train station and stops at several points downtown on its way up to the park. For the palace, use the Schloss Cecilienhof stop; for the KGB sites, use Glumestrasse (on northbound buses) or Periusstrasse (on southbound buses—returning from the palace to the center). On the way back to town, bus #603 also stops near the Dutch Quarter (Hebbelstrasse)—if you have time, hop off and explore this area, then walk back to Alter Markt and the train station. Bus line #603 comes closest to bus line #695 (serving Sanssouci Park) at the Reiterweg stop. The stops are a long block apart, across the bottom of the long park, making the transfer between these lines a little tricky (consider a taxi instead).

▲Cecilienhof

This early-20th-century villa was the site of the historic Potsdam Conference for two weeks in the summer of 1945. For Cold War buffs, it's worth ▲▲. Touring the rooms with an audioguide, you'll hear how, during those meetings, Harry Truman, Winston Churchill, and Joseph Stalin negotiated how best to punish Germany for dragging Europe through another devastating war. It was here that the postwar map of Europe was officially drawn, setting the stage for a protracted Cold War that would drag on for more than four decades. There's rarely a wait, and it pairs well with a drink or meal at the fine Meierei brewery and a visit to the KGB Prison Memorial—each less than a 10-minute walk away.

Cost and Hours: €6, includes audioguide, Tue-Sun 10:00-18:00, Nov-March until 17:00, closed Mon year-round, tel. 0331/969-4200, www.spsg.de.

Visiting the Palace: This Tudor-style villa—designed to appear smaller and more modest than it actually is—was built in 1912 to house Crown Prince Wilhelm and his wife Cecilie, who would have ruled Germany, had Kaiser Wilhelm II not lost World War I. For those into palace architecture, it's certainly less striking than Potsdam's other palaces. The real draw here is the 1945 history. You'll tour the palace using an excellent 45-minute audioguide, which (unlike the other palace audioguides) does a marvelous job of re-animating history. You'll hear all about those tense days in July 1945, including sound bites from meeting participants. You'll see the private offices of Stalin, Churchill, and Truman, as well as the grand meeting hall with the round table where they faced off to negotiate. It's both chilling and fitting to think that, just 20 years later, the Berlin Wall would run through the park right in front of the palace—cutting off idyllic views of the Wannsee. This was also where Truman issued the "Potsdam Declaration"—demanding that Japan surrender to end the war once and for all. Japan refused—and the US dropped atomic bombs on Hiroshima and Nagasaki.

Eating: The **$$ Meierei** ("Creamery") brewery, in the park near Cecilienhof, is an ideal spot for good beer and tasty food in an idyllic setting. Choose between its crowded interior or its fine beer garden, filling a terrace with tranquil views over the lake (Tue-Sun 12:00-22:00, closed Mon, less than a 10-minute stroll north of Cecilienhof—follow *Meierei* signs to Im Neuen Garten 10, tel. 0331/704-3211). The big open field to the right of the restaurant used to be part of the Berlin Wall.

▲KGB Prison Memorial at Leistikowstrasse (Gedenkstätte Leistikowstrasse Potsdam)

Standing in stark contrast to all of Potsdam's pretty palaces and Hohenzollern bombast, this crumbling concrete prison has been turned into a memorial and documentation center to the Cold War victims of USSR "counterintelligence."

Cost and Hours: Free, Tue-Sun 14:00-18:00, Nov-March 13:00-17:00, closed Mon year-round, Leistikowstrasse 1, tel. 0331/201-1540, www.gedenkstaette-leistikowstrasse.de.

Visiting the Memorial: On the nondescript Leistikowstrasse, a few steps from the lakeside park, the KGB established a base in August 1945 (mere days after the Potsdam Conference), which remained active until the fall of the USSR in 1991. The centerpiece of their "secret city" was this transit and remand prison, in which enemies of the Soviet regime were held and punished in horrible conditions before entering the USSR "justice" system—to be tried, executed, or shipped off to the notorious gulag labor camps. While most prisoners were Russian citizens, until 1955 the prison also held Germans who were essentially kidnapped by the USSR in retribution for their wartime activities.

From the blocky modern building at the corner, you'll enter the complex and head inside the prison, where today the hallways and cells are an eerie world of peeling paint, faded linoleum, and rusted hinges. The top floor hosts a well-presented permanent exhibit in English, explaining the history of the building (which was a vicarage before being seized by the Soviets) and profiling several of the individuals who were held here. Out in the yard, look for the bronze model that illustrates how this prison was just one part of an entire neighborhood of KGB-operated facilities—a "secret city" in the heart of one of East Germany's proudest cities.

NEAR POTSDAM
Babelsberg
Movie buffs might already know that the nearby suburb of Babelsberg (just east of Potsdam) hosts the biggest film studio in Germany, where classics such as *The Blue Angel* and *Metropolis,* as well as more recent films *The Reader* and *Inglourious Basterds,* were filmed (for visitor info, see www.filmpark-babelsberg.de).

Wannsee
To see Berliners at play on a hot summer day, consider hopping off the train at **Wannsee.** This big lake is a popular near-the-city getaway for urbanites who appreciate strolling, sunbathing, splashing, and *See*-faring on lazy cruises. As you go by on the train, you'll pass pea-patch gardens dotted with simple country homes, called *Datsche*—a Russian tradition (allowing even humble workers to escape periodically to the countryside) that caught on here in DDR times. These little pleasure shantytowns, while extremely basic, come with warm memories for many Berliners.

Nearby and accessible by ferry is **Peacock Island,** a favorite getaway where colorful birds run free around a palace built by Kaiser Wilhelm II. Modern art fans can also consider touring the **Liebermann-Villa,** showcasing the home and paintings of early-20th-century painter Max Liebermann, a founding member of the Berlin Secession movement (www.liebermann-villa.de).

Like most places in this part of Germany, romantic lake Wannsee has a sinister infamy: It was the site of the 1942 Wannsee Conference, when Nazi officials came up with their "Final Solution" to the "Jewish Question": wholesale extermination of all Jews.

Sachsenhausen Memorial and Museum

About 20 miles north of downtown Berlin, the small town of Oranienburg was the site of one of the most notorious Nazi concentration camps. Sachsenhausen's proximity to the capital gave it special status as the place to train camp

guards and test new procedures. It was also the site of the Third Reich's massive counterfeiting operation to destabilize Great Britain by flooding the monetary system with forged pound notes. Today the Sachsenhausen Memorial and Museum *(Gedenkstätte und Museum Sachsenhausen),* worth ▲▲, honors the camp's victims and survivors, and teaches visitors about the atrocities that took place here.

DAY TRIPS

GETTING TO SACHSENHAUSEN

Take a train to the town of Oranienburg (20-50 minutes, covered by zone ABC ticket); from there, it's a quick trip by bus or taxi to the camp, or a 20-minute walk. The whole journey takes just over an hour each way.

From Berlin Hauptbahnhof, a regional **train** speeds to Oranienburg (hourly, 25 minutes). Or you can take the S-Bahn (S1) line from various stops in downtown Berlin, including Potsdamer Platz, Brandenburger Tor, Friedrichstrasse, and Oranienburger Strasse (4/hour, 45-50 minutes).

At Oranienburg, the **bus** to the memorial departs from lane 4, right in front of the train station (on weekdays, hourly bus #804 is timed to meet most regional trains; on weekends it runs only every 2 hours, and doesn't sync with S-Bahn arrivals; direction: Malz; bus #821 also possible, runs 5/day, direction: Tiergarten; €1.70, covered by Berlin transit day pass for zones ABC, get off at Gedenkstätte stop). You can also take a **taxi** (€8, ask for the *Gedenkstätte*—geh-DENK-shteh-teh).

To **walk** 20 minutes to the memorial, turn right from the train station and head up Stralsunder Strasse for about two blocks. Turn right under the railroad trestle onto Bernauer Strasse, following signs for *Gedenkstätte Sachsenhausen.* At the traffic light, turn left onto André-Pican-Strasse, which becomes Strasse der Einheit.

After two blocks, turn right on Strasse der Nationen, which leads right to the camp.

PLANNING YOUR TIME

Make your pilgrimage to Sachsenhausen any day during the summer. The museums are closed on Monday from mid-October to mid-March (the grounds are open daily year-round). You'll need at least three hours to appreciate the many worthwhile exhibits here. Factoring in transit time, leave yourself at least five hours round-trip from central Berlin.

ORIENTATION TO SACHSENHAUSEN

Cost and Hours: Free, daily 8:30-18:00, mid-Oct-mid-March until 16:30, on Mon off-season only the grounds and visitors center are open, Strasse der Nationen 22.

Information: Tel. 03301/2000, www.gedenkstaette-sachsenhausen. de.

Visitor Information: The map in this book is sufficient, but the €0.50 map sold at the visitors center is worthwhile for the extra background information it includes. Skip the overlong €3 audioguide and instead make use of this chapter's self-guided tour and the ample English information posted within the camp.

Services: The visitors center has WCs, a bookshop, and a helpful information desk.

Tours from Berlin: A tour helps you understand the camp's complicated and important story. Virtually all walking-tour companies in Berlin offer side-trips to Sachsenhausen (meet in the city, then ride together by train to Oranienburg). The round-trip takes about six hours, much of which is spent in transit—but your time at the camp is made very meaningful by your guide's commentary.

Check walking-tour companies' websites or compare brochures to find an itinerary that fits your schedule (typically €14, April-Oct daily at 10:00, less frequent off-season). Options include **Original Berlin Walks** (www.berlinwalks.de) and **Insider Tour** (www.insidertour.com). Don't book a tour on an off-season Monday, when the grounds are open, but not the museum exhibits.

Eating: Pack a lunch or buy one en route, as dining choices at the camp are minimal. The little "Info Café" inside the camp offers small snacks, and Bistro To Go, just outside the visitors center, serves basic fare (wurst, soup).

Sachsenhausen

BURIAL GROUND

BRICK BARRACKS

MUSEUM

GUARD TOWER E

WC

SOVIET SPECIAL CAMP

100 Meters

100 Yards

PERIMETER FENCE

MEMORIAL

EXECUTION TRENCH

BURIAL GROUND

CREMATORIUM

KITCHEN BUILDING

EXHIBITS & FILM

WC

CAMP PRISON

BARRACKS 38 & 39

STATION Z

WC

GALLOWS

"BOOT TESTING RACK"

RECONSTRUCTED BARRACKS

INDUSTRIAL YARD

Appelplatz

FORMER BARRACKS

MAIN GUARD TOWER A

"ARBEIT MACHT FREI" GATE

CAFÉ

NEW MUSEUM

WC

ENTRANCE

R&R BUILDING

INFIRMARY

MORGUE

MASS GRAVES

SS COMMANDANT'S HOUSE

PERIMETER FENCE

Bus #804 (To/From Oranienburg Train Station)

WC

CAFÉ

CAMP STREET

CAMP MODEL

VISITORS CENTER

STANDING BUILDINGS

BUILDING FOUNDATIONS

STRASSE DER NATIONEN

To Oranienburg Train Station

T-BUILDING

DAY TRIPS

BACKGROUND

Completed in July of 1936, Sachsenhausen was the first concentration camp built under SS chief Heinrich Himmler. The triangle-shaped grounds, contained by three walls, enabled observation of the entire camp from a single point, the main guard tower. The design was intended to be a model for other camps, but it had a critical flaw that prevented its widespread adoption: It was very difficult to expand without interfering with sight lines.

Sachsenhausen was not, strictly speaking, a "death camp" for mass murder (like Auschwitz); it was a labor camp, intended to wring hard work out of the prisoners. Many toiled in a brickworks, producing materials to be used in architect Albert Speer's grandiose plans for erecting new buildings all over Berlin.

Between 1936 and 1945, about 200,000 prisoners did time at Sachsenhausen; about 50,000 died here, while numerous others were transported elsewhere to be killed (in 1942, many of Sachsenhausen's Jews were taken to Auschwitz). Though it was designed to hold 10,000 prisoners, by the end of its functional life the camp had up to 38,000 people. In the spring of 1945, knowing that the Red Army was approaching, guards took 35,000 able-bodied prisoners on a death march, leading them into the forest for seven days and nights with no rations. Rather than "wasting" bullets to kill them, SS troops hoped that the prisoners would expire from exhaustion. On the eighth day, after 6,000 had died, the guards abandoned the group in the wilderness. When Soviet troops liberated Sachsenhausen on April 22, 1945, they discovered an additional 3,000 prisoners who had been too weak to walk and were left there to die (all but 300 survived).

Just three months after the war, Sachsenhausen was converted into Soviet Special Camp No. 7 for the USSR's own prisoners. It was a notorious "silent camp," where prisoners would disappear—allowed no contact with the outside world and their imprisonment officially unacknowledged. The prisoners were Nazis as well as anti-Stalin Russians. By the time the camp closed in 1950, 12,000 more people had died here.

In 1961, Sachsenhausen became the first former concentration camp to be turned into a memorial. The East German government created the memorial mostly for propaganda purposes, to deflect attention from the controversial construction of the Berlin Wall and to exalt the USSR as the valiant antifascist liberators of the camp and all of Germany.

Since the end of the DDR, Sachsenhausen has been redeveloped into a true memorial, with updated museum exhibits and an emphasis on preservation—documenting and sharing the story of what happened here. While difficult to take in, as with all concentration camp memorials, the intention of Sachsenhausen is to share its story and lessons—and prevent this type of brutality from ever happening again.

● SELF-GUIDED TOUR

The camp's various exhibits are scattered throughout the grounds in various buildings, and offer more information than you probably have time to absorb. This outline covers the key parts of your visit.

Entrance

In the courtyard next to the visitors center, a **model** of the camp illustrates its unique triangular layout. Guards stationed in tower A (at the main gate) could see everything going on inside those three walls. Along the left (west) side of the triangle is the crematorium, called Station Z. Outside the main triangle are the workshops, factories, and extra barracks that were added when the camp ran out of room.

Walk up the dusty lane called Camp Street. On the right is the SS officers' R&R building, nicknamed the **"Green Monster,"** where prisoners dressed in nice clothes were forced to wait on their keepers. Officials mostly chose Jehovah's Witnesses for this duty, because they had a strong pacifist code and could be trusted not to attempt to harm their captors.

A left turn through the fence takes you into the courtyard in front of **guard tower A.** The clock on the tower is frozen at 11:07—the exact time that the Red Army liberated the camp. The building on the right—the **New Museum**—has an interesting DDR-era stained-glass window inside, as well as temporary exhibits and a small café.

Go through the gate cruelly marked *Arbeit Macht Frei*—"Work will set you free."

Main Grounds

Entering the triangular field, you can see that almost none of the original buildings still stand. Following the war, locals salvaged the barracks here for much-needed building materials. Tracing the perimeter, notice the electric fence and barbed wire. A few feet in front of the wall is a gravel track called the **neutral zone**—any prisoner setting foot here would be shot. This became a common way for prisoners to attempt suicide. Guards quickly caught on:

If they sensed a suicide attempt, they'd shoot to maim instead of kill. It was typical upside-down Nazi logic: Those who wanted to live would die, and those who wanted to die would live.

Every morning, after a 4:15 wake-up call, prisoners would scramble to eat, bathe, and dress in time to assemble in the

roll-call grounds in front of the guard tower by 5:00. Dressed in their thin, striped pajama-like uniforms and wooden clogs, prisoners would line up while guards, in long coats and accompanied by angry dogs, barked orders and accounted for each person, including those who had died in the barracks overnight. It could take hours, in any weather. A single misbehaving prisoner would bring about punishment for all others. One day, after a prisoner escaped, SS officer Rudolf Höss (who later went on to run Auschwitz-Birkenau) forced the entire population of the camp to stand here for 15 hours in a foot of snow and subzero temperatures. A thousand people died.

To the far right from the entrance, the wooden **barracks** (with good museum displays) are reconstructed from original timbers.

Barrack 38 focuses on the Jewish experience at Sachsenhausen, as well as the general mistreatment of German Jews under the Nazis (including anti-Semitic propaganda). Barrack 39 explains everyday life, with stories following 20 individual internees. You'll see how prisoners lived: long rows of bunks, benches for taking paltry meals, latrines crammed wall-to-wall with toilets, and communal fountains for washing. Inmates would jockey for access to these facilities. The strongest, meanest, most aggressive prisoners—often here because they had been convicted of a violent crime—would be named *Kapo*, the head of the barrack (to discourage camaraderie, the worst prisoners, rather than the best, were "promoted"). Like at many other camps, the camp leaders at Sachsenhausen ran a system of organized rape, whereby they brought in inmates from the women's-only Ravensbrück concentration camp and forced them to "reward good prisoners" at Sachsenhausen.

Next to the barracks is the **camp prison,** where political prisoners or out-of-line inmates were sent. It was run not by the SS, but by the Gestapo (secret police), who would torture captives to extract information. Other prisoners didn't know exactly what went on here, but they could hear screams from inside and knew it was no place they wanted to be. This was also where the Nazis held special hostages, including three Allied airmen who had participated in a bold escape from a Nazi prisoner-of-war camp (the basis for *The Great Escape;* they later managed to escape from Sachsenhausen as well, before being recaptured) and Joseph Stalin's son, Yakov Dzhugashvili, who had been captured during the fighting at Stalingrad. (The Nazis offered to exchange the young man for five German officers. Stalin refused, and soon after, Yakov died here under mysterious circumstances.) The cells contain exhibits about the prisoners and the methods used by their captors.

Just outside the back of the building stand three **posts** (out of an original 15) with iron pegs near the top. Guards cruelly executed people by tying their hands behind their backs, then hanging them on these pegs by their wrists until they died—a medieval method called *strappado.*

Walk around the inner semicircle toward the buildings in the middle of the camp. On this **"boot-testing track,"** prisoners were forced to put on boots two sizes too small and walk in a circle on uneven ground all day, supposedly to "test" the shoes for fighting at Stalingrad.

The rectangles of stones show where each of the original barrack buildings once stood. At the center, a marker represents the

location of the gallows, where prisoners would be publicly executed as a deterrent to others.

In the middle of the triangle, on the right, is the kitchen building, with exhibits that trace the chronological history of the camp. You'll learn how Sachsenhausen was built by prisoners and see original artifacts, including the gallows, a bunk from the barracks, uniforms, and so on. There are also photos, quotes, and a 22-minute film.

Memorial and Crematorium

Head back to the far end of the camp, which is dominated by the towering, 130-foot-tall, 1961 communist **DDR memorial** to the victims of Sachsenhausen. The 18 triangles at the top are red, the color designated for political prisoners (to the communists, they were more worthy of honor than the other victims who died here). At the base of the monument, two prisoners are being liberated by a noble Soviet soldier. The prisoners are unrealistically robust, healthy, and optimistic (they will survive and become part of the proud Soviet proletariat!). The **podium** in front was used by the East German army for speeches and rallies—exploiting Sachsenhausen as a backdrop for their propaganda.

From here, head left and go through the gap in the fence to find the execution trench, used for mass shootings. When this system proved too inefficient, the Nazis built "Station Z," the nearby **crematorium,** where they could execute and dispose of prisoners more systematically. Its ruins are inside the white building (prior to the camp's liberation by Soviet troops, Nazi guards destroyed the crematorium to remove evidence of their crimes).

The crematorium's ramp took prisoners down into the "infirmary," while the three steps led up to the dressing room. This is where, on five occasions, the Nazis tested Zyklon-B (the chemical later responsible for killing hundreds of thousands at Auschwitz). Most of the building's victims died in the room with the double row of bricks (for soundproofing; the Nazis also blasted classical music to mask noise). Victims would report here for a "dental check," to find out if they had gold or silver teeth that could be taken. They would then stand against the wall to have their height measured—and a guard would shoot them through a small hole in the wall with a single bullet to the back of the skull. (The Nazis found it was easier for guards to carry out their duties if they didn't have to see their victims face-to-face.)

Bodies were taken to be incinerated in the ovens (which still stand). Notice the statue of the emaciated prisoner—a much more accurate depiction than the one at the DDR monument. Outside, a burial ground is filled with ashes from the crematorium.

The Rest of the Camp

Back inside the main part of the camp you can head left, up to the tip of the triangle (behind the big monument) to find a museum about the postwar era, when Sachsenhausen served as a **Soviet**

Special Camp. Nearby is a burial ground for victims of that camp. At this corner of the triangle, the gate in the fence—called **tower E**—holds a small exhibit about the relationship between the camp and the town of Oranienburg.

Heading back toward the main guard tower, along the wall toward the front corner, are the long, green barracks of the **infirmary,** used for medical experiments on inmates (as explained by the exhibits inside). This was also where Soviet soldiers found the 3,000 remaining survivors when they liberated the camp. The small building in back was the morgue—Nazis used the long ramp to bring in the day's bodies via wheelbarrows. Behind that is a field with six stones, each marking 50 bodies for the 300 prisoners who died after the camp was freed.

Wittenberg

You need only look at its official name—Lutherstadt Wittenberg—to know this small city's claim to fame. The adopted hometown of Martin Luther, and the birthplace of his Protestant Reformation, little Wittenberg has a gigantic history that belies its straightforward townscape. With a pair of historic churches—the Town Church of St. Mary, where Luther preached, and the Church of All Saints (Castle Church), where he famously hammered his 95 Theses to the door—and an excellent museum about Luther's life (Luther House), Wittenberg can be a worthwhile stop even for those unfamiliar with the Great Reformer. And for Lutherans, it's a pilgrimage. The notable painter Lucas Cranach the Elder, a contemporary and friend of Luther who also lived and worked in Wittenberg, left behind a slew of masterful paintings and woodcuts, and you can see where he lived as well.

Centuries of Germans have celebrated Wittenberg for its ties to Luther. In 1983, which marked Martin Luther's 500th birthday, Wittenberg was part of communist East Germany, whose atheistic regime was tearing down proud old churches elsewhere. But ignoring the Luther anniversary would have made the East German government, already unpopular, seem woefully out of touch. (The government also sensed an opportunity to attract Luther tourists and much-needed hard Western currency.) So the communists swallowed hard and rehabilitated the memory of Luther, tidying up the sights devoted to him. This may be why Wittenberg emerged from communism in better shape than many other East German towns.

The city received another round of upgrades in 2017, when it celebrated the 500th anniversary of Luther's famous 95 Theses—

Wittenberg in the Early 1500s

As you explore Wittenberg, mentally time-travel to the days of Luther—the first few decades of the 16th century. The Renaissance was percolating to the south in Italy (where Michelangelo and Raphael were hard at work redecorating the Vatican), and a spirit of new ideas was also beginning to take hold in Germany.

The influential prince elector Frederick III "the Wise" (1463-1525), who had inherited half of Saxony from his father, chose sleepy Wittenberg as his royal seat. He built a stout castle here in 1492 (not open to visitors, but viewable from the park just beyond the town gate), and began remaking this humble fishing village into a proper Renaissance town. (That explains Wittenberg's grid of streets, compared with the twisty medieval muddle of many other German towns.) Frederick the Wise hired Lucas Cranach the Elder to be his official court painter. Cranach—along with his wife, Barbara, and son Lucas Cranach the Younger—lived in a big mansion on Market Square (today a museum; his statue—pictured above—is in the courtyard). Frederick also founded a university here (in 1502) and stocked it with some of the brightest minds of his time, including the promising young theologian Martin Luther and the brilliant classical-languages specialist Philipp Melanchthon. Cranach, Luther, Melanchthon, and others were good friends who regularly socialized and swapped ideas.

Although he remained a devout Catholic until the end of his life, Frederick the Wise supported Luther and the reformers in their darkest hour, likely saving them from obscurity or worse. Wittenberg would not be famous if not for Luther—but, most likely, if not for Frederick the Wise, Luther would not be famous, either.

it's newly spiffed up and sparkling. Most tourists here are Germans (and American Lutherans), and the town is also a stop for riverboat cruise groups heading from Hamburg to Dresden and Prague. And yet, Wittenberg isn't unpleasantly touristy. Its pedestrianized main street feels quiet—sometimes almost deserted—and its sights are satisfying and quickly seen. Wittenberg city works perfectly as a side-trip from Berlin (offering a refreshing small-town break from the intense city), and also works well on the way between Berlin and Leipzig, Erfurt, or even Dresden (handy lockers at Wittenberg train station).

GETTING TO WITTENBERG

It's a speedy 40 minutes from Berlin on ICE trains, or 1.5 hours on cheaper regional (RE) trains. All trains depart from the Berlin Hauptbahnhof; some regional trains also stop at Potsdamer Platz. If you're a small group day-tripping from Berlin, and are willing to take the slower regional trains (not valid on ICE), you can save a bundle with the **Brandenburg-Berlin-Ticket.** Available through Deutsche Bahn, this covers unlimited regional train travel throughout the Brandenburg region during one day, for up to five people, all for €29.

PLANNING YOUR TIME

Wittenberg's sights can be seen in just a few hours. For an efficient visit, from the train station ride the public bus to Marktplatz, start at the TI and Castle Church, then work your way downhill through town—sightseeing and possibly having lunch as you go. From the last couple of sights—Luther House and Asisi Panorama it's about a 15-minute, downhill walk back to the train station.

Background on Martin Luther

Luther lived a turbulent life. In early adulthood, the newly ordained Catholic priest suffered a crisis of faith before finally emerging as "born again." In 1517, he openly protested against Church corruption and was later excommunicated. Defying both the pope and the emperor, he was declared a heretic and hid out in a friendly prince's castle, watching as his ideas sparked peasant riots. In his castle refuge he translated the New Testament from Greek to German. He later composed hymns such as "A Mighty Fortress Is Our God," sparred with fellow Reformers, and tried to harness and guide the religious, social, and political firestorm he helped ignite.

Early Life

Luther was born on November 10, 1483, in Eisleben, south of Berlin. His dad owned a copper smelter, affording Luther a middle-class upbringing—a rarity in the medieval hierarchy of nobles, clergy, and peasants.

Luther enrolled at the University of Erfurt in 1501. There he earned a liberal-arts degree, entered law school, and earned himself

DAY TRIPS

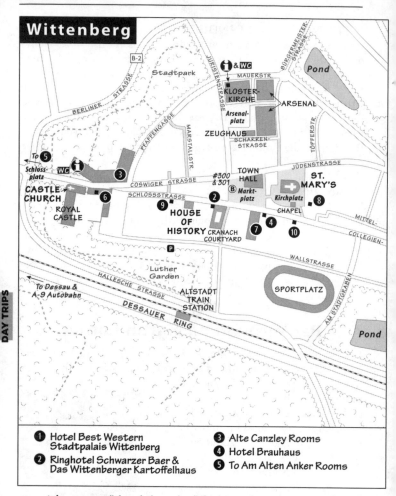

Wittenberg

B-2

Stadtpark

BERLINER STRASSE

PFAFFENGASSE

MARSTALLSTR.

JÜRGENSTRASSE

BÜRGERMEISTER-STRASSE

Pond

MAUERSTR.

ℹ & WC

KLOSTER-KIRCHE

Arsenal-platz

ARSENAL

ZEUGHAUS

SCHARREN-STRASSE

TÖFFERSTR.

JÜDENSTRASSE

To ⑤ Schloss-platz

WC ℹ

③

COSWIGER STRASSE

#300 & 301

TOWN HALL

B Markt-platz

ST. MARY'S

SCHLOSSSTRASSE

Kirchplatz

⑧

CASTLE CHURCH

⑥

②

ROYAL CASTLE

⑨

HOUSE OF HISTORY

CRANACH COURTYARD

CHAPEL

⑦ ④

⑩

MITTEL-COLLEGIEN-

P

Luther Garden

HALLESCHE STRASSE

WALLSTRASSE

To Dessau & A-9 Autobahn

ALTSTADT TRAIN STATION

SPORTPLATZ

AM STADTGRABEN

DESSAUER RING

Pond

DAY TRIPS

❶ Hotel Best Western Stadtpalais Wittenberg

❷ Ringhotel Schwarzer Baer & Das Wittenberger Kartoffelhaus

❸ Alte Canzley Rooms

❹ Hotel Brauhaus

❺ To Am Alten Anker Rooms

two nicknames—"the philosopher" for his wide-ranging mind, and "the king of hops" for his lifelong love affair with beer.

Then came July 2, 1505. While riding through the countryside, Luther was caught up in an intense thunderstorm, and a bolt of lightning knocked him to the ground. Luther cried out, "St. Anne, save me, and I will become a monk!" Surviving the storm, Luther was determined to make good on his promise. He returned to Erfurt, sold his possessions, and told his friends, "After this day, you will see me no more." The next morning, he knocked on the door of Erfurt's Augustinian Monastery and dedicated his life to Christianity.

But Luther soon realized that pious monastic life did not suit his inquisitive nature. He returned to academia, was ordained a

6 Lutherstadt Wittenberg Youth Hostel

7 Brauhaus Wittenberg & Reinsdorfer

8 Trattoria Toscana

9 Hanami Restaurant

10 Super Döner

priest in 1507 in Erfurt's cathedral, and by 1508 was teaching theology part-time at the university in nearby Wittenberg.

In 1509, Luther set out for Rome on foot, a pilgrimage that would change him forever. Upon arriving in the Eternal City, he

was dismayed to find rich, corrupt priests and bishops selling "indulgences," which supposedly guaranteed entry to heaven to those able to pay the price. This was the Rome of Pope Julius II, who was in the midst of an expensive, over-the-top remodel of Vatican City—and the lucrative sale of indulgences helped refill the papal treasury. At the time of Luther's visit, Michelangelo was lying aloft on his back in the Sistine Chapel, executing detailed frescoes on the ceiling, while

Raphael was slathering nearby hallways with his own Renaissance masterpieces.

This traffic in indulgences and luxury clashed violently with Luther's deeply held belief that people's faith, not their pocketbook, would determine the final destination of their souls. Indulgences were an insult to his worldview—and, to Luther, a betrayal of the Christian faith.

Professor and Preacher

After returning to Germany in 1512, Luther received his doctorate and got a job teaching theology at the university in Wittenberg. The prince elector of Saxony, Frederick the Wise, had decided to make this backwater town his royal seat, so he invited the region's best and brightest to populate his dynamic new burg. Here, Luther mingled with other great thinkers (including fellow professor Philipp Melanchthon) and artists (most notably Lucas Cranach the Elder).

During these early years, Luther was consumed with the notion that he was a sinner. He devoured the Bible, looking for an answer and finding it in Paul's letter to the Romans. Luther concluded that God makes sinners righteous through their faith in Jesus Christ, not by earning it through good deeds. As this concept of "unearned grace" took hold, Luther said, "I felt myself to have been born again."

Energized, he began a series of Bible lectures at Wittenberg's Town Church of St. Mary. The pews were packed as Luther quoted passages directly from the Bible. Speaker and audience alike began to see discrepancies between what the Bible said and what the Church was doing. Coincidentally, a friar happened to arrive in Wittenberg around this time, selling letters of indulgence that promised "forgiveness for all thy sins, transgressions, and excesses, howsoever enormous they may be"...a bargain at twice the price.

Outraged at the idea that God's grace could be bought, Luther thought the subject should be debated openly. On October 31, 1517, he nailed his now-famous 95 Theses (topics for discussion) to the door of Wittenberg's Castle Church. The theses questioned indulgences and other Church practices and beliefs. Thesis #82 boldly asked: "If the pope redeems a number of souls for the sake of miserable money with which to buy a church, why doesn't he empty purgatory for the sake of holy love?" With the newfangled printing presses belonging to Lucas Cranach, Luther's propositions were turned into pamphlets that became the talk of Germany.

Excommunication

Luther didn't set out to start a new church; he wanted to reform the existing one. He preached throughout the region, spreading his provocative ideas and publicly debating his positions in such venues as Leipzig's town hall. In 1520, a furious Pope Leo X sent the rebellious monk a papal bull threatening excommunication. Luther burned the edict on the spot, and soon after, Leo X formally excommunicated him.

Luther was branded a heretic and ordered to Rome to face charges, but he refused to go. Finally, the most powerful man in Europe, Emperor Charles V, stepped in to arbitrate, calling an Imperial Diet (congress) at Worms in 1521. Luther made a triumphal entry into Worms, greeted by cheering crowds. The Diet convened, and Luther took his place in the center of the large hall, standing next to a stack of his writings. Inquisitors grilled him while the ultra-conservative Charles looked on. Luther refused to disavow his beliefs.

The infuriated emperor declared Luther an outlaw and a heretic. Being "outside the law" meant that he could be killed at will. After leaving Worms, Luther disappeared. He was kidnapped—by supporters—and given refuge in Frederick the Wise's Wartburg Castle. There Luther wore a beard to disguise himself as Junker Jörg ("Squire George"). He spent 10 months fighting depression and translating the Bible's New Testament from the original Greek into German. This "September Testament" was revolutionary, bringing the Bible to the masses and shaping the modern German language.

Meanwhile, Luther's ideas caught on back home in Wittenberg, where his followers had continued to pursue reform. By the time Luther returned to the city in 1522, popular uprisings led by more radically minded reformers were undermining law and order.

Later Life

In 1525, Luther's friend and follower Thomas Müntzer used Luther's writings to justify an uprising known as the Peasants' Revolt. Poor farmers attacked their feudal masters with hoes and pitchforks, fighting for more food, political say-so, and respect. Thousands of peasants died, and Müntzer was executed. Luther decried the uprising, preaching that Church corruption did not justify outright societal rebellion. In fact, he supported the violent suppression of the Peasants' Revolt.

In 1525, the 41-year-old ex-priest married a 26-year-old ex-nun, Katharina von Bora, "to please my father and annoy the pope." (Their wedding set the precedent of allowing Protestant clergy to marry.) They moved into the former Wittenberg monastery where Luther had once lived (today's Luther House, the best museum anywhere on the Reformation and Luther), where they rented rooms to students. Luther turned his checkbook over to "my lord Katie," who ran the family farm and raised their six children and 11 adopted orphans.

Luther traveled, spreading the Protestant message. In 1529, at Marburg Castle (just north of Frankfurt), he attended a summit of leading Protestants to try and forge an alliance against Catholicism. They agreed on everything except a single theological point: whether Christ was present in the wine and bread of Communion in a physical sense (according to Luther) or symbolic sense (per the Swiss reformer Ulrich Zwingli). The disagreement doomed the Protestant movement to splinter into dozens of sects.

In 1534, Luther finished translating the Bible. Lucas Cranach illustrated it with woodcuts and published it on his printing presses. The Martin Luther Bible was to German-speaking Christians what the King James Bible would be to English-speaking Christians—essentially codifying an entire language. Luther also wrote a German Mass, catechisms, and several hymns, including the still-beloved "A Mighty Fortress Is Our God."

In his fifties, Luther's health declined and he grew bitter, a fact made clear in such writings as "Against the Papacy at Rome Founded by the Devil" and "Of the Jews and Their Lies." A general tone of anti-Judaism pollutes his later work. Luther was less concerned with the ethnicity of Jews—as the Nazis later were—than he was by their refusal to accept Christianity. Luther's words were later invoked to justify anti-Semitic speech and actions during the early days of Nazism.

Martin Luther died on February 18, 1546, and was buried in Wittenberg. To read more about Luther's legacy, see the sidebar on page 358. And watch my one-hour public television special, Rick Steves' *Luther and the Reformation* (www.ricksteves.com/luther).

Orientation to Wittenberg

Literally "White Hill," Wittenberg (Germans say VIT-tehn-behrk, pop. 50,000) sits atop a gentle rise above the Elbe River. The tourists' Wittenberg is essentially a one-street town: Its main drag runs about three-quarters of a mile from the Luther House (where the street is called Collegienstrasse) to the Castle Church (where it's called Schlossstrasse). The rest of the Old Town consists only of a few side streets. The modern part of town sprawls mostly to the north and east.

Don't confuse Wittenberg with Wittenberge, a town north of Berlin. (The correct Wittenberg sometimes shows up as "Kleinwittenberg" on GPS maps or "Lutherstadt Wittenberg" on some websites.)

TOURIST INFORMATION

Wittenberg's TI is at the far end of town from the train station, across the street from Castle Church (April-Oct daily 9:00-18:00; Nov-March Mon-Fri 10:00-16:00, Sat-Sun until 14:00; Schlossplatz 2, tel. 03491/498-610, www.lutherstadt-wittenberg.de). The TI rents a town audioguide (€7, 2 hours of commentary—must return before closing time), and there's a pay WC next door. A second, less comprehensive branch of the TI is at the northern edge of the Old Town, in the Stadthaus (shorter hours than main TI).

ARRIVAL IN WITTENBERG

Wittenberg's **main train station** (listed on schedules as Lutherstadt Wittenberg) is a dull 15-minute walk from the Luther Museum and a 25-minute walk from the TI and Castle Church. (The smaller Lutherstadt Wittenberg Altstadt station, while closer to the Old Town, only serves trains on a small branch line.) The station building has handy lockers, a café, and a ticket office. Nearby (on the other side of the big, white tent) are **bus**

stops for the ride into town. Look for bus #300 (toward Coswig) or bus #301 (toward Straach); these leave from bus stop #1 (every 30 minutes, 10-minute ride, €1.30/ride, €2.50/day pass, buy tickets from driver). Stops aren't announced; you want the Marktplatz stop, right at the Old Town's main square (ask the driver to confirm). A **taxi** from the station to Schlossplatz (near the TI) should cost about €10 (if no taxis are waiting, call 03491/666-666). To **walk,** head left from the station, walk beneath the overpass, and look for signs directing you to the city center.

Drivers will find plenty of free on-street **parking** just outside the mostly pedestrianized town center.

HELPFUL HINTS

Festivals: Various festivals dot Wittenberg's calendar, including a three-day celebration of the wedding of Luther and Katharina (second weekend in June) and special events for **Reformation Day** (Oct 31, when Luther nailed his 95 Theses to the church door).

Tours: Most walking-tour options (you'll likely see costumed Martin Luthers and Katharina von Boras leading groups through town) are in German only. For an English tour, hire your own local guide—gracious **Katja Köhler** does a great job telling Wittenberg's story (€80/2-hour tour, €130/4-hour tour, mobile 0177-688-8218, katjakoehler@gmx.net).

English Worship Services: Local Lutherans offer English-language services in historic Wittenberg churches during the summer (April-Oct Wed-Fri at 16:00 in small Corpus Christi chapel next to Town Church of St. Mary; Sat at 17:00 in either Castle Church or Town Church of St. Mary; confirm times at www.wittenbergenglishministry.com).

Classical Concerts: It seems like there's always a concert on in one of the town's churches. If you're spending the night, check at the TI to find out when and where you can enjoy some classical music. (Luther—who said "to sing is to pray double"—loved music.)

Sights in Wittenberg

MARTIN LUTHER SIGHTS

I've organized these sights roughly in order from the TI end of town (with the Castle Church) to the Luther House end of town.

▲▲Castle Church (Schlosskirche)

This Church of All Saints was the site of one of the most important moments in European history: Martin Luther nailing his 95 Theses to the church door. That door—and most of the church as it existed in Luther's time—are long gone (destroyed in 1760, during the Seven Years' War). But in the late 19th century, as Germany was uniting as a nation for the first time, the church and the door were rebuilt in the Romantic style as a temple to Luther and his fellow reformers. You'll find Luther's humble tombstone inside.

Cost and Hours: Free; April-Oct daily 10:00-18:00; Nov-March Tue-Sat 10:00-16:00, Sun 11:30-16:00, closed Mon; Schlossplatz, tel. 03491/402-585, www.schlosskirche-wittenberg.de.

Visiting the Church: Before entering, take a close look at that famous **side door** (in the middle of the church, to the left of the present-day entrance). According to most accounts, on October 31, 1517, a frustrated Martin Luther nailed a handwritten copy of 95 Theses—topics for discussion—to the wooden door that was here then. (What you see is a 19th-century bronze door engraved with the Latin theses.) The act wasn't quite as defiant as it sounds—the door served as a sort of community bulletin board. But the strong arguments Luther made about ending the practice of indulgences and other forms of Church corruption were revolutionary...as was his timing. Normally, Wittenbergers worshipped at the Town Church of St. Mary, but the day after Luther's act—All Saints' Day—was the one day each year that the Castle Church's interior was open to the public, who were invited to come inside, view Frederick the Wise's vast collection of relics, and purchase indulgences. Historians quibble over the exact day Luther made his theses public and whether he actually nailed them to the door, but there's no doubt that his work spurred a nascent sentiment of reform and cemented his role as that movement's leader.

Above the door is a glittering image of the crucified Christ flanked by Luther (on the left) and his fellow Reformer Philipp Melanchthon (on the right), with the skyline of Wittenberg behind them.

Go inside, walk down the **nave,** and look up. Notice the colorful coats of arms on the upper stained-glass windows, which represent German cities that became Protestant when they joined Luther's Reformation. The carved coats of arms on the railing honor larger principalities that also adopted Protestantism. The lower stained-glass windows, with images of Reformers, were grudgingly added for Luther's 500th birthday, in 1983, by the aggressively atheistic East German government... and it shows.

In the middle of the church, to the right (in front of the pulpit, with a raised plaque), you'll see the flower-bedecked **tomb of Martin Luther.** On the wall behind it is a replica of the large bronze tomb marker that originally covered Luther's remains. While this wasn't his home church (that would be the Town Church of St. Mary, just up the street and described later), this university church was traditionally where professors like Luther were entombed. On the left side of the nave is a similar raised plaque marking the grave of Luther's right-hand man and fellow professor, **Philipp Melanchthon**.

Proceed to the front of the church. In front of the high altar are large tomb markers for the **prince electors** who called Wittenberg home and provided safe harbor for Luther's provocative ideas. On the left is Frederick the Wise, and on his right is his younger brother, John the Steadfast. While Frederick remained devoutly

DAY TRIPS

Catholic throughout his life, his support for Luther, Melanchthon, and the early Protestant Reformers never wavered. Frederick's successor, John, converted to Protestantism and, in a fit of iconoclasm, destroyed his brother's impressive collection of relics. Flanking these markers are larger plaques and statues (from the original church) that depict these important brothers.

▲Market Square (Marktplatz)

This wide square is much the same today as it was in Luther's time. An all-purpose space back then, it was used for everything from tournaments to executions. The square is dominated by the Renaissance-style **Town Hall** (Rathaus). Notice the seven small, filled-in doors at the right side of the building,

which led to a shopping gallery back when the building's cellar hosted a little marketplace (today the Town Hall houses a 20th-century Christian art collection). In one corner of the square you'll find a metal model of Wittenberg's Old Town. In the middle of the square are 19th-century **statues** of Martin Luther (pictured here) and Philipp Melanchthon (pictured on page 352).

The main street through town is lined by delightful gurgling **canals,** as in a few other German cities, like Freiburg and Augsburg. When Luther first moved to Wittenberg, he was disgusted by these, which carried drinking water (on the way into town) and smelly sewage (on the way out). Years later, they were covered over by the modern street. But recently they were opened up to the air to evoke the ambience of Luther's time.

Cranach Courtyard (Cranachhof)

Find the big beige Renaissance building at Schlossstrasse 1, in one corner of the square, with a pharmacy (the Lucas-Cranach-Apotheke) on the ground floor. This building, circling a surprisingly large courtyard, was the residence of the artist Lucas Cranach the Elder. Enter the court-yard to see a statue of Cranach sketching at the far end (see the photo on page 340).

As the official court painter for Frederick the Wise, Cranach was one of the most esteemed men in town, but he was also an entrepreneur who dabbled in endeavors like printing and running a pharmacy. Cranach and Luther were fast friends. The artist was the only painter who had permission to do portraits of Luther and his family (Cranach and his school produced and reproduced some 2,000 Luther portraits), and he was one of the first printers of Luther's writings. Cranach's house is also where Luther's future bride, Katharina von Bora, lived when she first came to Wittenberg (fresh out of the convent).

For decades, this space sat in ruins (see the pre-1989 photo in the entry arch.) But it's been converted into a kind of cultural center, hosting artists' studios, a small bar, a gift shop, comfort-able hotel rooms, and—at the far end of the courtyard—an old-fashioned print shop *(Druckerstube)*. Operated by a quirky printer who speaks some English and enjoys explaining the importance of Luther's statement, "This is a German nation—the people speak German," the shop uses traditional methods to create postcards and replicas of works by Luther and Cranach (closed Sun). There's a small Cranach museum a few doors away (at #4 on Market Square).

DAY TRIPS

▲▲Town Church of St. Mary (Stadtkirche St. Marien)

Towering over a row of buildings at the end of Market Square, this is the oldest building in town and an impressively historic place to be surrounded by Luther lore.

Before stepping inside, notice that the tops of the twin towers don't quite match the rest of the building. Former-ly pointy Gothic steeples, these were knocked down during a 1546 battle. They were later rebuilt in the round Renaissance style you see today.

Cost and Hours: Free to enter, Mon-Sat 10:00-18:00, Sun from 11:30, Nov-Easter daily until 16:00, free organ concerts May-Oct Fri at 18:00, tel. 03491/62830, www.stadtkirchengemeinde-wittenberg.de.

Visiting the Church: The interior of the Town Church of St. Mary is striking for its pure, uncluttered feel. Once ornately paint-ed and slathered with chapels, statues, and ornamentation, it was cleaned out when it became Lutheran. Sit in a pew and enjoy the Doublemint freshness of the space.

Philipp Melanchthon (1497-1560)

While everyone who comes to Wittenberg has heard of Martin Luther, many are surprised to find another important figure celebrated here with almost equal reverence: Philipp Melanchthon. The Garfunkel to Luther's Simon, Melanchthon was a brainy university professor who also played a critical role in the Protestant Reformation.

Born Philipp Schwartzerdt in southern Germany, he later changed his name to its Greek translation, Melanchthon ("black soil"). Although he was short, young, sickly, and notoriously unattractive, Melanchthon impressed everybody in Wittenberg with his keen intellect. In fact, when Melanchthon became disillusioned with Wittenberg and threatened to move away, Frederick the Wise persuaded him to stay by arranging a marriage for him (to the mayor's daughter, no less). While Luther was no intellectual slouch, Melanchthon was even more brilliant—he taught several topics (specializing in ancient languages, pedagogy, and theology) and encouraged women to pursue university study. Particularly gifted with languages, he provided Luther with invaluable assistance when translating the Bible into German from the original Greek and Hebrew texts.

For most of his life, this was Luther's home church—where he was married, where his children were baptized, and where he preached over 2,000 times. This is where what many consider to be the first-ever Protestant service took place, on Christmas Day in 1521 (although Martin Luther wasn't in attendance—he was hiding out at Wartburg Castle). The readings were in German (not Latin), communion was taken by everyone (not just priests), and hymns were sung by the congregation—actually quite radical at the time.

At the front of the church, the **baptismal font** is where Luther's own children were baptized. Notice the tube extending from the basin directly down toward the ground. This allowed water, after having washed away sin, to be drained directly into what was a sandy floor, so it could be transmitted, unimpeded, to hell. Around the lower legs of the font, notice the many demons attempting to reach the baby being baptized up top—but their progress is blocked by the righteous saints.

The focal point of the church is the colorful, engaging, almost whimsical **altar painting** by Lucas Cranach the Elder, the Younger, and their school (completed in 1547, the year after Luther died).

The gang's all here: All the big-name early Protestants and their buddies have showed up to reenact classic ecclesiastical scenes. In the spirit of the Reformation, these aren't saints or royals—they're just people.

The bottom panel shows Martin Luther preaching from a pulpit, one hand on the Bible and the other pointing to Christ, as he engages an enthralled group of worshippers. The fluttering loincloth of Jesus helps to convey the message from preacher to parishioner. But notice that, true to life, some of those people aren't paying attention—they're chatting and looking around. The woman watching Luther most intently is his wife, Katharina. She's surrounded by their many children. Cranach (with the big white beard) is in the back.

The panel on the left shows Philipp Melanchthon (who was not a priest) baptizing a baby. The early reformers believed that lay people—not exclusively priests—could perform baptisms. In the foreground, the extravagantly dressed woman with her back to us is Cranach's wife, Barbara. Supposedly, she grew frustrated that her husband was always painting Luther, Katharina, and others, but never her. "Fine," he said. "I'll include you in the altarpiece."

On the right panel, Johannes Bugenhagen (among reformers, he ranks third after Luther and Melanchthon) is hearing confession from two very different people. Over the head of the obviously distraught and repentant man on the left, Bugenhagen holds the key of heaven—the sinner has done right by confessing and will reap eternal rewards. The man on the right, however, is trying to buy his way into heaven—but his hands are tied and the key of heaven is behind him, indicating he can't purchase paradise.

The central panel features the Last Supper, with the reformers standing in for the apostles. Notice the round table, which symbolizes how, in Protestantism, all are equal. People from all walks of life are actively engaging each other. It's easy to pick out Judas in the foreground (he wears yellow, as evildoers often do in Cranach paintings). On the opposite side of the table, Martin Luther (clad in black, wearing the bearded disguise of Junker Jörg) is being handed a chalice by Lucas Cranach the Younger. In contrast to

Catholic worship at the time, Protestant services invited everybody to participate in communion.

Circle behind the painting and look at the lower panel, which appears as though it's been defaced by some no-good teenagers. It was...centuries ago. Around Luther's time, students of theology came here at the end of their studies and scratched their names or initials into the painting: on the left, in the river of knowledge, if they'd done well—or on the right, in hell, if they'd flunked. Looking carefully among the damned (higher up, on a skull), you can find the name "Johannes Luther"—Martin's son. (Thankfully, he had more success after he switched to law.)

The zone behind the altar has several interesting paintings. Most important is a painting labeled *Epitaph for Paul Eber and his Family* (better known as ***The Vineyard of the Lord***), by Lucas Cranach the Younger. This work's propaganda-for-the-Reformation motives are obvious: On the right, the reformers tend to the garden of the Lord (that's Martin Luther raking and Philipp Melanchthon pulling water from the well—just as the reformers went back to the original source to translate their Bible). On the left, the pope and his cronies (in their excessively opulent robes) trash all their hard work. In the lower-left corner, everyone lines up to receive their reward from Jesus. The pope (wearing yellow, again symbolizing evil) has already received his, but keeps

his hand outstretched, expecting more than his share. In the lower right, the reformers (in their simple black robes) pray reverently.

As you head back up the nave to exit, look up: The grand **organ** dates from the communist period (1983), and booms out short organ concerts in summer. Luther's greatest musical hit, "A Mighty Fortress Is Our God," was first sung here.

Exiting the way you came in, turn left and go to the back corner of the church. Look up at the bottom of the roofline to find the relief of a pig, called the **Judensau** ("Jewish sow"). This bit of medieval anti-Semitic propaganda was designed to intimidate Wittenberg's Jews, who lived in the area just behind the church. Look carefully at the pig, which is considered unclean in the Jewish faith: Jewish children are suckling from it, and a rabbi seems to be peering inquisitively into its rear end. When restoring the church, church authorities asked the Jewish community in Berlin what they should do with this painful remnant of a less-enlightened time. Rather than cover it, they suggested leaving it here as a part of the town's heritage, and adding a modern monument: Look for the plaque in the cobbles directly below the pig, where four paving stones look as if they're being pried apart by something bubbling up from beneath. The message: You can't hide uncomfortable facts; they will find a way to see the light of day. The adjacent cedar tree was donated by students in Tel Aviv.

Behind you, go through the gap between the buildings near the pig to see one of Wittenberg's 16th-century **fountains.** Part of Frederick the Wise's improvements, this network of fountains (with wooden pipes) still works—but nobody knows quite how.

▲▲Luther House (Lutherhaus)

Luther's former home has been converted into an excellent museum displaying original paintings, manuscripts, and other Luther-era items—including the pulpit

from which Luther preached, famous portraits of Luther and the other reformers by Lucas Cranach, and Luther's original New Testament and Bible translations into High German. Everything is fully described, and touch-screen stations provide more depth.

Cost and Hours: €8, €10 combo-ticket with Melanchthon House; April-Oct daily 9:00-18:00; Nov-March Tue-Sun 10:00-17:00, closed Mon; Collegienstrasse 54, tel. 03491/420-3118, www.martinluther.de.

Visiting the House: From the street, step through the passage

(at #59) into the inner courtyard to see the giant, turreted building. Not really a "house," this was originally a monastery. Luther lived here first as a monk and again later, after he had married Katharina von Bora (the building was a wedding gift from a prince elector who took Luther under his wing). Katharina rented out rooms to students, and kept the family fed and watered by cultivating a garden, brewing beer, and even breeding cattle. In the middle of the courtyard is a **statue of Katharina.**

Erected on her 500th birthday in 1999, the sculpture symbolizes her leaving her former life at a nunnery and beginning a new one with Martin Luther.

Head inside through the gateway on your right. From the ticket desk, go straight into the first room to see a simplified model of Wittenberg during Luther's time; paintings by Lucas Cranach (including a portrait of Frederick the Wise, the prince elector who supported Luther); and a woodcut print of a knights' tournament at Market Square.

The next room juxtaposes several **historic items.** Flanking the door are an indulgence chest and an original letter of indulgence *(Ablassurkunde),* from 1492. Those who bought indulgences would supposedly be rescued from their sins...while generating substantial income for the Catholic Church. Money raised was applied directly to an ambitious building project at the Vatican: On the right, see the engraving of St. Peter's Basilica, with its spectacular dome still under construction. Albrecht of Brandenburg (as the archbishop of Mainz, he was Luther's direct superior) and Pope Leo X (both pictured at right), stunningly influential and wealthy, were part of a finely tuned business of selling forgiveness to mostly illiterate Christians frightened they'd spend eons in purgatory...or worse.

In contrast to the opulence in Roman Catholic churches, see Martin Luther's original lindenwood **pulpit** from the Town Church of St. Mary. Notice how relatively humble it is—imagine him climbing up to the top and bringing the Reformation message to a packed church. Nearby is the first printed version of Luther's troublemaking 95 Theses.

Continue into the **refectory,** where students would sit around a long table to dine. At the far end of this great hall is Cranach's wonderful painting *The Ten Commandments* (1516). This was originally designed for the Town Hall so that anybody could see it; today, as then, it's handy for a review of Sunday school lessons. See if you can iden-

tify each of the 10 commandments being broken (and followed)—and note that the same nobleman (in yellow and black) is responsible for half the sins. In each panel, an eerie-eyed demon prods the sinners.

In a side passage near the refectory, you can peruse a small but endearing exhibit with wood-carved figures acting out daily life in Luther's time.

Up on the **first floor** is a rare painting of a relatively young Martin Luther by Cranach (1520). In the little dimly lit alcove, find the Cranach-printed first edition (1522) of Luther's German translation of the New Testament, illustrated with Cranach woodcuts. Nearby is the "community chest," the first systematized charity for poor people—Protestants began steering donations to the needy rather than into Church coffers. (Compare this to the Church's indulgence chest we saw earlier.)

Pass through a lecture hall dominated by a fancy gilded lectern into the actual private **residence** of the Luther family (which still smells like the 16th century). Look for his-and-hers Cranach paintings of Martin and Katharina, three years after their wedding. Imagine the lifestyle of these newlyweds—he a former monk and priest, she a former nun. While the idealistic Luther took little or no payment for preaching and writing, and depended on the charity of wealthy local supporters, Katharina was a businesswoman who balanced the books and kept this huge household going. Look for the lockbox they used to protect their valuables. Katharina kept the key so Luther wouldn't give everything they owned to the poor.

The centerpiece is the **"Lutherstube"**—the room with benches, a stove, and the table where Luther engaged in spirited con-

versations with his colleagues. Notice the names scratched into the ceiling, left behind by visiting VIPs (on the door, protected by glass, is the John Hancock of Russian Czar Peter the Great). Luther's adjoining study contains a collection of his beer mugs (Luther loved his suds).

In the final room, see Luther's translation of the complete Bible from 1534, printed and illustrated by Cranach with 266 woodcuts, and a tiny hymnal from 1533. Luther, who believed that music should be an important part of worship, composed hymns that are still sung today.

An adjacent room features an old printing press and cases filled with booklets that Luther authored and Cranach illustrated. In this room you can find (on the wall) an etching of "the pope as Satan," a case full of anti-Jewish-themed books Luther wrote late in his life, and covers with more of Cranach's political cartoon etchings—designed so even the illiterate could get the gist of Luther's message. Perhaps the first PR genius to "go viral," Luther

Luther's Legacy

It'd be difficult to overstate the impact Luther and the Protestant Reformation he led had on European history.

Even during Luther's lifetime, the Reformation raged across northern Europe. In Holland, Protestant extremists marched into Catholic churches, lopped off the heads of holy statues, stripped gold-leaf angels from the walls, and shattered stained-glass windows in a fit of anti-Catholic iconoclasm. Switzerland—with its deep roots in democracy and self-rule—was a haven for free thinkers, led by Ulrich Zwingli (1484-1531) and the exiled Frenchman John Calvin (1509-1564), who established a theocratic government and inspired French followers called Huguenots. When England's charismatic King Henry VIII (r. 1509-1547) was excommunicated for divorcing Catherine of Aragon so he could marry Anne Boleyn, Henry "divorced" England from the Catholic Church, established the Church of England (or "Anglican Church") and "dissolved" (destroyed) England's many countryside abbeys.

The Vatican responded to these Protestant revolutions with the Counter-Reformation, which was an attempt to put the universal Catholic Church back together using a carrot-and-stick approach. On the one hand, the Church worked diligently to eliminate corruption from within, reach out to alienated members, do missionary work, and inspire the faithful with exalted Church art. This "Counter-Reformation" art, Baroque and bubbly, gave worshippers a glimpse of the heaven that awaited those who remained faithful. On the other hand, when need be, the Church resorted to propaganda, intimidation, and outright force—as doled out by the dreaded Inquisition.

The Reformation spawned a century of Catholic-versus-Protestant wars, with each side convinced that God favored them. When these wars finally ended, Western civilization realized what it should have known from the start: Catholics and Protestants would have to live together. The Peace of Westphalia (1648) decreed that the leader of each country would decide the religion of his nation. Ultimately this divided Europe in half: the generally Protestant north (Scandinavia, the Low Countries, northern Germany, and England), and the predominantly Catholic south (Spain, Portugal, Italy, and southern Germany).

It's clear that Luther's legacy lives on. If you are a Lutheran, Presbyterian, Methodist, Baptist, Episcopalian—or any one of a number of other Protestant faiths—you're the spiritual descendant of this German monk.

sold more than a quarter-million books and was the best-selling German author of the 16th century.

Now climb the stairs to the **top floor,** which features a small treasury filled with 16th-century documents (including a small printed indulgence from 1515 with empty blanks for the purchaser to fill in, and a big indulgence from 1492 worth 100 fewer days in purgatory). This exhibit finishes with an intriguing exhibit of images showing how Luther has been represented in the centuries after his death. At the very end, check out Luther posters from Hitler's time and from communist days (including the 1982 East German illustration showing Luther conversing at a table with Che Guevara and other revolutionaries). The East German government decided that it was OK to tell Luther's story—as long as it was linked to the ideals of socialist revolution.

Luther Sights near Luther House

Several other Reformation sights cluster along Collegienstrasse, at the Luther House end of town:

Leaving the Luther House, turn right down Collegienstrasse with your back toward the town center (toward the ring road). At the big roundabout (see map), at the edge of the park on the left, is the famous **"Luther Oak" tree** marking the spot where Luther burned the papal bull that threatened him with excommunication.

About a block toward Market Square from the Luther House are two other buildings of interest to Lutherans. At #60 (with the rounded gables) is the **Melanchthon House** (Melanchthonhaus)—given to Philipp Melanchthon to persuade him to stay in Wittenberg when he threatened to move elsewhere, and now a museum about his life. Nothing survives from Melanchthon's household, but the museum tries hard to bring him to life, and everything is described in English (€4, €10 combo-ticket with Luther House; April-Oct daily 10:00-18:00; Nov-March Tue-Sun until 17:00, closed Mon; tel. 03491/420-3110).

At #62a, duck through the doorway into the **university court-yard.** These are some of the original buildings where Luther, Melanchthon, and their colleagues worked. Wall plaques ringing the courtyard celebrate famous professors and alumni.

▲Wittenberg 360 Panorama: Luther 1517

Berlin artist Yadegar Asisi—who has created these immersive, 360-degree panorama paintings around eastern Germany—has arrived in Wittenberg. A giant bunker-like structure in a park near the Luther House is home to this nearly 12,000-square-foot work that wraps entirely around the viewer. Using a combination of photographed models and digitally reconstructed historic buildings, Asisi recreates a day in the life of the grubby, crowded, and colorful town on the cusp of the Reformation—standing right in front

DAY TRIPS

of the Castle Church. Light and sound effects highlight different parts of the giant illustration, inviting you to tune into various details (pick up the leaflet, which explains some of the tableaus you'll see). You can climb up the metal tower in the middle of the room for a higher vantage point. Panorama paintings like this one were all the rage in the 19th century, and Asisi does a good job of updating the magic for the modern era. While certainly overpriced, this could be worth the splurge to round out your Luther experience.

Cost and Hours: €11, daily 10:00-18:00, Lutherstrasse 42, www.wittenberg360.de.

Luther Garden

This orchard of ecumenism, a short walk just south of Market Square, is a leafy statement that Christian communities—Protestant, Catholic, and Orthodox—can cooperate. Hundreds of trees from as many Christian communities from all over the world have been planted, and each has a sister tree planted in its community of origin.

OTHER WITTENBERG SIGHTS
▲House of History (Haus der Geschichte)

Those intrigued by the communist chapter of Wittenberg's history will enjoy this museum's three floors of everyday items from East German times (1949-1989). For Cold War buffs, it's worth ▲▲. The *Wende* (German reunification) in 1989 erased an entire culture, and in the space of a few years East German toys, food brands, cars, schoolbooks, and much more were replaced by Western ones—awakening nostalgia even in those who otherwise welcomed the end of communism. Over the past two decades, a dedicated staff has collected thousands of items that memorialize the world of their youth. The museum also includes a few rooms showing furnishings and fashions from the 1920s and 1930s. On the ground floor, you'll find a fully stocked communist-era grocery store, a cozy DDR pub, and an exhibit (German only) on the life of Soviet troops posted to East Germany. The museum is directed at nostalgic German visitors, but the €1 audioguide makes it more meaningful to outsiders.

Cost and Hours: €6, daily 10:00-18:00, Schlossstrasse 6, tel. 03491/409-004, www.pflug-ev.de.

Historical Town Information Center
(Historisches Stadtinformation)

This slick new facility—in two buildings facing Arsenalplatz, a couple of blocks north of Marktplatz—illustrates the history of Wittenberg beyond the life of its most famous resident. The Zeughaus (former armory) displays a large model of Wittenberg in 1873, offering a good look at its earthen ramparts and moat. Across the square—displayed in the enclosed ruins of the Klosterkirche (former Franciscan monastery)—are exhibits on the Ascanian dukes of Saxony, who ruled this area before Luther. (This building adjoins the Stadthaus, with a branch TI, a concert hall, and a free WC.) While presented with modern flair, there's only so much to say—making this, mostly, a "so what?" experience.

Cost and Hours: €2; April-Oct daily 9:00-18:00; Nov-March Tue-Sun 10:00-17:00, closed Mon; Zeughaus at Juristenstrasse 16a, Klosterkirche at Mauerstrasse 18.

Hundertwasserschule

This formerly drab communist-era public school, on the northeast outskirts of town, was redecorated in 1993 with wildly colorful and imaginative flair by Austrian architect Friedensreich Hundertwasser. Most intriguing to architecture buffs, it's a long 30-minute walk from the city center (interior closed to the public but exterior viewable anytime, officially called "Luther-Melanchthon-Gymnasium," Schillerstrasse 22a, www.hundertwasserschule.de).

Cruises and Biking the Elbe River Valley

While you can pay to take a brief cruise on the Elbe River, there's not much to see other than a panoramic view of town (details at TI). The Elbe Valley also attracts many bicycle tourists, following the bike path called the Elberadweg (cycling route info at www.elberadweg.de).

Sleeping in Wittenberg

Wittenberg has a wide range of charming hotels at fine prices. My listings (except Am Alten Anker) are right in the heart of the Old Town. Air-conditioning is rare.

$$$ Hotel Best Western Stadtpalais Wittenberg is a professional-feeling place with 78 rooms offering predictable business-class comfort right on the main drag, near the Luther House (some rooms have air-con, elevator, pay parking, Collegienstrasse 56, tel. 03491/4250, www.stadtpalais.bestwestern.de, info@stadtpalais.bestwestern.de).

$$ Ringhotel Schwarzer Baer ("Black Bear") has 32 modern, comfortable rooms—each a bit different, but all of them stylish—in a period building with hardwood floors right off Market Square (elevator, free parking, Schlossstrasse 2, tel. 03491/420-4344, www.ringhotels.de/wittenberg, wittenberg@ringhotels.de).

$$ Alte Canzley, right next to the TI and across from the Castle Church, has nine enormous, well-equipped (if somewhat dated) rooms above a restaurant in a historic building from 1391. You'll pay extra for a small kitchenette or a view of the Castle Church (elevator, free parking, pay sauna, Schlossplatz 3, tel. 03491/429-110, www.alte-canzley.com, info@alte-canzley.de).

$$ Hotel Brauhaus, a lesser value, rents 34 straightforward rooms over a restaurant and antique shop fronting Market Square (cash only, closed Nov-March, lots of stairs with no elevator, free parking, Markt 7, tel. 03491/443-3130, www.brauhaus-wittenberg. de, info@brauhaus-wittenberg.de).

$ Am Alten Anker, above a restaurant in a drab area at the far end of town (about a 15-minute walk beyond the TI, or a 30-minute walk or quick taxi ride from the train station), has 21 basic but comfortable rooms at a reasonable price (Dessauer Strasse 286, tel. 03491/768-760, www.amaltenanker.de, info@amaltenanker.de).

¢ Lutherstadt Wittenberg Youth Hostel, an official HI hostel, has 160 beds in 3- to 6-bed dorms, each with its own bath. This modern hostel is perfectly located, filling a sleek building by the Castle Church (private rooms available, elevator, pay Wi-Fi, lots of school groups, doors close at 22:00, lunch or dinner available, tucked behind Castle Church at Schlossstrasse 14, tel. 03491/505-205, www.jugendherberge-wittenberg.de, wittenberg@jugendherberge.de).

Eating in Wittenberg

You'll find a fun variety of good, affordable restaurants within a couple blocks of Market Square.

$$ Brauhaus Wittenberg serves up traditional meals and great local beer in a fun-loving beer garden that feels closer to Bavaria than to Saxony. From Market Square, you'll enter the classic old courtyard filled with jovial tables; at the end, go inside to find comfortable seating on two levels, surrounding big copper vats where they brew their own "Wittenberger Original" pilsner. The menu includes big portions of tasty German standards (daily 11:00-22:30, Markt 6, tel. 03491/433-130).

$$ Das Wittenberger Kartoffelhaus serves up hearty, heavy skillets piled high with potatoes, potatoes, potatoes, prepared in fun and creative ways. The interior is cozy and brimming with kitschy decor, and the outdoor seating is on the relaxing pedestrian drag, just off Market Square (Schlossstrasse 2, daily 11:00-22:00, tel. 03491/411-200).

$$ Trattoria Toscana is a popular choice for Italian meals. Tucked in a "Little Italy" corner of town behind the Town Church of St. Mary, it has a fancy interior, romantic piazza seating, and down-to-earth prices (kid-friendly, daily 11:00-24:00, Mittelstrasse 1, tel. 03491/433-188).

$ Hanami, a family-run spot with a classy dining room, specializes in Vietnamese cooking and sushi. Like many Asian restaurants in eastern Germany, the Vietnam connection dates back to the communist days (usually daily 11:00-15:00 & 17:00-21:00, Schlossstrasse 8, tel. 03491/459-7068).

$ Reinsdorfer is good for a quick lunch on the go—there's a bakery on one side of the shop (sandwiches made to order) and a butcher's counter on the other (grilled sausages and prepared side dishes sold from the counter's back end, take out or eat at simple tables, Mon-Fri 8:00-18:00, Sat until 12:00, closed Sun, Markt 6).

$ Super Döner serves up super *döner kebabs* to go from a hardworking little hole-in-the-wall just off Market Square at Collegienstrasse 86 (Mon-Sat 10:30-19:00, closed Sun).

Wittenberg Connections

From Wittenberg by Train to: Berlin (hourly on ICE, 40 minutes; also every 2 hours on slower regional train, 1.5 hours), **Leipzig** (6/day on ICE, 40 minutes; also hourly on regional trains, 1 hour, some with transfer in Bitterfeld), **Erfurt** (every 2 hours, 1.5 hours direct, more with transfer in Leipzig), **Eisenach** and Wartburg Castle (at least hourly, 2.5 hours, transfer in Erfurt or Leipzig), **Dresden** (1-2/hour, 2-3 hours, transfer in Leipzig and sometimes also Bitterfeld), **Frankfurt** (every 2 hours, 4 hours, transfer in Naumburg), **Hamburg** (nearly hourly direct on ICE, 3 hours; also possible about hourly with transfer in Berlin, 3.5 hours), and **Nürnberg** (every 2 hours direct on ICE, 4.5 hours). Train info: Toll tel. 0180-699-6633, www.bahn.com.

DAY TRIPS

GERMANY: PAST & PRESENT

A united Germany has only existed since 1871, but the cultural heritage of the German-speaking people stretches back 2,000 years.

Romans (A.D. 1-500)

German history begins in A.D. 9, when Roman troops were ambushed and driven back by the German chief Arminius. For the next 250 years, the Rhine and Danube rivers marked the border between civilized Roman Europe (to the southwest) and "barbarian" German lands (to the northeast). While the rest of Western Europe's future would be Roman, Christian, and Latin, most of Germany followed a separate, pagan path.

In A.D. 476, Rome fell to the Germanic chief Theodoric the Great (a.k.a. Dietrich of Bern). After that, Germanic Franks controlled northern Europe, ruling a mixed population of Romanized Christians and tree-worshipping pagans. Rome's imprint on Germany remains in place names like Cologne ("Colonia" was an important Roman city) and great monuments like Trier's Porta Nigra.

Charlemagne and the Franks (A.D. 500-1000)

For Christmas in A.D. 800, the pope gave Charlemagne the title of Holy Roman Emperor. Charlemagne, the king of the Franks, was the first of many German kings to be called *Kaiser* ("emperor," from "Caesar") over the next thousand years. Allied with the pope, Charlemagne ruled an empire that included Germany, Aus-

tria, France, the Low Countries, and
northern Italy.

Charlemagne (Karl der Grosse, or
Charles the Great, r. 768-814) stood a
head taller than his subjects, and his
foot became a standard unit of mea-
surement. The stuff of legend, Charlemagne had five wives and four con-
cubines, producing descendants with
names like Charles the Bald, Louis the
Pious, and Henry the Quarrelsome.
His eldest son, Pippin the Hunchback,
led a failed coup against Charlemagne
and was exiled to a monastery. When
Charlemagne died of pneumonia (814),
he lacked a clear heir. His united empire was divided into (what
would become) Germany, France, and the lands in between (Treaty
of Verdun, 843).

The Holy Roman Empire (1000-1500)

Chaotic medieval Germany was made up of more than 300 small,
quarreling dukedoms ruled by the Holy Roman Emperor. The
title was pretty bogus, implying that the German king ruled the
same huge European empire as the ancient Romans. In fact, he
was "Holy" because he was blessed by the pope, "Roman" to recall
ancient grandeur, and the figurehead "Emperor" of what was an
empire in name only.

Holy Roman Emperors had less hands-on power than other
kings around Europe. Because of the custom of electing emperors by nobles and archbishops, rather than by bestowing the title
through inheritance, they couldn't pass the crown from father to
son. In addition, there were no empire-wide taxes and no national
capital. This system gave nobles great power: Peasants had to huddle close to their local noble's castle for protection from attack by
the noble next door.

When Emperor Henry IV (r. 1056-1106) tried to assert his
power by appointing bishops, he was slapped down by the nobles,
and forced to repent to the pope by standing barefoot in the alpine
snow for three days at Canossa (in northern Italy, 1077).

Emperor Frederick I Barbarossa (1152-1190), blue-eyed and
red-bearded (hence *barba rossa*), gained an international reputation
as a valiant knight, gentleman, bon vivant, and lover of poetry and
women. Still, his great victories were away in Italy and Asia (on
the Third Crusade, where he drowned in a river), while back home
nobles wielded the real power.

This was the era of Germany's troubadours *(Meistersinger)*,

Why We Call Deutschland "Germany"

Our English name "Germany" comes from the Latin *Germania,* the Roman name for the lands north of the Alps where "barbarian" tribes lived. The French and Spanish call it *Allemagne* and *Alemania,* respectively, after the Alemanni tribe. Italians call the country *Germania,* but in Italy the German language is known as *tedesco.* The Slavic peoples of Eastern Europe have a perhaps simpler approach, calling Germany *Německo* (Czech), *Niemcy* (Polish), and other variations of a word that basically means "people who can't speak right." The Hungarians borrowed this word from the Slavs and call anything German *német.*

To Germans, their country is *Deutschland,* their language is *Deutsch,* and they themselves are *Deutsche.* A few hundred years ago, this word was spelled *Teutsch* (later, the "t" changed to a "d"). The English word Teutonic, the Italian *tedesco,* and the Scandinavian *tysk* all come from this earlier form. *Alles klar?*

who traveled from castle to castle singing love songs *(Minnesang)* and telling the epic tales of chivalrous knights (Tristan and Isolde, Parsifal, and the Nibelungen) that would later inspire German nationalism and Wagnerian operas.

While France, England, and Spain were centralizing power around a single ruling family to create nation-states, Germany remained a decentralized, backward, feudal battleground.

Medieval Growth

Nevertheless, Germany was strategically located at the center of Europe, and trading towns prospered. Berlin was born when inhabitants of the region of Brandenburg settled on a marshy island in the Spree River. Several northern towns (especially Hamburg and Lübeck) banded together into the Hanseatic League, promoting open trade around the Baltic Sea. To curry favor at election time, emperors granted powers and privileges to certain towns, which were designated "free imperial cities." Some towns, such as Cologne, Mainz, Dresden, and Trier, held higher status than many nobles, as hosts of one of the seven "electors" of the emperor. To this day, every German town keeps careful track of whether it was "free" during the Middle Ages—or answered to a duke, king, archbishop, or elector in another place.

Textiles, mining, and the colonization of lands to the east made Germany an economic powerhouse with a thriving middle class. In towns, middle-class folks (burghers), not aristocrats, began running things. In about 1450, Johann Gutenberg of Mainz figured out how to use moveable type for printing, an innovation

The History of Berlin

Berlin was a humble, marshy burg until prince electors from

the Hohenzollern dynasty made it their capital in the mid-15th century. Gradually their territory spread and strengthened, becoming the powerful Kingdom of Prussia in 1701. As the leading city of Prussia, Berlin dominated the northern Germanic world—both militarily and culturally—long before there was a united "Germany."

Thanks largely to Frederick the Great (1712-1786), the enlightened despot who was both a ruthless military tactician and a cultured lover of the arts, Prussia was well-positioned to lead the German unification movement in the 19th century. And when Germany became a unified modern nation in 1871, Berlin was its natural capital. The city boomed with Germany's industrialization, quadrupling its population over the next 40 years. After Germany's humiliating defeat in World War I, Berlin thrived as an anything-goes cultural capital of the Roaring Twenties. During World War II, the city was Hitler's headquarters—and the place where the Führer drew his final breath.

When the Soviet Army reached Berlin in 1945, the protracted fighting left the city in ruins. Berlin was divided by the victorious Allied powers—the American, British, and French sectors became West Berlin, and the Soviet sector, East Berlin. The city became the main battlefield of the nascent Cold War. In 1948, the Soviets tried to starve the 2.2 million residents of the western half in an almost medieval-style siege, which was broken by the Allies' Berlin Airlift (see page 63). Later, with the overnight construction of the Berlin Wall in 1961, an Iron (or, at least, concrete) Curtain completely encircled West Berlin—cutting Berlin in half (see page 212). While East Berliners lived through difficult times, West Berlin became a magnet for artists, punks, squatters, and free spirits.

Finally, on November 9, 1989, the Wall came down (see page 177). After wild celebration, Berlin faced a fitful transition to reunification. Two cities—and countries—became one at a staggering pace. Some "Ossies" (impolite slang for Easterners) missed their security. Some "Wessies" missed military deferrals, subsidized rent, and tax breaks for living in an isolated city surrounded by the communist world.

Today, going on 30 years later, the old East-West divisions are a distant memory. Berlin's local government has been eager to charge forward, with little nostalgia for the past. Big corporations and the national government have moved in, and the dreary swath of land that was the Wall has been transformed. Berlin is a new city—ready to welcome visitors.

GERMAN HISTORY

that would allow the export of a new commodity: ideas. Around this time, Berlin came under the rule of the powerful Hohenzollern family, who began a palace complex on what is now that city's "Museum Island." The Hohenzollern's influence soon spread throughout northern Germany (Prussia).

Sights
- Marien Church
- (Rebuilt) Nikolai Quarter
- Museum Island

Religious Struggles and the Thirty Years' War (1500-1700)

Martin Luther—German monk, fiery orator, and religious whistle-blower—sparked a century of European wars by speaking

out against the Catholic Church. Luther's protests ("Protestantism") threw Germany into a century of turmoil, as each local prince took sides between Catholics and Protestants. In the 1525 Peasant Revolt, peasants attacked their feudal masters with hoes and pitchforks, fighting for more food, political say-so, and respect. The revolt was brutally put down.

The Holy Roman Emperor, Charles V (r. 1519-1556), sided with the pope. Charles was the most powerful man in Europe, having inherited an empire that included Germany and Austria, plus the Low Countries, much of Italy, Spain, and Spain's New World possessions. But many local German nobles took the opportunity to go Protestant—some for religious reasons, but also as an excuse to seize Church assets and powers.

The 1555 Peace of Augsburg allowed each local noble to decide the religion of his realm. In general, the northern and eastern lands became Protestant, while the south (today's Bavaria, along with Austria) and west remained Catholic.

Unresolved religious and political differences eventually expanded into the Thirty Years' War (1618-1648). This Europe-wide war, fought mainly on German soil, involved Denmark, Sweden, France, and Bohemia (in today's Czech Republic), among others. It was one of history's bloodiest wars, fueled by religious extremism and political opportunism, and fought by armies of brutal mercenaries who worked on commission and were paid in loot and pillage.

By the war's end (Treaty of Westphalia, 1648), a third of all Germans had died, France was the rising European power, and the Holy Roman Empire was a medieval mess of scattered feudal states. In 1689, France's Louis XIV swept down the Rhine, gutting and leveling its once-great castles, and Germany ceased to be a major player in European politics until the modern era.

Sights
- Luther sights in Wittenberg

Austria and Prussia (1700s)
The German-speaking lands now consisted of three "Germanys": Austria in the south, Prussia in the north, and the rest in between.

Prussia—originally a largely Slavic region colonized by celibate ex-Crusaders called Teutonic Knights—was forged into a unified state by two strong kings. Frederick I (the "King Sergeant," r. 1701-1713) built a modern state around a highly disciplined army, a centralized government (with Berlin as its capital), and national pride.

His grandson, Frederick II "The Great" (r. 1740-1786), added French culture and worldliness, preparing militaristic Prussia to enter the world stage. A well-read, flute-playing lover of the arts and liberal ideals, Frederick also ruled with an iron fist—the very model of the "enlightened despot." Meanwhile, Austria thrived under the laid-back rule of the Habsburg family. The Habsburgs gained power in Europe by marrying it. They acquired the Netherlands, Spain, and Bohemia that way (a strategy that didn't work so well for Marie-Antoinette, who wed the doomed king of France).

In the 1700s, the Germanic lands became a cultural power-house, producing musicians (Bach, Haydn, Mozart, Beethoven), writers (Goethe, Schiller), and thinkers (Kant, Leibniz). Sophisticated Berlin became the epicenter of Prussian culture. But politically, feudal Germany was no match for the modern powers.

After the French Revolution (1789), Napoleon swept through Germany with his armies, deposing feudal lords, emancipating Jews, confiscating church lands, and forcing the Holy Roman Emperor to hand over his crown (1806). After a thousand years, the Holy Roman Empire was dead.

GERMAN HISTORY

Church Architecture

History comes to life when you visit a centuries-old church. Even if you wouldn't know your apse from a hole in the ground, learning a few simple terms will enrich your experience. Note that not every church has every feature, and a "cathedral" isn't a type of church architecture, but rather a designation for a church that's a governing center for a local bishop.

Aisles: The long, generally low-ceilinged arcades that flank the nave.

Altar: The raised area with a ceremonial table (often adorned with candles or a crucifix), where the priest prepares and serves the bread and wine for Communion.

Apse: The space beyond the altar, often bordered with small chapels.

Barrel Vault: A continuous round-arched ceiling that resembles an extended upside-down U.

Choir: A cozy area, often screened off, located within the church nave and near the high altar where services are sung in a more intimate setting.

Cloister: Covered hallways bordering a square or rectangular open-air courtyard, traditionally where monks and nuns got fresh air.

Facade: The front exterior surface of the church's main (west) entrance, viewable from outside and generally highly decorated.

Groin Vault: An arched ceiling formed where two equal barrel vaults meet at right angles. Less common usage: term for a medieval jock strap.

Narthex: The area (portico or foyer) between the main entry and the nave.

Nave: The long, central section of the church (running west to east, from the entrance to the altar) where the congregation sits or stands through the service.

Transept: In a traditional cross-shaped floor plan, the transept is one of the two parts forming the "arms" of the cross. The transepts run north-south, perpendicularly crossing the east-west nave.

West Portal: The main entry to the church (on the west end, opposite the main altar).

Sights
- Frederick the Great's Bebelplatz (Berlin State Opera, St. Hedwig's Cathedral)
- Humboldt Forum on Museum Island
- Charlottenburg Palace
- Sanssouci and New Palace at Potsdam

German Unification (1800s)

Napoleon's invasion helped unify the German-speaking peoples by rallying them against a common foreign enemy. After Napoleon's defeat, the Congress of Vienna (1815), presided over by the Austrian Prince Metternich, realigned Europe's borders. The idea of unifying the three Germanic nations—Prussia, Austria, and the German Confederation, a loose collection of small states in between—began to grow. By mid-century, most German-speaking people favored forming a modern nation-state; the only question was whether the confederation would be under Prussian or Austrian dominance.

Economically, Germany was becoming increasingly efficient and modern, with a unified trade organization (1834), railroads (1835), mechanical-engineering prowess, and booming factories benefiting from a surplus of labor. Berlin was changing into a world-class city graced by Neoclassical buildings designed by architect Karl Friedrich Schinkel (including many of today's museums). By 1850, with its Unter den Linden boulevard and the Brandenburg Gate, Berlin rivaled Paris as Europe's most elegant promenade.

Energetic Prussia took the lead in unifying the country. Otto von Bismarck (served 1862-1890), the strong minister of Prussia's weak king, used cunning politics to engineer a unified Germany under Prussian dominance. First, he started a war with Austria, ensuring that any united Germany would be under Prussian control. (Austria remains a separate country to this day.)

Next, Bismarck provoked a war with France (the Franco-Prussian War, 1870-1871), which united Prussia and the German Confederation against their common enemy, France.

Fueled by hysterical patriotism, German armies swept through France and, in the Hall of Mirrors at Versailles, crowned Prussia's Wilhelm I as Emperor *(Kaiser)* of a new German Empire, uniting Prussia and the German Confederation (but excluding Austria). Berlin was the obvious choice as the new imperial capital. This Sec-

GERMAN HISTORY

Germany in the Early 1800s

ond Reich (1871-1918) featured elements of democracy (an elected *Reichstag*—parliament), offset by a strong military and an emperor with veto powers.

A united and resurgent Germany was suddenly flexing its muscles in European politics. Berlin's population boomed, prompting the construction of Prenzlauer Berg, Kreuzberg, and other outlying districts. With strong industry, war spoils, overseas colonies, and a large and disciplined military, Germany sought its rightful place in the sun. Fueled by nationalistic fervor, patriotic *Volk* art flourished (Wagner's operas, Nietzsche's essays), reviving medieval German myths and Nordic gods. The rest of Europe saw Germany's rapid rise—and began arming themselves to the teeth. In Berlin, the imposing Berlin Cathedral was built, announcing the über-nationalism of Kaiser Wilhelm II that would lead Europe into World War I.

Sights
- Concert Hall on Gendarmenmarkt
- Neue Wache
- Museum Island
- Berlin Cathedral
- Prenzlauer Berg Walk

Nazi Terminology

Many Nazi military terms are familiar to English speakers. "Nazi" is an abbreviation for *Nationalsozialismus* (National Socialism), Hitler's political party. Other terms you'll probably recognize are SS (short for *Schutzstaffel,* or "protective unit"), *Luftwaffe* (air force), and *Blitzkrieg* ("lightning war"). Nazis also devised the *Endlösung* ("final solution") for doing away with Jewish and other "undesirable" people, by interning and killing them in *Konzentrationslager* (KZ, concentration camps). The *Widerstand* (resistance) stood up against the Nazis. *Vergangenheitsbewaltigung* (coming to terms with the past) continues to be a major issue in Germany. Many concentration camps and other wartime symbols have been turned into *Gedenkstätte* (memorials). At a *Dokumentationzentrum* (documentation center), locals and visitors can learn about Nazi atrocities. The message of these sites is *Vergesst es nie*—"Never forget."

World War I and Hitler's Rise (1914-1939)

When Archduke Franz Ferdinand, the heir to the Austro-Hungarian Empire, was assassinated in 1914, all of Europe took sides as the political squabble quickly escalated into World War I. Germany and Austria-Hungary attacked British and French troops in France, but were stalled at the Battle of the Marne. Both sides dug defensive trenches, then settled in for four brutal years of bloodshed, boredom, mud, machine-gun fire, disease, and mustard gas.

Finally, at 11:00 in the morning of November 11, 1918, the fighting ceased. Germany surrendered, signing the Treaty of Versailles in the Hall of Mirrors at Versailles. The war cost the defeated German nation 1.7 million men, precious territory, colonies, military rights, reparations money, and national pride.

A new democratic government called the Weimar Republic (1919) dutifully abided by the Treaty of Versailles, and tried to maintain order among Germany's many divided political parties. But after the humiliating defeat, the country was in ruins, its economy a shambles, and the war's victors demanded heavy reparations. Berlin attracted the disillusioned as the center of decadent cabaret nightlife—especially near today's Ku'damm and along Friedrichstrasse. Elsewhere, communists rioted in the streets, fascists plotted coups, and inflation drove the price of a loaf of bread to a billion marks. War vets grumbled in their beer about how their leaders had sold them out. All Germans, regardless of their political affiliations, were fervently united in their apathy toward the new democracy. When the worldwide depression of 1929 hit Germany with brutal force, the nation was desperate for a strong leader with answers.

Germany During World War II
(1939-1945)

1939: Soldiers singing *"Muss ich denn, Muss ich denn zum Städtele hinaus"* ("I must leave, I must leave my happy home") march off to war. On September 1, Germany invades Poland to seize the free city of Danzig (Gdańsk), sparking World War II. Germany, Italy, and Japan (the Axis) would eventually square off against the Allies—which included Britain, France, the United States, and the USSR.

1940: The Nazi Blitzkrieg (lightning war) quickly sweeps through Denmark, Norway, the Low Countries, and France; later it also conquers Yugoslavia and Greece. With fellow fascists ruling Italy (Mussolini), Spain (Franco), and Portugal (Salazar), the Continent is now dominated by fascists, creating a "fortress Europe."

1941: Hitler invades his former ally, the USSR. Bombastic victory parades in Berlin celebrate the triumph of the Aryan race over the lesser peoples of the world.

1942: Allied bombs begin falling on German cities. That autumn and winter, German families receive death notices from the horrific Battle of Stalingrad. The German army suffers around 850,000 casualties (by comparison, the US had roughly 214,000 casualties for the entire Vietnam War). Back home, Nazi officials begin their plan for the "final solution to the Jewish problem"—systematic execution of Europe's Jews in specially built death camps.

1943: Germany fights a two-front war: against tenacious Soviets on the bitter Eastern Front, and against Brits and Yanks advancing north through Italy on the Western Front. Germany's indus-

Adolf Hitler (1889-1945) was a disgruntled vet who had spent the post-World War I years homeless, wandering the streets of Vienna with sketchpad in hand, hoping to become an artist. In Munich, he joined other disaffected Germans to form the National Socialist German Workers' Party—the Nazis. In stirring speeches, Hitler promised to restore Germany to its rightful glory, blaming the country's current problems on communists, foreigners, and Jews. After an unsuccessful coup attempt (the Beer Hall Putsch in Munich, 1923), Hit- ler was sent to jail, where he wrote an influential book of his political ideas, titled *Mein Kampf (My Struggle)*.

By 1930, the Nazis—now wearing power suits and working within the system—had become a formidable political party trial output tries desperately to keep up with that of the Allies. The average German suffers through shortages, rationing, and frequent trips to the bomb shelter.

1944: Hitler's no-surrender policy is increasingly unpopular, and he narrowly survives an assassination attempt by members of his own military. After the Allies reach France on D-Day, Germany counterattacks with a last-gasp offensive (the Battle of the Bulge) that slows but doesn't stop the Allies.

1945: Soviet soldiers approach Berlin from the east, and Ameri-

cans and Brits advance from the west. Adolf Hitler commits suicide, and families lock up their daughters to protect them from rapacious Soviet soldiers. When Germany finally surrenders on May 8, the country is in ruins, occupied by several foreign powers, divided into occupation zones, and viewed by the world as an immoral monster.

War's Aftermath: German citizens are faced with the scope of the mass killings and atrocities committed by their leaders and accomplices. Over 11 million people have been systemically murdered—6 million Jews, as well as people with disabilities, homosexuals, prisoners of war, political dissidents, and ethnic minorities.

in Germany's democracy. They won 38 percent of the seats in the Reichstag in 1932, and Hitler was appointed chancellor (1933). Two months later, the Reichstag building was mysteriously set on fire—an apparent act of terrorism with a September 11-sized impact—and a terrified Germany gave Chancellor Hitler sweeping powers to preserve national security.

Hitler wasted no time in using this Enabling Act to jail opponents, terrorize the citizenry, and organize every aspect of German life under the watchful eye of the Nazi Party. Plumbers' unions, choral societies, schoolteachers, church pastors, filmmakers, and artists all had to account to a Nazi Party official about how their work furthered the Third Reich.

For the next decade, an all-powerful Hitler revived Germany's economy, building the autobahns and rebuilding the military. Defying the Treaty of Versailles and world opinion, Hitler proceeded with his Four-Year Plan to re-arm Germany: He occupied the Saar region (1935) and the Rhineland (1936), annexed

Austria and the Sudetenland (1938), and invaded Czechoslovakia (March 1939). The rest of Europe finally reached its appeasement limit—and World War II began—when Germany invaded Poland in September 1939 (see timeline on page 374). When the war was over (1945), countless millions were dead and most German cities had been bombed beyond recognition. The Third Reich was over.

Sights
- Former Air Ministry
- Topography of Terror
- Site of Hitler's Bunker
- German Resistance Memorial
- Kaiser Wilhelm Memorial Church
- Sachsenhausen Concentration Camp Memorial

Two Germanys...and Reunification (1945-2000)
After World War II, the Allies divided occupied Germany into two halves, split down the middle by an 855-mile border that Winston Churchill called an "Iron Curtain." By 1949, Germany was officially two separate countries. West Germany (the Federal Republic of Germany) was democratic and capitalist, allied with the powerful United States. East Germany (the German Democratic Republic, or DDR) was a communist state under Soviet control. The former capital, Berlin, sitting in East German territory, was itself split into two parts, allowing a tiny pocket of Western life in the Soviet-controlled East. In 1961, the East German government erected a 12-foot-high concrete wall through

the heart of Berlin—physically dividing the city in two, isolating West Berlin, and preventing East German citizens from fleeing to the West. Over the next decades, more than a hundred East Germans would die or be arrested trying to cross that Wall. The Berlin Wall came to symbolize a divided Germany.

In West Germany, Chancellor Konrad Adenauer (who had suffered imprisonment under the Nazis) tried to restore Germany's good name, paying war reparations and joining international organizations of nations. Thanks to US aid from the Marshall Plan, West Germany was rebuilt, democracy was established, and its "economic miracle" quickly exceeded pre-WWII levels. Adenauer was eventually succeeded in 1969 by the US-friendly Willy Brandt.

Postwar Berlin

FRENCH SECTOR

EAST BERLIN

EAST GERMANY (SOVIET SECTOR)

5 Kilometers
5 Miles

Havel R.

Tegel

To Frankfurt & Bonn

CITY LIMITS

COURSE OF BERLIN WALL 1961–89

BRITISH SECTOR

BRANDEN-BURG GATE

SOVIET SECTOR

To Moscow

WEST BERLIN

Tempelhof

Spree R.

Müggelsee

Wannsee

AMERICAN SECTOR

Potsdam

COURSE OF BERLIN WALL 1961–89

Schönefeld

EAST GERMANY (SOVIET SECTOR)

Meanwhile, East Germany was ruled with an iron fist by Walter Ulbricht (who had been exiled by the Nazis). In 1953, demonstrations and anti-government protests were brutally put down by Soviet—not German—troops. Erich Honecker (a kinder, gentler tyrant who had endured a decade of Nazi imprisonment) succeeded Ulbricht as ruler of the East in 1971.

Throughout the 1970s and 1980s, both the US and the Soviet Union used divided Germany as a military base. West Germans debated whether US missiles aimed at the Soviets should be placed in their country. Economically, West Germany just got stronger while East Germany stagnated.

As the Soviet Union collapsed, so did its client nation, East Germany. On November 9, 1989, East Germany unexpectedly opened the Berlin Wall. Astonished Germans from both sides climbed the Wall, hugged each other, shared bottles of beer, sang songs, and chiseled off souvenirs. At first, most Germans— West and East—simply looked forward to free travel and better relations between two distinct nations. But before the month was out, negotiations and elections to reunite the two Germanys had begun. October 3, 1990, was proclaimed German Unity Day, and Berlin resumed its status as the German capital in 1991.

In the decade that followed, in reunified Berlin, Potsdamer Platz, formerly part of the Berlin Wall's "death strip," was re-developed into a forest of skyscrapers. The glittering new dome atop the Reichstag—which had been damaged in World War II and sat unused for decades—formally opened, giving the German people a birds-eye view of their government at work. Formerly dilapidated neighborhoods (first Prenzlauer Berg, then Kreuzberg, now Friedrichshain) rapidly gentrified, and the city erected several monuments to the victims of both the Nazis and the Cold War divide. Germany was ready to leave its painful past behind.

Sights

- Berlin Wall Memorial
- Museum of the Wall at Checkpoint Charlie
- East Side Gallery
- Tempelhof Field
- Alexanderplatz (TV Tower and World Clock)
- Karl-Marx-Allee
- DDR Museum
- Everyday Life in the DDR Museum
- Stasi Museum
- Palace of Tears
- Potsdamer Platz
- Reichstag Dome
- Memorials near the Reichstag

Germany Today (2000-present)

Today Germany is a major economic and political force in Europe. It's a powerful member of the European Union—an

organization whose original chief aim was to avoid future wars by embracing Germany in the economic web of Europe. Recently, however, Germany has outgrown its role as a mere member state to become, thanks to its economic might, the EU's de facto leader. (While many other European countries were hard-hit by the economic crisis of the last decade, Germany—with the largest economy in the EU—emerged relatively unscathed.)

German elections in 2005 resulted in no clear victory,

The Many Faces of Berlin

Like any cosmopolitan city, Berlin has relatively few born-and-bred "original Berliners"—

many of the people you meet here aren't even from Germany. As you get to know the locals, you'll come to understand Berlin's melting pot.

Many Berliners are "internal expats" from elsewhere in Germany. The first wave of these came to West Berlin back when the Wall was up—lured by draft deferments and tax breaks designed to keep this little outpost of the West vital. West Berlin became home to a combination of granola peaceniks and tattooed-and-pierced punks, squatters, and graffiti artists. Still others came to West Berlin for business.

A second wave came just after the Wall fell, when East Berliners flocked to the West. East Berlin in 1990 enjoyed an "anything goes" anarchy that attracted German artists, students, recent graduates, and unattached singles. This was the heyday for squatting in—and eventually renovating—abandoned apartments (see "Squatters" on page 205).

A third wave of expats—both from inside and outside of Germany—came in the 2000s and 2010s, as Berlin put behind the chaos of reunification and blossomed as a 21st-century cultural capital and all-around cool place to live. Many Americans and Brits came to Berlin as backpackers, fell in love with the place, and decided to stick around.

And, of course, Berlin is also home to a vast number of immigrants and refugees from the Middle East and North Africa. In the post-WWII years, with a decimated population, West Germany needed help rebuilding. Through the 1960s and 1970s, the government invited guest workers from poorer nations to live and work in Germany. With approximately 200,000 residents of Turkish descent, Berlin is considered the largest "Turkish city" outside of Turkey. These families—some now in their second or third generation—are an integral part of Berlin society.

More recently, refugees have formed another strand of Berlin's cultural tapestry. In 2015, Chancellor Angela Merkel offered asylum to people fleeing war-torn Syria—and 1.1 million took her up on it, in that year alone. While many have since resettled elsewhere, hundreds of thousands remain in Germany. Syrian Berliners have opened Middle Eastern bakeries and restaurants, and the Pergamon Museum actively recruits Syrians as tour guides—allowing them to proudly show off the masterpieces of their homeland's ancient culture.

If you really want to understand Berlin...take the time to get to know some Berliners. And be sure to ask about their own personal story. You'll never hear the same one twice.

and both major parties formed a "Grand Coalition," sharing power equally under Germany's first female chancellor, Angela Merkel, whom the media like to call "Mutti" (Mommy). While representing the center-right Christian Democratic Union, Merkel's cautious, centrist, pro-business policies earned her broad support and re-election in both 2009 and 2013. Though she governs with a coalition partner, she is considered one of the world's most powerful people. If re-elected to her fourth term in September 2017, Merkel will become Europe's longest-serving elected female leader—breaking Margaret Thatcher's 11-year record.

Painfully aware of tensions that still linger even decades after World War II, many Germans have been reluctant to embrace their country's dominant role in Europe. But this hesitancy is slipping away. The 2006 World Cup is often cited as a turning point—not because Germany successfully hosted the huge event, but because that's when a new generation of Germans embraced their country's flag en masse. For the first time since World War II, Germans exhibited a national pride that they no longer feared would be confused with Nazi sentiment.

In 2014, the country's spirit got a huge boost when its soccer team won the World Cup, its first as a united nation. And while Chancellor Merkel's EU austerity measures have proved widely unpopular in many corners of Europe, her firm stance has been largely applauded by a German population that's increasingly comfortable calling the shots.

Merkel's popularity weakened somewhat in 2015 after she welcomed Syrian refugees fleeing that nation's civil war. About 1.1 million people claimed asylum, and the flood of refugees taxed Germany's social services. Her decision was praised by some (she was named *Time* magazine's Person of the Year) but sparked a backlash among others, concerned about Germany's ability to absorb so many newcomers.

Like the US and other European nations, Germany has been the target of isolated terrorist incidents. During New Year's Eve celebrations in 2015, an orchestrated series of sexual assaults and thefts rippled through German cities (especially Cologne); many of the perpetrators were determined to have been North African migrants. And in 2016, a 24-year-old Tunisian man plowed a tractor-trailer into Berlin's Christmas market, killing 12. These events increased pressure on Germany's leaders to take a tougher stance on immigration, though the country's population remains generally welcoming.

The long-term viability of the EU is another challenge facing Germany. As the biggest and staunchest EU booster, Germany must grapple with the implications of Brexit (Britain's decision to withdraw from the EU) and the rise of other European anti-EU movements.

For more on German history, consider *Europe 101: History and Art for the Traveler,* written by Rick Steves and Gene Openshaw (available at www.ricksteves.com).

PRACTICALITIES

This chapter covers the practical skills of European travel: how to get tourist information, pay for things, sightsee efficiently, find good-value accommodations, eat affordably but well, use technology wisely, and get between destinations smoothly. To round out your knowledge, check out "Resources from Rick Steves." For more information on these topics, see www.ricksteves.com/travel-tips.

Tourist Information

Germany's national tourist office **in the US** is a wealth of informa-

tion. Before your trip, scan their website (www.germany.travel) for maps, as well as information on festivals, biking, and regions. Travel brochures can also be downloaded from their website.

In Berlin, tourist information offices—abbreviated **TI** in this book—are well-organized and have English-speaking staff. But be aware that TIs are in business to help you enjoy spending money in their town. Most Berlin TIs have been privatized—they're essentially sales agents for big tours and hotels, and their "information" is unavoidably colored. While this corrupts much of their advice—and you can get plenty of information online—I still make a point to swing by the local TI to confirm sightseeing plans, pick up a city map, and get information on public transit (including bus and train schedules), walking tours, special events, and nightlife. Prepare a list of questions and a proposed plan to double-check.

Travel Tips

Emergency and Medical Help: In Germany, dial 112 for police help or a medical emergency. If you get sick, do as the Germans do and go to a pharmacist for advice. Or ask at your hotel for help—they'll know the nearest medical and emergency services.

Theft or Loss: To replace a passport, you'll need to go in person to an embassy (see page 437). If your credit and debit cards disappear, cancel and replace them (see "Damage Control for Lost Cards" on page 388). File a police report, either on the spot or within a day or two; you'll need it to submit an insurance claim for lost or stolen rail passes or travel gear, and it can help with replacing your passport or credit and debit cards. For more information, see www.ricksteves.com/help.

Time Zones: Germany, like most of continental Europe, is generally six/nine hours ahead of the East/West coasts of the US. The exceptions are the beginning and end of Daylight Saving Time: Europe "springs forward" the last Sunday in March (two weeks after most of North America) and "falls back" the last Sunday in October (one week before North America). For a handy online time converter, see www.timeanddate.com/worldclock.

Business Hours: In Berlin, most shops are open from about 9:00 until 18:00-20:00 on weekdays. Banks are generally open Monday to Friday from 9:00 to 15:00 (or even later, up to 19:00). Many museums and sights are closed on Monday.

Saturdays are virtually weekdays, though banks are closed, and smaller stores generally close early—anywhere between 12:00 and 17:00. Sundays have the same pros and cons as they do for travelers in the US: Sightseeing attractions are generally open, while shops and banks are closed, public transportation options are fewer, and there's no rush hour. Friday and Saturday evenings are lively; Sunday evenings are quiet.

A few shops are usually open later than other stores, including shops in train stations, which often have grocery stores that are open long hours.

Watt's Up? Europe's electrical system is 220 volts, instead of North America's 110 volts. Most newer electronics (such as laptops, battery chargers, and hair dryers) convert automatically, so you won't need a converter plug, but you will need an adapter plug with two round prongs, sold inexpensively at travel stores in the US. Avoid bringing older appliances that don't automatically convert voltage; instead, buy a cheap replacement in Europe.

Discounts: Discounts for sights are generally not listed in this book. However, seniors (age 60 and over), youths under 18, and students and teachers with proper identification cards (www.isic. org) can get discounts at many sights. Always ask. Some discounts are available only for citizens of the European Union (EU).

Online Translation Tips: Google's Chrome browser instantly translates websites. You can also paste text or the URL of a foreign website into the translation window at Translate.google.com. The Google Translate app converts spoken English into most European languages (and vice versa) and can also translate text it "reads" with your smartphone's camera.

Money

Here's my basic strategy for using money in Europe:
- Upon arrival, head for a cash machine (ATM) at the airport and load up on local currency, using a debit card with low international transaction fees.
- Withdraw large amounts at each transaction (to limit fees) and keep your cash safe in a money belt.
- Pay for most items with cash.
- Pay for larger purchases with a credit card with low (or no) international fees.

PLASTIC VERSUS CASH

Although credit cards are widely accepted in Europe, day-to-day spending is generally more cash-based than in the US. I find cash is the easiest—and sometimes only—way to pay for cheap food, bus fare, taxis, tips, and local guides. Some businesses (especially smaller ones, such as B&Bs and mom-and-pop cafés and shops) may charge you extra for using a credit card—or might not accept credit cards at all. Having cash on hand helps you out of a jam if your card randomly doesn't work.

I use my credit card to book hotel reservations, to buy advance tickets for events or sights, and to cover major expenses (such as car rentals or plane tickets). It can also be smart to use plastic near the end of your trip, to avoid another visit to the ATM. But keep in mind that some shops and restaurants in Germany accept only the local "EC" debit cards—not American credit cards. Larger hotels,

---

Exchange Rate

1 euro (€) = about $1.10

To convert prices in euros to dollars, add about 10 percent: €20=about $22, €50=about $55. (Check www.oanda.com for the latest exchange rates.) Just like the dollar, one euro (€) is broken down into 100 cents. Coins range from €0.01 to €2, and bills from €5 to €200 (bills over €50 are rarely used; €500 bills are being phased out).

---

restaurants, and shops that do take US cards more commonly accept Visa and MasterCard than American Express.

WHAT TO BRING

I pack the following and keep it all safe in my money belt.

Debit Card: Use this at ATMs to withdraw local cash.

Credit Card: Use this to pay for larger items (at hotels, larger shops and restaurants, travel agencies, car-rental agencies, and so on).

Backup Card: Some travelers carry a third card (debit or credit; ideally from a different bank), in case one gets lost, demagnetized, eaten by a temperamental machine, or simply doesn't work.

US Dollars: I carry $100-200 US as a backup. While you won't use it for day-to-day purchases, American cash in your money belt comes in handy for emergencies, such as if your ATM card stops working.

What NOT to Bring: Resist the urge to buy euros before your trip or you'll pay the price in bad stateside exchange rates. Wait until you arrive to withdraw money. I've yet to see a European airport that didn't have plenty of ATMs.

BEFORE YOU GO

Use this pre-trip checklist.

Know your cards. Debit cards from any major US bank will work in any standard European bank's ATM (ideally, use a debit card with a Visa or MasterCard logo).

Newer credit and debit cards have chips that authenticate and secure transactions. In Europe, the cardholder inserts the chip card into the payment machine slot, then enters a PIN. (In the US, you provide a signature to verify your identity.)

Any American card, whether with a chip or an old-fashioned magnetic stripe, will work at Europe's hotels, restaurants, and shops. I've been inconvenienced a few times by self-service payment machines in Europe that wouldn't accept my card, but it's never caused me serious trouble.

If you're concerned, ask if your bank offers a true chip-and-PIN card. Cards with low fees and chip-and-PIN technology include those from Andrews Federal Credit Union (www.andrewsfcu.org) and the State Department Federal Credit Union (www.sdfcu.org).

Report your travel dates. Let your bank know that you'll be using your debit and credit cards in Europe, and when and where you're headed.

Know your PIN. Make sure you know the numeric, four-digit PIN for all of your cards, both debit and credit. Request it if you don't have one and allow time to receive the information by mail.

Adjust your ATM withdrawal limit. Find out how much you can take out daily and ask for a higher daily withdrawal limit if you want to get more cash at once. Note that European ATMs will withdraw funds only from checking accounts; you're unlikely to have access to your savings account.

Ask about fees. For any purchase or withdrawal made with a card, you may be charged a currency conversion fee (1-3 percent), a Visa or MasterCard international transaction fee (1 percent), and—for debit cards—a $2-5 transaction fee each time you use a foreign ATM (some US banks partner with European banks, allowing you to use those ATMs with no fees—ask).

If you're getting a bad deal, consider getting a new debit or credit card. Reputable no-fee cards include those from Capital One, as well as Charles Schwab debit cards. Most credit unions and some airline loyalty cards have low-to-no international transaction fees.

IN EUROPE
Using Cash Machines

European cash machines have English-language instructions and work just like they do at home—except they spit out local currency instead of dollars, calculated at the day's standard bank-to-bank rate.

In most places, ATMs are easy to locate—in Germany ask for a *Geldautomat*. When possible, withdraw cash from a bank-run ATM located just outside that bank. Ideally use it during the bank's opening hours; if your card is munched by the machine, you can go inside for help.

If your debit card doesn't work, try a lower amount—your request may have exceeded your withdrawal limit or the ATM's limit. If you still have a problem, try a different ATM or come back later—your bank's network may be temporarily down.

Avoid "independent" ATMs, such as Travelex, Euronet, Moneybox, Cardpoint, and Cashzone. These have high fees, can be less secure than a bank ATM, and may try to trick users with "dynamic currency conversion" (see below).

Exchanging Cash

Avoid exchanging money in Europe; it's a big rip-off. In a pinch you can always find exchange desks at major train stations or airports—convenient but with crummy rates. Banks in some countries may not exchange money unless you have an account with them.

Using Credit Cards

European cards use chip-and-PIN technology, while most cards issued in the US use a chip-and-signature system. But most European card readers can automatically generate a receipt for you to sign, just as you would at home. If a cashier is present, you should have no problems. Some card readers will instead prompt you to enter your PIN (so it's important to know the code for each of your cards).

At self-service payment machines (transit-ticket kiosks, parking, etc.), results are mixed, as US chip-and-signature cards aren't configured for unattended transactions. If your card won't work, look for a cashier who can process your card manually—or pay in cash.

Drivers Beware: Be aware of potential problems using a credit card to fill up at an unattended gas station, enter a parking garage, or exit a toll road. Carry cash and be prepared to move on to the next gas station if necessary. When approaching a toll plaza, use the "cash" lane.

Dynamic Currency Conversion

Some European merchants and hoteliers cheerfully charge you for converting your purchase price into dollars. If it's offered, refuse this "service" (called dynamic currency conversion, or DCC). You'll pay extra for the expensive convenience of seeing your charge in dollars. Some ATM machines also offer DCC, often in confusing or misleading terms. If an ATM offers to "lock in" or "guarantee" your conversion rate, choose "proceed without conversion." Other prompts might state, "You can be charged in dollars: Press YES for dollars, NO for euros." Always choose the local currency.

Security Tips

Pickpockets target tourists. To safeguard your cash, wear a money belt—a pouch with a strap that you buckle around your waist like a belt and tuck under your clothes. Keep your cash, credit cards, and passport secure in your money belt, and carry only a day's spending money in your front pocket or wallet.

Before inserting your card into an ATM, inspect the front. If anything looks crooked, loose, or damaged, it could be a sign of a card-skimming device. When entering your PIN, carefully block other people's view of the keypad.

Don't use a debit card for purchases. Because a debit card pulls

PRACTICALITIES

funds directly from your bank account, potential charges incurred by a thief will stay on your account while the fraudulent use is investigated by your bank.

To access your accounts online while traveling, be sure to use a secure connection (see page 416).

Damage Control for Lost Cards

If you lose your credit or debit card, report the loss immediately to the respective global customer-assistance centers. Call these 24-hour US numbers collect: Visa (tel. 303/967-1096), MasterCard (tel. 636/722-7111), and American Express (tel. 336/393-1111). In Germany, to make a collect call to the US, dial 0-800-225-5288. Press zero or stay on the line for an English-speaking operator. European toll-free numbers (listed by country) can be found at the websites for Visa and MasterCard.

You'll need to provide the primary cardholder's identification-verification details (such as birth date, mother's maiden name, or Social Security number). You can generally receive a temporary card within two or three business days in Europe (see www. ricksteves.com/help for more).

If you report your loss within two days, you typically won't be responsible for unauthorized transactions on your account, although many banks charge a liability fee of $50.

TIPPING

Tipping in Germany isn't as automatic and generous as it is in the US. For special service, tips are appreciated, but not expected. As in the US, the proper amount depends on your resources, tipping philosophy, and the circumstances, but some general guidelines apply.

Restaurants: You don't need to tip if you order your food at a counter. At German restaurants that have a wait staff, it's common to tip by rounding up (about 10 percent) after a good meal. For details on tipping in restaurants, see page 402.

Taxis: For a typical ride, round up your fare a bit (for instance, if your fare is €4.70, pay €5). If the cabbie hauls your bags and zips you to the airport to help you catch your flight, you might want to toss in a little more. But if you feel like you're being driven in circles or otherwise ripped off, skip the tip.

Services: In general, if someone in the service industry does a super job for you, a small tip of a euro or two is appropriate...but not required. If you're not sure whether (or how much) to tip, ask a local for advice.

GETTING A VAT REFUND

Wrapped into the purchase price of your German souvenirs is a value-added tax (VAT) of 19 percent. You're entitled to get most of that tax back if you purchase more than €25 (about $28) worth of goods at a store that participates in the VAT-refund scheme. Typically, you must ring up the minimum at a single retailer—you can't add up your purchases from various shops to reach the required amount. (If the store ships the goods to your US home, VAT is not assessed on your purchase.)

Getting your refund is usually straightforward...and worthwhile if you spend a significant amount on souvenirs.

Get the paperwork. Have the merchant completely fill out the necessary refund document, called a "Tax-Free Shopping Check." You'll have to present your passport. Get the paperwork done before you leave the store to ensure you'll have everything you need (including your original sales receipt).

Get your stamp at the border or airport. Process your VAT document at your last stop in the European Union (such as at the airport) with the customs agent who deals with VAT refunds. Arrive an additional hour before you need to check in to allow time to find the customs office—and to stand in line. Some customs desks are positioned before airport security; confirm the location before going through security.

It's best to keep your purchases in your carry-on. If they're too large or dangerous to carry on (such as knives), pack them in your checked bags and alert the check-in agent. You'll be sent (with your tagged bag) to a customs desk outside security; someone will examine your bag, stamp your paperwork, and put your bag on the belt. You're not supposed to use your purchased goods before you leave. If you show up at customs wearing your new lederhosen, officials might look the other way—or deny you a refund.

Collect your refund. Many merchants work with services, such as Global Blue or Premier Tax Free, that have offices at major airports, ports, or border crossings (either before or after security, probably strategically located near a duty-free shop). These services, which extract a 4 percent fee, can refund your money immediately in cash or credit your card (within two billing cycles). Other refund services may require you to mail the documents from home, or more quickly, from your point of departure (using an envelope you've prepared in advance or one that's been provided by the merchant). You'll then have to wait—it can take months.

CUSTOMS FOR AMERICAN SHOPPERS

You can take home $800 worth of items per person duty-free, once every 31 days. Many processed and packaged foods are allowed, including: vacuum-packed cheeses, dried herbs, jams, baked goods, candy, chocolate, oil, vinegar, mustard, and honey. Fresh fruits and vegetables and most meats are not allowed, with exceptions for some canned items. As for alcohol, you can bring in one liter duty-free (it can be packed securely in your checked luggage, along with any other liquid-containing items).

To bring alcohol (or liquid-packed foods) in your carry-on bag on your flight home, buy it at a duty-free shop at the airport. You'll increase your odds of getting it onto a connecting flight if it's packaged in a "STEB"—a secure, tamper-evident bag. But stay away from liquids in opaque, ceramic, or metallic containers, which usually cannot be successfully screened (STEB or no STEB).

For details on allowable goods, customs rules, and duty rates, visit http://help.cbp.gov.

Sightseeing

Sightseeing can be hard work. Use these tips to make your visits to Berlin's finest sights meaningful, fun, efficient, and painless.

MAPS AND NAVIGATION TOOLS

A good map is essential for efficient navigation while sightseeing. The maps in this book are concise and simple, designed to help you locate recommended destinations, sights, and local TIs, where you can pick up more in-depth maps. Maps with even more detail are sold at newsstands and bookstores.

You can also use a mapping app on your mobile device. Be aware that pulling up maps or turn-by-turn walking directions on the fly requires an Internet connection: To use this feature, it's smart to get an international data plan (see page 411). With Google Maps or City Maps 2Go, it's possible to download a map while online, then go offline and navigate without incurring data-roaming charges, though you can't search for an address or get real-time walking directions. A handful of other apps—including Apple Maps, OffMaps, and Navfree—also allow you to use maps offline.

PLAN AHEAD

Set up an itinerary that allows you to fit in all your must-see sights. For a one-stop look at opening hours, see "Berlin at a Glance" (page 30). Most sights keep stable hours, but you can easily confirm the latest by checking with the TI or visiting museum websites.

Don't put off visiting a must-see sight—you never know when a place will close unexpectedly for a holiday, strike, or restoration. Given how precious your vacation time is, I recommend getting reservations for any must-see sight that offers them (see page 5). Many museums are closed or have reduced hours at least a few days a year, especially on holidays such as Christmas, New Year's, and

Labor Day (May 1). A list of holidays is on page 437; check online for possible museum closures during your trip. In summer, some sights may stay open late; in the off-season, hours may be shorter.

Going at the right time helps avoid crowds. This book offers tips on the best times to see specific sights. Try visiting popular sights very early or very late. Evening visits (when possible) are usually peaceful, with fewer crowds.

If you plan to hire a local guide, reserve ahead by email. Popular guides can get booked up.

Study up. To get the most out of the self-guided tours and sight descriptions in this book, read them before you visit.

AT SIGHTS

Here's what you can typically expect:

Entering: Be warned that you may not be allowed to enter if you arrive less than 30 to 60 minutes before closing time. And guards start ushering people out well before the actual closing time, so don't save the best for last.

Many sights have a security check, where you must open your bag or send it through a metal detector. Allow extra time for these lines in your planning. Most museums in Germany require you to check any bag bigger than a purse, and sometimes even purses. Museum lockers are free, but be prepared to pay a €2 deposit.

Photography: If the museum's photo policy isn't clearly posted, ask a guard. Generally, taking photos without a flash or tripod is allowed. Some sights ban selfie sticks; others ban photos altogether.

Temporary Exhibits: Museums may show special exhibits in addition to their permanent collection. Some exhibits are included in the entry price, while others come at an extra cost (which you may have to pay even if you don't want to see the exhibit).

Expect Changes: Artwork can be on tour, on loan, out sick, or

shifted at the whim of the curator. Pick up a floor plan as you enter, and ask museum staff if you can't find a particular item.

Audioguides and Apps: Most of Berlin's top museums are run by the government, and offer excellent audioguides that are included in admission (though you'll need to leave an ID as a deposit). Other, privately run museums charge a rental fee, often $3-5. If you bring along your earbuds, you can enjoy better sound. To save money, bring a Y-jack and share one audioguide with your travel partner. Museums and sights often offer free apps that you can

PRACTICALITIES

download to your mobile device (check their websites). And, I've produced a free, downloadable audio tour for my Best of Berlin City Walk; look for the 🎧 symbol in this book. For more on my audio tours, see page 6.

Services: Important sights may have a reasonably priced on-site café or cafeteria (handy places to rejuvenate during a long visit). Berlin's state-run museums offer free loaner stools, inviting you to camp out and really ponder your favorite work of art. The WCs at sights are free and generally clean.

Before Leaving: At the gift shop, scan the postcard rack or thumb through a guidebook to be sure that you haven't overlooked something that you'd like to see.

Every sight or museum offers more than what is covered in this book. Use the information in this book as an introduction—not the final word.

Sleeping

I favor hotels and restaurants that are handy to your sightseeing activities. Rather than list hotels scattered throughout Berlin, I choose hotels in my favorite neighborhoods. My recommendations run the gamut, from dorm beds to fancy rooms with all the comforts.

Extensive and opinionated listings of good-value rooms are a major feature of this book's Sleeping chapter. I like places that are clean, central, relatively quiet at night, reasonably priced, friendly, small enough to have a hands-on owner or manager and stable staff, and run with a respect for German traditions. I'm more impressed by a convenient location and a fun-loving philosophy than flat-screen TVs and a fancy gym. Most places I recommend fall short of perfection. But if I can find a place with most of these features, it's a keeper.

Book your accommodations as soon as your itinerary is set, especially if you want to stay at one of my top listings or if you'll be traveling during busy times, such as Easter weekend, the first weekend and Ascension weekend in May, Green Week in mid-January, the ITB travel show in mid-March, or Germany Unity Day on October 3. See page 437 for a list of major holidays and festivals in Germany; for tips on making reservations, see page 396. Many German hotel chains have multiple branches scattered across a city; be sure you're booking the one you want.

RATES AND DEALS

I've categorized my recommended accommodations based on price, indicated with a dollar-sign rating (see sidebar). The price ranges suggest an estimated cost for a one-night stay in a standard dou-

Sleep Code

Hotels are classified based on the average price of a standard double room with breakfast in high season.

$$$$	**Splurge:**	Most rooms over €170
$$$	**Pricier:**	€130-170
$$	**Moderate:**	€90-130
$	**Budget:**	€50-90
¢	**Backpacker:**	Under €50
RS%	**Rick Steves discount**	

Unless otherwise noted, credit cards are accepted, hotel staff speak basic English, and free Wi-Fi is available. Comparison-shop by checking prices at several hotels (on each hotel's own website, on a booking site, or by email). For the best deal, *book directly with the hotel*. Ask for a discount if paying in cash; if the listing includes **RS%,** request a Rick Steves discount.

ble room with a private toilet and shower in high season, include breakfast, and assume you're booking directly with the hotel (not through a booking site, which extracts a commission and logically closes the door on special deals). Room prices can fluctuate significantly with demand and amenities (size, views, room class, and so on), but these relative price categories remain constant.

Room rates are especially volatile at larger hotels that use "dynamic pricing" to set rates. Prices can skyrocket during festivals and conventions, while business hotels can have deep discounts on weekends when demand plummets. Of the many hotels I recommend, it's difficult to say which will be the best value on a given day—until you do your homework.

Once your dates are set, check the specific price for your preferred stay at several hotels. You can do this either by comparing prices online on the hotels' own websites, or by emailing several hotels directly and asking for their best rate. Even if you start your search on a booking site such as TripAdvisor or Booking.com, you'll usually find the best deal through a hotel's own website. (While many hotels are contractually obligated not to undercut booking site prices, when you go direct, the hotel avoids the 15-20 percent commission, giving them wiggle room to treat you better—offering perhaps a nicer room or free breakfast.)

Some hotels offer a discount to those who pay cash or stay longer than three nights. To cut costs further, try asking for a cheaper room (for example, with a shared bathroom or no window) or offer to skip breakfast.

Additionally, some accommodations offer a special discount for Rick Steves readers, indicated in this guidebook by the abbreviation **"RS%."** Discounts vary: Ask for details when you reserve.

Generally, to qualify you must book directly (that is, not through a booking site), mention this book when you reserve and show it upon arrival, and sometimes pay cash or stay a certain number of nights. In some cases, you may need to enter a discount code (which I've provided in the listing) in the booking form on the hotel's website. Rick Steves discounts apply to readers with ebooks as well as printed books. Understandably, discounts do not apply to promotional rates.

Berlin hoteliers charge a daily tourist tax (5 percent of the room rate). This may be included in the room price or may appear as an extra charge on your bill.

TYPES OF ACCOMMODATIONS
Hotels

Chain hotels can be a good value, especially in Berlin; along with those listed in the Sleeping in Berlin chapter, the Europe-wide Ibis/Mercure chain has many options (www.accorhotels.com). I'm also impressed with the homegrown, Hamburg-based German chain called Motel One, which specializes in affordable style and has several branches in Berlin (www.motel-one.com).

In this book, the price for a double room in a hotel ranges from €50 (very simple, toilet and shower down the hall) to €400-plus (maximum plumbing and the works). Breakfast is generally not included in the quoted rate, but you can usually add or remove a breakfast option when booking (sometimes continental, but often buffet; see page 401).

Some hotels can add an extra bed (for a small charge) to turn a double into a triple; some offer larger rooms for four or more people (I call these "family rooms" in the listings). If there's space for an extra cot, they'll cram it in for you. In general, a triple room is cheaper than the cost of a double and a single. Three or four people can economize by requesting one big room.

Arrival and Check-In: Hotel elevators are becoming more common, though some older buildings still lack them. Bigger hotels commonly have elevators. When you're inside an elevator, press "E" to descend to the "ground floor" *(Erdgeschoss)*. You may have to climb a flight of stairs to reach the elevator (if so, you can ask the front desk for help carrying your bags up). Elevators are typically very small—pack light, or you may need to send your bags up without you.

When you check in, the receptionist will normally ask for your passport and keep it for anywhere from a couple of minutes to a couple of hours. The EU requires that hotels collect your name, nationality, and ID number. Relax. Americans are notorious for making this chore more difficult than it needs to be.

If you're arriving in the morning, your room probably won't be ready. Check your bag safely at the hotel and dive right into sightseeing.

In Your Room: In Germany, as elsewhere in northern Europe, beds don't come with a top sheet or blankets, but only with a comforter. A double bed comes with two comforters—rather than one bigger one. It also frequently has two separate mattresses and sometimes two separate (but adjacent) frames—even if the bed is intended for couples. (A "real" double bed with a single mattress is called a *Französisches Bett*—a French bed.) Rooms with truly separate twin beds are less common in German hotels. When Americans request separate beds, German hotels sometimes give them normal doubles with complete sincerity—reasoning that the mattresses, though adjacent, are separate. More pillows and blankets are usually in the closet or available on request. Towels and linens aren't always replaced every day. Hang your towel up to dry.

Most hotel rooms have a TV, telephone, and free Wi-Fi (although in old buildings with thick walls, the Wi-Fi signal doesn't always make it to the rooms; sometimes it's only available in the lobby). There's often a guest computer with Internet access in the lobby. Simpler places rarely have a room phone, but often have free Wi-Fi.

Air-conditioning is rarely needed, and rare at smaller hotels. If you're here during a heat spell, ask to borrow a fan. Learn how the windows work: You'll often find the windows tipped open from the top to air out the room, with the window handle pointing up. To close the window, push it in and rotate the handle so it points down. The third handle position is horizontal, which lets you swing the entire window open.

Most hotels have gone completely nonsmoking. Some hotels have nonsmoking rooms or floors—let them know your preference when you book.

Checking Out: While it's customary to pay for your room upon departure, it can be a good idea to settle your bill the day before, when you're not in a hurry and while the manager's in. That way you'll have time to discuss and address any points of contention.

Hotelier Help: Hoteliers can be a good source of advice. Most know their city well, and can assist you with everything from public transit and airport connections to finding a good restaurant, the nearest launderette, or a late-night pharmacy. English works in all but the cheapest places.

PRACTICALITIES

Making Hotel Reservations

Reserve your rooms as you've pinned down your travel dates. For busy national holidays, it's wise to reserve far in advance (see page 437).

Requesting a Reservation: It's easiest and generally cheaper to book your room through the hotel's official website. If there's no reservation form, or for complicated requests, send an email. Most recommended hotels take reservations in English.

Here's what the hotelier wants to know:
- type(s) of rooms you need and size of your party
- number of nights you'll stay
- your arrival and departure dates, written European-style as day/month/year (for example, 18/06/19 or 18 June 2019);
- special requests (such as en suite bathroom vs. down the hall, cheapest room, twin beds vs. double bed, quiet room)
- applicable discounts (such as a Rick Steves reader discount, cash discount, or promotional rate)

Confirming a Reservation: Most places will request a credit-card number to hold your room. If they don't have a secure online reservation form—look for the https—you can email it (I do), but it's safer to share that confidential info via a phone call or fax.

Canceling a Reservation: If you must cancel, it's courteous—and smart—to do so with as much notice as possible, especially for smaller family-run places. Cancellation policies can be strict; read the fine print or ask about these before you book. Many discount deals require prepayment, with no cancellation refunds.

Hotel Hassles: Even at the best places, mechanical breakdowns occur: Sinks leak, hot water turns cold, toilets may gurgle or smell, the Wi-Fi goes out, or the air-conditioning dies when you need it most. Report your concerns clearly and calmly at the front desk. For more complicated problems, don't expect instant results. Above all, keep a positive attitude. Remember, you're on vacation. If your hotel is a disappointment, spend more time out enjoying the place you came to see.

If you suspect night noise will be a problem (if, for instance, your room is over a café), ask for a quieter room in the back or on an upper floor. To guard against theft in your room, keep valuables out of sight. Some rooms come with a safe, and other hotels have safes at the front desk. I've never bothered using one, and in a lifetime of travel, I've never had anything stolen out of my room.

Short-Term Rentals

A short-term rental—whether an apartment, house, or room in a local's home—is an increasingly popular alternative, especially if you plan to settle in one location for several nights. For stays longer

From: rick@ricksteves.com
Sent: Today
To: info@hotelcentral.com
Subject: Reservation request for 19-22 July

Dear Hotel Central,

I would like to stay at your hotel. Please let me know if you have a room available and the price for:
• 2 people
• Double bed and en suite bathroom in a quiet room
• Arriving 19 July, departing 22 July (3 nights)

Thank you!
Rick Steves

Reconfirming a Reservation: Always call or email to reconfirm your room reservation a few days in advance. For pensions or very small hotels, I call again on my day of arrival to tell my host what time to expect me (especially important if arriving late—after 17:00).

Phoning: For tips on how to call hotels overseas, see page 412.

than a few days, you can usually find a rental that's comparable to—and even cheaper than—a hotel room with similar amenities. Plus, you'll get a behind-the-scenes peek into how locals live.

Many places require a minimum-night stay, and compared to hotels, rentals usually have less-flexible cancellation policies. And you're generally on your own: There's no hotel reception desk, breakfast, or daily cleaning service.

Finding Accommodations: Aggregator websites such as Airbnb, FlipKey, Roomorama, Booking.com, and the Home-Away family of sites (HomeAway, VRBO, and VacationRentals) let you browse properties and correspond directly with European property owners or managers. If you prefer to work from a curated list of accommodations, consider using a rental agency such as InterhomeUSA.com or RentaVilla.com. Agency-represented apartments typically cost more, but this method often offers more help and safeguards than booking directly.

Before you commit, be clear on the details, location, and amenities. I like to virtually "explore" the neighborhood using the Street View feature on Google Maps. Also consider the proximity to public transportation, and how well connected the property is with the rest of the city. Ask about amenities (elevator, laundry, coffee maker, Wi-Fi, parking, etc.). Reviews from previous guests can help identify trouble spots.

Be clear about the kind of experience you want: Just a key and an affordable bed...or a chance to get to know a local? There are typically two kinds of hosts: those who want minimal interaction with their guests, and hosts who are friendly and may want to interact with you. Read the promotional text and online reviews to help shape your decision.

Apartments: If you're staying somewhere for four nights or longer, it's worth considering an apartment (shorter stays aren't worth the hassle of arranging key pickup, buying groceries, etc.). Apartment rentals can be especially cost-effective for groups and families. European apartments, like hotel rooms, tend to be small by US standards. But they often come with laundry machines and small, equipped kitchens, making it easier and cheaper to dine in. If you make good use of the kitchen (and Europe's great produce markets), you'll save on your meal budget.

Private and Shared Rooms: Renting a room in someone's home is a good option for those traveling alone, as you're more likely to find true single rooms—with just one single bed, and a price to match. Beds range from air-mattress-in-living-room basic to plush-B&B-suite posh. Some places allow you to book for a single night; if staying for several nights, you can buy groceries just as you would in a rental house. While you can't expect your host to also be your tour guide—or even to provide you with much info—some may be interested in getting to know the travelers who come through their homes.

Other Options: Swapping homes with a local works for people with an appealing place to offer, and who can live with the idea of having strangers in their home (don't assume where you live is not interesting to Europeans). A good place to start is HomeExchange. To sleep for free, Couchsurfing.com is a vagabond's alternative to Airbnb. It lists millions of outgoing members, who host fellow "surfers" in their homes.

Confirming and Paying: Many places require you to pay the entire balance before your trip. It's easiest and safest to pay through the site where you found the listing. Be wary of owners who want to take your transaction offline to avoid fees; this gives you no recourse if things go awry. Never agree to wire money (a key indicator of a fraudulent transaction).

Hostels

A hostel *(Jugendherberge)* provides cheap beds where you sleep alongside strangers for about €25 per night. Travelers of any age

The Good and Bad of Online Reviews

User-generated review sites and apps such as Yelp, Booking. com, and TripAdvisor can give you a consensus of opinions about everything from hotels and restaurants to sights and nightlife. If you scan reviews of a hotel and see several complaints about noise or a rotten location, it tells you something important that you'd never learn from the hotel's own website.

But as a guidebook writer, my sense is that there is a big difference between the uncurated information on a review site and a guidebook. A user-generated review is based on the experience of one person, who likely stayed at one hotel in a given city and ate at a few restaurants there (and who doesn't have much of a basis for comparison). A guidebook is the work of a trained researcher who, year after year, visits many alternatives to assess their relative value. I recently checked out some top-rated user-reviewed hotel and restaurant listings in various towns; when stacked up against their competitors, some were gems, while just as many were duds.

Both types of information have their place, and in many ways, they're complementary. If something is well-reviewed in a guidebook, and also gets good ratings on one of these sites, it's likely a winner.

are welcome if they don't mind dorm-style accommodations and meeting other travelers. Most hostels offer kitchen facilities, guest computers, Wi-Fi, and a self-service laundry. Hostels almost always provide bedding, but the towel's up to you (though you can usually rent one for a small fee). Family and private rooms are often available.

Independent hostels tend to be easygoing, colorful, and informal (no membership required; www.hostelworld.com). You may pay slightly less by booking directly with the hostel.

Official hostels are part of Hostelling International (HI) and share an online booking site (www.hihostels.com). HI hostels typically require that you be a member or pay extra per night.

Eating

Germanic cuisine is heavy, hearty, and—by European standards—inexpensive. Each region has its specialties, which are often good values. Order house specials whenever possible. Though it's tasty, German food can get monotonous unless you look beyond the schnitzel and wurst. Fortunately, German chefs are increasingly adopting international influences, picking up previously unknown spices and ingredients to jazz up "Modern German" cuisine. Be adventurous.

PRACTICALITIES

Restaurant Code

I've assigned each eatery a price category, based on the average cost of a typical main course. Drinks, desserts, and splurge items (steak and seafood) can raise the price considerably.

$$$$ **Splurge:** Most main courses over €20
$$$ **Pricier:** €15-20
$$ **Moderate:** €10-15
$ **Budget:** Under €10

In Germany, a wurst stand or other takeout spot is **$**; a beer hall, *Biergarten,* or basic sit-down eatery is **$$**; a casual but more upscale restaurant is **$$$**; and a swanky splurge is **$$$$**.

I look for restaurants that are convenient to your hotel and sightseeing. When restaurant hunting, choose a spot filled with locals, not the place with the big neon signs boasting, "We Speak English and Accept Credit Cards." Venturing even a block or two off the main drag leads to higher-quality food for a better price.

RESTAURANT PRICING

I've categorized my recommended eateries based on price, indicated with a dollar-sign rating (see sidebar). The price ranges suggest the average price of a typical main course—but not necessarily a complete meal. Obviously, expensive items (like steak and seafood), fine wine, appetizers, and dessert can significantly increase your final bill.

The categories also indicate a place's personality:

Budget eateries include street food, takeaway, order-at-the-counter shops, basic cafeterias, and bakeries selling sandwiches.

Moderate eateries are nice (but not fancy) sit-down restaurants, ideal for a straightforward, fill-the-tank meal. Most of my listings fall in this category—great for a good taste of local cuisine on a budget.

Pricier eateries are a notch up, with more attention paid to the setting, presentation, and cuisine. These are ideal for a memorable meal that doesn't break the bank. This category often includes affordable "destination" or "foodie" restaurants. And **splurge** eateries are dress-up-for-a-special-occasion-swanky—typically with an elegant setting, polished service, pricey and intricate cuisine, and an expansive (and expensive) wine list.

I haven't categorized places where you might assemble a picnic, snack, or graze: supermarkets, delis, ice cream-stands, cafés or bars specializing in drinks, chocolate shops, and so on.

BREAKFAST

Most Berlin hotels offer breakfast for an extra fee (it's generally not included in the base room price). German hotels pride themselves

on laying out an attractive buffet spread. Expect sliced bread, rolls, pastries, cereal, yogurt (both plain and with fruit), cold cuts, cheese, and fruit. You'll always find coffee, tea, and some sort of *Saft* (juice). Along with orange, apple, and grapefruit, multivitamin juice is popular. This sweet, smooth blend of

various fruits is less acidic than a citrus juice. A bottle of mineral water is standing by to mix with any juice to turn it into a *Schorle* (spritzer).

For breakfast, most Germans prefer a sandwich with cold cuts and/or a bowl of *Müsli* (an oat cereal like granola, but less sweet), sometimes mixed with corn flakes. Instead of pouring milk over cereal, most Germans begin with a dollop of yogurt (or *Quark*—sweet curds that resemble yogurt), then sprinkle the cereal on top. If it's not sweet enough, drizzle on some *Honig* (honey). *Bircher Müsli* is a healthy mix of oats, nuts, yogurt, and fruit. To make a German-style sandwich for breakfast, layer *Aufschnitt* (cold cuts), *Schinken* (ham), *Streichwurst* (meat spread, most often *Leberwurst*—liver spread), and *Käse* (cheese) on a slice of bread or a roll.

If a buffet has eggs, they're most likely soft-boiled *(weich gekochte Eier)*. To eat it as the Germans do, set the egg in its stand, gently break the shell around its perimeter, remove the top half of the shell, salt it, and eat it as if from a tiny bowl. Hard-boiled eggs *(hartgekochte Eier)* are often served with rémoulade (similar to tartar sauce). Occasionally a buffet will have *Rühreier* (scrambled eggs) or *Spiegeleier* (fried eggs—literally "mirror eggs"—typically sunny-side up).

In some hotels, a small garbage can is set on the table for you to dispose of trash as you eat.

LUNCH AND DINNER

Traditional restaurants go by many names. For basic, stick-to-the-ribs meals—and plenty of beer—look for a beer hall *(Brauhaus)* or beer garden *(Biergarten)*. *Gasthaus, Gasthof, Gaststätte,* and *Gaststube* all loosely describe an informal, inn-type eatery. A *Kneipe* is a bar, and a *Keller* (or *Ratskeller*) is a restaurant or tavern located in a cellar. A *Weinstube* serves wine and usually traditional food as well.

Germans are health-conscious and quite passionate about choosing organic *(Bio)* products: *Bio* fruits and vegetables, and

PRACTICALITIES

even *Bio* bread, ice cream, and schnitzel. You'll often see footnotes on restaurant menus marking which dishes have artificial ingredients. However, despite Germans' healthy ways, many starchy, high-fat, high-calorie traditional foods remain staples of the national diet. (For a rundown of common German foods, see "Traditional German Fare," later.)

Most eateries have menus tacked onto their front doors, with an English menu inside. If you see a *Stammtisch* sign hanging over a table at a restaurant or pub, it means that it's reserved for regulars—don't sit here unless invited. Once you're seated, take your time—only a rude waiter will rush you. Good service is relaxed (slow to an American).

To wish others "Happy eating!" offer a cheery *"Guten Appetit!"* When you want the bill, say, *"Die Rechnung, bitte"* (dee REHKH-noong, BIT-teh).

Tipping: You only need to tip at restaurants that have table service. If you order your food at a counter, don't tip. At restaurants with wait staff, it's common to tip after a good meal by rounding up (roughly 10 percent). Rather than leaving coins behind on the table (considered slightly rude), Germans usually pay directly: When the server comes by with the bill, simply hand over paper money, stating the total you'd like to pay. For example, if paying for a €10 meal with a €20 bill, while handing your money to the server, say "Eleven, please" (or *"Elf, bitte"* if you've got your German numbers down). The server will keep a €1 tip and give you €9 in change.

Lately, many restaurants—especially those in well-touristed areas—have added a "Tip is not included" line, in English, to the bottom of the bill. This is misleading, as the prices on any menu in Germany *do* include service. I wouldn't tip one cent more at a restaurant that includes this note on the bill. (Supposedly the trend's been prompted by an influx of tourists from cultures where it's not customary to round up...though I've seen servers circle the "tip not included" line before presenting the bill to Americans, who are known to overtip.) Many Germans are rebelling by tipping far less generously at eateries using this approach.

Budget Tips

It's easy to eat a meal for €10 or less here. At lunchtime, locals grab a sandwich (around €2.50) and perhaps a pastry (€1-2) from one of the ubiquitous bakeries, which often have tables to sit at (but not table service). If there aren't any sandwiches on display at the bakery counter, ask to have one made for you.

Department-store cafeterias (usually on the top floor with a view) are common and handy, and they bridge the language barrier by letting you see your options. A *Schnellimbiss* is a small fast-food takeaway stand where you can get a bratwurst or other grilled sausage (usually less than €2, including a roll); for a rundown of common sausages, see page 405.

All schnitzeled out? Ethnic restaurants provide a welcome break from Germanic fare. Italian, Turkish, and Asian food are generally good values. A freshly baked pizza, a Turkish sandwich, or a rice or noodle dish will cost you €4-7, and can be packed up to enjoy on a park bench or in your room.

Stands and shops selling Turkish-style *döner kebab*—gyro-like, pita-wrapped rotisserie meat—are common (€4 at any time of day). Turkish cafés abound, selling not only the basic *döner kebab*, but also several variations on the theme (see sidebar on page 278), plus falafel (chickpea croquettes), "Turkish pizzas," and much more.

Some restaurants offer inexpensive €6-9 weekday hot-lunch specials that aren't listed on the regular menu (look for the *Tages-karte* or *Tagesangebot*, or just ask—sometimes available at dinner, too). For smaller portions, order from the *kleine Hunger* (small hunger) section of the menu. Simple dishes of wurst with sauerkraut and bread tend to run €6-8.

TRADITIONAL GERMAN FARE
Here are some typical dishes you'll see at German eateries.

Specialties
Traditional German dishes tend to be meat-heavy. The classic dish is sausage—hundreds of varieties of bratwurst, *Weisswurst*, and other types of wurst are served with sauerkraut as an excuse for a vegetable (see page 405 for a list of common types of wurst).

Many traditional eateries serve some kind of meat on the bone, such as pork knuckle *(Sch-weinshaxe)* or shoulder, which has been roasted tender and goes down well with a big mug of beer. The fish and venison here are also good.

Another ubiquitous meat dish is schnitzel (a meat cutlet that's been pounded flat, breaded, and fried). Though traditionally made with veal, pork schnitzel is cheaper and more common.

You'll often see stuck on the beginning and end of menu items a form of the word *Braten* (which can mean "roasted" or "grilled" or "fried")—as in *Bratkartoffeln* (roasted potatoes), *Schweinebraten* (roasted pork), or *Bratwurst* (grilled sausage).

Here are a few other specialties—both regional and nationwide—to look for:

Aal Grün: Boiled eel served with *Spreewaldsauce* (parsley, dill, and cream sauce).

Buletten: Giant pan-fried meatball, sometimes flattened like a hamburger.

Dampfnudeln: Steamed bread roll with various toppings (also available sweet).

Eisbein (or **Hachse, Haxe, Schweinshaxe**): Boiled ham hock.

Flammkuchen (or **Dünnele**): German version of white pizza, on a thin, yeastless dough; the classic version is topped with bacon and onions.

Geschnetzeltes: Strips of veal or chicken braised in a rich sauce and served with noodles.

Kassler (or **Kasseler**): Salted, slightly smoked pork.

Kohlrouladen: Cabbage leaves stuffed with minced meat.

Königsberger Klopse (or **Sossklopse**): Meatball with capers and potatoes in a white sauce (a staple of eastern Germany).

Kümmelbraten: Crispy roast pork with caraway.

Labskaus: Mushy mix of salted meat, potatoes, often beets, and sometimes herring, onions, and sour cream.

Leber Berliner Art: Pan-fried veal liver served with sautéed apple rings and onions.

Maultaschen ("mouth pockets"): Ravioli with various fillings, such as veal, cheese, and spinach.

Mett (or **Hackepeter**): Raw, minced pork spread onto a roll.

Ratsherrentopf: Stew of roasted meat with potatoes.

Rollmops: Pickled herring fillets wrapped around a filling of pickled cucumber or onion. A popular hangover cure.

Rostbrätel: Marinated and grilled pork neck.

Rouladen (or **Rinderrouladen**): Strip of beef rolled up with bacon, onion, and pickles, then braised.

Sauerbraten: "Sour"-marinated and roasted cut of beef (sometimes pork), typically served with red cabbage and potato dumplings.

Saure Zipfel: Bratwurst cooked in vinegar and onions.

Schäufele: Oven-roasted pork shoulder with gravy.

Schlachtplatte (or **Schlachtschüssel**): "Butcher's plate"—usually blood sausage, *Leberwurst,* and other meat over hot sauerkraut.

Schnitzel Holstein: Schnitzel topped with a fried egg, capers, and anchovies.

Schweinebraten (or **Schweinsbraten**): Roasted pork with gravy.

Senfeier: Hard-boiled eggs in mustard sauce served with potatoes (classic eastern German dish).

Spargel: Big, white asparagus in season in May and June.

Speckpfannkuchen: Large, savory crêpe with bacon.

Stolle (or *Butterbrot*): Simple open-faced sandwich with butter and one topping.

Stolzer Heinrich: Grilled sausage in beer sauce (Berlin).

Best of the Wurst

Sausage (wurst) is a fast, tasty staple of the Germanic diet. Most restaurants offer it (often as the cheapest thing on the menu), but it's more commonly eaten at takeout fast-food stands (called *Würstchenbude* in Germany). Options go far beyond the hometown hot dog. Most are pork-based. Generally, the darker the weenie, the spicier it is.

Sausages can be boiled or grilled. The generic term *Bratwurst* (or *Rostbratwurst*) simply means "grilled sausage." *Brühwurst* means boiled. *Kochwurst* describes sausage made of precooked ingredients, then lightly steamed. While some types of wurst can be found all over, others are unique to a particular area (as noted below).

When surveying your options at a sidewalk sausage stand or butcher *(Metzgerei),* these terms may help:

Blutwurst (or *Blunzen*): Made from congealed blood. Variations include *Schwarzwurst, Rotwurst,* and *Beutelwurst.*

Bockwurst: Thick pork-and-veal sausage with a mild, grassy flavor and a toothsome, smoky casing.

Bosna: Spicy sausage with onions and sometimes curry (Austrian).

Cervelat: Smoky, mild, chewy sausage that's butterflied at each end before grilling (mostly Swiss).

Currywurst: Grilled pork sausage (usually *Bockwurst*), often chopped into small pieces, with ketchup/curry sauce, served *mit* or *ohne Darm* (with or without skin; with skin tastes smokier). Though this dish originated in Berlin, it's popular all over.

Frankfurter: A skinny, pink, boiled sausage—the ancestor of our hot dog (also called *Wienerwurst, Wienerwürstchen,* or simply *Wiener*).

Jagdwurst: Baloney-like "hunter's sausage"—smoked pork with garlic and mustard.

Käsekrainer: Boiled, with melted cheese inside (Austrian).

Knackwurst (or *Knockwurst*): Short, stubby, garlicky beef or pork sausage with a casing that "cracks" *(knackt)* when you bite into it.

Krakauer: Type of Polish sausage *(kiełbasa).*

Landjäger: Skinny, spicy, air-dried (almost withered) salami. *Ahle Wurst* is similar.

Leberkäse: Literally "liver cheese," this pâté is made of pork and beef (but, confusingly, no cheese and often no liver). *Leberkäse-semmel* is a pâté sandwich.

Leberwurst: Usually made from pig or calf livers and customarily served as a spread on open-face sandwiches, often with mustard or pickled cucumber.

Mettwurst: Made of minced pork that's cured and smoked.

Milzwurst: Made of pig spleen *(Milzstückchen)*.

Saumagen: "Sow's stomach" stuffed with meat, vegetables, and spices.

Teewurst: Air-dried, often smoked pork sausage similar to prosciutto, traditionally spread on bread and eaten at teatime (hence the name). It can also be grilled.

Thüringer: Long, skinny, peppery, and wedged into a much shorter roll. *Thüringer Rotwurst* is a blood-sausage variation.

Weisswurst: Boiled white sausage (peel off the casing before you eat it), served with sweet mustard and a pretzel (traditionally from Munich but served at any Bavarian-themed restaurant). If it's *frisch* (fresh), you're supposed to "eat it before the noon bell tolls."

Zwiebelmettwurst: Spicy, soft sausage made with raw pork and onions; usually spread on bread, it comes *fein* (smooth) or *grob* (chunky).

Accompaniments: Sauces and sides include *Senf* (mustard; ask for *süss*—sweet; or *scharf*—hot), ketchup, curry-ketchup, or *Currysauce* (a tasty curry-infused ketchup), Kraut (sauerkraut), and sometimes horseradish (called *Meerrettich* in the north, *Kren* in the south and Austria).

At sausage stands, wurst usually comes with a roll (*Semmel*—not your typical hot-dog bun). The sausage might be inside the roll, or it may come on a plate with the roll to the side. You might be given the choice of a slice of bread *(Brot)*, a pretzel *(Brezel)*, or in restaurants, potato salad.

Starches

Besides bread *(Brot)* and potatoes (*Kartoffeln;* boiled, fried, or grilled), other typical starches include:

Kartoffelsalat: Potato salad.

Knödel: Large dumplings, usually made from potatoes but also from wheat, sourdough, semolina, or even liver; baseball-size dumplings are called *Klöss.*

Schupfnudeln: Stubby, diamond-shaped potato noodles.

Spätzle: Little noodles made from egg dough scraped through a wide-holed sieve; often served with melted cheese and fried onions as a standalone meal *(Käsespätzle).*

Salads

Germans make excellent salads, and most menus feature big, varied, dinner-size salad plates. Besides *grüner Salat* (mostly lettuce), you'll likely come across these options:

Bauernsalat: Greek salad, sometimes with sausage.

Bohnensalat: Bean salad.

Fleischsalat: Chopped cold cuts mixed with pickles and mayonnaise.

Gemischter Salat (or *Bunter Salat*): A mixed salad of lettuce, fresh and (often) pickled veggies, and a tasty dressing.

Gurkensalat: Cucumber salad—usually just cukes in vinegar.

Nudelsalat: Pasta salad.

Ochsenmaulsalat: "Ox-mouth salad" with vinegar, onion, and herbs.

Oliviersalat: Russian-style salad—potatoes, eggs, vegetables, and mayonnaise.

Wurstsalat: Chopped sausage in onion and vinegar.

Snacks

Pretzels (*Brezeln* or—in Bavaria—*Brez'n*), either plain or buttered, make for an inexpensive snack. The brown crust comes from dunking them in water boiled with baking soda or lye.

Brotzeit ("bread time") is the all-purpose word for a light between-meals snack that's served cold. *Brotzeit* involves cold cuts, cheeses, breads, and other cold snacks, such as salads and some sausages. Other snack items include:

Kartoffelkäse: "Potato cheese" spread made of mashed potatoes, onion, and sour cream (but no cheese).

Krautsalat: "Coleslaw," basically cold sauerkraut.

Matjesfilet: Raw herring in yogurt.

Obatzda: Pungent Bavarian cheese spread with paprika and onions.

Schmalzbrot: Bread smeared with lard.

Schnittlauchbrot: Bread with cream cheese and diced chives.

Streichwurst: Meat spread; the most popular is *Leberwurst,* made from liver.

Sweets

Make sure to visit a bakery *(Bäckerei)* or pastry shop *(Konditorei)* to browse the selection of fresh pastries *(Feingebäck)* and cakes. Pastries can include the familiar *Apfelstrudel* and *Croissant* (sometimes called *Gipfel*, "peak"). Pastries often have a filling; these can include jam (*Marmelade* or *Konfitüre*), apple *(Apfel)*, cherry *(Kirsche)*, raisins *(Rosinen)*, nut *(Nuss)*, almond *(Mandel)*, poppy seeds *(Mohn)*, or the sweet cheese curds called *Quark*. Don't mistake *Mohn* for cinnamon, which resembles *Mohn* but is far less common in German desserts. Here are some other sweets you might see:

Amerikaner: A flat, round doughnut with a thick layer of glaze frosting on top.

Berliner Luft: An airy dessert made of cream, eggs, and gelatin, and served with raspberry sauce.

Berliner Pfannkuchen: A jelly-filled doughnut, known simply as a *"Berliner"* elsewhere in Germany (so JFK was really saying, "I am a jelly doughnut").

Rohrnudel: Roll-like sweet dumpling with raisins.

Schnecken: "Snail"-shaped pastry roll with raisins and nuts.

Gummi Bears from the German candy company Haribo are everywhere and taste better here, close to the source. Ice-cream stores, often run by Italian immigrants, abound. While you can always get a cone to go (ask for *eine Kugel*, a scoop—literally "ball"), many Germans sit down to enjoy their ice cream, ordering fancy sundaes in big glass bowls.

BEVERAGES
Water, Juice, and Soft Drinks

At restaurants, waiters aren't exactly eager to bring you *Leitungswasser* (tap water), preferring that you buy *Mineralwasser* (*mit/ohne Gas*—with/without carbonation). Half-liter mineral-water bottles are available everywhere for about €1. (I refill my water bottle with tap water.)

Popular soft drinks include *Apfelschorle* (half apple juice, half sparkling water) and *Spezi* (cola and orange soda). Menus list drink sizes by the tenth of a liter, or deciliter (dl): 0.2 liters is a small glass, and 0.4 or 0.5 is a larger one. Buy juice at a grocery store in cheap liter boxes, then drink some and store the extra in your water bottle.

At stores, most bottled water and soft drinks require a deposit (*Pfand;* usually €0.15 or €0.25—listed in small print on the shelf's price label), which is refunded if you return the bottle for recycling. You can generally return bottles to any supermarket, provided the bottle is a type they sell. Some supermarkets have vending machine-like bottle-return stations (marked *Leergutrückgabe* or *Leergutannahme*) that issue a coupon after you insert your bottles (redeem when you pay for your groceries). If you don't want to bother getting your deposit back but do care about recycling, set the bottle on top of or right next to any trash can, whether on the street or in your hotel room. Chances are someone will collect it for the extra cash.

Beer

The average German drinks 40 gallons of beer a year and has a tremendous variety to choose from. *Flaschenbier* is bottled, and *vom Fass* is on tap. For more on Berlin's beer scene, see page 280. Broadly speaking, most German beers fall into four main categories:

Helles Bier: Closest to American-style beer, this is the generic name for pale lager. Light-colored (but not "lite" as in low-calorie), a *helles Bier* is similar to a *Pilsner*, but with more malt. *Helles Bier* is usually served either in a straight glass (*Stange*, meaning "rod," which its shape resembles) or a mug. Unfiltered lager (like cask ale) is *Kellerbier* or *Zwickelbier*.

Dunkles Bier: This is a general term for dark beer. Munich-style *dunkles* is sweet and malty, while farther north it's drier and hoppier. Variations include *Schwarzbier* (a "black" lager with a chocolaty flavor), *Rauchbier* (with a "smoky" flavor, from Bamberg), and *Weihnachsbier* (or *Festbier*—a seasonal Christmas beer). *Dunkles Bier*, like *helles Bier*, is typically served in a straight glass or mug.

Weissbier or *Weizenbier:* "White" or "wheat" beer (better known in North America as *Hefeweizen*) is a yeasty, highly caloric beer. It is poured slowly to build a frothy head in a tall, rounded-top glass and served with a lemon wedge. Unfiltered *Weissbier*, especially common in the south, is cloudy (and usually called *Hefeweizen*). *Kristallweizen* is a clear, filtered, yeast-free wheat beer. *Roggenbier* is darker-colored and made with rye.

Pilsner (a.k.a. *Pilsener* or simply *Pils*): This is a barley-based, bottom-fermented, flavorful, hoppy, light-colored beer. Particularly common in the north, a *Pilsner* is usually served in a tall, slender, tapered, and sometimes stemmed glass. If it takes a while for the beer to arrive, it's because they're waiting for the head to die down.

Other Beer Drinks: *Radler* (literally "bicyclist"—designed to be refreshing and not too intoxicating for a biker on a hot day) is half lager and half lemon soda. Wheat beer and lemon soda is *Russ* (or *Russ'n*). Cola-beer mixes are also common: *Diesel* (a.k.a. *Schmutziges* or *Krefelder*) is cola and lager, and *Colaweizen* is cola and wheat beer.

Nährbier ("Near Beer") is just that—low-alcohol lager. The closest thing to our "lite" beer is *leichtes Bier*—a low-calorie, low-alcohol wheat beer.

Nonalcoholic Beer: While virtually all nonalcoholic brews in the US are watery, bitter lagers, Germany produces some excellent alcohol-free white/wheat beers *(Weisses)*, which have a somewhat

PRACTICALITIES

sweeter flavor—very smooth drinking on a hot day. Teetotalers, or anyone who wants a refreshing beer at lunch without being tipsy all afternoon, can look for *"ohne Alkohol"* or *"alkoholfrei."* There's also the drink called *Malztrunk* (or *Malzbier*)—the sweet, malted beverage (resembling dark beer) that children quaff before they start drinking the real thing.

Wine

Though famous for its beer, Germany also has excellent wine. The best-known white wines are from the Rhine and Mosel, and there are some good reds (usually from the south), including *Dornfelder* (velvety, often oaky, sometimes sweet) and *Spätburgunder* (or *Blauburgunder;* German for "pinot noir").

You can order *Wein* by the glass simply by asking for *ein Glas,* or to clarify that you don't want much, *ein kleines Glas* (about an eighth of a liter, or 4 oz). For a mini-pitcher of wine, ask for *ein Viertel* (quarter-liter, about two glasses' worth). For a half-liter pitcher (about four glasses), request *ein Halber.* For white wine, ask for *Weisswein;* red wine is *Rotwein.* Order your wine *lieblich* (sweet), *halbtrocken* (medium), or *trocken* (dry).

Here are some of the white wines you may see:

Eiswein: Ultra-sweet dessert white made from frozen shriveled grapes.

Gewürztraminer: Aromatic, intense, and "spicy."

Grauburgunder: German for "pinot gris"—a soft, full-bodied white.

Liebfraumilch: Semisweet "beloved maiden's milk" blending Riesling with Silvaner and Müller-Thurgau.

Müller-Thurgau: Light and flowery, best when young, smooth, and semisweet.

Riesling: Fruity, fragrant, elegant.

Silvaner (or **Grüner Silvaner**): Acidic, fruity white from Franconia, comes in jug-shaped bottle.

Weinschorle: A spritzer of white wine pepped up with a little sparkling water.

Many hotels serve the inexpensive *Sekt,* or German champagne, at breakfast. In winter, *Glühwein* (hot mulled wine) is popular.

Staying Connected

One of the most common questions I hear from travelers is, "How can I stay connected in Europe?" The short answer is: more easily and cheaply than you might think.

The simplest solution is to bring your own device—mobile phone, tablet, or laptop—and use it just as you would at home (fol-

Hurdling the Language Barrier

German—like English, Dutch, Swedish, and Norwegian—is a Germanic language, making it easier on most American ears than Romance languages (such as Italian and French). These tips will help you pronounce German words: The letter *w* is always pronounced as "v" (e.g., the word for "wonderful" is *wunderbar*, pronounced VOON-der-bar). The vowel combinations *ie* and *ei* are pronounced like the name of the second letter—so *ie* sounds like a long *e* (as in *hier* and *Bier,* the German words for "here" and "beer"), while *ei* sounds like a long *i* (as in *nein* and *Stein,* the German words for "no" and "stone"). The vowel combination *au* is pronounced "ow" (as in *Frau*). The vowel combinations *eu* and *äu* are pronounced "oy" (as in *neu, Deutsch,* and *Bräu,* the words for "new," "German," and "brew"). To pronounce *ö* and *ü,* purse your lips when you say the vowel; the other vowel with an umlaut, *ä,* is pronounced the same as *e* in "men." (In written German, these can be depicted as the vowel followed by an *e—oe, ue,* and *ae,* respectively.) The letter Eszett (ß) represents *ss.* Written German capitalizes all nouns.

Though most young or well-educated Germans—especially those in the tourist trade and in big cities—speak at least some English, you'll get more smiles if you learn and use German pleasantries. Study the German survival phrases on page 445. Give it your best shot. The locals will appreciate your efforts.

For more tips on hurdling the language barrier, consider the *Rick Steves German Phrase Book* (available at www.ricksteves.com).

lowing the tips below, such as connecting to free Wi-Fi whenever possible). Another option is to buy a European SIM card for your mobile phone—either your US phone or one you buy in Europe. Or you can use European landlines and computers to connect. Each of these options is described below, and more details are at www.ricksteves.com/phoning. For a very practical one-hour talk covering tech issues for travelers, see www.ricksteves.com/mobile-travel-skills.

USING A MOBILE PHONE IN EUROPE

Here are some budget tips and options.

Sign up for an international plan. Using your cellular net-

How to Dial

International Calls

Whether phoning from a US landline or mobile phone, or from a number in another European country, here's how to make an international call. I've used one of my recommended Berlin hotels as an example (tel. 030/780-089-760).

Initial Zero: Drop the initial zero from international phone numbers—except when calling Italy.

Mobile Tip: If using a mobile phone, the "+" sign can replace the international access code (for a "+" sign, press and hold "0").

US/Canada to Europe

Dial 011 (US/Canada international access code), country code (49 for Germany), and phone number.

▶ To call the Berlin hotel from home, dial 011-49-30/780-089-760.

Country to Country Within Europe

Dial 00 (Europe international access code), country code, and phone number.

▶ To call the Berlin hotel from Spain, dial 00-49-30/780-089-760.

Europe to the US/Canada

Dial 00, country code (1 for US/Canada), and phone number.

▶ To call from Europe to my office in Edmonds, Washington, dial 00-1-425-771-8303.

Domestic Calls

To call within Germany (from one German landline or mobile phone to another), simply dial the phone number, including the initial 0 if there is one.

▶ To call the Berlin hotel from Munich dial 030/780-089-760.

More Dialing Tips

German Phone Numbers: Local phone numbers in Germany can vary in length (4-8 digits), as can area codes (3-5 digits). I keep it simple by always dialing the full number. Mobile phone numbers start with 015, 016, or 017, and cost more to

PRACTICALITIES

work in Europe on a pay-as-you-go basis can add up (about $1.70/minute for voice calls, 50 cents to send text messages, 5 cents to receive them, and $10 to download one megabyte of data). To stay connected at a lower cost, sign up for an international service plan through your carrier. Most providers offer a simple bundle that includes calling, messaging, and data. Your normal plan may already include international coverage (T-Mobile's does).

Before your trip, call your provider or check online to confirm that your phone will work in Europe, and research your provider's call than landlines. Area codes are listed in this book, or you can get them from directory assistance (tel. 11833).

Toll and Toll-Free Calls: Some numbers, typically those that start with 018 (including some train and airline informa-tion numbers), are premium toll calls and cost more than a regular landline call. The per-minute charge should be listed in small print next to the phone number. International rates apply to US toll-free numbers dialed from Germany—they're not free.

More Phoning Help: See www.howtocallabroad.com.

European Country Codes		Ireland & N. Ireland	353 / 44
Austria	43	Italy	39
Belgium	32	Latvia	371
Bosnia-Herzegovina	387	Montenegro	382
Croatia	385	Morocco	212
Czech Republic	420	Netherlands	31
Denmark	45	Norway	47
Estonia	372	Poland	48
Finland	358	Portugal	351
France	33	Russia	7
Germany	49	Slovakia	421
Gibraltar	350	Slovenia	386
Great Britain	44	Spain	34
Greece	30	Sweden	46
Hungary	36	Switzerland	41
Iceland	354	Turkey	90

PRACTICALITIES

international rates. Activate the plan a day or two before you leave, then remember to cancel it when your trip's over.

Use free Wi-Fi whenever possible. Unless you have an un-limited-data plan, you're best off saving most online tasks for Wi-Fi. You can access the Internet, send texts, and make voice calls over Wi-Fi.

Most accommodations in Europe offer free Wi-Fi, but some—especially expensive hotels—charge a fee. Many cafés (including Starbucks and McDonald's) have free hotspots for customers; look for signs offering it and ask for the Wi-Fi password when you buy something. You'll also often find Wi-Fi at TIs, city squares, major museums, public-transit hubs, airports, and aboard trains and buses.

Minimize the use of your cellular network. Even with an international data plan, wait until you're on Wi-Fi to Skype, download apps, stream videos, or do other megabyte-greedy tasks. Using a navigation app such as Google Maps over a cellular network can take lots of data, so do this sparingly or use it offline.

Limit automatic updates. By default, your device constantly checks for a data connection and updates apps. It's smart to disable these features so your apps will only update when you're on Wi-Fi, and to change your device's email settings from "auto-retrieve" to "manual" (or from "push" to "fetch").

When you need to get online but can't find Wi-Fi, simply turn on your cellular network just long enough for the task at hand. When you're done, avoid further charges by manually turning off data roaming or cellular data (either works) in your device's Settings menu. Another way to make sure you're not accidentally using data roaming is to put your device in "airplane" mode (which also disables phone calls and texts), and then turn your Wi-Fi back on as needed.

It's also a good idea to keep track of your data usage. On your device's menu, look for "cellular data usage" or "mobile data" and reset the counter at the start of your trip.

Use Wi-Fi calling and messaging apps. Skype, Viber, FaceTime, and Google+ Hangouts are great for making free or low-cost voice and video calls over Wi-Fi. With an app installed on your phone, tablet, or laptop, you can log on to a Wi-Fi network and contact friends or family members who use the same service. If you buy credit in advance, with some of these services you can call any mobile phone or landline worldwide for just pennies per minute.

Many of these apps also allow you to send messages over Wi-Fi to any other person using that app. Be aware that some apps, such as Apple's iMessage, will use the cellular network if Wi-Fi isn't available: To avoid this possibility, turn off the "Send as SMS" feature.

USING A EUROPEAN SIM CARD

With a European SIM card, you get a European mobile number and access to cheaper rates than you'll get through your US carrier. This option works well for those who want to make a lot of voice calls or need faster connection speeds than their US carrier provides. Fit the SIM card into a cheap phone you buy in Europe (about $40 from phone shops anywhere), or swap out the SIM card in an "unlocked" US phone (check with your carrier about unlocking it).

SIM cards are sold at mobile-phone shops, department-store electronics counters, some newsstands, and vending machines. Costing about $5-10, they usually include prepaid calling/messaging credit, with no contract and no commitment. Expect to pay $20-40 more for a SIM card with a gigabyte of data. If you travel with this card to other countries in the European Union, there should be no extra roaming fees.

I like to buy SIM cards at a phone shop where there's a clerk to help explain the options. Certain brands—including Lebara and Lycamobile, both of which operate in multiple European countries—are reliable and economical. Ask the clerk to help you insert your SIM card, set it up, and show you how to use it. In some countries—including Germany—you'll be required to register the SIM card with your passport as an antiterrorism measure (which may mean you can't use the phone for the first hour or two).

Find out how to check your credit balance. When you run out of credit, you can top it up at newsstands, tobacco shops, mobile-phone stores, or many other businesses (look for your SIM card's logo in the window), or online.

PUBLIC PHONES AND COMPUTERS

It's possible to travel in Europe without a mobile device. You can make calls from your hotel (or the increasingly rare public phone), and check email or browse websites using public computers.

Most **hotels** charge a fee for placing calls—ask for rates before you dial. You can use a prepaid international phone card (available at post offices, newsstands, street kiosks, tobacco shops, and train stations) to call out from your hotel. Dial the toll-free access number, enter the card's PIN code, then dial the number. Even small hotels in Germany tend to have a direct-dial system, so callers can reach you without going through reception. Ask the staff for your room's specific telephone number.

You'll see **public pay phones** in post offices and train stations. The phones generally come with multilingual instructions; most don't take coins but instead require insertable phone cards (sold at post offices, newsstands, etc.). With the exception of Great Britain, each European country has its own insertable phone card—so your German card won't work in a French phone.

Avoid using an international phone card at a German pay phone—a surcharge for their use effectively eliminates any savings.

Most hotels have **public computers** in their lobbies for guests to use; otherwise you can find them at Internet cafés (ask your ho-

Tips on Internet Security

Make sure that your device is running the latest versions of its operating system, security software, and apps. Next, ensure that your device and key programs (like email) are password- or passcode-protected. On the road, use only secure, password-protected Wi-Fi hotspots. Ask the hotel or café staff for the specific name of their Wi-Fi network, and make sure you log on to that exact one.

If you must access your financial info online, use a banking app rather than accessing your account via a browser. A cellular connection is more secure than Wi-Fi. Avoid logging onto personal finance sites on a public computer.

Never share your credit-card number (or any other sensitive information) online unless you know that the site is secure. A secure site displays a little padlock icon, and the URL begins with *https* (instead of the usual *http*).

telier or the TI for the nearest location). German keyboards are a little different from ours; to type an @ symbol, press the "Alt Gr" key and Q at the same time. If you can't locate a special character (such as @), simply copy it from a Web page and paste it into your email message.

MAIL

You can mail one package per day to yourself worth up to $200 duty-free from Europe to the US (mark it "personal purchases"). If you're sending a gift to someone, mark it "unsolicited gift." For details, visit www.cbp.gov, select "Travel," and search for "Know Before You Go."

Get stamps at the neighborhood post office, newsstands within fancy hotels, and some minimarts and card shops. Avoid standing in line at the post office by using the handy yellow stamp *(Briefmarke)* machines found just outside the building. Warning: These machines give change only in stamps, not in coins.

The German postal service works fine, but for quick transatlantic delivery (in either direction), consider services such as DHL (www.dhl.com).

Transportation

If your trip will cover more of Germany than just Berlin, you may need to take a long-distance train or bus, rent a car, or fly. I give some specifics on all of those options here. For more detailed information on transportation throughout Europe, see www.ricksteves.com/transportation.

TRAINS

German trains—most operated by the Deutsche Bahn (DB), Germany's national railway—are speedy, comfortable, and nonsmok-

ing. Though German trains are fairly punctual, very tight connections can be a gamble. Once the obvious choice for long-distance travel within Germany, trains now face competition from buses offering ultra-low fares (described later).

If you have a rail pass, you can hop on any train without much forethought (though for a small fee, you can reserve a seat on a fast train). Without a rail pass, you can save a lot of money by understanding the difference between fast trains and cheaper "regional" trains.

Types of Trains

Germany's three levels of trains differ in price, speed, and comfort. **ICE** trains (white with red trim and streamlined noses) are the fastest, zipping from city to city in air-conditioned comfort, and costing proportionately more. Midlevel **IC** and **EC** trains are also white with red trim, but look older than the ICEs. **Regional trains** (mostly red and labeled RB, RE, IRE, or S on schedules) are slowest but cost much less. Milk-run S and RB trains stop at every station.

If you have a rail pass, take the fastest train available; rail-pass holders don't pay a supplement for the fast ICE trains. If you're buying point-to-point tickets, taking a slower train can save a lot of money. You also save with day-pass deals valid only on slower trains.

Schedules

Schedules change by season, weekday, and weekend. Verify train times listed in this book at www.bahn.com. This website also includes public transport in cities (buses, trams, and subways). The DB Navigator app is also a useful tool.

At staffed train stations, attendants will print out a step-by-step itinerary for you, free of charge. You can also produce an itinerary yourself by using the trackside machines marked *Fahrkarten* (usually silver, red, and blue). The touch-screen display gives you an English option; choose "Timetable Information," indicate your point of departure and destination, and then hit "Print" for a personalized schedule, including transfers and track numbers.

If you're changing trains en route and have a tight connection,

German Public Transportation

North Sea

50 Kilometers
50 Miles

To Copenhagen
Westerland
Tønder
Tinglev
Niebüll
Flensburg
Husum
Schleswig
Heide
Rendsburg
Kiel
Neumünster
Cuxhaven
Norden
Wilhelmshaven
Bremerhaven
Emden
Bremen
Hamburg
Groningen
Leer
Weener
Oldenburg
Lüneburg
Den Helder
Uelzen
NETHERLANDS
Celle
Wolfsburg
Haarlem
Amsterdam
Schiphol
Hengelo
Bad Bentheim
Osnabrück
Hannover
Braunschweig
The Hague
Utrecht
Rheine
Rotterdam
Arnhem
Emmerich
Münster
Antwerp
Duisburg
Essen
Dortmund
GERMA
Brussels
Venlo
Hagen
Wuppertal
Göttingen
To Brussels
Mönchengladbach
Düsseldorf
Maastricht
Cologne
Kassel
Namur
Liege
Aachen
Siegen
Bonn
Siegburg
BELGIUM
Marburg
Bebra
Moselkern
(BURG ELTZ)
Koblenz
Giessen
Eisenach
LUX.
Cochem
Hahn
St. Goar
Mainz
Frankfurt
Fulda
Meiningen
Luxembourg
Beilstein
Bacharach
Trier
Worms
Darmstadt
Würzburg
Metz
Mannheim
Heidelberg
To Paris
Saarbrücken
Steinach
Nürnberg
Forbach
Rothenburg
ob der Tauber
Ansbach
Nancy
Baden-Baden
Oos
Karlsruhe
Crailsheim
Ellwangen
Dinkelsbühl
Strasbourg
Kehl
Baden-Baden
Nordlingen
Treuchtlingen
FRANCE
Offenburg
Stuttgart
Ingolstadt
Colmar
Triberg
Ulm
Dachau
Augsburg
Munich
Titisee
Bad Kroz.
Freiburg
Singen
Mulhouse
Staufen
Fried.
Kempten
Buchloe
Belfort
Konstanz
Lindau
Oberammergau
Basel
Bregenz
Murn.
SWITZERLAND
Zürich
Reutte
Füssen
Feldkirch
Mitt.
To Bern
To Lausanne
To Interlaken
Luzern
To Lugano
LIECH.
Garmisch
Innsbruck
To Italy

PRACTICALITIES

PRACTICALITIES

note the numbers of the platforms (*Bahnsteig* or *Gleis*) where you will arrive and depart (listed on itineraries). This will save you precious time hunting for your connecting train.

To reach Germany's train information number from anywhere in the country, dial toll tel. 0180-699-6633 and ask for an English speaker.

Rail Passes

The single-country German Rail Pass can be a great value, often saving money while allowing you to hop on trains at your convenience (for the most part, most daytime routes in Germany, including fast ICE trains, do not require seat reservations). Rail passes are an even better deal if you're under 28 (you qualify for a youth pass) or traveling with a companion (you save with the "twin" rate). For only shorter hops, a rail pass probably isn't worth it, especially if you get discounts on point-to-point tickets and day passes (explained below).

If you're traveling in a neighboring country, two-country Eurail Select Passes allow you to pair Germany with Austria, Switzerland, France, the Benelux region, Denmark, Poland, or the Czech Republic. Three- and four-country versions of the Select Pass add more connecting countries (but not Poland). All passes allow up to two kids (ages 4-11) to travel free with an adult.

Your rail pass covers certain extras, including travel on city S-Bahn systems (except in Berlin, where it's only good on S-Bahn lines between major train stations), German buses marked "Deutsche Bahn" or "DB" (run by the train company), and international express buses operated by Deutsche Bahn (covered by either a German Rail Pass or a pass for both countries of travel).

For more detailed advice on figuring out the smartest rail-pass options for your train trip, visit www.ricksteves.com/rail.

Point-to-Point Tickets

Ticket fares are shown in the "Rail Passes and Train Travel in Germany" sidebar, and for some journeys, at www.bahn.com (though not for most trains outside of Germany). Deutsche Bahn can charge a wide variety of fares for the same journey, depending on the time of day, how far ahead you purchase the ticket, and other considerations. Know your options to get the best deal.

First Class vs. Second Class: First-class tickets usually cost 50 percent more than second-class tickets. While first-class cars are a bit more spacious and quieter than second class, the main advantage of a first-class ticket is the lower chance that the cars will fill up. Riding in second class gets you there at the same time, and with the same scenery. As second-class seating is still comfortable and quiet, most of my readers find the extra cost of first class

Rail Passes and Train Travel in Germany

A **German Rail Pass** lets you travel by train in Germany for 3 to 15 days (consecutively or not) within a one-month period. Discounted "twin" rates are offered for two people traveling together. Germany can also be included in a Eurail **Select Pass,** which allows travel in two to four neighboring countries over two months, and it's covered (along with most of Europe) by the classic Eurail **Global Pass.**

Rail passes are available through travel agents in the US or from Rick Steves' Europe; the German Rail Pass (unlike Eurail-brand passes) is also sold at main train stations and airports in Germany. For more on the ins and outs of rail passes, including prices, download my **free guide to Eurail Passes** (www.ricksteves.com/rail-guide) or go to www.ricksteves.com/rail.

If you're taking just a couple of train rides, buying individual **point-to-point tickets** may save you money over a pass. Use this map to add up approximate pay-as-you-go fares for your itinerary, and compare that to the price of a rail pass. Keep in mind that significant discounts on point-to-point tickets may be available with advance purchase.

This map shows approximate costs, in US$, for one-way, second-class tickets on faster trains.

PRACTICALITIES

isn't worth it. Germans tell me they never ride in first class unless someone else is paying for it.

Full-Fare Tickets *(Normalpreis):* The most you'll ever have to pay for a journey is the unrestricted *Normalpreis.* This full-fare ticket allows you to easily change your plans and switch to an earlier or later train, without paying a penalty. (If you buy a *Normal-*

preis ticket for a slower train, though, you can't use it on a fast one without paying extra.)

Discount Fares *(Sparpreis):* If you reserve a ticket on a fast train at least a day in advance and are comfortable committing to specific departure times, you can usually save 25-75 percent over the *Normalpreis.* But these tickets are more restrictive; you must take the train listed on the ticket or pay a €17.50 change fee. Discounted fares go on sale nine months in advance and remain available until one day before departure, though the cheap seats often sell out earlier.

Savings on Slow Trains: You can always save money on point-to-point tickets if you're willing to skip Germany's high-speed trains (IC, EC, and ICE) and limit yourself to regional trains (most commonly labeled RB, RE, IRE, or S, but also a range of region-specific names). For example, Freiburg to Baden-Baden might cost €30 by ICE, €25 by EC, and €20 by RE train. To limit your search to these slower, cheaper trains, select "only local transport" on the Deutsche Bahn website or at ticket machines.

Day Passes

You may save even more with three types of extremely popular day passes valid only on slow trains: the various Länder-Tickets, the Schönes-Wochenende-Ticket, and the Quer-durchs-Land-Ticket. They are most cost-effective for groups of two to five people, but single travelers can benefit from them, too.

With a **Länder-Ticket,** up to five people traveling together get unlimited travel in second class on regional trains for one day at a very cheap price. There are a few restrictions: A Länder-Ticket only covers travel within a certain *Land* (Germany's version of a US state, such as Brandenburg, where Berlin is), doesn't work for the fastest classes of trains (ICE, IC, EC), and doesn't cover travel on weekdays before 9:00. Still, Länder-Tickets offer big savings, don't require advance purchase, and are also valid on local transit. For example, a Brandenburg-Berlin-Ticket covers five people traveling between Berlin and Wittenberg or Berlin and Potsdam for €29.

The **Quer-durchs-Land-Ticket** works like a Länder-Ticket, but gives you the run of the whole country. It's valid on any regional train anywhere in Germany, but doesn't include city transit (first person-€44, each additional passenger-€8, maximum of 5 travelers, only valid weekdays after 9:00).

The **Schönes-Wochenende-Ticket** is a cheaper weekend version of the Quer-durchs-Land Ticket, with looser conditions: It's valid on all regional trains on a Saturday or Sunday (starting at midnight, not 9:00), it does cover local transit in some areas (buses, trams, subways—check specifics when you buy), and additional travelers pay only €4 extra (first person-€40, maximum 5 travelers).

Kids ages 6-14 travel free with a parent or grandparent, but the ticket needs to list the number of children (unless purchased from a regional-train ticket machine). Kids under age 6 don't need tickets.

Buying Tickets

At the Station: Major German stations have a handy *Reisezentrum* (travel center) where you can ask questions and buy tickets (with a

€2 markup for the personal service). You can also buy tickets from machines, which come in three types.

The silver, red, and blue touch-screen machines (marked with the Deutsche Bahn logo and *Fahrkarten,* which means "tickets") are user-friendly. They sell both short- and long-distance train tickets; and print schedules for free. Touch the flag to switch to English (some rare screens are German-only). You can pay with bills, coins, or credit cards—but US credit cards may not work. There's one exception: Any trip that is entirely within the bounds of a regional transport network (i.e., Berlin-Potsdam) is considered local: Tickets can only be bought on the day of travel, and you must pay cash.

Each German city and region also has its own machines that sell only same-day tickets to nearby destinations (usually including Länder-Ticket day passes). In cities, these machines also sell local public transit tickets. At some smaller, unstaffed stations, these machines are the only ticket-buying option. You'll see the logo of the city or regional transport network on the machine. Increasingly, these machines are multilingual, with touch screens, and some even take American cards with a PIN (though others take only cash and German cards).

Some cities and regions still have older, silver ticket machines with smaller screens and plenty of buttons. To buy a train ticket from these machines, press the flag button until it gives you a screen in English. Then look for your destination on the long list of towns on the left side. If your destination isn't on the list (because it's too far away), you can buy the ticket on board (let the conductor know where you boarded so you won't have to pay the small markup for buying a ticket on the train). If your destination *is* on the list, note its four-digit code and enter it on the number pad. The machine defaults to a one-way *(Einfache)* second-class ticket, but you can alter that with the buttons below the keypad (press *Hin- und Rückfahrt* for a round-trip ticket, and *1./2. Klasse* for first class; also note the buttons for Länder-Ticket day passes and children's tickets). Feed the machine cash (small bills are OK, but it won't take credit cards), then collect your ticket and change. *Gut gemacht!* (Well done!)

On the Train: If you have enough cash, you can buy a ticket on board from the conductor for a long-distance journey by paying a small markup (US credit cards won't work unless they have a chip). But if you're riding a local (short distance) train, you're expected to board with a valid ticket...or you can get fined. Note that ticket-checkers on local trains aren't necessarily in uniform.

Online: You can buy German train tickets online and print them out, or have them sent to your phone as an eticket; visit www. bahn.com and create a login and password. If you print out your ticket, the conductor will also ask to see your passport. You can also book seat reservations (optional) with a rail pass for trips within Germany—start to buy a regular ticket, then check the box for "reservation only."

Getting a Seat

As you board or exit a train, you'll usually have to push a button or flip a lever to open the door. Watch locals and imitate.

On the faster ICE, IC, and EC trains, it costs €4.50 extra per person to reserve a seat, which you can do at a station ticket desk, a touch-screen machine, or online (especially useful with a rail pass or a second-class ticket). If buying a first-class ticket on these trains, you can add a seat assignment for free at the time of purchase. German trains generally offer ample seating, but popular routes do fill up, especially on holiday weekends. If your itinerary is set, and you don't mind the small fee, seat reservations can be worth it for the peace of mind. They're especially smart for small groups and families (€9 reservation cap for families).

On ICE trains, families with small children can book special compartments called *Kleinkindabteil,* which have extra room for strollers and diaper changing, for the regular seat-reservation price.

With rare exceptions, there's no need to go through a US agent to make a seat reservation in advance of your trip; just do it online or at a German station. Reservations may be required on international trains and buses (specified in schedule). Slower regional trains don't even accept them.

If you have a seat reservation, while waiting for your train to arrive, note the departure time and *Wagen* (car) number and look along the train platform for the diagram *(Wagenstandanzeiger)* showing what sector of the platform the car will arrive at (usually A through F). Stand in that sector to avoid a last-minute dash to the right car or a long walk through the train to your seat. This is especially important for ICE trains, which are often divided into two unconnected parts.

If you're traveling without a reservation and are looking for an open seat, check the displays (or, in older trains, the slips of paper) that mark reserved seats. If you have a hard time finding an unreserved seat, take a closer look at the reservations—if you find a seat that's reserved for a leg of the journey that doesn't overlap with yours, you're free to take the seat.

In stations without elevators, you can take advantage of the luggage belts along the stairs to each platform. They start automatically when you put your bag on the bottom or top of the belt.

Bikes on Board
Your bike can travel with you for €5 per day on regional trains or €9 per trip on fast trains. Deutsche Bahn's helpful website even has a list of bike-rental shops that are in or near train stations. Rentals usually run about €10-15 a day, and some rental outfits offer easy "pick up here and drop off there" plans.

LONG-DISTANCE BUSES
While most American travelers still find the train to be the better option (mainly because rail passes make German train travel affordable and no-hassle), ultra-low-fare long-distance buses are worth considering.

While buses don't offer as extensive a network as trains, they do cover the most popular cities for travelers, often with a direct connection. The primary disadvantage to buses is a lack of travel flexibility: Buses are far less likely than trains to have a seat available for those who show up sans ticket (especially on either end of a weekend). And compared to trains, buses also offer fewer departures per day, though your options probably aren't too shabby on major routes served by multiple operators. Trains also beat buses in travel time and convenience, although often not by much.

Bus tickets are sold on the spot (on board and/or at kiosks at some bus terminals), but because the cheapest fares often sell out, it's best to book online as soon as you're sure of your plans (at a minimum, book a few days ahead to nab the best prices). The main bus operators to check out are FlixBus (with the most extensive network, www.flixbus.de) and Berlin Linien Bus (www.berlinlinienbus.de).

Though not as comfortable as trains, each company's brightly colored buses are surprisingly well outfitted and make for a more pleasant ride than your average Greyhound trip. Most offer free Wi-Fi and onboard snack bars and WCs.

Bus terminals vary; you may find a true depot with ticket kiosks and overhead shelter, or just a stretch of street with a cluster of bus stops. Serious bus stations are labeled across Germany as "ZOB" (for *Zentraler Omnibusbahnhof*—central bus station). While most cities' bus terminals are usually a block or two from the train station, in some bigger cities (such as Munich and Berlin), bus travelers have to go a little farther afield to catch their ride.

TAXIS AND UBER

Most European taxis are reliable and cheap. In many cities, couples can travel short distances by cab for little more than two bus or subway tickets. Taxis can be your best option for getting to the airport for an early morning flight or to connect two far-flung destinations. If you like ride-booking services like Uber, these apps usually work in Europe just like they do in the US: You request a car on your mobile device (connected to Wi-Fi or a data plan), and the fare is automatically charged to your credit card. For more about taxis in Berlin, see page 21.

RENTING A CAR

Rental companies require you to be at least 21 years old and to have held your license for one year. Drivers under the age of 25 may incur a young-driver surcharge, and some rental companies do not rent to anyone 75 or older. If you're considered too young or old, look into leasing (covered later), which has less-stringent age restrictions.

Research car rentals before you go. It's cheapest to arrange most car rentals from the US. Consider several companies to compare rates.

Most of the major US rental agencies (including Avis, Budget, Enterprise, Hertz, and Thrifty) have offices throughout Europe. Also consider the two major Europe-based agencies, Europcar and Sixt. It can be cheaper to use a consolidator, such as Auto Europe/Kemwel (www.autoeurope.com—or the often cheaper www.autoeurope.eu) or Europe by Car (www.europebycar.com), which compares rates at several companies to get you the best deal—but because you're working with a middleman, it's especially important to ask in advance about add-on fees and restrictions.

Always read the fine print or query the agent carefully for add-on charges—such as one-way drop-off fees, airport surcharges, or mandatory insurance policies—that aren't included in the "total price."

For the best deal, rent by the week with unlimited mileage. Be aware that diesel cars may not be allowed in Berlin, Munich, or other big cities—confirm with your rental company. I normally rent the smallest, least-expensive model with a stick shift (generally cheaper than an automatic). Almost all rentals are manual by default, so if you need an automatic, request one in advance; be aware that these cars are usually larger models (not as maneuverable on narrow, winding roads).

Figure on paying roughly $250 for a one-week rental. Allow extra for supplemental insurance, fuel, tolls, and parking. For trips of three weeks or more, leasing can save you money on insurance and taxes. Be warned that international trips—say, picking up in Berlin and dropping off in Prague—while efficient, can be expensive (it depends partly on distance).

As a rule, always tell your car-rental company up front exactly which countries you'll be entering. Some companies levy extra insurance fees for trips taken in certain countries with certain types of cars (such as BMWs, Mercedes, and convertibles). Double-check with your rental agent that you have all the documentation you need before you drive off (especially if you're crossing borders into non-Schengen countries, such as Croatia, where you might need to present proof of insurance).

Picking Up Your Car: Compare pickup costs (downtown can be less expensive than the airport) and explore drop-off options. Always check the hours of the location you choose: Many rental offices close from midday Saturday until Monday morning and, in smaller towns, at lunchtime.

When selecting a location, don't trust the agency's description of "downtown" or "city center." In some cases, a "downtown" branch can be on the outskirts of the city—a long, costly taxi ride from the center. Before choosing, plug the addresses into a mapping website. You may find that the "train station" location is handier. Returning a car at a big-city train station or downtown agency can be tricky; get precise details on the car drop-off location and hours, and allow ample time to find it.

When you pick up the car, check it thoroughly and make sure any damage is noted on your rental agreement. Rental agencies in Europe tend to charge for even minor damage, so be sure to mark everything. Before driving off, find out how your car's gearshift, lights, turn signals, wipers, radio, and fuel cap function, and know what kind of fuel the car takes (diesel vs. unleaded). When you return the car, make sure the agent verifies its condition with you. Some drivers take pictures of the returned vehicle as proof of its condition.

Car Insurance Options

When you rent a car, you are liable for a very high deductible, sometimes equal to the entire value of the car. Limit your financial risk with one of these three options: Buy Collision Damage Waiver (CDW) coverage with a low or zero deductible from the car-rental company, get coverage through your credit card (free, if your card automatically includes zero-deductible coverage), or get collision insurance as part of a larger travel-insurance policy.

Basic **CDW** includes a very high deductible (typically $1,000-1,500), costs $15-30 a day (figure roughly 30-40 percent extra) and reduces your liability, but does not eliminate it. When you reserve or pick up the car, you'll be offered the chance to "buy down" the basic deductible to zero (for an additional $10-30/day; this is sometimes called "super CDW" or "zero-deductible coverage").

If you opt for **credit-card coverage,** you'll technically have to decline all coverage offered by the car-rental company, which means they can place a hold on your card (which can be up to the full value of the car). In case of damage, it can be time-consuming to resolve the charges with your credit-card company. Before you decide on this option, quiz your credit-card company about how it works.

If you're already purchasing a **travel-insurance policy** for your trip, adding collision coverage can be an economical option. For example, Travel Guard (www.travelguard.com) sells affordable renter's collision insurance as an add-on to its other policies; it's valid everywhere in Europe except the Republic of Ireland, and some Italian car-rental companies refuse to honor it, as it doesn't cover you in case of theft.

For more on car-rental insurance, see www.ricksteves.com/cdw.

Leasing

For trips of three weeks or more, consider leasing (which automatically includes zero-deductible collision and theft insurance). By technically buying and then selling back the car, you save lots of money on tax and insurance. Leasing provides you a new car with unlimited mileage and a 24-hour emergency assistance program. You can lease for as little as 21 days to as long as five and a half months. Car leases must be arranged from the US. Two of many companies offering affordable lease packages are Europe by Car and Auto Europe.

Navigation Options

If you'll be navigating using your phone or a GPS unit from home, remember to bring a car charger and device mount.

Your Mobile Device: The mapping app on your mobile phone works fine for navigation in Europe, but for real-time turn-by-turn directions and traffic updates, you'll generally need Internet access. And driving all day while online can be very expensive. Helpful exceptions are Google Maps, Here WeGo, and Navmii, which provide turn-by-turn voice directions and recalibrate even when they're offline.

Download your map before you head out—it's smart to select a large region. Then turn off your cellular connection so you're not charged for data roaming. Call up the map, enter your destination, and you're on your way. View maps in standard view (not satellite view) to limit data demands.

GPS Devices: If you prefer the convenience of a dedicated GPS unit, consider renting one with your car ($10-30/day). These units offer real-time turn-by-turn directions and traffic without the data requirements of an app. Note that the unit may only come loaded with maps for its home country; if you need additional maps, ask. Also make sure your device's language is set to English before you drive off.

A less-expensive option is to bring a GPS device from home. Be aware that you'll need to buy and download European maps before your trip.

Maps and Atlases: Even when navigating primarily with a mobile app or GPS, I always make it a point to have a paper map. It's invaluable for getting the big picture, understanding alternate routes, and filling in when my phone runs out of juice. The free maps you get from your car-rental company usually don't have enough detail. It's smart to buy a better map before you go, or pick one up at European gas stations, bookshops, newsstands, and tourist shops.

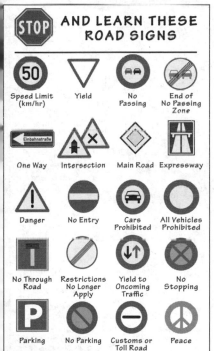

STOP AND LEARN THESE ROAD SIGNS

Speed Limit (km/hr)	Yield	No Passing	End of No Passing Zone
One Way	Intersection	Main Road	Expressway
Danger	No Entry	Cars Prohibited	All Vehicles Prohibited
No Through Road	Restrictions No Longer Apply	Yield to Oncoming Traffic	No Stopping
Parking	No Parking	Customs or Toll Road	Peace

Driving

Road Rules: Be aware of typical European road rules; for example, many countries require headlights to be turned on at all times, and nearly all forbid talking on a mobile phone without a hands-free headset. In Germany, kids under age 12 (or less than about 5 feet tall) must ride in an appropriate child-safety seat. Seat belts are mandatory for all, and two beers under those belts are enough to land you in jail. You're required to use low-beam headlights if it's overcast, raining, or snowing. In Europe, you're not allowed to turn right on a red light, unless a sign or signal specifically authorizes

Note: Your times may vary based on traffic, construction, and road conditions.

m = miles
h = hours
...... = ferry

North Sea

To Copenhagen 200m 4h

Flensburg

95m · 1.25h

NETHERLANDS

Hamburg

Amsterdam

165m · 2.5h

265m · 4.25h

310m · 4.5h

360m · 5.5h

GER

Brussels

90m · 1.5h

Cologne

40m · .75h

Aachen

230m · 3.5h

Erfurt

BELGIUM

55m · .75h

Koblenz

25m · .5h

140m · 2.25h

LUX.

Cochem

30m .5h

Bacharach

55m 1h

Trier

70m · 1h

60m · 1h

Frankfurt

60m · 1h

125m · 2h

200m · 3.25h

175m · 2.5h

135m · 2.5h

100m · 1.5h

Würzburg

40m .5h

Rothenburg

70m 1.25h

Nürnberg

Strasbourg

40m 1h

Baden-Baden

135m · 2h

100m · 1.75h

FRANCE

60m · 1.25h

200m · 3.25h

150m · 2h

Colmar

35m 1h

Freiburg

260m · 4h

175m · 3.75h

Munich

Füssen

95m · 1.75h

Zürich

55m · 1h

95m · 2.25h

70m 1.5h

45m · 1h

70m 1.75h (via Reutte)

100m

Appenzell

Bern

70m · 1.25h

SWITZERLAND

LIECH.

Innsbruck 20m .25h

To Brenner Pass

PRACTICALITIES

Driving in Germany

DENMARK

To Copenhagen

100m • 1.75h

Rødby
Puttgarten

100m • 1.5h

Rostock

Sassnitz

Baltic Sea

MANY

180m • 3h

140m • 2.25h

200m • 3.25h

50 Kilometers

50 Miles

Berlin

60m • 1.25h

305m • 6h
To Warsaw

Frankfurt
an der
Oder

200m • 3.25h

75m • 1.25h

120m • 2.25h

POLAND

Wittenberg

45m • 1h

Leipzig

95m • 1.75h

70m • 1.5h

Dresden

70m • 1.25h

Görlitz

195m • 3h

95m • 3h

190m • 3h

Prague

CZECH
REPUBLIC

105m • 2.253h

185m • 3.25h

240m • 4h

Český
Krumlov

135m • 2.5h

140m • 3.25h

80m • 1.25h

Salzburg

125m • 2h

Melk

55m • 1.25h

Vienna

SLOVAKIA

50m • 1.5h

15m
.5h

Hallstatt

110m • 2h

Berchtesgaden

AUSTRIA

HUNGARY

it, and on expressways it's illegal to pass drivers on the right. Ask your car-rental company about these rules, or check the US State Department website (www.travel.state.gov, search for your country in the "Learn about your destination" box, then click on "Travel & Transportation").

Fuel: Unleaded gasoline comes in "Super" (95 octane) and "Super Plus" (98 octane). Pumps marked "E10" or "Super E10" mean the gas contains 10 percent ethanol—make sure your rental can run on this mix. You don't have to worry about learning the German word for diesel. Your US credit and debit cards may not work at self-service gas pumps. Pay the attendant or carry enough euros.

Navigation: Use good local maps and study them before each drive. Learn which exits you need to look out for, which major cities you'll travel toward, where the ruined castles lurk, and so on. Every long drive between my recommended destinations is via the autobahn (super-freeway), and nearly every scenic backcountry drive is paved and comfortable. Learn the universal road signs (explained in charts in most road atlases and at service stations). To get to the center of a city, follow signs for *Zentrum* or *Stadtmitte*. Ring roads go around a city.

The Autobahn: The shortest distance between any two points is the autobahn (no speed limit in many sections, toll-free within Germany). Blue signs direct you to the autobahn. To understand this complex but super-efficient freeway, look for the *Autobahn Service* booklet at any autobahn rest stop (free, lists all stops, services, road symbols, and more). Learn the signs: *Dreieck* ("three corners") means a Y-intersection; *Autobahnkreuz* is where two expressways cross. Exits are spaced about every 20 miles and often have a gas station, a restaurant, a minimarket, and sometimes a tourist information desk. Exits and intersections refer to the next major city or the nearest small town. Peruse the map and anticipate which town names to look out for. Know what you're looking for—miss it, and you're long autobahn-gone. When navigating, you'll see *Nord, Süd, Ost,* and *West.* Electronic signs warning of dangerous conditions may include one of these words: *Unfall* (accident), *Nebel* (fog), or *Stau* (congestion).

Autobahns in Germany are famous for having no speed limit, but some sections actually do have a limit, particularly in urban areas and near complicated interchanges. Sometimes there are electronic signs with "dynamic" limits that change depending on traffic conditions. There are also cameras that take pictures of the speeder's license plate—so obey the law or be prepared to pay. In areas without an "official" maximum speed, you will commonly see a recommended speed posted. While no one gets a ticket for ignoring this recommendation, exceeding this speed means your car insurance no longer covers you in the event of an accident.

It's important to stay alert on the autobahn: Everything happens much more quickly, and the speed differential between lanes can be dangerous for unaccustomed drivers. Watch for potential lane changers, whether from your right or from behind—a roaring Mercedes can appear out of thin air in your rearview mirror.

Even if you're obeying posted limits, don't cruise in the passing lane; stay right. Since it's illegal to pass on the right on the autobahn, drivers will angrily flash their lights, and possibly tailgate, if you drive in a passing lane. Obstructing traffic on the autobahn is against the law—so running out of gas, or even cruising in the far-left lane—is not only dangerous, it can earn you a big ticket. In fast-driving Germany, the backed-up line caused by an insensitive slow driver is called an *Autoschlange,* or "car snake." What's the difference between a car snake and a real snake? According to locals, "On a real snake, the ass is in the back."

***Umweltplakette* for Driving in German Cities:** To drive into specially designated "environmental zones" *(Umweltzone)* in the centers of many German cities—including Berlin—you are required to display an *Umweltplakette* sticker. Literally "environmental sticker," these already come standard with most German rental cars (ask when you pick up your car). If you're renting a car outside of Germany and plan to enter one of these cities, be sure you have one (sold cheap—around €10—at the border and at gas stations; you'll need the registration and legal paperwork that came with your rental; see www.umwelt-plakette.de).

Parking: To park on the street, pick up a cardboard clock (*Parkscheibe,* available free at gas stations, police stations, and *Tabak* shops). Display your arrival time on the clock and put it on the dashboard, so parking attendants can see you've been there less than the posted maximum stay. Your US credit and debit cards may not work at automated parking garages—bring cash.

Theft: Thieves easily recognize rental cars and assume they are filled with a tourist's gear. Be sure all your valuables are out of sight and locked in the trunk, or even better, with you or in your room.

FLIGHTS

The best comparison search engine for both international and intra-European flights is Kayak.com. An alternative is Google Flights, which has an easy-to-use system to track prices. For inexpensive flights within Europe, try Skyscanner.com.

Flying to Europe: Start looking for international flights about four to six months before your trip, especially for peak-season travel. Off-season tickets can usually be purchased a month or so in advance. Depending on your itinerary, it can be efficient to fly into one city and out of another. If your flight requires a connection in Europe, see my hints on navigating Europe's top hub airports at www.ricksteves.com/hub-airports.

Flying within Europe: If you're considering a train ride that's more than five hours long, a flight may save you both time and money. When comparing your options, factor in the time it takes to get to the airport and how early you'll need to arrive to check in.

Well-known cheapo airlines include EasyJet and Ryanair. Others with strong presence in Germany are Air Berlin, Euro-wings, Condor, WizzAir, and TUIfly. But be aware of the potential drawbacks of flying with a discount airline: nonrefundable and nonchangeable tickets, minimal or nonexistent customer service, pricey and time-consuming treks to secondary airports, and stingy baggage allowances with steep overage fees. If you're traveling with lots of luggage, a cheap flight can quickly become a bad deal. To avoid unpleasant surprises, read the small print before you book. These days you can also fly within Europe on major airlines affordably—and without all the aggressive restrictions—for around $100 a flight. For the best fares on these (which are often not changeable or refundable), you'll want to book well in advance.

Flying to the US and Canada: Because security is extra tight for flights to the US, be sure to give yourself plenty of time at the airport. It's also important to charge your electronic devices before you board because security checks may require you to turn them on (see www.tsa.gov for the latest rules).

Resources from Rick Steves

Begin your trip at www.ricksteves.com: My mobile-friendly **website** is *the* place to explore Europe. You'll find thousands of fun articles, videos, photos, and radio interviews organized by country; a wealth of money-saving tips for planning your dream trip; monthly travel news dispatches; a video library of my travel talks; my travel blog; and my latest guidebook updates (www.ricksteves.com/update).

Our **Travel Forum** is an immense yet well-groomed collection of message boards, where our travel-savvy community answers questions and shares their personal travel experiences—and our well-traveled staff chimes in when they can be helpful (www.ricksteves.com/forums).

Our **online Travel Store** offers travel bags and accessories that I've designed specifically to help you travel smarter and lighter. These include my popular carry-on bags (which I live out of four months a year), money belts, totes, toiletries kits, adapters, other accessories, and a wide selection of guidebooks and planning maps (www.ricksteves.com/shop).

Choosing the right **rail pass** for your trip—amid hundreds of options—can drive you nutty. Our website will help you find the perfect fit for your itinerary and your budget: We offer easy, one-stop shopping for rail passes, seat reservations, and point-to-point tickets (www.ricksteves.com/rail).

Small Group Tours: Want to travel with greater efficiency and less stress? We offer more than 40 itineraries and have over 900 departures annually reaching the best destinations in this book... and beyond. We offer a 13-day Best of Germany tour; a 14-day tour of Germany, Austria, and Switzerland; a 12-day tour of Berlin, Prague, and Vienna; an 8-day tour of Munich, Salzburg, and Vienna; and a My Way: Alpine Europe in 12 days "unguided" tour (covering hotel and transportation) of alpine destinations in Germany, Austria, Italy, Switzerland, and France. You'll enjoy great guides, a fun bunch of travel partners (with small groups of 24 to 28 travelers), and plenty of room to spread out in a big, comfy bus when touring between towns. You'll find European adventures to fit every vacation length. For all the details, and to get our Tour Catalog, visit www.ricksteves.com/tours or call us at 425/608-4217.

Books: *Rick Steves Berlin* is one of many books in my series on European travel, which includes country guidebooks, city and regional guidebooks, Snapshot guidebooks (excerpted chapters from my country guides), Pocket guidebooks (full-color little books on big cities), "Best Of" guidebooks (condensed country guides in a full-color, easy-to-scan format), and my budget-travel skills handbook, *Rick Steves Europe Through the Back Door.* Most of my titles are available as ebooks.

My phrase books—for German, French, Italian, Spanish, and Portuguese—are practical and budget-oriented. My other books include *Europe 101* (a crash course on art and history designed for travelers); *Mediterranean Cruise Ports* and *Northern European Cruise Ports* (how to make the most of your time in port), and *Travel as a Political Act* (a travelogue sprinkled with tips for bringing home a global perspective). A more complete list of my titles appears near the end of this book.

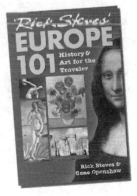

TV Shows: My public television series, *Rick Steves' Europe,* covers Europe from top to bottom with over 100 half-hour episodes, and we're working on new shows every year. We have seven episodes on Germany—that's over three hours of vivid video coverage of one of my favorite countries. To watch full episodes online for free, see www.ricksteves.com/tv.

Travel Talks on Video: You can raise your travel I.Q. with video versions of our popular classes (including talks on travel skills, packing smart, cruising, tech for travelers, European art for travelers, travel as a political act, and individual talks covering most European countries). See www.ricksteves.com/travel-talks.

Radio: My weekly public radio show, *Travel with Rick Steves,* features interviews with travel experts from around the world. It airs on 400 public radio stations across the US, and you can also listen to it as a podcast on iTunes, iHeartRadio, Stitcher, Tune In, and other platforms. A complete archive of programs (over 400 in all) is available at www.soundcloud.com/rick-steves.

Audio Tours on My Free App: I've also produced dozens of free, self-guided audio tours of the top sights in Europe, including a City Walk tour in Berlin. My audio tours and other audio content are available for free through my **Rick Steves Audio Europe app,** an extensive online library organized into handy geographic playlists. For more on my app, see page 6.

APPENDIX

Useful Contacts

Emergency Needs
Police, Fire, and Ambulance: 112 (Europe-wide in English)

Embassies
US Embassy in Berlin: Open by appointment only Mon-Fri 8:00-12:00, closed Sat-Sun and last Thu of month; Clayallee 170, tel. 030/83050, http://de.usembassy.gov

Canadian Embassy in Berlin: Consular services open Mon-Fri 9:00-12:00, closed Sat-Sun; Leipziger Platz 17, tel. 030/203-120, www.germany.gc.ca

Holidays and Festivals

This list includes selected festivals in Berlin and Wittenberg, plus national holidays observed throughout Germany. Many sights and banks close on national holidays—keep this in mind when planning your itinerary. Verify dates by checking the festival's website, Berlin's national tourist office (www.visitberlin.de), or my "Upcoming Holidays and Festivals in Germany" web page (www.ricksteves.com/europe/germany/festivals).

Jan 1	New Year's Day
Jan 6	Epiphany (Heilige Drei Könige)
Feb	Berlinale (international film festival, www.berlinale.de)
Feb 8-14	Fasching (carnival season; parties, parades leading up to Ash Wednesday)
March 30-April 1	Easter weekend (Good Friday-Easter Monday)
May 1	May Day (maypole dances)
May 10	Ascension
May 17-21	Carnival of Cultures (four-day street festival of international music and dance culminating in a parade through Kreuzberg's Blücherplatz on Pentecost Sunday, www.karneval-berlin.de)
May 20-21	Pentecost (Pfingsten) and Pentecost Monday (Pfingstmontag)
Mid-June (second weekend)	Luther's Wedding festival, Wittenberg
July	Open Air Festival, Berlin (six days of music on Gendarmenmarkt, www.classicopenair.de)
Early Aug (first weekend)	International Beer Festival (www.bierfestival-berlin.de), Berlin
Aug 15	Assumption (Mariä Himmelfahrt)
Sept	International Literature Festival (www.literaturfestival.com), Berlin
Late Sept-mid Oct	Berliner Oktoberfest (www.schaustellerverband-berlin.de)
Oct 3	German Unity Day (Tag der Deutschen Einheit); party along Unter den Linden in Berlin
Mid-Oct	Festival of Lights, Berlin (landmark buildings artistically lit, www.festival-of-lights.de)
Oct 31	Reformation Day celebration, Wittenberg
Nov	Jazzfest Berlin (www.berlinerfestspiele.de)
Nov-Dec	Christmas Garden Berlin (light show in Botanical Gardens, http://christmas-garden.de)
Dec 6	St. Nikolaus Day
Dec 24	Christmas Eve (Heiliger Abend), when Germans celebrate Christmas
Dec 25	Christmas
Dec 31	New Year's Eve (Silvester, fireworks)

APPENDIX

Books and Films

To learn more about Berlin past and present, check out a few of these books and films.

Nonfiction

Berlin Diary: The Journal of a Foreign Correspondent (William Shirer, 1941). Stationed in Berlin from 1934 until 1940, CBS radio broadcaster Shirer delivers a vivid and harrowing day-by-day account of the rise of Nazi Germany.

Berlin Now—The City After the Wall (Peter Schneider, 2014). A long-time resident and journalist explores aspects of Berlin since 1989, including the Stasi legacy, the debate about how to preserve sections of the Wall, the city's frenetic club scene, thorny urban planning issues, and the ongoing BER airport debacle.

Berlin—Portrait of a City Through the Centuries (Rory MacLean, 2014). MacLean's colorful look at this pivotal and resilient city focuses on the people (from Frederick the Great to JFK to David Bowie) who were instrumental to its narrative—and its unique soul.

Culture Shock! Germany (Richard Lord, 2008). Lord provides cultural insights on German customs and etiquette.

Here I Stand: A Life of Martin Luther (Roland Bainton, 1950). Bainton delivers an authoritative biography of the man who initiated the Reformation.

In the Garden of Beasts (Erik Larson, 2011). Larson captures Berlin during the rise of the Nazis, as seen through the eyes of a reserved US ambassador to Germany and his socialite daughter.

Martin Luther: A Life (Martin E. Marty, 2004). Marty offers a short, vivid biography of the irascible German reformer who transformed Western Christianity.

Stasiland: Stories from Behind the Berlin Wall (Anna Funder, 2002). Funder delivers a powerful account about the secrets of the Stasi, the East German Ministry for State Security, and how it affected the citizens of East Germany.

When in Germany, Do as the Germans Do (Hyde Flippo, 2002). Want to fit in? This lighthearted and helpful guide details the do's and don'ts of being German.

Fiction

1632 (Eric Flint, 2000). This sci-fi/time travel book sends West Virginians back to 17th-century Germany.

Berlin Noir (Philip Kerr, 1993). An ex-policeman-turned-detective struggles with secrets and crime in 1930s and '40s Berlin.

The Berlin Stories: The Last of Mr. Norris and Goodbye to Berlin

(Christopher Isherwood, 1945). Composed of two novellas published in the 1930s, these stories capture the freewheeling early '30s Berlin and inspired the Broadway musical/motion picture *Cabaret*.

Winter (Len Deighton, 1987). Deighton's engrossing historical novel traces the lives of a German family from 1899 to 1945. The book also serves as a prequel to Deighton's masterful nine-part Cold War spy series, which kicks off with *Berlin Game* (1983).

Film and TV

The Baader Meinhof Complex (2008). The still-fragile German democracy is rocked in 1967 by acts of terrorism committed by radicalized Germans.

Cabaret (1972). With Hitler on the rise and anti-Semitism growing, the only refuge in Berlin during the 1930s is in the cabaret. (This musical won multiple Academy Awards.)

The Counterfeiters (2007). This Oscar-winning film tells the story of Sachsenhausen Concentration Camp inmates forced to run a counterfeiting ring to undermine the British pound.

Downfall (2004). Bruno Ganz delivers a frightening performance as Hitler in this story of Der Führer's final days in his Berlin bunker.

Good Bye, Lenin! (2003). In this funny, poignant film, a son struggles to re-create a pre-unification Berlin for his ailing communist mother.

Hannah Arendt (2012). This biographical drama examines the life of the German-Jewish philosopher who reported on Adolf Eichmann's 1961 Nazi war crimes trial for the *New Yorker*.

The Lives of Others (2006). In this gripping, Oscar-winning drama, a member of East Germany's secret police becomes too close to those whose lives he surveils.

Valkyrie (2008). This historical thriller chronicling the July 20, 1944 attempt to assassinate Hitler includes scenes shot on location in Berlin's Bendlerblock, the nerve center of the failed coup and now a memorial to the resistance effort.

Wings of Desire (1987). Set in the former West Berlin, Wim Wenders' romantic fantasy tells the story of an angel who falls in love with a human. The story concludes in Wenders' 1993 sequel, *Faraway, So Close*.

Conversions and Climate

Numbers and Stumblers

- Europeans write a few of their numbers differently than we do. 1 = $\mathcal{1}$, 4 = $\mathcal{4}$, 7 = $\mathcal{7}$.
- In Europe, dates appear as day/month/year, so Christmas 2019 is 25/12/19.
- Commas are decimal points and decimals are commas. A dollar and a half is 1,50, one thousand is 1.000, and there are 5.280 feet in a mile.
- When counting with fingers, start with your thumb. If you hold up your first finger to request one item, you'll probably get two.
- What Americans call the second floor of a building is the first floor in Europe.
- On escalators and moving sidewalks, Europeans keep the left "lane" open for passing. Keep to the right.

Metric Conversions

A **kilogram** equals 1,000 grams (about 2.2 pounds). One hundred **grams** (a common unit at markets) is about a quarter-pound. One **liter** is about a quart, or almost four to a gallon.

A **kilometer** is six-tenths of a mile. To convert kilometers to miles, cut the kilometers in half and add back 10 percent of the original (120 km: 60 + 12 = 72 miles). One **meter** is 39 inches—just over a yard.

1 foot = 0.3 meter	1 square yard = 0.8 square meter
1 yard = 0.9 meter	1 square mile = 2.6 square kilometers
1 mile = 1.6 kilometers	1 ounce = 28 grams
1 centimeter = 0.4 inch	1 quart = 0.95 liter
1 meter = 39.4 inches	1 kilogram = 2.2 pounds
1 kilometer = 0.62 mile	32°F = 0°C

Clothing Sizes

When shopping for clothing, use these US-to-European comparisons as general guidelines (but note that no conversion is perfect).

Women: For pants and dresses, add 30 in Germany (US 10 = German 40). For blouses and sweaters, add 8 for most of Europe (US 32 = European 40). For shoes, add 30-31 (US 7 = European 37/38).

Men: For shirts, multiply by 2 and add about 8 (US 15 = European 38). For jackets and suits, add 10. For shoes, add 32-34.

Children: Clothing is sized by height—in centimeters (2.5 inches = 1 cm), so a US size 8 roughly equates to 132-140. For shoes up to size 13, add 16-18, and for sizes 1 and up, add 30-32.

Germany's Climate

First line, average daily high; second line, average daily low; third line, average days without rain. For more detailed weather statistics for destinations in this book (as well as the rest of the world), check www.wunderground.com.

	J	F	M	A	M	J	J	A	S	O	N	D
Berlin												
	35°	37°	46°	56°	66°	72°	75°	74°	68°	56°	45°	38°
	26°	26°	31°	39°	47°	53°	57°	56°	50°	42°	36°	29°
	14	13	19	17	19	17	17	17	18	17	14	16

Fahrenheit and Celsius Conversion

Europe takes its temperature using the Celsius scale, while we opt for Fahrenheit. For a rough conversion from Celsius to Fahrenheit, double the number and add 30. For weather, remember that 28°C is 82°F—perfect. For health, 37°C is just right. At a launderette, 30°C is cold, 40°C is warm (usually the default setting), 60°C is hot, and 95°C is boiling. Your air-conditioner should be set at about 20°C.

Packing Checklist

Whether you're traveling for five days or five weeks, you won't need more than this. Pack light to enjoy the sweet freedom of true mobility.

Clothing

- ❑ 5 shirts: long- & short-sleeve
- ❑ 2 pairs pants (or skirts/capris)
- ❑ 1 pair shorts
- ❑ 5 pairs underwear & socks
- ❑ 1 pair walking shoes
- ❑ Sweater or warm layer
- ❑ Rainproof jacket with hood
- ❑ Tie, scarf, belt, and/or hat
- ❑ Swimsuit
- ❑ Sleepwear/loungewear

Money

- ❑ Debit card(s)
- ❑ Credit card(s)
- ❑ Hard cash ($100-200 in US dollars)
- ❑ Money belt

Documents

- ❑ Passport
- ❑ Tickets & confirmations: flights, hotels, trains, rail pass, car rental, sight entries
- ❑ Driver's license
- ❑ Student ID, hostel card, etc.
- ❑ Photocopies of important documents
- ❑ Insurance details
- ❑ Guidebooks & maps
- ❑ Notepad & pen
- ❑ Journal

Toiletries Kit

- ❑ Basics: soap, shampoo, toothbrush, toothpaste, floss, deodorant, sunscreen, brush/comb, etc.
- ❑ Medicines & vitamins
- ❑ First-aid kit
- ❑ Glasses/contacts/sunglasses
- ❑ Sewing kit
- ❑ Packet of tissues (for WC)
- ❑ Earplugs

Electronics

- ❑ Mobile phone
- ❑ Camera & related gear
- ❑ Tablet/ebook reader/media player
- ❑ Laptop & flash drive
- ❑ Headphones
- ❑ Chargers & batteries
- ❑ Smartphone car charger & mount (or GPS device)
- ❑ Plug adapters

Miscellaneous

- ❑ Daypack
- ❑ Sealable plastic baggies
- ❑ Laundry supplies: soap, laundry bag, clothesline, spot remover
- ❑ Small umbrella
- ❑ Travel alarm/watch

Optional Extras

- ❑ Second pair of shoes (flip-flops, sandals, tennis shoes, boots)
- ❑ Travel hairdryer
- ❑ Picnic supplies
- ❑ Water bottle
- ❑ Fold-up tote bag
- ❑ Small flashlight
- ❑ Mini binoculars
- ❑ Small towel or washcloth
- ❑ Inflatable pillow/neck rest
- ❑ Tiny lock
- ❑ Address list (to mail postcards)
- ❑ Extra passport photos

German Survival Phrases

In the phonetics, ī sounds like the long i in "light," and bolded syllables are stressed.

English	German	Pronunciation
Good day.	Guten Tag.	**goo**-tehn tahg
Do you speak English?	Sprechen Sie Englisch?	**shprehkh**-ehn zee **ehgn**-lish
Yes. / No.	Ja. / Nein.	yah / nīn
I (don't) understand.	Ich verstehe (nicht).	ikh fehr-**shtay**-heh (nikht)
Please.	Bitte.	**bit**-teh
Thank you.	Danke.	**dahng**-keh
I'm sorry.	Es tut mir leid.	ehs toot meer līt
Excuse me.	Entschuldigung.	ehnt-**shool**-dig-oong
(No) problem.	(Kein) Problem.	(kīn) proh-**blaym**
(Very) good.	(Sehr) gut.	(zehr) goot
Goodbye.	Auf Wiedersehen.	owf **vee**-der-zayn
one / two	eins / zwei	īns / tsvī
three / four	drei / vier	drī / feer
five / six	fünf / sechs	fewnf / zehkhs
seven / eight	sieben / acht	**zee**-behn / ahkht
nine / ten	neun / zehn	noyn / tsayn
How much is it?	Wieviel kostet das?	**vee**-feel **kohs**-teht dahs
Write it?	Schreiben?	**shrī**-behn
Is it free?	Ist es umsonst?	ist ehs oom-**zohnst**
Included?	Inklusive?	in-kloo-**zee**-veh
Where can I buy / find...?	Wo kann ich kaufen / finden...?	voh kahn ikh **kow**-fehn / **fin**-dehn
I'd like / We'd like...	Ich hätte gern / Wir hatten gern...	ikh **heh**-teh gehrn / veer **heh**-tehn gehrn
...a room.	...ein Zimmer.	īn **tsim**-mer
...a ticket to ____.	...eine Fahrkarte nach ____.	ī-neh **far**-kar-teh nahkh
Is it possible?	Ist es möglich?	ist ehs **mur**-glikh
Where is...?	Wo ist...?	voh ist
...the train station	...der Bahnhof	dehr **bahn**-hohf
...the bus station	...der Busbahnhof	dehr **boos**-bahn-hohf
...the tourist information office	...das Touristen- informations- büro	dahs too-**ris**-tehn- in-for-maht-see-**ohns**- **bew**-roh
...the toilet	...die Toilette	dee toh-**leh**-teh
men	Herren	**hehr**-rehn
women	Damen	**dah**-mehn
left / right	links / rechts	links / rehkhts
straight	geradeaus	geh-**rah**-deh-**ows**
What time does this open / close?	Um wieviel Uhr wird hier geöffnet / geschlossen?	oom **vee**-feel oor veerd hoor geh-**urf**-neht / geh-**shloh**-sehn
At what time?	Um wieviel Uhr?	oom **vee**-feel oor
Just a moment.	Moment.	moh-**mehnt**
now / soon / later	jetzt / bald / später	yehtst / bahld / **shpay**-ter
today / tomorrow	heute / morgen	**hoy**-teh / **mor**-gehn

In a German Restaurant

English	German	Pronunciation
I'd like / We'd like...	Ich hätte gern / Wir hätten gern...	ikh **heh**-teh gehrn / veer **heh**-tehn gehrn
...a reservation for...	...eine Reservierung für...	ī-neh reh-zer-**feer**-oong fewr
...a table for one / two.	...einen Tisch für eine Person / zwei Personen.	ī-nehn tish fewr ī-neh pehr-zohn / tsvī pehr-**zoh**-nehn
Non-smoking.	Nichtraucher.	**nikht**-rowkh-er
Is this seat free?	Ist hier frei?	ist heer frī
Menu (in English), please.	Speisekarte (auf Englisch), bitte.	**shpī**-zeh-kar-teh (owf **ehng**-lish) **bit**-teh
service (not) included	Trinkgeld (nicht) inklusive	**trink**-gehlt (nikht) in-kloo-**zee**-veh
cover charge	Eintritt	**īn**-trit
to go	zum Mitnehmen	tsoom **mit**-nay-mehn
with / without	mit / ohne	mit / **oh**-neh
and / or	und / oder	oont / **oh**-der
menu (of the day)	(Tages-) Karte	(**tah**-gehs-) **kar**-teh
set meal for tourists	Touristenmenü	too-**ris**-tehn-meh-**new**
specialty of the house	Spezialität des Hauses	shpayt-see-ah-lee-**tayt** dehs **how**-zehs
appetizers	Vorspeise	**for**-shpī-zeh
bread / cheese	Brot / Käse	broht / **kay**-zeh
sandwich	Sandwich	**zahnd**-vich
soup	Suppe	**zup**-peh
salad	Salat	zah-**laht**
meat	Fleisch	flīsh
poultry	Geflügel	geh-**flew**-gehl
fish	Fisch	fish
seafood	Meeresfrüchte	**meh**-rehs-**frewkh**-teh
fruit	Obst	ohpst
vegetables	Gemüse	geh-**mew**-zeh
dessert	Nachspeise	**nahkh**-shpī-zeh
mineral water	Mineralwasser	min-eh-**rahl**-vah-ser
tap water	Leitungswasser	**lī**-toongs-vah-ser
milk	Milch	milkh
(orange) juice	(Orangen-) Saft	(oh-**rahn**-zhehn-) zahft
coffee / tea	Kaffee / Tee	kah-**fay** / tay
wine	Wein	vīn
red / white	rot / weiß	roht / vīs
glass / bottle	Glas / Flasche	glahs / **flah**-sheh
beer	Bier	beer
Cheers!	Prost!	prohst
More. / Another.	Mehr. / Noch eins.	mehr / nohkh īns
The same.	Das gleiche.	dahs **glīkh**-eh
Bill, please.	Rechnung, bitte.	**rehkh**-noong **bit**-teh
tip	Trinkgeld	**trink**-gehlt
Delicious!	Lecker!	**lehk**-er

For more user-friendly German phrases, check out *Rick Steves' German Phrase Book and Dictionary* or *Rick Steves' French, Italian & German Phrase Book*.

INDEX

MAP INDEX

Our website enhances this book and turns

Explore Europe

At ricksteves.com you can browse through thousands of articles, videos, photos and radio interviews, plus find a wealth of money-saving travel tips for planning your dream trip. And with our mobile-friendly website, you can easily access all this great travel information anywhere you go.

TV Shows

Preview the places you'll visit by watching entire half-hour episodes of Rick Steves' Europe (choose from all 100 shows) on-demand, for free.

ricksteves.com

your travel dreams into affordable reality

Radio Interviews

Enjoy ready access to Rick's vast library of radio interviews covering travel

tips and cultural insights that relate specifically to your Europe travel plans.

Travel Forums

Learn, ask, share! Our online community of savvy travelers is a great resource for first-time travelers to Europe, as well as seasoned pros. You'll find forums on each country, plus travel tips and restaurant/hotel reviews. You can even ask one of our well-traveled staff to chime in with an opinion.

Travel News

Subscribe to our free Travel News e-newsletter, and get monthly updates from Rick on what's happening in Europe.

Audio Europe™

Rick's Free Travel App

Get your FREE **Rick Steves Audio Europe**™ app to enjoy...

- Dozens of self-guided tours of Europe's top museums, sights and historic walks
- Hundreds of tracks filled with cultural insights and sightseeing tips from Rick's radio interviews
- All organized into handy geographic playlists
- For Apple and Android

With Rick whispering in your ear, Europe gets even better.

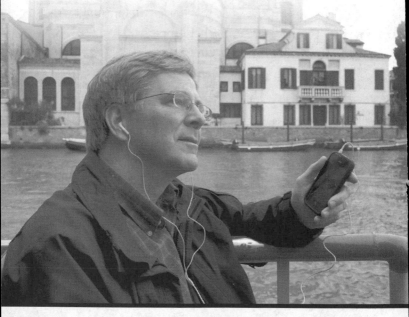

Find out more at ricksteves.com

Pack Light and Right

Gear up for your next adventure at ricksteves.com

Light Luggage

Pack light and right with Rick Steves' affordable, custom-designed rolling carry-on bags, backpacks, day packs and shoulder bags.

Accessories

From packing cubes to moneybelts and beyond, Rick has personally selected the travel goodies that will help your trip go smoother.

Save time and energy

This guidebook is your independent-travel toolkit. But for all it delivers, it's still up to you to devote the time and energy it takes to manage the preparation and logistics that are essential for a happy trip. If that's a hassle, there's a solution.

Rick Steves Tours

A Rick Steves tour takes you to Europe's most interesting places with great

great tours, too!

with minimum stress

guides and small groups of 28 or less. We follow Rick's favorite itineraries, ride in comfy buses, stay in family-run hotels, and bring you intimately

close to the Europe you've traveled so far to see. Most importantly, we take away the logistical headaches so you can focus on the fun.

travelers—nearly half of them repeat customers—along with us on four dozen different itineraries, from Ireland to Italy to Athens. Is a Rick Steves tour the right fit for your travel dreams? Find out at ricksteves.com, where you can also request Rick's latest tour catalog. Europe is best experienced with happy travel partners. We hope you can join us.

Join the fun

This year we'll take thousands of free-spirited

See our itineraries at ricksteves.com

A Guide for Every Trip

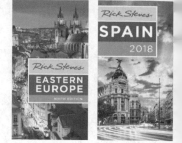

BEST OF GUIDES

Full color easy-to-scan format, focusing on Europe's most popular destinations and sights.

Best of France
Best of Germany
Best of England
Best of Europe
Best of Ireland
Best of Italy
Best of Spain

COMPREHENSIVE GUIDES

City, country, and regional guides with detailed coverage for a multi-week trip exploring the most iconic sights and venturing off the beaten track.

Amsterdam & the Netherlands
Barcelona
Belgium: Bruges, Brussels, Antwerp & Ghent
Berlin
Budapest
Croatia & Slovenia
Eastern Europe
England
Florence & Tuscany
France
Germany
Great Britain
Greece: Athens & the Peloponnese
Iceland
Ireland
Istanbul
Italy
London
Paris
Portugal
Prague & the Czech Republic
Provence & the French Riviera
Rome
Scandinavia
Scotland
Spain
Switzerland
Venice
Vienna, Salzburg & Tirol

THE BEST OF ROME

, Italy's capital, is studded with
n remnants and floodlit-fountain
s. From the Vatican to the Colos-
with crazy traffic in between, Rome
erful, huge, and exhausting. The
the heat, and the weighty history

of the Eternal City where Caesars walked
can make tourists wilt. Recharge by taking siestas, gelato breaks, and after-dark
walks, strolling from one atmospheric
square to another in the refreshing evening air.

*Pantheon—which
dome until the
2,000 years old
ver 1,500).*

*thens in the Vat-
the humanistic*

*liators fought
ner, entertaining*

*me rintorante.
t St. Peter's
iously.*

Rick Steves guidebooks are published by Avalon Travel,
an imprint of Perseus Books, a Hachette Book Group company.

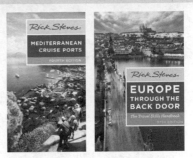

POCKET GUIDES

Compact, full color city guides with the essentials for shorter trips.

Amsterdam
Athens
Barcelona
Florence
Italy's Cinque Terre
London
Munich & Salzburg

Paris
Prague
Rome
Venice
Vienna

SNAPSHOT GUIDES

Focused single-destination coverage.

Basque Country: Spain & France
Copenhagen & the Best of Denmark
Dublin
Dubrovnik
Edinburgh
Hill Towns of Central Italy
Krakow, Warsaw & Gdansk
Lisbon
Loire Valley
Madrid & Toledo
Milan & the Italian Lakes District
Naples & the Amalfi Coast
Northern Ireland
Normandy
Norway
Reykjavik
Sevilla, Granada & Southern Spain
St. Petersburg, Helsinki & Tallinn
Stockholm

CRUISE PORTS GUIDES

Reference for cruise ports of call.

Mediterranean Cruise Ports
Northern European Cruise Ports

Complete your library with...

TRAVEL SKILLS & CULTURE

Study up on travel skills and gain insight on history and culture.

Europe 101
European Christmas
European Easter
European Festivals
Europe Through the Back Door
Postcards from Europe
Travel as a Political Act

PHRASE BOOKS & DICTIONARIES

French
French, Italian & German
German
Italian
Portuguese
Spanish

PLANNING MAPS

Britain, Ireland & London
Europe
France & Paris
Germany, Austria & Switzerland
Ireland
Italy
Spain & Portugal

Credits

Contributors

To help write this book, Rick relied on...

Cameron Hewitt

Born in Denver and raised in central Ohio, Cameron settled in Seattle in 2000. Ever since, he has spent three months each year in Europe, contributing to guidebooks, tours, radio and television shows, and other media for Rick Steves' Europe, where he serves as content manager. Cameron married his high school sweetheart (and favorite travel partner), Shawna, and enjoys taking pictures, trying new restaurants, and planning his next trip.

Gene Openshaw

Gene has co-authored a dozen *Rick Steves* books, specializing in writing walks and tours of Europe's cities, museums, and cultural sights. He also contributes to Rick's public television series, produces tours for Rick Steves Audio Europe, and is a regular guest on Rick's public radio show. Outside of the travel world, Gene has co-authored *The Seattle Joke Book*. As a composer, Gene has written a full-length opera called *Matter*, a violin sonata, and dozens of songs. He lives near Seattle with his daughter, enjoys giving presentations on art and history, and roots for the Mariners in good times and bad.

Acknowledgements

Many Berliners—and others with a passion for Berlin—helped shape this book. *Vielen herzlichen Dank* to Gretchen Strauch, Lee Evans, Holger Zimmer, Carlos Meissner, Torben Brown, Maisie Hitchcock, Caroline Marburger, Nick Gay, and Robyn Stencil for informing and inspiring us over many years of visits.

Photo Credits

Avalon Travel
Hachette Book Group
1700 Fourth Street
Berkeley, CA 94710

ISBN 978-1-63121-674-9
First Edition

For the latest on Rick's lectures, guidebooks, tours, public television series, and public
radio show, contact Rick Steves' Europe, 130 Fourth Avenue North, Edmonds, WA
98020, 425/771-8303, www.ricksteves.com, rick@ricksteves.com.

Rick Steves' Europe

Managing Editor: Jennifer Madison Davis
Special Publications Manager: Risa Laib
Assistant Managing Editor: Cathy Lu
Editors: Glenn Eriksen, Tom Griffin, Katherine Gustafson, Suzanne Kotz, Carrie
   Shepherd
Editorial & Production Assistant: Jessica Shaw
Editorial Intern: Alexandra Ivy
Contributors: Cameron Hewitt, Gene Openshaw
Graphic Content Director: Sandra Hundacker
Maps & Graphics: David C. Hoerlein, Lauren Mills, Mary Rostad

Avalon Travel

Senior Editor and Series Manager: Madhu Prasher
Editor: Jamie Andrade
Associate Editor: Sierra Machado
Editorial Intern: Rachael Sablik
Copy Editor: Maggie Ryan
Proofreader: Becca Freed
Indexer: Stephen Callahan
Production & Typesetting: Rue Flaherty, Jane Musser, Sarah Wildfang
Cover Design: Kimberly Glyder Design
Maps & Graphics: Kat Bennett, Mike Morgenfeld

Let's Keep on Travelin'

Your trip doesn't need to end.

Follow Rick on social media!